Demography

Demography

Demography

Measuring and Modeling Population Processes

Samuel H. Preston
Patrick Heuveline
Michel Guillot

BLACKWELL
Publishers

First published 2001

2 4 6 8 10 9 7 5 3 1

Blackwell Publishers Ltd
108 Cowley Road
Oxford OX4 1JF
UK

Blackwell Publishers Inc.
350 Main Street
Malden, Massachusetts 02148
USA

British Library Cataloguing in Publication Data
A CIP catalogue record for this book is available from the British Library.

Library of Congress Cataloging-in-Publication Data

Preston, Samuel H.
    Demography: measuring and modeling population processes / Samuel H. Preston,
    Patrick Heuveline, Michel Guillot.
        p. cm.
    Includes bibliographical references and index.
    ISBN 1-55786-214-1 (alk. paper)—ISBN 1-55786-451-9 (pb: alk. paper)
        1. Demography. 2. Population research. I. Heuveline, Patrick. II. Guillot, Michel.
    III. Title.

    HB849.4 .P73 2000
    304.6'07'2—dc21   00-033721

Typeset in 10 on 12 pt Times Roman
by Newgen Imaging Systems (P) Ltd, Chennai, India

This book is printed on acid-free paper.

Contents

Boxes

Tables

Figures

Preface

This volume is designed to be an introduction to demography, the study of population processes. It attempts to impart an understanding of the behavior of human populations by describing carefully the basic measures, models, and observational procedures devised by generations of demographers.

Our greatest debt is to the five giants of twentieth-century demography: William Brass, Ansley Coale, Louis Henry, Nathan Keyfitz, and Alfred Lotka. Their influence is reflected in every chapter of the volume. While inventing numerous tools of practical analytic value, perhaps their greatest contribution was to create a subject that, at its best, radiates a compelling order and elegance. We owe a more direct debt to our own mentors, a list that includes Nicolas Brouard, Ansley Coale, Thomas Espenshade, Douglas Ewbank, Henri Leridon, Roland Pressat, and James Trussell.

Writing a text that covers a sizable field is fraught with dangers of omission. No matter how much they would like to avoid such responsibility, the authors appear to be distinguishing between more important and less important work. So let us be very explicit: whatever the underlying merits of the work, the authors are also distinguishing between work with which they are more and less familiar – and the work with which they are most familiar is inevitably their own. Readers who seek supplementary coverage of the field are referred to Shryock and Siegel (1973) and to the extensive compilation of original contributions in Bogue et al. (1993). Smith and Keyfitz (1977) provide more detailed information about the origins of technical demography.

Much of the material appearing in these pages was rehearsed in a graduate class in demography at the University of Pennsylvania. We are grateful to the hundreds of students in this class whose queries sharpened the arguments and exposition that they encountered. We are also grateful for comments received from George Alter, Tom Burch, Irma Elo, Herbert Smith, James Vaupel, and John Wilmoth. Ken Hill's astute reading of the entire manuscript helped prevent many perplexing moments for both authors and readers. The preparation of this volume was supported by a grant from the National Institute of Aging, AG 10168.

Readers are invited to contribute comments, annotated references, problem sets, or other material to the volume's website, www.demographytext.upenn.edu.

Samuel H. Preston
Patrick Heuveline
Michel Guillot

Acknowledgments

The publishers and authors are grateful to the following for permission to reproduce material:

The Population Association of America, for *Demography* vol. 3, no. 2 (1966), table 10.1, "Accuracy of stated age in years, 1963 Ghana registration system," by J. C. Caldwell; vol. 25, no. 3 (1988), figure 8.4, "Age-specific growth rates by years since mortality decline began," by S. Horiuchi and S. H. Preston; vol. 28, no. 1 (1991), figure 7.9, "Momentum and evolution of age-groups," by Y. J. Kim, R. Schoen, and P. Sarma; vol. 31, no. 3 (1994), figure 10.2, "1930 census and extinct generation estimates, African–American females," by I. T. Elo, and S. H. Preston.

Oxford University Press, for tables 3.1 and 3.4 from J. Bongaarts, T. Burch, and K. Wachter, *Family Demography: Methods and their Applications*, Oxford, 1987, by permission.

The United Nations, for material from *Model Life Tables for Developing Countries*, 1982; *Manual X: Indirect Techniques for* Demographic Estimation, 1983; G. A. Condran, C. Himes, and S. H. Preston, *Population Bulletin of the United Nations*, 1991; *World Population Prospects*, 1999.

The London School of Hygiene and Tropical Medicine, University of London, for material from CPS Research Paper no. 88–1, "Indirect estimation of maternal mortality: the sisterhood method," by W. Graham, W. Brass, and R. Snow.

The Academic Press, Inc. for material from A. J. Coale and P. Demeny, *Regional Model Life Tables and Stable Populations*, 1983.

The Office of Population Research, Princeton University and *Population Index* for material from *Population Index* vol. 44, no. 2 (1978), "Technical note: finding two parameters," by A. J. Coale and J. Trussell.

Princeton University Press for material from A. J. Coale, *The Growth and Structure of Human Populations*. Copyright ©1972 by Princeton University Press. Reprinted by permission of Princeton University Press.

The International Institute for Applied Systems Analysis, Laxenburg, Austria for material from A. Rogers and L. J. Castro, *Model Migration Schedules*, 1981.

Every effort has been made to trace the appropriate copyright holders, but in the event that any copyright holders have been overlooked the publisher will be pleased to rectify the error at the earliest opportunity.

1 Basic Concepts and Measures

1.1 Meaning of "Population"

To a statistician, the term "population" refers to a collection of items, for example, balls in an urn. Demographers use the term in a similar way to denote the collection of persons alive at a specified point in time who meet certain criteria. Thus, they may refer to the "population of India on April 1, 1995," or to the "population of American black females in the Northeast on June 1, 1900." In both cases the criteria for inclusion in the population need further elaboration: do we count "legal residents" or simply those who can be found within the borders on that date? What do we mean by "black," or by "Northeast"? Do we refer to midnight or noon on the specified date? It is clear that "the population of India on April 1, 1995" is a shorthand description of what may be a rather long set of operational choices designed to minimize blurriness at the boundaries.

But demographers also use the term "population" to refer to a different kind of collectivity, one that persists through time even though its members are continuously changing through attrition and accession. Thus, "the population of India" may refer to the aggregate of persons who have ever been alive in the area we define as India and possibly even to those yet to be born there. The collectivity persists even though a virtually complete turnover of its members occurs at least once each century.

Demographic analysis focuses on this enduring collectivity. It is particularly addressed to studying changes in its size, its growth rates, and its composition. But while the emphasis is on understanding aggregate processes, demography is also attentive to the implications of those processes for individuals. Many of the indexes in common use in demography, such as life expectancy at birth and the total fertility rate, translate aggregate-level processes into statements about the demographic circumstances faced by an average or randomly-chosen individual. In turn, a frequent concern in demography is to trace out the consequences of changes in individual-level behavior for aggregate processes. Demography is one of the social science disciplines where micro- and macro-level analyses find perhaps their most complete and satisfactory articulation.

1.2 The Balancing Equation of Population Change

No matter how a population is defined, there are only two ways of entering it: being born into it; or migrating into it. If the definition of the population includes a social element in addition to the customary geographic/temporal elements, then "migration" can include a change in the social label, a process often referred to as "social mobility." For example, the population of American high school graduates can be entered by achieving a high school diploma, a form of social migration or mobility. Note in this example that the population cannot be entered at birth since the acquisition of the label of high school graduate requires the investment of years of life. Populations defined by marital status or occupation are other examples of populations that cannot normally be entered by birth (except for the default options, unmarried and no occupation). On the other hand, populations defined by characteristics fixed at birth, such as sex, race, or nativity, cannot be entered through migration but only through birth. So there are *at most* two ways of entering a population, birth and in-migration (= immigration).

Likewise, there are at most two ways of leaving a population, death and out-migration (= emigration). All populations can be left through death, but only those defined by characteristics not fixed at birth can be exited through migration. If one is born in the United States, one cannot leave the population of persons born in the United States by migration, but one can obviously leave the population resident in the United States by migration.

Because there are only four possible ways of entering or leaving a population, we can be sure that changes in the size of the population must be attributable to the magnitude of these flows. In particular,

$$N(T) = N(0) + B[0, T] - D[0, T] + I[0, T] - O[0, T], \qquad (1.1)$$

where

$N(T)$ = number of persons alive in the population at time T,
$N(0)$ = number of persons alive in the population at time 0,
$B[0, T]$ = number of births in the population between time 0 and time T,
$D[0, T]$ = number of deaths in the population between time 0 and time T,
$I[0, T]$ = number of in-migrations between time 0 and time T,
$O[0, T]$ = number of out-migrations from the population between time 0 and time T.

The unit of time in this equation, and throughout the book unless otherwise noted, is number of years. Thus, the time period in which births, deaths, and migrations are occurring is T years in length. T may be fractional and need not be an integer number.

Kenneth Boulding has called this equation the most fundamental in the social sciences. It is clearly an *identity* rather than an approximation or a hypothesized relation. However, when data are used to estimate the elements of this equation, it is no longer the case that both sides must be equal. Error in measuring any element will cause an imbalance in the equation, unless two or more errors happen to be exactly offsetting. An imbalance in the equation is sometimes

---

Box 1.1 *The Balancing Equation of Population Change*

$N(T) = N(0) + B[0, T] - D[0, T] + I[0, T] - O[0, T]$

Example: Sweden, 1988

Ending population Jan. 1, 1989	Starting population Jan. 1, 1988	Births between Jan. 1, 1988 and Jan. 1, 1989	Deaths between Jan. 1, 1988 and Jan. 1, 1989	In-migrations between Jan. 1, 1988 and Jan. 1, 1989	Out-migrations between Jan. 1, 1988 and Jan. 1, 1989

$N(1989.0) = N(1988.0) + B[1988.0, 1989.0] - D[1988.0, 1989.0] + I[1988.0, 1989.0] - O[1988.0, 1989.0]$

$8,461,554$	$= 8,416,599$	$+ 112,080$	$- 96,756$	$+ 51,092$	$- 21,461$

Data source: United Nations, *Demographic Yearbook* (various years).

---

referred to as an "error of closure." Box 1.1 demonstrates the application of the equation to data from Sweden, which are among the world's most reliable.

1.3 The Structure of Demographic Rates

The balancing equation of population change breaks down the changes in the size of the population into four flows. Each flow is the sum of events or transitions occurring to individuals. Three of the four types of events can be related to an individual present in the population prior to the event. While death and out-migration can be related to one individual, birth can be related to two individual parents, assuming that both belong to the population of interest. Analytical insight can be gained by relating the size of these flows (number of occurrences) to the size of the population producing them. This task is normally accomplished by constructing a demographic "rate."

The term "rate" is used in many fields and its meaning is not consistent. An unemployment rate, for example, is simply a *ratio* of the unemployed to the total labor force at a moment in time. In demography, rates are normally (but not invariably) what are known in statistical parlance as "occurrence/exposure rates." The typical form of demographic rates reflects the fact that the frequency of occurrences can be expected to be higher in a larger population, and that the total number of occurrences can also be expected to be higher the longer the members of the population are exposed to the "risk" of the occurrence. The amount of exposure in the denominator of an occurrence/exposure rate combines these two features – the number of persons in the population and the length of the time frame in which exposure is counted. The most conventional occurrence/exposure rate in demography takes the form of:

$$Rate = \frac{Number\ of\ Occurrences}{Person\text{-}years\ of\ Exposure\ to\ the\ Risk\ of\ Occurrence}$$

Demographic rates thus contain in the numerator a count of the number of events occurring within some defined time period, and in the denominator an estimate of the number of "person-years" lived in the population during that time period. The number of person-years functions in part as an indicator of the population's amount of exposure to the risk of the event, hence the term *occurrence/exposure rate*. When person-years are used in the denominator, a rate is referred to as an "annualized" rate.

Unlike occurrences, the number of person-years lived is rarely directly observed or counted. Nevertheless, the concept is central in demography. To deal with the concept in a population that is continuously changing its membership, it is useful to represent individual exposures as "life-lines." A life-line extends from an individual's birth (A) to the point where he or she experiences some terminal event (B), usually death. Occurrences of interest, θ_i, can be added to the life-line, as illustrated below:

In order to better connect events and exposure to the risk of experiencing the event, a life-line is sometimes restricted: if we are interested in the risk of giving birth, for instance, we may restrict analysis of life-lines to a certain age range. In our exposition, event A and B are simply birth and death respectively, but the concept can readily be extended to other types of bounding events.

For a group of individuals, however the group might be defined, the concept of the occurrence/exposure rate can be illustrated by a set of life-lines for each member of the group G:

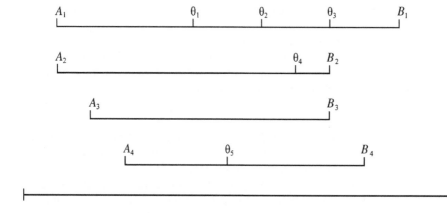

where θ_j are the event occurrences in group G and A_i and B_i represent the birth and death of individual i in the group. The rate for the group defined over their entire lifetimes is

$$Rate^G = \frac{\sum_{i \in G} N_i}{\sum_{i \in G} T_i}$$

where N_i is the total number of occurrences in the lifetime of individual i, T_i is the length of time between A_i and B_i, and $\sum_{i \in G}$ is an instruction to take the sum across all individuals (i) who are a member of group G.

1.4 Period Rates and Person-years

A period rate for a population is constructed by limiting the count of occurrences and exposure times to those pertaining to members of the population during a specified period of time:

$$Rate\,[0,\,T] = \frac{Number\ of\ Occurrences\ between\ Time\ 0\ and\ T}{Person\text{-}years\ Lived\ in\ the\ Population\ between\ Time\ 0\ and\ T}$$

If a person lives one year between time 0 and time T, he or she has contributed one person-year to the denominator of the period rate. If a person lives 24 hours between 0 and T, he or she has contributed 1/365th of a person-year. The contributions from all individuals who were alive in the population at any time between 0 and T are simply added together in order to produce the denominator for our rates.

The idea is easily grasped by referring again to life-lines. If we are interested in period 0 to T, all life-lines can be truncated to the "window" 0 to T, since we will not count any occurrences outside that interval. Figure 1.1 shows the life-lines of 7 individuals in a small hypothetical population during the period from 12:00 A.M., January 1, 1981 to 12:00 A.M. on January 1, 1982.

Person 1, for example, is a member of the population for the entire year, whereas person 6 is born on April 1 and dies on October 1, thereby contributing only 6 months or one-half of a person-year to the sum of person-years. Adding exposure across individuals would be a convenient way to estimate person-years lived in country that had a population register which recorded exact dates of birth, death, and migration for each individual.

An alternative method of computing period person-years is to ignore individual histories, such as those provided by a population register, and simply record the number of persons alive

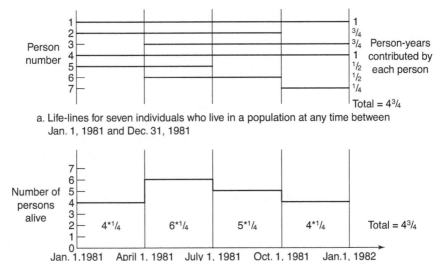

a. Life-lines for seven individuals who live in a population at any time between Jan. 1, 1981 and Dec. 31, 1981

b. Life-lines converted into numbers of persons alive at each moment

Figure 1.1   Demonstration of the equivalence of the two methods for recording person-years

at various points in time during the year. In our example, there were 4 persons alive from January 1, 1981 to April 1, 1981, so that this quarter-year contributed $4(\frac{1}{4}) = 1$ person year. The next quarter contributed $6(\frac{1}{4}) = 1.5$ person-years, and so on to a total of 4.75 person-years contributed during all of 1981. This value is of course the same number derived by following personal histories, as demonstrated in figure 1.1.

In this alternative approach, what we have done is to estimate the area under the $N(t)$ curve between January 1, 1981 and January 1, 1982. $N(t)$ is defined as the number of persons alive at time t. An area is found by taking the height of a figure times its width. In our case, $N(t)$ is the height and the proportion of the year that corresponds to our measurement of $N(t)$ is the width. Since height represents persons and width represents fractions of a year, it is natural to measure the product in units of person-years.

In our example the number of person-years was:

$$PY[1981.00, 1982.00] = 4(.25) + 6(.25) + 5(.25) + 4(.25) = 4.75$$

This sum can be written in conventional notation as:

$$PY[1981.00, 1982.00] = \sum_{i=1}^{4} N_i \cdot \Delta_i$$

where N_i is the number of persons alive in the ith quarter and Δ_i is the fraction of a year represented by that quarter. Had we measured the size of the population each *day* instead of each quarter, the sum would be represented as:

$$PY[1981.00, 1982.00] = N(Jan. 1, 1981) \cdot \frac{1}{365}$$

$$+ N(Jan. 2, 1981) \cdot \frac{1}{365}$$

$$+ \cdots$$

$$+ N(Dec. 31, 1981) \cdot \frac{1}{365}$$

$$= \sum_{i=1}^{365} N_i \cdot \Delta_i$$

If we were able to measure the height, $N(t)$, in tiny intervals of time dt, where dt represents the width of the interval, the area under the curve could be represented more accurately as:

$$PY[1981.00, 1982.00] = \int_{1981.00}^{1982.00} N(t) \cdot dt$$

Here an integral sign has replaced the summation sign and for the fraction of a year represented by the time interval, dt has replaced Δ_i.

We have seen that areas under a curve can be represented in two ways, using either algebraic or calculus notation. In demography, algebraic notation satisfies a practical need that arises when measurement occurs in discrete intervals. But calculus is often preferred for its compact notation and for its far more extensive body of theorems having direct applicability to population processes. We will use algebra and calculus interchangeably in this volume. One of the most frequent uses of calculus will occur in the issue we have already encountered, representing the area under a curve.

1.5 Principal Period Rates in Demography

We can now apply the concept of period rate to demographic events of interest, in particular the four components of the balancing equation of population change. When the elements of equation (1.1), the balancing equation of population growth, are each divided by the number of person-years lived between 0 and T, we define four rates:

The Crude Birth Rate between times 0 and T:

$$CBR\,[0, T] = \frac{\text{Number of births in the population between times 0 and } T}{\text{Number of person-years lived in the population between times 0 and } T}$$

The Crude Death Rate between times 0 and T:

$$CDR\,[0, T] = \frac{\text{Number of deaths in the population between times 0 and } T}{\text{Number of person-years lived in the population between times 0 and } T}$$

The Crude Rate of In-migration between times 0 and T:

$$CRIM\,[0, T] = \frac{\text{Number of in-migrations into the population between times 0 and } T}{\text{Number of person-years lived in the population between times 0 and } T}$$

The Crude Rate of Out-migration between times 0 and T:

$$CROM\,[0, T] = \frac{\text{Number of out-migrations from the population between times 0 and } T}{\text{Number of person-years lived in the population between times 0 and } T}$$

We could label the crude birth rate as we have defined it as the "true" crude birth rate, since it includes the actual births and actual person-years in the numerator and denominator, respectively. Throughout the book, the term "rates" will refer to the true or actual rates prevailing in a population. These should be distinguished from the "recorded" or "estimated" rates that are produced when data are used to estimate the value of the true rate.

A person is normally counted as having migrated during the period 0 to T if he or she has changed his or her principal place of residence during the period in a way that crosses the administrative boundaries defining "the population" of a region.

As is especially clear from our definition of the crude rate of in-migration, the connection between exposure and event is not always very precise in demography. No member of a population is literally exposed to the risk of in-migrating into that same population; those at risk are all outside of the population. Like any definitions, these contain an element of arbitrariness, and we could have chosen to put another element in the denominator. What the crude rate of in-migration expresses is the rate at which the population is growing as a result of in-migration. The other rates also indicate the rate at which the population is changing as a result of births, deaths, or out-migration. Using person-years as the denominator for all the major rates in demography provides a firm basis for developing and integrating many different functions and formulas involving population growth. This advantage should become evident in the course of this volume.

It is important to keep in mind the distinction between the reference period to which a rate pertains (i.e., the period for which the values are calculated) and the unit in which exposure time is measured. As noted, the conventional practice is to count exposure in the form of person-years lived, thus creating "annualized" rates. They express the number of events occurring *per year* of exposure. But a period rate need not refer to a single year of the population's experience. For example, we can readily define a crude death rate for 1990–1. Here the number of events in the numerator would include all deaths for calendar years 1990 and 1991, and the denominator would include all person-years lived in 1990 as well as those lived in 1991. Since both the numerator and denominator are, in size, approximately double what they would be if they referred to only a single calendar year, defining the rate over a 2-year period does not affect the scale of the rate. It is still an annualized rate, expressing the number of events per person-year. Likewise, we could define a crude death rate for May 1992, in which both numerator and denominator would be approximately one-twelfth of their value for all of 1992. The scale of the rate, and its annualized nature, is preserved.

Although a period rate in demography apparently can accommodate any length of reference period, it is important to recognize that it must have *some* reference period. The phrase, "the crude birth rate of the United States," has no meaning and there is no way to calculate its value. We must know in what period to count births for the numerator and person-years for the denominator.

1.6 Growth Rates in Demography

1.6.1 Crude growth rate

Let us rearrange the balancing equation of population change (1.1), by subtracting $N(0)$ from both sides and then dividing both sides by the total of person-years lived between 0 and T, $PY[0, T]$:

$$\frac{N(T) - N(0)}{PY[0, T]} = \frac{B[0, T]}{PY[0, T]} - \frac{D[0, T]}{PY[0, T]} + \frac{I[0, T]}{PY[0, T]} - \frac{O[0, T]}{PY[0, T]}$$

$$CGR[0, T] = CBR[0, T] - CDR[0, T] + CRIM[0, T] - CROM[0, T] \qquad (1.2)$$

$$= CRNI[0, T] \qquad + \qquad CRNM[0, T]$$

Here we have defined the crude growth rate between 0 and T, $CGR[0, T]$, as the change in the size of population divided by person-years lived between 0 and T. If $N(T)$ exceeds $N(0)$, then the growth rate will be positive; if $N(0)$ exceeds $N(T)$, it will be negative. Clearly, the crude growth rate as we have defined it is simply equal to the crude birth rate minus the crude death rate plus the crude rate of in-migration minus the crude rate of out-migration.

The difference between the crude birth rate and the crude death rate is usually termed the crude rate of natural increase (*CRNI*); also, the difference between the crude rate of in-migration and the crude rate of out-migration is usually termed the crude rate of net migration (*CRNM*). So the crude growth rate will equal the crude rate of natural increase plus the crude rate of net migration. Box 1.2 illustrates the calculation of crude demographic rates, again using the Swedish data in box 1.1 and estimating the person-years lived in 1988 by the population size on July 1, 1988. Table 1.1 presents the estimated value of demographic rates for major regions of the world.

Box 1.2 *Principal Period Rates in Demography*

$$\frac{N(T) - N(0)}{PY[0, T]} = \frac{B[0, T]}{PY[0, T]} - \frac{D[0, T]}{PY[0, T]} + \frac{I[0, T]}{PY[0, T]} - \frac{O[0, T]}{PY[0, T]}$$

$$CGR[0, T] = CBR[0, T] - CDR[0, T] + CRIM[0, T] - CROM[0, T]$$

$$= CRNI[0, T] + CRNM[0, T]$$

Example: Sweden, 1988

Person-years lived in Sweden between January 1, 1988 and January 1, 1989 = 8,438,477 (mid-year population)

$$\frac{N(1989.0) - N(1988.0)}{PY[1988.0, 1989.0]} = \frac{B[1988.0, 1989.0]}{PY[1988.0, 1989.0]} - \frac{D[1988.0, 1989.0]}{PY[1988.0, 1989.0]} + \frac{I[1988.0, 1989.0]}{PY[1988.0, 1989.0]} - \frac{O[1988.0, 1989.0]}{PY[1988.0, 1989.0]}$$

$$CGR[1988.0, 1989.0] = CBR[1988.0, 1989.0] - CDR[1988.0, 1989.0] + CRIM[1988.0, 1989.0] - CROM[1988.0, 1989.0]$$

$$\frac{8,461,554 - 8,416,599}{8,438,477} = \frac{112,080}{8,438,477} - \frac{96,756}{8,438,477} + \frac{51,092}{8,438,477} - \frac{21,461}{8,438,477}$$

$$0.00533 = 0.01328 - 0.01147 + 0.00605 - 0.00254$$

$$CGR[1988.0, 1989.0] = CRNI[1988.0, 1989.0] + CRNM[1988.0, 1989.0]$$

$$0.00533 = 0.00182 + 0.00351$$

Data source: United Nations, *Demographic Yearbook* (various years).

The crude growth rate is only one of several types of growth rate encountered in demography. The term "growth rate" is used to refer to other measures as well, and it is important to distinguish the various forms.

1.6.2 Instantaneous growth rate

As any rate, the crude growth rate can be computed for any period of time. What happens when we compute the growth rate during a very short period of time, between time t and $t + \Delta t$, as Δt approaches 0? Denote the population change, $N(t + \Delta t) - N(t)$, as $\Delta N(t)$ and the growth rate as $r(t)$. Since the person-years lived over the period $[t, t + \Delta t]$ is now $N(t)\Delta t$, the crude growth rate for the period is $r(t) = \Delta N(t)/N(t)\Delta t$. But the limit of $\Delta N(t)/\Delta t$ when Δt approaches 0 is simply the derivative of the $N(t)$ function, designated $dN(t)/dt$. Therefore:

$$r(t) = \lim_{\Delta t \to 0} \frac{\Delta N(t)}{N(t)\, \Delta t} = \frac{\frac{dN(t)}{dt}}{N(t)} = \frac{d \ln[N(t)]}{dt} \tag{1.3}$$

where "ln" refers to the natural logarithm. The time interval is very short, dt years, so that $r(t)$ pertains to the tiny interval of time between t and $t + dt$. Because it is measured in time units of years, $r(t)$ continues to be an annualized rate. It is referred as "the growth rate at time t" or "the instantaneous growth rate at time t." It is, of course, also the crude growth rate in the tiny interval of time from t to $t + dt$.

Table 1.1: *Population size and components of change in major areas of the world, 1995–2000*

Major area	Population size (thousands)		Births (thousands)	Deaths (thousands)	Net international migrants (thousands)	Crude growth rate (percentage)	Crude birth rate (per 1000)	Crude death rate (per 1000)	Crude rate of natural increase (per 1000)	Crude rate of net migration (per 1000)
	1995	2000	1995–2000	1995–2000	1995–2000	1995–2000	1995–2000	1995–2000	1995–2000	1995–2000
World	5,666,360	6,055,049	649,050	260,360	0	1.33	22.1	8.9	13.2	0.0
Africa	696,963	784,445	140,575	51,655	−1,435	2.37	38.0	13.9	24.1	−0.4
Asia	3,436,281	3,682,550	389,765	137,460	−6,035	1.38	21.9	7.7	14.2	−0.3
Europe	727,912	728,887	37,465	41,240	4,750	0.03	10.3	11.3	−1.0	1.3
Latin America and the Caribbean	479,954	519,143	57,770	16,225	−2,355	1.57	23.1	6.5	16.6	−0.9
Northern America	296,762	309,631	20,860	12,640	4,650	0.85	13.8	8.3	5.5	3.1
Oceania	28,488	30,393	2,635	1,135	405	1.30	17.9	7.7	10.2	2.8

Source: United Nations, 1999.

The concept of the instantaneous growth rate enables us to develop a new expression for population change over a longer time interval. Integrating formula (1.3) between exact times 0 and T (also measured in years), gives:

$$\int_0^T r(t)\, dt = \int_0^T \frac{d\ln N(t)}{dt}\, dt = \ln N(t) \Big]_0^T$$

So:

$$\int_0^T r(t)\, dt = \ln\left(\frac{N(T)}{N(0)}\right) \qquad (1.4)$$

Taking exponentials on both sides we have:

$$e^{\int_0^T r(t)\, dt} = \frac{N(T)}{N(0)}$$

or

$$N(T) = N(0)e^{\int_0^T r(t)\, dt} \qquad (1.5)$$

Formula (1.5) is extremely important in demography. It appears in many guises in many different applications. It expresses the change in population size during a particular discrete time period (in this case from 0 to T) as a simple function of the set of instantaneous growth rates that prevailed during that period. Note that the proportionate growth in population over the period, $N(T)/N(0)$, is a simple function of the sum of growth rates. The order in which those growth rates are applied is immaterial; all that matters is their sum.

Viewing $r(t)$ as a continuously varying function raises questions about the commonly encountered term, "exponential growth." Any growth that occurs, including zero growth or negative growth, must obey equation (1.5). An exponential appears in that formula because we have *defined* our measure of growth – the growth rate – in proportionate terms. In this sense the term "exponential growth" is a redundancy; all growth is exponential by our measure of growth as the proportionate rate of change in population size. When people use the term "exponential growth" they are often (but not invariably) referring to an $N(t)$ sequence produced by a *constant positive* growth rate within some time interval. Such a sequence is probably more precisely characterized by the term Malthus chose for it, "geometric growth," or by "constant growth rate." If the instantaneous growth rate is in fact constant between time 0 and time T at some value r^*, then equation (1.5) simplifies to:

$$N(T) = N(0)e^{r^* \cdot T} \qquad (1.6)$$

This formula follows from the fact that:

$$\int_0^T r^*\, dt = r^* \Big]_0^T = r^* \cdot T - r^* \cdot 0 = r^* \cdot T$$

Rearranging equation (1.6) and taking natural logarithms gives:

$$r^* = \frac{\ln \left(\dfrac{N(T)}{N(0)} \right)}{T} \tag{1.7}$$

Equation (1.7) shows that, if the instantaneous growth rate is constant during the interval 0 to T, one can solve for its value by observing the population size at the beginning and end of the interval.

1.6.3 Mean annualized growth rate

If we divide both sides of equation (1.4) by T, the length of the time interval over which growth is occurring, we have:

$$\frac{\int_0^T r(t)\,dt}{T} = \frac{\ln \left[\dfrac{N(T)}{N(0)} \right]}{T}$$

The left-hand side of this equation is simply the mean value of the instantaneous growth rate over the period 0 to T, which we will designate as $\bar{r}[0, T]$. It is the area under the $r(t)$ function between 0 and T, divided by the length of the time interval. Thus:

$$\bar{r}[0, T] = \frac{\ln \left[\dfrac{N(T)}{N(0)} \right]}{T} \tag{1.8}$$

Note that the right-hand side of equation (1.8) is identical to that of (1.7); if the growth rate is constant between 0 and T, equation (1.8) provides a way of estimating its value. But (1.8) is clearly a more general expression since it requires no assumption of constancy. Performing the simple operation given by the right-hand side of equation (1.8) provides the "mean annualized growth rate between 0 and T."

1.6.4 Doubling time

If population size doubles between time 0 and time T, then $N(T)/N(0) = 2$ and:

$$\ln[N(T)/N(0)] = \ln[2] = .693$$

A population thus doubles in size beyond some initial date whenever the sum of its annualized growth rates beyond that date equals 0.693. If the growth rate is constant at r^*, the population will double whenever the product of r^* and T, the length of time (in years) over which it is applied, is 0.693.

So with constant growth rate r^*,

$$Doubling\ time = \frac{.693}{r^*}$$

Under a constant annual growth rate of 0.03, the population will double in $.693/.03 = 23.1$ years. With a constant growth rate of 0.01, it will double in $.693/.01 = 69.3$ years. Since $e^{-.693} = 1/e^{.693} = 0.5$, a population will be reduced to half of its initial size whenever the sum of annual growth rates equals $-.693$.

1.6.5   Comparison of crude growth rate and mean annualized growth rate

We have now developed two formulas for period growth rates over the discrete interval between 0 and T: the crude growth rate and the mean annualized growth rate. This section, which is included for completeness and can be skipped by many readers, compares the two rates. The basic lesson is that the two growth rates will be the same when the instantaneous growth rate is constant during the period 0 to T. Otherwise, the two rates will not, in general, have the same value. However, differences between them can usually be ignored for practical purposes unless the period of measurement is very long (say, longer than 10 years) *and* the growth rate function, $r(t)$, is very irregular.

From (1.2), the crude growth rate between 0 and T can be written as:

$$CGR[0, T] = \frac{B[0, T] - D[0, T] + I[0, T] - O[0, T]}{\int_0^T N(t)\, dt}$$

$$= \frac{N(T) - N(0)}{\int_0^T N(t)\, dt} \tag{1.9}$$

As is clear in (1.8), $\bar{r}[0, T]$ does not depend on the order in which growth rates occur between 0 and T. The numerator of $CGR[0, T]$ in (1.9) is also independent of the order in which growth rates occur. But the denominator of $CGR[0, T]$ in (1.9), person-years lived between 0 and T, *does* depend on the order in which growth rates occur. A distribution of positive growth rates that is heavily skewed toward the beginning of the period will raise person-years lived relative to a distribution that is skewed toward the end of the period. This tendency is illustrated in figure 1.2.

So it is clear that, in general, there can be no equality between CGR and $\bar{r}$. An "early" distribution of growth rates will lower CGR relative to $\bar{r}$, and a "late" distribution will

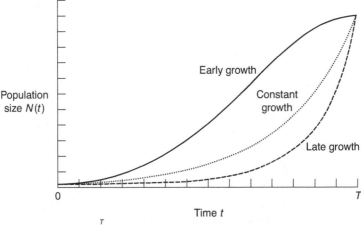

The sum of growth rates, $\int_0^T r(t)dt$, is the same in the three cases, since $N(0)$ and $N(T)$ are the same.

Person-years lived – the area under the $N(t)$ curve – are different, however.

Figure 1.2   Population growth sequences between times 0 and T under three different assumptions about the time sequence of growth rates

raise CGR relative to $\bar{r}$. There is, however, one circumstance in which CGR will equal $\bar{r}$. This occurs when the growth rates are constant between 0 and T. Suppose that $r(t) = r^*$ for $0 \le t \le T$. Then:

$$\int_0^T N(t)\,dt = \int_0^T N(0)e^{r^*t}\,dt = N(0) \int_0^T e^{r^*t}\,dt$$

$$= N(0) \cdot \frac{1}{r^*} \cdot e^{r^*t}\Big]_0^T = \frac{N(0) \cdot e^{r^*t}\big]_0^T}{r^*}$$

$$= \frac{N(T) - N(0)}{r^*} \qquad\qquad (1.10)$$

Substituting expression (1.10) for person-years lived between 0 and T into equation (1.9) gives:

$$CGR[0, T] = \frac{N(T) - N(0)}{\left[\dfrac{N(T) - N(0)}{r^*}\right]} = r^*$$

In the case of a constant growth rate, we also have:

$$\bar{r}[0, T] = \frac{1}{T} \int_0^T r^*\,dt = r^*$$

So in the case of constant growth rates – and, except for rare circumstances, only in this case – the crude growth rate will equal $\bar{r}$. Differences between the two will normally be trivial in size unless the growth rate sequence is extremely erratic and the time period (0 to T) very long, say a decade or more.

If one wants to ensure that the crude growth rate calculated by (1.9) is in fact equal to the mean of annualized growth rates, then a simple rule for computing person-years is indicated: compute person-years lived during the period as though the growth rate were constant throughout. Under this circumstance, the denominator for calculating all crude rates would be:

$$\int_0^T N(t)\,dt = \begin{cases} \dfrac{N(T) - N(0)}{\bar{r}[0, T]} = \dfrac{[N(T) - N(0)] \cdot T}{\ln\left(\dfrac{N(T)}{N(0)}\right)}, & \text{if } \bar{r} \neq 0 \\[3ex] T \cdot N(0), & \text{if } \bar{r} = 0 \end{cases}$$

Although we defined the "mean annualized growth rate" as the average of period rates, in equation (1.8) it does not have person-years in the denominator, which was said to be a typical feature of a demographic rate. In this format, it shares the characteristic of many rates in common usage, such as a mean rate of speed or mean rate of inflation. But under the simplifying assumption that the "mean annualized growth rate" is constant during the interval of measurement, its value is in fact identical to that of the crude growth rate, which does explicitly contain person-years in the denominator.

1.7 Estimating Period Person-years

The above argument suggests that, if one knew nothing about the path of $N(t)$, or $r(t)$, during a particular year, one should assume constancy of the growth rate during the period and estimate person-years lived during the year as:

$$PY[0, 1] = \frac{N(1) - N(0)}{r[0, 1]} = \frac{N(1) - N(0)}{\ln\left[\dfrac{N(1)}{N(0)}\right]}$$

More generally, when the period is not necessarily one year long,

$$PY[0, T] = \frac{[N(T) - N(0)] \cdot T}{\ln\left[\dfrac{N(T)}{N(0)}\right]} \tag{1.11}$$

Using equation (1.11) to estimate person-years has the advantage of forcing consistency between the crude growth rate for the period and the mean annualized growth rate for that period, and it would be exactly correct if the growth rate were constant during the period. But it does require observations on population size at the beginning and end of the period. It is often the case (e.g., in the United States) that population size estimates are only available at mid-year. It will usually be perfectly acceptable to use the mid-year population size as an estimate of person-years lived during the year. The mid-year approximation to person-years will be exactly correct if the $N(t)$ sequence is linear between the beginning and end of the year, as demonstrated in figure 1.3. Even if the $N(t)$ sequence is a product of a constant growth rate, the error in using the mid-year approximation will be very small. For example, if $r = 0.03$ (rapid by historical standards), the ratio of true person-years lived in a year to the mid-year population will be 1.00004. The mid-year population will always underestimate the true number of person-years lived if the population is changing at a constant rate, whether positive or negative.

More caution is necessary in using mid-period approximations to estimate person-years when the interval of time for which an estimate is sought extends far beyond a year. For example, if we estimate the person-years lived during a 10-year period in a population growing at 3 percent a year by taking the mid-period population times 10 (i.e., mid-height times width), then the ratio of true person-years lived to our estimated person-years will be 1.0038. This error of about four-tenths of 1 percent is too large to ignore for most purposes. Note that if we had used the arithmetic mean of beginning and end-period populations (times 10) as our estimate of person-years lived in this example, we would have *overestimated* true person-years by the factor 1.0075. So this procedure provides an even poorer estimate of person-years than does the mid-period population in a population having a constant positive growth rate.

If mid-year population estimates are available for each year during a 10-year period, a sensible way to estimate person-years lived during the period would be simply to add up the 10 estimates. If observations are available at the beginning, middle, and end of the period, then it is possible to ascertain whether growth is more nearly linear or exponential and to use the corresponding approximation for each half-period.

Although it is convenient and fairly accurate to estimate person-years lived during a particular year as the population size in the middle of the year, it is important to remember that the resulting demographic rate should not be expressed as a number of occurrences divided by a

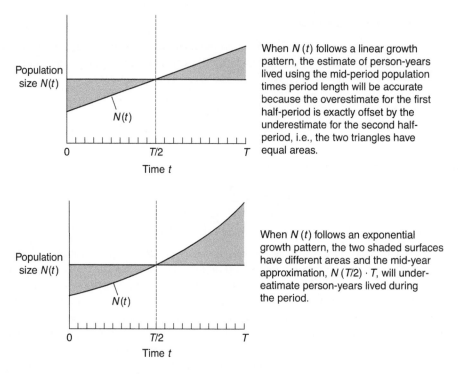

When $N(t)$ follows a linear growth pattern, the estimate of person-years lived using the mid-period population times period length will be accurate because the overestimate for the first half-period is exactly offset by the underestimate for the second half-period, i.e., the two triangles have equal areas.

When $N(t)$ follows an exponential growth pattern, the two shaded surfaces have different areas and the mid-year approximation, $N(T/2) \cdot T$, will underestimate person-years lived during the period.

Figure 1.3 Approximation of person-years lived by midperiod population times period length

number of people. The unit in which exposure-time is measured (usually, person-years) must not disappear, or confusion is inevitable. We are using the mid-year population as an *estimate* of person-years lived during the period, and not as a *substitute* for person-years. The risk of confusion is greatest when an annualized rate is being estimated for a period that is not one year in length. Box 1.3 illustrates the computation of growth rates and person-years lived during a 10-year period in a hypothetical population with a constant annualized growth rate of 0.03.

1.8 The Concept of a Cohort

Almost as important to demography as the concept of a population is the concept of a cohort. A cohort is the aggregate of all units that experience a particular demographic event during a specific time interval. As in the case of a population, a cohort always has some specific geographic referent, whether it is explicit or implicit. A cohort usually consists of people, but it may also consist of entities (e.g., marriages) formed by a demographic event. The cohort is usually identified verbally both by the event itself and by the time period in which it is experienced. Some examples of cohorts are:

"US birth cohort of 1942," which refers to all persons born as US citizens in calendar year 1942;

Box 1.3 *Illustration of Calculation of Growth Rates and Person-years*

Suppose that a population had 100,000 persons at time 0 and that it grew at a constant annualized growth rate of 0.03. Then:

$$N(0) = 100,000$$

$$N(5) = 100,000 \cdot e^{5 \cdot .03} = 116,183$$

$$N(10) = 100,000 \cdot e^{10 \cdot .03} = 134,986$$

1. Calculating the mean annualized growth rate between $t = 0$ and $t = 10$:

$$\bar{r}[0, 10] = \frac{\ln\left(\dfrac{N(10)}{N(0)}\right)}{10} = \frac{\ln\left(\dfrac{134,986}{100,000}\right)}{10} = 0.0300$$

2. Estimating person-years lived between $t = 0$ and $t = 10$:

   a) Assuming a constant growth rate:

   $$PY[0, T] = \frac{N(T) - N(0)}{\bar{r}[0, T]} = \frac{N(10) - N(0)}{\bar{r}[0, 10]} = \frac{134,986 - 100,000}{0.03} = 1,166,200$$

   b) Assuming growth is linear and using the mid-period approximation:

   $$PY[0, T] = N(T/2) \cdot T$$
   $$PY[0, 10] = N(5) \cdot 10 = 116,183 \cdot 10 = 1,161,830$$

   c) Assuming growth is linear and using the mean of initial and final population sizes:

   $$PY[0, T] = \left[\frac{N(0) + N(T)}{2}\right] \cdot T$$
   $$PY[0, 10] = \left[\frac{N(0) + N(10)}{2}\right] \cdot 10$$
   $$= \left[\frac{100,000 + 134,986}{2}\right] \cdot 10 = 1,174,930$$

3. Calculating crude growth rates based upon various estimates of person-years lived:

   a) $CGR[0, T] = \dfrac{34,986}{1,166,200} = 0.0300$

   b) $CGR[0, T] = \dfrac{34,986}{1,161,830} = 0.0301$

   c) $CGR[0, T] = \dfrac{34,986}{1,174,930} = 0.0298$

"French marriage cohort of 1990," which refers to all marriages contracted in France during the calendar year 1990;

"French female marriage cohort of 1990," which refers to all women who married in France in 1990;

"Austrian immigrant cohort of 1995," which refers to all immigrants into Austria in 1995.

The most frequently encountered type of cohort is a birth cohort. Persons who are born during the same period are destined to pass through life together, in the sense that they will reach their xth birthday during a period exactly x years beyond that which defined their cohort membership. For the US birth cohort of 1942, all would reach their 10th birthday (assuming that they survived) in 1952, their 15th birthday in 1957, and so on. The time period that circumscribes the cohort need not be one year in length; it is common to deal with such entities as the US birth cohort of 1918–22, for example.

To calculate a rate for a cohort, we simply restrict the counting of occurrences and person-years of exposure to people who were born during the period that defines membership in the cohort. The lines below show the counting schema for a birth cohort defined by birth in the period a_0 to a_1:

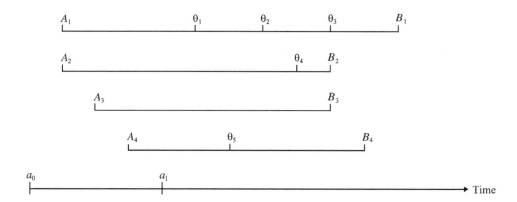

Although those life-lines refer to a birth cohort, the concept can clearly be extended to other types of cohorts.

1.9 Probabilities of Occurrence of Events

We can define an additional concept for a cohort that is impossible for a population: the concept of a probability. The term is used in demography in a manner similar to its usage in statistics. It refers to the *chance* that some event will occur, rather than to the rate at which it occurs. Thus, for example, we may compute the probability that a marriage would end in a divorce for a given birth cohort by counting, over all members of the cohort, the number of marriages and the number of divorces over the cohort's lifetime:

$$q^D = \frac{Number\ of\ Divorces}{Number\ of\ Marriages}$$

In doing so, we have used a "relative frequency" approach to estimating the probability of divorce. We have said, in effect, that our best guess about the true underlying probability of divorce in the cohort is the observed frequency of divorce. The situation is analogous to drawing balls out of a very large urn. If we draw a sample of 10 balls and 2 of them are red, then the relative frequency of red balls in that drawing is 0.2. This relative frequency is also the maximum likelihood estimator of the true proportion of balls in the entire urn that are red, assuming that the outcome of drawings is independent. That is, a proportion in the entire urn of 0.2 is more likely than any other proportion to have given rise to the observed sample of 10 balls of which 2 are red. Many introductory statistics texts contain a clear discussion of maximum likelihood estimation.

The structure of a probability in demography is thus quite different from the structure of a rate:

$$Rate = \frac{Number\ of\ Occurrences}{Number\ of\ Person\text{-}years\ Lived}$$

$$Probability = \frac{Number\ of\ Occurrences}{Number\ of\ Preceding\ Events\ or\ Trials}$$

The denominator of the probability indicates that it is not possible to define a probability unless there is some *event* or *trial* (equivalent to the act of drawing balls out of an urn). Since each occurrence in the numerator (e.g., divorce) must be preceded by an event in the denominator (marriage), the number of occurrences cannot exceed the number of preceding events. Thus the probability cannot exceed one and, since we are only dealing with positive quantities, probabilities cannot be negative.

Populations do not have probabilities except insofar as they pertain to cohorts that are included in the population. Although we could count the number of marriages in a population during some calendar year and the number of divorces during that year, the two numbers combined do not give a sensible estimate of the probability of divorce because they don't apply to the same cohort. We are, in effect, counting events (or trials) in one urn and occurrences in another. If we happened to choose a year in a small population where no one married but there was a divorce, our population's probability of divorce q^D would be $1/0 = \infty$, an obviously absurd outcome. Only when we count the events pertaining to the cohort at risk of the event can we properly define a probability.

The concepts of cohorts and of probabilities that certain events will occur to cohorts can be applied to a vast number of situations extending well beyond demography's customary range. They are central to all analysis of longitudinal data in the social and health sciences. Perhaps their major utility derives from the fact that they translate aggregate-level measures into implications for individuals. They help "locate" the individual in an otherwise amorphous and undifferentiated population.

Despite its conceptual simplicity, analysis of data on actual cohorts suffers from several major practical limitations. First, computing cohort rates and probabilities requires complete information on each individual until he or she has died (or at least has ceased to be "at risk" of the event of interest). We may lose track of some individuals, for instance, when they move out of the area of the study. Out-migration is part of a more general problem called "loss to follow-up." We deal with one way of coping with this problem in chapter 4. A more serious practical problem is that, by the time the cohort's experience is completely observed, much of the experience may be ancient. In order to provide more timely information, demographers rely primarily on data for recent periods. The measures that are constructed from period rates include life expectancy, expected years to be lived in the single state, total fertility rate, net reproduction rate and gross reproduction rate. They also include probabilities of dying, giving birth, migrating, and so on. In constructing these and other measures, demographers rely on the concept of a cohort, but adapt that concept to deal with data pertaining to a period. The principal adaptation is the introduction of "hypothetical cohorts," a concept that will be encountered frequently in the remainder of this volume.

2 Age-specific Rates and Probabilities

In nearly every population, the rate of occurrence of demographic events varies very sharply with age. In fact, the rates defined in chapter 1 are called "crude" rates precisely because they fail to account for age variation in the underlying rate schedules. In the case of mortality and fertility, this variation mainly reflects age differences in physiological capacity. Age variation in migration rates seems to reflect primarily age differences in the economic and social gains from movement.

Because of this age variation, it is common to define and study age-specific rates. These have the same structure as crude rates, with a count of events in the numerator and of person-years in the denominator. However, the age range within which the events and person-years are to be tallied is restricted.

2.1 Period Age-specific Rates

The following notation is conventional for defining a period age-specific death rate:

$$_nM_x[0, T] = \frac{\text{Number of deaths in the age range } x \text{ to } x + n \text{ between time 0 and } T}{\text{Number of person-years lived in the age range } x \text{ to } x + n \text{ between time 0 to } T}$$

Note that, just like the crude death rate, a period age-specific death rate must pertain to some specified time period.

It is clear from the definition that x, the right subscript of $_nM_x[0, T]$, refers to the age at the beginning of the age interval and n, the left subscript, to the length of the interval. Both are measured in *exact number of years*. That is, they refer to the elapsed time since one's birth in years, including decimal or fractional years. So $_5M_{30}$, the death rate between ages 30 and 35, refers to events occurring to and person-years lived by persons who are aged 30.0000 to 34.9999 in exact years since birth. This concept of exact years of age differs from the one in normal use in most countries. When asked their age, most people give a number indicating how many years of life they have *completed*. That is, they omit the decimals altogether. This latter concept of age is sometimes termed "age last birthday." If the data one uses are classified in terms of age last birthday, then the ages (at last birthday) to which $_5M_{30}$ pertains are 30, 31, 32, 33, and 34. Often the analyst will have to determine which age grouping is being used in published data by observing whether the age ranges are stated as 30–5, 35–40, 40–5... (i.e., in exact age) or as 30–4, 35–9, 40–4... (age at last birthday).

Table 2.1 displays the number of deaths by age for females in Sweden, 1992, as well as the estimated mid-year population by age. The format uses age last birthday. The data are converted into age-specific death rates in the fourth column (M_i^{Sw}), using the mid-year population as the estimate of person-years lived in an age interval. The table also shows the same information for Kazakhstan, 1992.

Note that the crude death rate, shown at the bottom of the table as the death rate for "all" ages, is higher in Sweden than in Kazakhstan (0.01055 vs. 0.00742). This result seems on the face of it inconsistent with the fact that the age-specific death rates in Sweden are lower than those in Kazakhstan *at every age*. To understand this apparent anomaly, let us show explicitly how the crude death rate is related to age-specific death rates. Designate $_nN_x$ as the number

Table 2.1: *Comparison of crude death rates and age-specific death rates in two populations*

	Sweden, females, 1992					Kazakhstan, females, 1992			
Age group i	Mid-year population	Deaths during year	Death rate	Proportion in age category	Age group i	Mid-year population	Deaths during year	Death rate	Proportion in age category
	N_i^{Sw}	D_i^{Sw}	M_i^{Sw}	C_i^{Sw}		N_i^{K}	D_i^{K}	M_i^{K}	C_i^{K}
0	59,727	279	0.00467	0.0136	0	174,078	3,720	0.02137	0.0200
1–4	229,775	42	0.00018	0.0524	1–4	754,758	1,220	0.00162	0.0868
5–9	245,172	31	0.00013	0.0559	5–9	879,129	396	0.00045	0.1011
10–14	240,110	33	0.00014	0.0548	10–14	808,510	298	0.00037	0.0929
15–19	264,957	61	0.00023	0.0604	15–19	720,161	561	0.00078	0.0828
20–4	287,176	87	0.00030	0.0655	20–4	622,988	673	0.00108	0.0716
25–9	311,111	98	0.00032	0.0709	25–9	733,057	752	0.00103	0.0843
30–4	280,991	140	0.00050	0.0641	30–4	732,312	965	0.00132	0.0842
35–9	286,899	197	0.00069	0.0654	35–9	612,825	1,113	0.00182	0.0704
40–4	308,238	362	0.00117	0.0703	40–4	487,996	1,405	0.00288	0.0561
45–9	320,172	643	0.00201	0.0730	45–9	284,799	1,226	0.00430	0.0327
50–4	242,230	738	0.00305	0.0552	50–4	503,608	2,878	0.00571	0.0579
55–9	210,785	972	0.00461	0.0481	55–9	301,879	3,266	0.01082	0.0347
60–4	216,058	1,640	0.00759	0.0493	60–4	374,317	5,212	0.01392	0.0430
65–9	224,479	2,752	0.01226	0.0512	65–9	256,247	6,866	0.02679	0.0295
70–4	222,578	4,509	0.02026	0.0508	70–4	154,623	6,182	0.03998	0.0178
75–9	184,102	6,745	0.03664	0.0420	75–9	149,917	8,199	0.05469	0.0172
80–4	140,667	9,587	0.06815	0.0321	80–4	88,716	9,013	0.10159	0.0102
85+	110,242	17,340	0.15729	0.0251	85+	58,940	10,627	0.18030	0.0068
All	4,385,469	46,256	0.01055	1.0000	All	8,698,860	64,572	0.00742	1.0000
CDR		10.55 p. 1,000			CDR		7.42 p. 1,000		

Data source: United Nations, *Demographic Yearbook* (various years).

of persons aged x to $x + n$ at mid-year and use it as an estimate of person-years lived in the age interval x to $x + n$ during the year. N is the size of the total population and functions as an estimate of total person-years lived. D is the total number of deaths during the year. To simplify the notation, we will not use any indicator of the time period to which the rate pertains.

The crude death rate, using this simplified notation, is:

$$CDR = \frac{D}{N} = \frac{\sum_{x=0}^{\infty} {}_nD_x}{N} = \frac{\sum_{x=0}^{\infty} \frac{{}_nD_x}{{}_nN_x} \, {}_nN_x}{N}$$

$$= \sum_{x=0}^{\infty} \frac{{}_nD_x}{{}_nN_x} \cdot \frac{{}_nN_x}{N} = \sum_{x=0}^{\infty} {}_nM_x \cdot {}_nC_x \tag{2.1}$$

where ${}_nC_x = {}_nN_x/N =$ the proportion of total population that belongs to the age interval x to $x + n$.

This equation says that the crude death rate is determined by two functions: the set of age-specific death rates $({}_nM_x)$ and the proportionate age distribution of the population $({}_nC_x)$. In particular, the crude death rate is a weighted average of age-specific death rates, where the weights are supplied by a population's proportionate age distribution (strictly speaking, the proportionate distribution of person-years lived). The sum of these weights, of course, must be unity:[1]

$$\sum_{x=0}^{\infty} {}_nC_x = \sum_{x=0}^{\infty} \frac{{}_nN_x}{N} = \frac{N}{N} = 1.000$$

Now it is easy to see how Kazakhstan could have a lower crude death rate than Sweden even though Sweden had a lower death rate at each age: Sweden's age distribution gives greater weight to the older ages, where age-specific death rates are higher, than did Kazakhstan's.

An equation equivalent to (2.1) can be written with regard to any categorization of the population into subgroups. For example, we could express the crude death rate in terms of height-specific death rates and the proportion of the population that falls into various height classes. There are four reasons for emphasizing the role of age composition:

1. Death rates show very great variation with age, as demonstrated in table 2.1;
2. Human populations differ very considerably from one another in age composition, also as illustrated in table 2.1;[2]
3. The age distribution of the population is itself a demographic variable, being uniquely determined by a population's history of birth, death, and migration rates by age;
4. Data on age-specific deaths and population size are commonly available.

Just as there is nothing unique to age in the derivation in equation (2.1), neither is there anything in it that restricts its applicability to the crude death rate. The development there shows explicitly how any rate (or proportion) in a population is determined by category-specific rates (or proportions) weighted by the proportions of the population that fall into various categories.

Another common way of writing a sum over different ages in demography is to use i to denote the ith age group. So the age group used for the youngest age group becomes $i = 1$; the next youngest becomes $i = 2$, and so on. The sum can go to the highest interval or simply to ∞, since beyond the highest interval the values of any age series are zero. So equation (2.1) can also be written as:

$$CDR = \sum_{i=1}^{\infty} M_i \cdot C_i$$

The main advantage of using the i notation instead of notation with x and n subscripts is that the i notation can accommodate age groups of irregular size. It is common for deaths to be tabulated in age (last birthday) intervals of 0, 1–4, 5–9, 10–14... A series of death rates in such intervals cannot be represented using the summation sign with $_n M_x$ because n is of variable length (1, 4, and 5 years in the first three age intervals). To show explicitly how the age-specific death rates and population proportions shown for Sweden in table 2.1 combine to produce its crude death rate, we used the i notation.

2.2 Age-standardization

The example of Sweden and Kazakhstan showed that differing age structures in the two populations were having a major influence on the comparison of crude death rates. In comparing the levels of mortality in two populations, it is often desirable to eliminate or at least minimize the influence of age composition. One way of making such a comparison would be to assume that Kazakhstan, for example, had the same proportionate age composition as Sweden. The formula for the crude death rate that would result under these circumstances is straightforward:

$$CDR^* = \sum_{i} M_i^K \cdot C_i^{Sw}$$

CDR^* is the estimated death rate in Kazakhstan if it retained its own age-specific death rates but had the age distribution of Sweden. In making this estimate we have assumed that adopting the age distribution of Sweden would have no influence on the age-specific death rate schedule in Kazakhstan. CDR^* is a special case of what is commonly termed an age-standardized rate. An age-standardized crude death rate for population j, which we will denote as $ASCDR^j$, has the following structure:

$$ASCDR^j = \sum_{i=1}^{\infty} M_i^j \cdot C_i^s$$

where C_i^s is the proportion of the population that falls in the ith age interval in some population chosen as a "standard." Of course,

$$\sum_{i=1}^{\infty} C_i^s = 1.00$$

What we have done by choosing some population's age distribution as a standard is simply to weight the age-specific rate schedule in population j not by its own age distribution (such a weighing would just reproduce its observed crude death rate), but by that of another, "standard," population.

Standardization is normally used to control or "standardize" the effects of "extraneous" influences when comparing conditions among populations. In the case of age standardiza-tion, the extraneous influence that is "standardized" among the populations involved in the comparisons is their age composition. The procedure is applicable to any rate or proportion. For example, the age-standardized proportion literate (ASPL) in population j would be:

$$ASPL^j = \sum_{i=1}^{\infty} L_i^j \cdot C_i^s$$

where L_i^j is the proportion literate in the ith age interval in population j. This index indicates what population j's proportion literate for all ages combined would be if it had the standard age distribution.

As noted above, there is nothing about standardization that restricts its applicability to age. We might, for example, want to standardize the effects of differences in birth-order distributions between two populations whose infant death rates we are comparing. Infant death rates usually vary with birth order and for some purposes it is desirable to control for differences in birth order distributions in making infant death rate comparisons. The birth-order standardized infant death rate in population j is:

$$BOSIDR^j = \sum_{i=1}^{\infty} {}_1M_{0,i}^j \cdot C_i^s$$

where ${}_1M_{0,i}^j$ = death rate between exact ages 0 and 1 in population j for births of order i,

and C_i^s = proportion of all births in a "standard" population which are of order i.

Note that the i index now refers to the birth order rather than to age. As before:

$$\sum_{i=1}^{\infty} C_i^s = 1.00$$

Most price indexes, such as the Consumer Price Index computed by the US Bureau of Labor Statistics, have the form of a standardized rate. They are weighted averages of prices of different goods, with the weights supplied by a "standard market basket of goods."

In performing a standardization, the question arises of what population structure to adopt as a standard. To illustrate that this selection can be consequential, let us examine Mexican and English crude death rates standardized using two different standards (table 2.2). One is a young population age distribution, the other old.[3]

When a young standard is used, both countries' crude death rates decline; when an old standard is used (with relatively high fraction in the older ages), both rates rise. But the curious result is that when a young standard is used, England has a lower age-standardized crude death rate than Mexico's; but when an older standard is used, Mexico has the lower rate. Obviously,

Table 2.2: *Comparison of crude death rates and age-standardized crude death rates using a "young" and an "old" age distribution as standard*

Female population	Crude death rate (per 1000 persons)	Age-standardized crude death rate (per 1000 persons) by standard age distribution used	
		"Young" distribution	"Old" distribution
Mexico, 1964	9.30	9.20	11.50
England and Wales, 1931	11.61	8.76	13.13

Data source: Preston, Keyfitz, and Schoen, 1972: 254 and 458.

the choice of standard here affects not only the *amount* of difference between standardized rates but even the *direction* of that difference. Such a result could occur only if England had higher death rates at older ages and Mexico had higher death rates at younger ages; the age-specific death rates functions must cross at least once on the age axis. In this case, Mexico's death rates are higher than England's at young ages and lower at old ages.

In view of the possible sensitivity of results to the choice of a standard, it is regrettable that there are no simple rules for selecting one. In fact, the selection inevitably has a large element of arbitrariness. Arbitrariness is scientifically unhealthy, since it allows the researcher to manipulate results to his or her own taste. So let us set down a pair of rules:

a) When comparing only two populations, A and B, use the average of the two population compositions as the standard:

$$C_i^s = \frac{C_i^A + C_i^B}{2}$$

Since both C_i^A and C_i^B sum to unity, so must C_i^s. This procedure for selecting a standard has some important interpretive advantages, as we will see in the next section. Box 2.1 illustrates the application of standardization for a two-population comparison by applying the procedure to the data for Sweden and Kazakhstan shown in table 2.1. Once age-standardized, the CDR for Kazakhstan becomes higher than the CDR for Sweden, reflecting the higher mortality conditions in Kazakhstan.

b) When comparing many populations, use a standard that is close to the mean or median of population structures in the populations under investigation. The only instance where this rule should be ignored is when some peculiarity in structures makes the average or median somehow unrepresentative of human experience. For example, population compositions may be quite distorted by a recent war and a more "normal" structure might be sought for a standard.

It should be clear that the technique of standardization is useful when three conditions are met:

1. One is comparing an aggregate-level variable (usually a rate or proportion) among two or more populations, or in the same population over time;
2. The variable takes on different values from subgroup to subgroup within each population (e.g., from age group to age group);
3. One wishes to minimize the effect on the comparison of differences in the composition of the population according to these subgroups.

Standardization requires data by subgroup both on the composition of population and on the number of events of interest, e.g. on both population and deaths by age group. It is clear from equation (2.1) that an operation closely related to age standardization can be performed. Instead of asking what population A's crude death rate would be if it had population B's age distribution, we could ask what it would be if it had population B's age-specific death rates.

This type of question is frequently asked if data are lacking on age-specific death rates in population A itself. The answer provides a means of indirectly comparing the (unknown) rate schedule in A to the (known) schedule in B. A ratio of the actual number of deaths in A to the expected number based on B's rate schedule is sometimes called a Comparative Mortality Ratio (CMR):

$$CMR = \frac{\sum_i N_i^A \cdot M_i^A}{\sum_i N_i^A \cdot M_i^B} = \frac{D^A}{\sum_i N_i^A \cdot M_i^B}$$

Box 2.1 *Example of Age-standardization*

Formulas:

$$ASCDR^{Sw} = \sum_{i=1}^{\infty} M_i^{Sw} \cdot C_i^s = \text{Age-standardized crude death rate for Sweden}$$

$$ASCDR^{K} = \sum_{i=1}^{\infty} M_i^{K} \cdot C_i^s = \text{Age-standardized crude death rate for Kazakhstan}$$

$$C_i^s = \left(\frac{C_i^{Sw} + C_i^{K}}{2}\right) = \text{Average age distribution}$$

Example: Sweden and Kazakhstan, females, 1992

Age group i	Age distribution of Sweden C_i^{Sw}	Age distribution of Kazakhstan C_i^{K}	Average age distribution $\frac{C_i^{Sw}+C_i^{K}}{2}$	Age-specific death rate in Sweden M_i^{Sw}	$M_i^{Sw} \cdot \frac{C_i^{Sw}+C_i^{K}}{2}$	Age-specific death rate in Kazakhstan M_i^{K}	$M_i^{K} \cdot \frac{C_i^{Sw}+C_i^{K}}{2}$
0	0.0136	0.0200	0.0168	0.00467	0.00008	0.02137	0.00036
1–4	0.0524	0.0868	0.0696	0.00018	0.00001	0.00162	0.00011
5–9	0.0559	0.1011	0.0785	0.00013	0.00001	0.00045	0.00004
10–14	0.0548	0.0929	0.0738	0.00014	0.00001	0.00037	0.00003
15–19	0.0604	0.0828	0.0716	0.00023	0.00002	0.00078	0.00006
20–4	0.0655	0.0716	0.0686	0.00030	0.00002	0.00108	0.00007
25–9	0.0709	0.0843	0.0776	0.00032	0.00002	0.00103	0.00008
30–4	0.0641	0.0842	0.0741	0.00050	0.00004	0.00132	0.00010
35–9	0.0654	0.0704	0.0679	0.00069	0.00005	0.00182	0.00012
40–4	0.0703	0.0561	0.0632	0.00117	0.00007	0.00288	0.00018
45–9	0.0730	0.0327	0.0529	0.00201	0.00011	0.00430	0.00023
50–4	0.0552	0.0579	0.0566	0.00305	0.00017	0.00571	0.00032
55–9	0.0481	0.0347	0.0414	0.00461	0.00019	0.01082	0.00045
60–4	0.0493	0.0430	0.0461	0.00759	0.00035	0.01392	0.00064
65–9	0.0512	0.0295	0.0403	0.01226	0.00049	0.02679	0.00108
70–4	0.0508	0.0178	0.0343	0.02026	0.00069	0.03998	0.00137
75–9	0.0420	0.0172	0.0296	0.03664	0.00108	0.05469	0.00162
80–4	0.0321	0.0102	0.0211	0.06815	0.00144	0.10159	0.00215
85+	0.0251	0.0068	0.0160	0.15729	0.00251	0.18030	0.00288
Sum	1.0000	1.0000	1.0000		0.00737		0.01188

$$ASCDR^{Sw} = 7.37 \text{ p. } 1{,}000 \qquad ASCDR^{K} = 11.88 \text{ p. } 1{,}000$$

Data source: United Nations, *Demographic Yearbook* (various years).

where

D^A = recorded deaths at all ages combined in A,

N_i^A = number of persons in the ith age interval in A,

M_i^B = death rate in the ith age interval in B.

This index was used for many years by the Registrar-General of Great Britain to compare the death rates of different occupational groups. If the ratio is greater than one, the implication is that the (unknown) age-specific death rates are in general higher in A than in B, though strictly speaking this need be true only in one age interval. This procedure is part of a demographic method called "indirect standardization" that is now rarely used in its complete form (see Shryock and Siegel, 1973: 421–2). The truncated portion of the procedure just described finds extensive application in historical studies of fertility (see section 5.1).

2.3 Decomposition of Differences between Rates or Proportions

A closely-related question is, "How much of the difference between death rates in A and B is attributable to differences in their age distributions?" This latter question is addressed through a technique known as decomposition (Kitagawa, 1955).

We should note at the outset that there is no unique answer to the question addressed by decomposition. There are many ways to decompose a difference and the choice among them is, to an important extent, arbitrary. However, one technique has an advantage of economy and expositional cleanness, and that is what we shall develop here. Let us suppose that we are interested in decomposing the difference between crude death rates in populations A and B. Define the original difference as Δ.

$$\Delta = CDR^B - CDR^A = \sum_i C_i^B \cdot M_i^B - \sum_i C_i^A \cdot M_i^A$$

Now we will divide each of these terms into two equal parts and add and subtract certain additional terms, thereby keeping the difference (Δ) constant:

$$\Delta = \frac{\sum_i C_i^B \cdot M_i^B}{2} + \frac{\sum_i C_i^B \cdot M_i^B}{2} - \frac{\sum_i C_i^A \cdot M_i^A}{2} - \frac{\sum_i C_i^A \cdot M_i^A}{2}$$
$$+ \frac{\sum_i C_i^B \cdot M_i^A}{2} - \frac{\sum_i C_i^B \cdot M_i^A}{2} + \frac{\sum_i C_i^A \cdot M_i^B}{2} - \frac{\sum_i C_i^A \cdot M_i^B}{2}$$

We now combine the eight terms in Δ into four and then into two:

$$\Delta = \sum_i C_i^B \cdot \left[\frac{M_i^B + M_i^A}{2}\right] - \sum_i C_i^A \cdot \left[\frac{M_i^B + M_i^A}{2}\right]$$
$$+ \sum_i M_i^B \cdot \left[\frac{C_i^A + C_i^B}{2}\right] - \sum_i M_i^A \cdot \left[\frac{C_i^A + C_i^B}{2}\right]$$
$$= \sum_i \left(C_i^B - C_i^A\right) \cdot \left[\frac{M_i^B + M_i^A}{2}\right] + \sum_i \left(M_i^B - M_i^A\right) \cdot \left[\frac{C_i^A + C_i^B}{2}\right]$$

$$= \begin{bmatrix} \text{difference in age} \\ \text{composition} \end{bmatrix} \cdot \begin{bmatrix} \text{weighted by average} \\ \text{age-specific mortality} \end{bmatrix} + \begin{bmatrix} \text{difference in rate} \\ \text{schedules} \end{bmatrix} \cdot \begin{bmatrix} \text{weighted by} \\ \text{average age} \\ \text{composition} \end{bmatrix}$$

$$= \begin{array}{c} \text{contribution of age compositional} \\ \text{differences to } \Delta \end{array} + \begin{array}{c} \text{contribution of rate schedule} \\ \text{differences to } \Delta \end{array}$$

We have decomposed the difference into two terms, one of which is clearly interpretable as the contribution of age distributional differences and the other as the contribution of rate schedule differences. Between them, they completely account for the original difference. Note that the "contribution of rate schedule differences" term is precisely the difference between age-standardized death rates in B and A, when the "standard" population age composition applied to both populations is the *average* age composition in A and B.

Interpreting this version of decomposition is straightforward. Any other decompositional procedure introduces a residual, or interaction, term whose meaning is not always clear-cut. For example, by including a different set of terms in the expansion of Δ and then rearranging and simplifying again, we can develop an alternative formula:

$$\Delta = \sum_i C_i^B \cdot \left(M_i^B - M_i^A \right) + \sum_i M_i^B \cdot \left(C_i^B - C_i^A \right) - \sum_i \left(M_i^B - M_i^A \right) \cdot \left(C_i^B - C_i^A \right)$$

The right-most summation term in this expression looks something like a covariance term; it is positive if M_i^A tends to be high relative to M_i^B at ages where C_i^A is high relative to C_i^B. Such a pattern would contribute *negatively* to Δ (since the sign of the last term is negative), because Δ was expressed as the crude death rate in B minus the crude death rate in A.

But it is awkward and unnecessary, in general, to deal with residual terms. The earlier procedure obviated the need for them. And it used an approach to decomposition that is perhaps least arbitrary, since it accepted the average of their rate schedules to weight their age-compositional differences and the average of age structures to weight their rate differences. For most applications, it seems preferable.

Box 2.2 demonstrates the application of the recommended procedure to the decomposition of differences between the crude death rates in France, 1991, and Japan, 1992. France's crude death rate is higher than Japan's by 0.003116. Differences in age composition account for 75 percent (.002333/.003116) of the difference between crude death rates and differences in rate schedules account for the remaining 25 percent. In this case, both factors contribute in the same direction to the difference. But in many applications, one of the factors will account for more than 100 percent of the original difference. This happens when the two factors work in opposite directions, and there is no reason to expect that they will normally work in concert.

Both standardization and decomposition procedures can be applied simultaneously to more than one variable (see Das Gupta, 1993, for a thorough development of multivariate standardization and decomposition). The same standard can also be applied to many populations to produce standardized rates. However, the decompositional procedure described above must be limited to the two populations being directly compared. Comparisons among more than two populations require more complex procedures (Das Gupta, 1993; Smith et al., 1996).

Note that, as in the case of standardization, there is nothing to require that age be one of the variables involved in decomposition. For example, one could decompose a difference between two nations' infant death rates into differences due to birth-order distributions and differences due to rate-schedule differences (that is, differences in their death rates for children of the same birth order). When age is one of the variables in a standardization or decomposition of demographic rates, it is strongly recommended that age categories be no wider than 5 years when data permit. Age variation in vital rates is sufficiently great that the age composition *within* a 10-year age interval can have a substantial effect on the value of an age-specific rate pertaining to that interval.

Box 2.2 *Decomposition of Differences between Rates*

$\Delta = CDR^F - CDR^J$ = difference between crude death rates in France and Japan

$$= \sum_i \left(C_i^F - C_i^J \right) \cdot \left[\frac{M_i^F + M_i^J}{2} \right] + \sum_i \left(M_i^F - M_i^J \right) \cdot \left[\frac{C_i^F + C_i^J}{2} \right]$$

Example: France, 1991 and Japan, 1992, females

Age group i	C_i^F	C_i^J	M_i^F	M_i^J	$\left(C_i^F - C_i^J \right) \cdot \left[\frac{M_i^F + M_i^J}{2} \right]$	$\left(M_i^F - M_i^J \right) \cdot \left[\frac{C_i^F + C_i^J}{2} \right]$
0	0.0133	0.0089	0.0061	0.0040	0.000022	0.000023
1–4	0.0467	0.0349	0.0004	0.0004	0.000005	0.000000
5–9	0.0508	0.0734	0.0002	0.0001	−0.000003	0.000006
10–14	0.0541	0.0720	0.0002	0.0001	−0.000003	0.000006
15–19	0.0746	0.0811	0.0003	0.0002	−0.000002	0.000008
20–4	0.0686	0.0674	0.0005	0.0003	0.000000	0.000014
25–9	0.0730	0.0703	0.0006	0.0003	0.000001	0.000021
30–4	0.0749	0.0618	0.0007	0.0004	0.000007	0.000021
35–9	0.0794	0.0581	0.0009	0.0007	0.000017	0.000014
40–4	0.0768	0.0789	0.0014	0.0011	−0.000003	0.000023
45–9	0.0533	0.0677	0.0022	0.0016	−0.000027	0.000036
50–4	0.0507	0.0649	0.0029	0.0024	−0.000038	0.000029
55–9	0.0551	0.0602	0.0042	0.0037	−0.000020	0.000029
60–4	0.0544	0.0554	0.0064	0.0056	−0.000006	0.000044
65–9	0.0528	0.0470	0.0096	0.0090	0.000054	0.000030
70–4	0.0317	0.0365	0.0184	0.0158	−0.000083	0.000089
75–9	0.0360	0.0286	0.0279	0.0303	0.000216	−0.000078
80–4	0.0298	0.0197	0.0589	0.0587	0.000596	0.000005
85+	0.0240	0.0132	0.1605	0.1356	0.001599	0.000462
Sum	1.0000	1.0000			0.002333	0.000783

$$CDR^F = \sum_i C_i^F \cdot M_i^F = 0.008996$$

$$CDR^J = \sum_i C_i^J \cdot M_i^J = 0.005880$$

Original difference = $CDR^F - CDR^J$ = 0.008996 − 0.005880 = 0.003116
Contribution of age compositional differences = 0.002333
Contribution of age-specific rate differences = 0.000783
Total contribution = 0.002333 + 0.000783 = 0.003116
Proportion of difference attributable to differences in age composition = 0.002333/0.003116 = 0.749
Proportion of difference attributable to differences in rate schedules = 0.000783/0.003116 = 0.251

Data source: United Nations, *Demographic Yearbook* (various years).

2.4 The Lexis Diagram

We can define cohort age-specific rates by restricting occurrences and exposures to the relevant ages, exactly as we did for period age-specific rates. Thus, the age-specific death rate between ages 25 and 30 for a cohort born in 1940 (denoted with a 1940 superscript) is:

$$_5M_{25}^{1940c} = \frac{\text{Number of deaths to the 1940 cohort between ages 25 and 30}}{\text{Number of person-years lived by the 1940 cohort between ages 25 and 30}}$$

Note that counting deaths and person-years for this cohort requires including experience that stretches from calendar year 1965 (when they all reach age 25) through calendar year 1970 (when they all reach age 30), or over a span of 6 calendar years (1965, 1966, 1967, 1968, 1969, and 1970).

As noted already, cohort rates and period rates have the same structure but take into account different exposure segments. The Lexis diagram (Lexis, 1875) is a useful device to clarify relations between exposure segments for cohorts and exposure segments for periods. It is simply a two-dimensional figure in which age (in this case) is one dimension and calendar time the other. Units of age and time are normally the same (e.g., years), and these units are displayed in equal increments along both axes. What goes onto the diagram varies from one application to the next. Sometimes it is counts of events; sometimes it is symbols that represent counts; and sometimes it is life-lines.

On a Lexis diagram with the same time unit on both the time and age axis, a cohort advances through life along a 45° line. The exposure of interest in a cohort rate is thus delineated by two 45° lines that demarcate the time interval that defines membership in the cohort. Figure 2.1 delineates the age-time exposure region pertaining to the cohort born between 1.000 and 3.999.

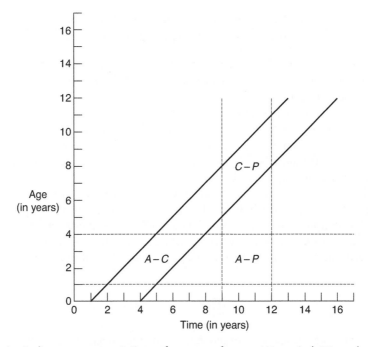

Figure 2.1 Lexis diagram representations of exposure for age (*A*), period (*P*), and cohort (*C*)

Period rates would be constructed from regions of exposure delineated by two vertical lines, shown on the figure for the period between 9.000 and 11.999.

An age-specific cohort rate thus restricts measuring exposure and counting occurrences to a parallelogram formed by two 45° lines defining the cohort and the two horizontal lines defining the age range (A–C on figure 2.1). An age-specific period rate restricts the measurement of exposure and occurrences to a rectangle formed by the two vertical lines defining the period and the two horizontal lines defining the age-range (A–P on figure 2.1). One can also define a cohort-specific period rate, which restricts exposure and occurrences of interest to a parallelogram delineated by two vertical lines defining the period and two 45° lines defining the cohort (C–P in figure 2.1). This latter construction is rarely encountered.

2.5 Age-specific Probabilities

Just as in the case of rates, the computation of probabilities can also be restricted to a certain age range. The conventional notation for a probability of dying between age x and $x + n$ (with both x and n measured in exact age) is $_nq_x$. The probability that a birth in the 1940 cohort would die before reaching age one is thus:

$$_1q_0^{1940\,c} = \frac{\text{Number of deaths to 1940 birth cohort between ages 0 and 1}}{\text{Number of births in the 1940 birth cohort}}$$

In the above example, the events (or "trials") that were counted in the denominator were the number of births in the 1940 cohort. If we had been dealing instead with the probability that a member of the 1940 birth cohort who reached age 25 died before he or she reached age 30, we would have:

$$_5q_{25}^{1940\,c} = \frac{\text{Number of deaths to 1940 birth cohort between ages 25 and 30}}{\text{Number of persons in the 1940 birth cohort who reached their 25th birthday}}$$

Recall that the calculation of a probability requires having a number of events in the denominator. The number of events in the denominator of $_5q_{25}^{1940\,c}$ is the number of 25th birthdays achieved by the 1940 cohort.

The infant deaths occurring to the birth cohort of 1940 will stretch over two calendar years, 1940 and 1941 (since the cohort will reach its first birthday, on average, about halfway through 1941). Likewise, the infant deaths occurring in 1941 will pertain to two annual birth cohorts, those born in 1940 and those born in 1941. The counting rules for calculating probabilities are also usefully displayed on a Lexis diagram.

Figure 2.2.a is a Lexis diagram containing life-lines of 6 persons during a two-year segment of age and time that begins with birth in calendar year 1995. The 1995 cohort's life-lines clearly must all fall within a parallelogram formed by two 45° lines that originate on January 1, 1995 and on January 1, 1996. A line ends when a person dies. Two persons out of the original cohort of 6 persons die before reaching age 1, so the probability of infant death for the cohort born in 1995 is

$$_1q_0^{1995\,c} = \frac{2}{6} = .3333$$

We cannot calculate, on the basis of the information presented, the probability that a person who reaches age 1 in 1996 dies before reaching age 2 because some of the members of the

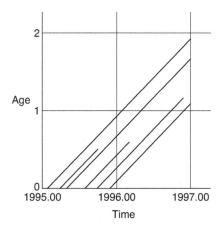

Figure 2.2a Lexis diagram containing life-lines for a birth cohort of 1995
Note: Time = 1995.00 refers to January 1, 1995.

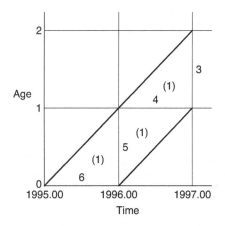

Figure 2.2b Lexis diagram containing counts of events pertaining to a birth cohort of 1995
Notes: From a birth cohort of 6 births in 1995: (1) death in 1995 and 5 survivors to the beginning of calendar year 1996; (1) death at age 0 in 1996 and 4 survivors at age 1 (4 first birthdays in the cohort, all occurring in 1996); (1) death to the cohort at age 1 during 1996 and 3 survivors to the beginning of calendar year 1997.

cohort may have died, before reaching age 2, in calendar year 1997. That year is not shown on the Lexis diagram.

The mortality experience represented by those 6 life-lines is summarized in a series of counts presented on figure 2.2.b, where the interpretation of the various numbers is also presented. The counts are placed within the same parallelogram that contains the cohort's experience. If a census were taken on January 1, 1996, it should have counted 5 persons aged 0 (last birthday); the only persons aged 0 at that date would have to have been born during calendar year 1995. A census taken at any time other than the beginning of a year would mix persons from two different birth cohorts at age 0. Counts adjacent to horizontal lines show the numbers arriving at a particular age in the cohort (6 births and 4 first birthdays).

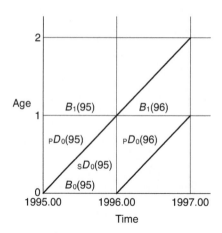

$B_0(95)$ = Number of births in 1995.
$B_1(95)$ = Number of first birthdays in 1995.
$B_1(96)$ = Number of first birthdays in 1996.
$_sD_0(95)$ = Number of deaths at age 0 in 1995 to people who reached age 0 in the same year.
$_pD_0(95)$ = Number of deaths at age 0 in 1995 to people who reached age 0 in the previous year.
$_pD_0(96)$ = Number of deaths at age 0 in 1996 to people who reached age 0 in the previous year.

Figure 2.2c Lexis diagram containing main symbols used to represent counts of events

Part c of figure 2.2 presents symbols that can be used to represent the counts presented in part b. For example,

$$_sD_0(95) = \text{number of deaths at age 0 in 1995 to persons who reached age 0}$$
(i.e., who were born) in the *same* year that they died

$$= 1$$

So $D_x(Y)$ is the total number of deaths at age x (last birthday) in year Y. The S and P subscripts on the left divide those deaths between those occurring to the birth cohorts who reached age x during the *same* year in which they died (S) and those occurring to the cohort that reached age x during the *previous* year (P). The "separation factor" at age x, year Y, separates the deaths at age x last birthday into two birth cohorts to which they occur. The separation factor at age x, year Y, is the proportion of deaths at age x (last birthday) in year Y occurring to persons who reached age x during year Y:

$$SF_x(Y) = \frac{_sD_x(Y)}{D_x(Y)} = \frac{_sD_x(Y)}{_sD_x(Y) + _pD_x(Y)}$$

In terms of these symbols, the probability of death before reaching age one for the birth cohort of 1995 is:

$$_1q_0^{1995\,c} = \frac{_sD_0(95) + _pD_0(96)}{B_0(95)}$$

Box 2.3 *Calculating Rates and Probabilities*

$$_nM_x^{cohort\ c} = \frac{Number\ of\ deaths\ to\ the\ cohort\ c\ between\ ages\ x\ and\ x+n}{Number\ of\ person\text{-}years\ lived\ by\ the\ cohort\ c\ between\ ages\ x\ and\ x+n}$$

$$_nM_x^{year\ t} = \frac{Number\ of\ deaths\ in\ the\ age\ range\ x\ to\ x+n\ during\ year\ t}{Number\ of\ person\text{-}years\ lived\ in\ the\ age\ range\ x\ to\ x+n\ during\ year\ t}$$

$$_nq_x^{cohort\ c} = \frac{Number\ of\ deaths\ to\ the\ cohort\ c\ between\ ages\ x\ and\ x+n}{Number\ of\ persons\ in\ the\ cohort\ c\ who\ reached\ their\ x^{th}\ birthday}$$

The probability of dying before reaching age 2 for the birth cohort of 1995 is:

$$_2q_0^{1995\ c} = \frac{_sD_0(95) + _pD_0(96) + _sD_1(96) + _pD_1(97)}{B_0(95)}$$

The probability of dying before reaching age 2 for a member of the 1994 birth cohort who survived to age 1 is:

$$_1q_1^{1994\ c} = \frac{_sD_1(95) + _pD_1(96)}{B_0(94) - _sD_0(94) - _pD_0(95)}$$

This type of measure cannot be computed without data that separate deaths occurring during a certain calendar year at a particular age into the two birth cohorts that contribute those deaths.

Box 2.3 summarizes the main cohort and period mortality indexes developed in this and previous sections.

2.6 Probabilities of Death Based on Mortality Experience of a Single Calendar Year

For many purposes it is desirable to have measures of mortality that pertain to a particular time period rather than to a particular cohort. But we have seen that two annual birth cohorts contribute to the deaths recorded during any year at any particular age. How are these two cohorts' experiences to be synthesized in producing an estimate of age-specific mortality for that calendar year? Such a synthesis for infants is facilitated by writing the probability of death before age 1 as:

$$_1q_0 = \begin{matrix} \text{probability that a} \\ \text{child dies in his} \\ \text{calendar year of birth} \end{matrix} + \begin{matrix} \text{probability that a} \\ \text{child survives his} \\ \text{calendar year of birth} \end{matrix} \cdot \begin{matrix} \text{probability that if a child} \\ \text{survives his year of birth, he} \\ \text{dies in the next calendar year} \\ \text{before reaching age 1} \end{matrix}$$

Let us insert the appropriate elements in this formula and show that it produces a correct formula for a cohort born in year Y:

$$_1q_0^{Y\ c} = \frac{_sD_0(Y)}{B_0(Y)} + \frac{B(Y) - _sD_0(Y)}{B_0(Y)} \cdot \frac{_pD_0(Y+1)}{B_0(Y) - _sD_0(Y)} = \frac{_sD_0(Y) + _pD_0(Y+1)}{B_0(Y)}$$

The idea underlying the synthesis is to take all the death terms in the numerator from the same calendar year, rather than from two different years (as required for calculating a cohort's probability). Thus we can write the probability of dying between ages 0 and 1 for calendar year Y as:

$$_1q_0(Y) = \frac{_sD_0(Y)}{B_0(Y)} + \frac{B(Y) - _sD_0(Y)}{B_0(Y)} \cdot \frac{_pD_0(Y)}{B_0(Y-1) - _sD_0(Y-1)} \qquad (2.2)$$

A more general formula appropriate for any age interval x to $x + 1$ would replace age 0 with age x in equation (2.2) and would use $B_x(Y)$ as the number of xth birthdays achieved in year Y.

A closely related concept is the "infant mortality rate," one of the most common indexes used in demography. The conventionally defined infant mortality rate for year Y is defined as infant deaths in year Y divided by births in year Y:

$$IMR(Y) = \frac{D_0(Y)}{B_0(Y)} = \frac{_sD_0(Y) + _pD_0(Y)}{B_0(Y)} \qquad (2.3)$$

Unfortunately, this infant mortality "rate" is structured as a probability rather than as a conventional demographic rate, since it has a count of events in the denominator. But in fact it not only fails as a rate but as a probability: it is counting trials in one urn (births in year Y) but events from parts of two (deaths to births that occurred in years Y and $Y - 1$). It will equal the probability of dying before age one for the *cohort* born in year Y only if $_pD_0(Y) = _pD_0(Y + 1)$. Such equivalence would occur if births were constant from year to year and if age-specific mortality conditions were also constant. Under these restricted circumstances, the infant mortality rate will also equal the period probability of dying before age 1 given by (2.2).

But the infant mortality rate is simple to define and materials for its calculation do not require the division of infant deaths by calendar year of birth. Its value should not be seriously misleading as an estimate of the probability of dying before age 1 (assuming that data are accurate) unless the number of births varies greatly from year to year. As a simple expedient, it probably deserves tolerance more than condemnation. Table 2.3 presents estimates of infant mortality rates in major regions of the world in recent years, and box 2.4 defines other conventional measures of fetal and early-life mortality.

An alternative procedure for converting data on mortality in a particular period into estimated probabilities of dying is used more frequently than the method described in this section. It is developed in the next chapter.

Table 2.3: *Infant mortality rates in major areas, 1995–2000 (deaths per 1,000 live births)*

Major area	IMR 1995–2000
Africa	87
Asia	57
Europe	12
Latin America and the Caribbean	36
Northern America	7
Oceania	24

Source: United Nations, 1999.

Box 2.4 *Conventional Measures of Fetal and Early-infancy Mortality*

Fetal mortality rate:

$$\frac{\text{Fetal Deaths during year } t}{\text{Fetal Deaths} + \text{Births during year } t}$$

Perinatal mortality rate:

$$\frac{(\text{Fetal Deaths} \geq 28 \text{ weeks of pregnancy}) + (\text{Deaths} < 1\text{week of age}) \text{ during year } t}{\text{Births} + (\text{Fetal Deaths} \geq 28 \text{ weeks}) \text{ during year } t}$$

Neonatal mortality rate:

$$\frac{\text{Deaths} < 1 \text{ month of age during year } t}{\text{Births during year } t}$$

Post-neonatal mortality rate:

$$\frac{\text{Deaths } 1\text{--}11 \text{ months of age during year } t}{\text{Births during year } t}$$

Infant mortality rate:

$$\frac{\text{Deaths} < 1 \text{ year of age during year } t}{\text{Births during year } t}$$

NOTES

1. In equation (2.1), the *CDR* can be seen as the sum of a mortality level indicator and of a covariance between two distributions: the population by age and the age-specific death rates. Indeed, (2.1) can be rewritten as:

$$CDR = \sum_{x=0}^{\omega}[(_nM_x - \overline{M}) \cdot (_nC_x - \overline{C})] + \overline{M}$$

   where $\overline{M}$ is the (unweighted) mean of age-specific death rates and $\overline{C}$ is the (unweighted) mean of proportions of the population in an age interval. For a given set of age-specific death rates, the *CDR* is thus higher the higher is the covariance of the population by age with these age-specific rates.

2. Age composition only matters as long as the variable of interest varies with age. If age-specific mortality rates were constant by age, the *CDR* would not depend on the age structure of the population. If $_nM_x = M$ at all ages, then equation (2.1) becomes: $CDR = \sum M \cdot {_nC_x} = M \cdot \sum {_nC_x} = M$ (since $\sum {_nC_x} = 1$). The assumption of constant age-specific rates is an unrealistic assumption for mortality.

3. In particular, the "young" structure is that of a model "West" female stable population with $r = .02$ and life expectancy at birth of 45 years; the old structure has an $r = .01$ and life expectancy at birth of 65 years (Coale and Demeny, 1983: 46 and 64). The concept of a stable population is developed in chapter 7 below and model life tables are described in chapter 9.

3 The Life Table and Single Decrement Processes

The life table is one of the most important devices used in demography. In its classical form, it is a table that displays various pieces of information about the dying out of a birth cohort. One column of a classical life table is invariably "age." The remaining columns tabulate age-related functions pertaining to mortality, such as the number of survivors to various ages, deaths in particular age intervals, age-specific death rates, probabilities of death in various age intervals, and so on. The life *table* is only one way of summarizing a cohort's mortality experience; other ways, for example, are in graphical form or in the form of a mathematical function.

As an accounting device, the life table poses few conceptual difficulties. However, the profusion of columns and functions creates a cumbersome notational baggage. Probably the easiest way to elucidate the life table is to return to the concept of life-lines. These are normally displayed on a Lexis diagram. But if we imagine that a cohort is all born at the same instant of time, then the two dimensions of a Lexis diagram (age and time) can be collapsed into one. Figure 3.1 displays the life-lines of 10 individuals born on January 1, 1800. From these life-lines alone, all of the information available in a life table can be derived. Table 3.1 displays the life table corresponding to the 10 life-lines shown on figure 3.1.

The verbal description of life table columns is included on table 3.1, so there is no need to reiterate them in the text. The most frequently-used column of a life table is probably "expectation of life at age x" or "life expectancy at age x," usually denoted e_x^o. It refers to

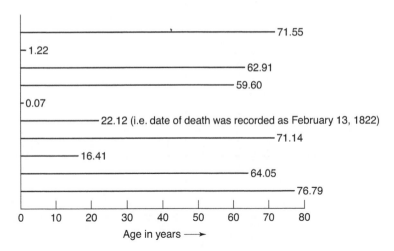

Figure 3.1 Age at death and life-lines of a hypothetical cohort of births (10 in all); date of birth: January 1, 1800

the average number of *additional* years that a survivor to age x will live beyond that age. It is calculated simply by dividing the total number of person-years lived by the cohort above exact age x by the number of survivors to that age.[1] Life expectancy at birth (e_0^o), the sum of all person-years lived by the cohort divided by the original number in the cohort, is also equal to the average age at death for the cohort, since life ends at the exact age when death occurs. The average age at death for someone who survives to age 50 is equal to $50 + e_{50}^o$, or 67.673 in table 3.1. Note that life expectancy at age 1 in this table exceeds that at age 0, a phenomenon that is not uncommon. Very high levels of infant mortality often mean that those who survive this hazardous year can actually look forward to more years of *additional* life than could newborns themselves.

The other column that needs an introduction is the $_na_x$ column. This refers to the average number of person-years lived in the interval x to $x + n$ by those dying in the interval. It is found by dividing the total number of person-years lived in the interval x to $x + n$ by those dying in that interval by the total number dying in the interval. For example, in age interval 60–70, two people died, at ages 62.91 and 64.05. Thus, they lived $(2.91 + 4.05) = 6.96$ years in the interval. So $_{10}a_{60} = 6.96/2 = 3.48$. The utility of this column is not obvious at this point but will become so in the next section.

It should be clear that some functions (l_x, T_x, e_x^o) refer to a single (exact) age, while other functions ($_nd_x$, $_np_x$, $_nq_x$, $_nm_x$, $_na_x$) refer to age intervals that begin with exact age x and extend for exactly n years. The length of these intervals need not be, and usually is not, constant within the same life table. Perhaps the most conventional format for a life table has a length of 1 year for the first age interval (i.e., the functions in the first row pertain either to exact age 0 or to the age interval 0 to 1); a length of 4 years for the second age interval (i.e., the functions in the second row pertain either to exact age one or to the age interval 1 to 5); and a length of 5 years thereafter (i.e., functions in the third row pertain either to exact age 5 or to age interval 5 to 10). Another convention is to use lower-case letters to refer to the number of deaths ($_nd_x$) and deaths rates ($_nm_x$) in a cohort whose experience is summarized in a life table, rather than using the $_nD_x$ and $_nM_x$ notation that pertains to equivalent functions in a population.

Table 3.1: *Life table for hypothetical cohort of 10 births shown in figure 3.1*

Exact age	Number left alive at age x	Number dying between ages x and x+n	Probability of dying between ages x and x+n	Probability of surviving from age x to age x+n	Person-years lived between ages x and x+n	Person-years lived above age x	Expectation of life at age x	Death rate in the cohort between ages x and x+n	Average person-years lived in the interval by those dying in the interval
x	l_x	$_nd_x$	$_nq_x$	$_np_x$	$_nL_x$	$T_x = \sum_{a=x}^{\infty} {_nL_a}$	$e_x^o = T_x/l_x$	$_nm_x$	$_na_x$
0	10	1	1/10	9/10	$9 + .07$ $= 9.07$	$436.79 + 9.07$ $= 445.86$	$\dfrac{445.86}{10}$ $= 44.586$	$\dfrac{1}{9.07}$	.07
1	9	1	1/9	8/9	$8 \cdot 4 + .22$ $= 32.22$	$404.57 + 32.22$ $= 436.79$	$\dfrac{436.79}{9}$ $= 48.532$	$\dfrac{1}{32.22}$	.22
5	8	0	0	1	$8 \cdot 5 = 40$	$364.57 + 40$ $= 404.57$	$\dfrac{404.57}{8}$ $= 50.571$	0	—
10	8	1	1/8	7/8	$7 \cdot 10 + 6.41$ $= 76.41$	$288.16 + 76.41$ $= 364.57$	$\dfrac{364.57}{8}$ $= 45.571$	$\dfrac{1}{76.41}$	6.41
20	7	1	1/7	6/7	$6 \cdot 10 + 2.12$ $= 62.12$	$226.04 + 62.12$ $= 288.16$	$\dfrac{288.16}{7}$ $= 41.166$	$\dfrac{1}{62.12}$	2.12

30	6	0	0	1	$6 \cdot 10 = 60$	$166.04 + 60$ $= 226.04$	$\dfrac{226.04}{6}$ $= 37.673$	0	—
40	6	0	0	1	$6 \cdot 10 = 60$	$106.04 + 60$ $= 166.04$	$\dfrac{166.04}{6}$ $= 27.673$	0	—
50	6	1	1/6	5/6	$5 \cdot 10 + 9.60$ $= 59.60$	$46.44 + 59.60$ $= 106.04$	$\dfrac{106.04}{6}$ $= 17.673$	$\dfrac{1}{59.60}$	9.60
60	5	2	2/5	3/5	$3 \cdot 10 + 6.96$ $= 36.96$	$9.48 + 36.96$ $= 46.44$	$\dfrac{46.44}{5}$ $= 9.288$	$\dfrac{2}{36.96}$	$(2.91 + 4.05)/2$ $= 6.96/2$ $= 3.48$
70	3	3	3/3	0	9.48	9.48	$\dfrac{9.48}{3}$ $= 3.16$	$\dfrac{3}{9.48}$	$(1.55 + 1.14 + 6.79)/3$ $= 9.48/3$ $= 3.16$
80	0	0	—	—					

Because the columns of the life table are so closely related to one another, there are many arithmetic relations among the columns. For example:

$$_nd_x = l_x - l_{x+n},$$

i.e., the number of deaths between age x and age $x + n$ is equal to the difference between the number of survivors to age x and the number of survivors to age $x + n$;

$$_nd_x = l_x \cdot {}_nq_x,$$

i.e., the number of deaths between age x and age $x + n$ is equal to the number of survivors to age x times the probability of dying between age x and age $x + n$; and

$$_np_x = \frac{l_{x+n}}{l_x} = \frac{l_x - {}_nd_x}{l_x} = 1 - {}_nq_x,$$

i.e., the probability of surviving between age x and age $x + n$ is equal to one minus the probability of dying between those ages.

3.1 Period Life Tables

As illustrated in table 3.1, the construction of a life table for a cohort poses little difficulty. But because cohort data might be outdated, unavailable, or incomplete, actuaries and demographers have developed what is termed a "period" life table (sometimes also referred to as a "current" life table). This table presents exactly the same type of information as that contained in a cohort life table. But the information attempts to show what *would happen* to a cohort *if* it were subjected for all of its life to the mortality conditions of that period. Such a cohort is usually termed a "synthetic" or "hypothetical" cohort, as opposed to a "real" cohort consisting of actual births. Whereas the *cohort* life table (i.e., that pertaining to a real birth cohort) simply *records* information about what actually happened to that cohort, a *period* life table is a *model* of what would happen to a hypothetical cohort if a certain set of mortality conditions pertained throughout its life.

How should the period's "mortality conditions" be operationalized to produce a period life table? Almost always, the answer is "by the set of age-specific death rates for that period." These rates must then be transformed into other columns of the table. The key to this transformation is a conversion from the set of observed period age-specific death rates, $_nM_x$, to a set of age-specific probabilities of dying, $_nq_x$. This conversion is usually accomplished by referring to the relation between age-specific death rates and age-specific probabilities of dying in an actual cohort:

$$_nm_x = \frac{_nd_x}{_nL_x}$$

$$= \frac{Number\ of\ deaths\ in\ the\ cohort\ between\ ages\ x\ and\ x + n}{Number\ of\ person\text{-}years\ lived\ in\ the\ cohort\ between\ ages\ x\ and\ x + n}$$

$$_nq_x = \frac{_nd_x}{l_x}$$

$$= \frac{Number\ of\ deaths\ in\ the\ cohort\ between\ ages\ x\ and\ x + n}{Number\ of\ survivors\ to\ age\ x\ in\ the\ cohort}$$

The formula for the conversion can be derived by replacing the l_x term in the formula for $_nq_x$ by an equivalent expression. Note that:

$$_nL_x \qquad = \qquad n \cdot l_{x+n} \qquad + \qquad _nA_x,$$

Number of person-years lived by the cohort between ages x and $x+n$	Number of person-years lived in the interval by members of the cohort who survive the interval	Number of person-years lived in the interval by members of the cohort who die in the interval

or

$$_nL_x \qquad = \qquad n \cdot l_{x+n} \qquad + \qquad _na_x \qquad \cdot \qquad _nd_x$$

		Mean number of person-years lived in the interval by those dying in the interval	Number of members of the cohort dying in the interval

Rewriting this equation, we have:

$$_nL_x = n(l_x - {_nd_x}) + {_na_x} \cdot {_nd_x}$$

$$n \cdot l_x = {_nL_x} + n \cdot {_nd_x} - {_na_x} \cdot {_nd_x}$$

$$l_x = \frac{1}{n}[{_nL_x} + (n - {_na_x}) \cdot {_nd_x}]$$

Now substituting this expression for l_x into the formula for $_nq_x$, we have:

$$_nq_x = \frac{_nd_x}{l_x} = \frac{n \cdot {_nd_x}}{{_nL_x} + (n - {_na_x}){_nd_x}}$$

Finally, we divide both numerator and denominator of this last expression by $_nL_x$, giving:

$$_nq_x = \frac{n \cdot \dfrac{_nd_x}{_nL_x}}{\dfrac{_nL_x}{_nL_x} + (n - {_na_x})\dfrac{_nd_x}{_nL_x}} = \frac{n \cdot {_nm_x}}{1 + (n - {_na_x}){_nm_x}} \qquad \textbf{(3.1)}$$

Equation (3.1), due to Greville (1943) and Chiang (1968), says that, for a cohort, the conversion from $_nm_x$ to $_nq_x$ depends on only one parameter: $_na_x$, the average number of person-years lived in the interval by those dying in the interval. No other information is required to perform this conversion, and any other information is redundant.

If persons dying in the interval do so, on average, half-way through the interval, then equation (3.1) becomes:

$$_nq_x = \frac{n \cdot {_nm_x}}{1 + \dfrac{n}{2}{_nm_x}} = \frac{2n \cdot {_nm_x}}{2 + n \cdot {_nm_x}} \qquad \textbf{(3.2)}$$

The $_na_x$ function is of little interest in a cohort life table because $_nq_x$ and $_nm_x$ can both, in principal, be directly observed. It gains its importance from its utility in making the $_nm_x \rightarrow {_nq_x}$

conversion for use in a period life table. In particular, if it is assumed that the hypothetical cohort in a period life table is to experience an observed set of period age-specific death rates, $_nM_x$, then all that remains to complete the period life table is the adoption of a set of $_na_x$ values in order to make the $_nM_x \rightarrow {_nq_x}$ conversion. If we choose this common route, then we have assumed that the observed period age-specific death rates $(_nM_x)$ are to be reproduced in the hypothetical cohort passing through life in the period life table $(_nm_x)$. All that remains is to convert the $_nm_x{'}$s to $_nq_x{'}$s. Whether the strategy is implicit or explicit, techniques for period life table construction that start out with a set of $_nm_x$s are focused upon the choice of a set of $_na_x$ values. We now mention several diverse strategies that are sometimes employed.

3.2 Strategies for Choosing a Set of $_na_x$ Values and/or for Making the $_nm_x \rightarrow {_nq_x}$ Conversion

3.2.1 Direct observation

If data on exact ages at death are available for a population (e.g. 60.19, 23.62, . . .), then it is clearly possible to take all of the deaths during a period that fall within a particular n-year wide age interval and compute $_na_x$ directly. Note that this value would pertain to a population, rather than to a cohort. Such information is rarely available, and even if it were it is not always advisable to use it. The reason is that the $_na_x$ values observed in a population are influenced by that population's age distribution within the n-year wide age interval. Suppose, to take an extreme example, that a certain population had 100 times as many people aged 60 as those in the combined age-group 61–4. Then $_5a_{60}$ would almost certainly lie between ages 60.00 and 61.00, regardless of mortality conditions. But it would not, in general, be sensible to suppose that those dying in a *cohort* passing from ages 60 to 65 would all die before age 61. For reasons discussed below, using observed $_na_x{'}$s will usually reinforce biases already present in data subject to age-distributional anomalies.

3.2.2 Graduation of the $_nm_x$ function

The level and slope of the $_nm_x$ function itself provide strong clues about the ages of persons dying within an age interval. Given two populations with the same $_5m_{60}$ values, the population in which mortality rises more rapidly with age during the interval will have a higher concentration of deaths at the upper part of that interval and, hence, a higher value of $_5a_{60}$. While we cannot normally observe the slope of death rates *within* the 5-year age interval 60 to 65, we can observe the general slope of death rates based on, for example, $_5m_{55}, _5m_{60},$ and $_5m_{65}$. In addition to being affected by the slope of the death rate function, the value of $_na_x$ is also affected by the level of mortality. Given a certain slope, the higher is mortality within a particular age interval, the more will deaths be concentrated at the beginning of that interval because fewer people will survive to be at risk of death near the end of the interval. This is the logic on which several systems of life table construction are based. Greville (1943) assumed that age-specific death rates were log-linearly related to age (a hypothesis first set forth in Gompertz' law of mortality, as we will see in section 9.1), and then showed how the $_nm_x \rightarrow {_nq_x}$ conversion could be made once the slope of that log-linear relation was ascertained.

Another approach consists of estimating $_na_x$ from information on the age distribution of deaths in the life table, assuming that this distribution, $d(a)$, follows a polynomial function of the second degree in the interval $x - n$ to $x + 2n$ (Keyfitz, 1966):

$$d(a) = A + Ba + Ca^2, \quad \text{for } x - n \leq a \leq x + 2n$$

Under this assumption, one can show that

$$
{}_n a_x = \frac{-\frac{n}{24}{}_n d_{x-n} + \frac{n}{2}{}_n d_x + \frac{n}{24}{}_n d_{x+n}}{{}_n d_x}
$$

Note that this equation produces an estimate of ${}_n a_x = n/2$ when deaths are symmetrically distributed in the three relevant age groups. This equation for ${}_n a_x$ requires having estimates of ${}_n d_x$, which is usually estimated from the ${}_n M_x \rightarrow {}_n q_x$ conversion itself and thus requires information on ${}_n a_x$. To solve this circularity problem, one must use iteration. It makes most sense to begin by taking ${}_n a_x = n/2$ in the ${}_n M_x \rightarrow {}_n q_x$ conversion to obtain a first set of ${}_n d_x$ estimates, and then using these ${}_n d_x$ to obtain a new set of ${}_n a_x$ estimates with the above equation. This new set of ${}_n a_x$ values can then be reused in the ${}_n M_x \rightarrow {}_n q_x$ conversion until stable estimates of ${}_n a_x$ and ${}_n d_x$ are obtained. Two or three iterations are typically sufficient to produce stable estimates. Limitations of the method are that it does not permit the estimation of ${}_n a_x$ in the first and last age groups and it requires that all age groups used in the estimation have the same width, n.

Keyfitz and Frauenthal (1975) have developed another approach to estimating ${}_n q_x$ which assumes that the age distribution and age-specific death rates are both linear between ages $(x-n)$ and $(x+2n)$, conditions that may be mutually inconsistent. These assumptions produce the following estimation equation:

$$
\frac{l_{x+n}}{l_x} = \exp\left[-n\,{}_n M_x - \frac{n}{48\,{}_n N_x}({}_n N_{x-n} - {}_n N_{x+n})({}_n M_{x+n} - {}_n M_{x-n})\right]
$$

where ${}_n N_x = $ population aged x to $x + n$.

Keyfitz and Frauenthal's equation appears to produce satisfactory results in situations where the age distribution is rather smooth, but it does not necessarily give better estimates than other methods when the age distribution is erratic (Pressat, 1995).

3.2.3 Borrowing ${}_n a_x$ values from another population

If there are reasons to believe that the level and shape of the ${}_n m_x$ curve is similar to that of another population for which ${}_n a_x$ values have been accurately estimated, then a simple and reasonable expedient is to adopt that set of values. The borrowed values should correspond to the sex for which they are being used because ${}_n a_x$ values vary significantly between the sexes. Keyfitz and Flieger (1968 and 1990) provide sets of ${}_n a_x$ values for populations based on graduation techniques above age 10. Examples of several sets of these functions are shown in table 3.2. Note that at older ages the values of ${}_5 a_x$ tend to exceed 2.5 years, reflecting the rapid rise in mortality with age so that deaths are concentrated towards the upper end of the age range. At the very highest ages, the values of ${}_5 a_x$ start to decline as the increasingly high mortality levels leave fewer survivors available to die at the upper end of an age range.

A traditional method of life table construction due to Reed and Merrell (1939) amounts to borrowing ${}_n a_x$ values from another population, although it is not usually recognized in this guise. Reed and Merrell used life tables for the US in which ${}_n a_x$ had been estimated for actual cohorts, based upon very detailed US vital statistics. They compared the ${}_n m_x$ values to the ${}_n q_x$ values in the resulting life tables and fit a statistical relation between the two series. They then recommend inserting the values of ${}_n m_x$ into the resulting equation in order to derive ${}_n q_x$. This operation is equivalent to reproducing (with an error term) the ${}_n a_x$ values in the US life tables

Table 3.2: *Average person-years lived between ages x and x + n for persons dying in the interval ($_na_x$)*

e_0^o	Sweden, 1900		Sweden, 1985		United States, 1985		Guatemala, 1985	
	Males	*Females*	*Males*	*Females*	*Males*	*Females*	*Males*	*Females*
	51.528	54.257	73.789	79.830	71.266	78.422	60.582	64.415
Age *x*	Average person-years lived for people dying in the interval *x* to *x + n*							
0	0.358	0.375	0.083	0.081	0.090	0.086	0.165	0.150
1	1.235	1.270	1.500	1.500	1.500	1.500	1.500	1.500
5	2.500	2.500	2.500	2.500	2.500	2.500	2.500	2.500
10	2.456	2.469	3.006	2.773	3.014	2.757	2.469	2.390
15	2.639	2.565	2.749	2.617	2.734	2.644	2.711	2.665
20	2.549	2.536	2.569	2.578	2.564	2.552	2.628	2.601
25	2.481	2.514	2.561	2.665	2.527	2.588	2.573	2.563
30	2.505	2.509	2.600	2.649	2.571	2.632	2.593	2.627
35	2.544	2.521	2.638	2.625	2.622	2.678	2.545	2.566
40	2.563	2.522	2.695	2.662	2.666	2.706	2.541	2.543
45	2.572	2.561	2.705	2.722	2.688	2.702	2.604	2.592
50	2.574	2.578	2.706	2.694	2.684	2.683	2.596	2.627
55	2.602	2.609	2.687	2.670	2.657	2.671	2.623	2.661
60	2.602	2.633	2.673	2.689	2.626	2.650	2.635	2.623
65	2.591	2.628	2.643	2.697	2.608	2.642	2.616	2.676
70	2.561	2.585	2.607	2.706	2.571	2.631	2.557	2.607
75	2.500	2.517	2.547	2.650	2.519	2.614	2.486	2.532
80	2.415	2.465	2.471	2.607	2.460	2.596	2.409	2.447
85+	3.488	3.888	4.607	5.897	5.455	6.969	4.611	4.836

Source: Keyfitz and Flieger, 1968: 491; and 1990: 310, 348 and 528.

on which their statistical relation was based. Since there is no special reason to believe in the widespread applicability of this US table, it seems better, in general, to borrow from a more suitable lender.

3.2.4 Using rules of thumb

There are two rules of thumb that are commonly implemented in choosing $_na_x$. Except for infancy and possibly age 1, each of these works extremely well – leads to trivial error – when data are arrayed in one-year wide age intervals. One rule of thumb is that $_na_x = n/2$: deaths are assumed to occur, on average, halfway through the interval. This assumption leads immediately to equation (3.2).

The other assumption is that the age-specific death rate is constant in the age interval *x* to *x + n*. In this case, as will be shown below,

$$_np_x = 1 - _nq_x = e^{-n \cdot _n m_x}$$

Here no conversion involving $_na_x$ is required. Of course, a value of $_na_x$ is implicit in this conversion formula; in particular, for this assumption,

$$_na_x = n + \frac{1}{_n m_x} - \frac{n}{1 - e^{-n \cdot _n m_x}}$$

It can be shown that $_na_x$ in this case is necessarily less than $n/2$. The reason is that, with a constant death rate in the interval, the number of deaths at any point in that interval will be proportional to the number of survivors, a number which declines throughout the interval. So there must be more deaths in the first half of the interval than in the second half.

The shape of the human mortality curve is sharply upward-sloping beyond age 30 or so. Therefore, the second rule of thumb tends not to be very attractive for this set of ages. It is often used, however, in nonmortality applications and has convenient aggregation properties.

Which of these four strategies should be used? The answer depends on data quality and on the demographic conditions generating the observations. Graduation is the most time-consuming alternative but perhaps the one in which most confidence can be invested. Adoption of a set of $_na_x$ values from another, similar, population is probably a close second in terms of accuracy, and is exceedingly easy to apply. Direct computation is usually difficult and, in a population subject to age distributional disturbances, not advisable.

The strategy chosen should depend in part upon the sensitivity of results to error in choosing $_na_x$. Here the results are reassuring. Examining the formula for the $_nm_x \rightarrow {_nq_x}$ conversion,

$$_nq_x = \frac{n \cdot {_nm_x}}{1 + (n - {_na_x})_nm_x}$$

we see that $_na_x$ is being multiplied by $_nm_x$ before it enters into the formula. With a death rate of 0.012, which is about that prevailing in the world at present, an error of as much as 0.2 years in $_na_x$, which is relatively large error, would affect $_nq_x$ in the proportion of only $0.2(.012) = .0024$, or about a quarter of 1 percent. Of course, if that error is repeated over and over again from age group to age group, it will cumulate in its effects. But even if *every* age has an $_na_x$ that is in error by 0.2 in the same direction, life expectancy at birth will be in error by only about 0.2 years. We can agree with the World Health Organization (1977: 70) in its conclusion that "Although these various methods [of life table construction] are based upon very different assumptions, when applied to actual mortality rates they do not result in significant differences of importance to mortality analysis."

3.3 The Very Young Ages

Life expectancy estimates are most sensitive to procedures used in the very young, high mortality ages. When estimation of $_nq_x$ for these ages can be made by assigning deaths to the appropriate birth cohorts, as described in chapter 2, it is usually best to do so. But when converting a death rate into a probability of dying, it is important to recognize that the value of $_na_x$ is (empirically) a function of the level of mortality itself. Generally speaking, the lower the level of mortality, the more heavily will infant deaths be concentrated at the earliest stages of infancy; the influence of the prenatal and perinatal environment becomes increasingly dominant relative to the postnatal environment. Coale and Demeny (1983: 20) have reviewed this relation in many populations and have fit a line to the international and intertemporal data. In particular, they have fit the relation between values of $_1a_0$ and $_4a_1$ and the values of $_1q_0$. We have adapted these relations to the typical circumstances encountered in life table construction. Results are shown in table 3.3. In the absence of other information, the formulas presented in this table can be recommended for use in deriving $_na_x$ values below age 5.

Table 3.3: *Values of $_na_x$ for use below age 5*

	Males	Females
Value of $_1a_0$		
If $_1m_0 \geq .107$	.330	.350
If $_1m_0 < .107$	$.045 + 2.684 \cdot {}_1m_0$	$.053 + 2.800 \cdot {}_1m_0$
Value of $_4a_1$		
If $_1m_0 \geq .107$	1.352	1.361
If $_1m_0 < .107$	$1.651 - 2.816 \cdot {}_1m_0$	$1.522 - 1.518 \cdot {}_1m_0$

Source: Adapted from Coale and Demeny (1983) West model life tables.

3.4 The Open-ended Age Interval

The formulas presented so far are incapable of dealing with the open-ended (or terminal) age interval. In this interval n is, in effect, infinity. A conventional way of dealing with this interval is to return to the formula for the death rate in a cohort. Since

$$_nm_x = \frac{_nd_x}{_nL_x},$$

when $n = \infty$ we must have

$$_\infty m_x = \frac{_\infty d_x}{_\infty L_x} \quad \text{or} \quad _\infty L_x = \frac{_\infty d_x}{_\infty m_x}.$$

But the number of persons dying in the cohort above age x, whether the cohort is real or hypothetical, must equal the number of persons surviving to age x $(_\infty d_x = l_x)$, so:

$$_\infty L_x = \frac{l_x}{_\infty m_x}.$$

$_\infty m_x$ is observed and l_x can be calculated on the basis of mortality at all ages below x. So the number of person years lived above x can be calculated and used to complete the life table. Of course, $_\infty q_x = 1.00$ and $_\infty p_x = 0.00$.

Procedures for dealing with the open-ended interval have become increasingly important as more people have survived to its beginning. The most commonly encountered open-ended interval begins with age 85, to which age nearly half of females in recent period life tables for developed countries will survive. Where data permit, the analyst should clearly adopt a high enough age for starting the open-ended interval that only a small fraction of the population survives to that age. In section 7.8, we will describe a more elaborate procedure for estimating person-years in the open-ended age interval.

3.5 Review of Steps for Period Life Table Construction

a. Calculate the set of age-specific death rates to be used ($_nm_x$). The usual procedure is to assume, for each age-interval, that $_nm_x = {}_nM_x$. This equality means that we choose to reproduce, in the life table $_nm_x$ values, the set of $_nM_x$ values observed in a population during a particular period.

Box 3.1 *Period Life Table Construction*

A. Observed data:

$_nN_x$ = mid-year population in age interval x to $x + n$

$_nD_x$ = deaths between ages x and $x + n$ during the year

B. Steps for period life table construction:

1. $_nm_x \simeq {}_nM_x = \dfrac{_nD_x}{_nN_x}$

2. $_na_x$:

   calculated from Coale and Demeny equations
   shown in table 3.3 under age 5, borrowed
   from Keyfitz and Flieger above age 5

3. $_nq_x = \dfrac{n \cdot {}_nm_x}{1 + (n - {}_na_x) \cdot {}_nm_x}$

   $_\infty q_{85} = 1.00$

4. $_np_x = 1 - {}_nq_x$

5. $l_0 = 100,000$

   $l_{x+n} = l_x \cdot {}_np_x$

6. $_nd_x = l_x - l_{x+n}$

7. $_nL_x = n \cdot l_{x+n} + {}_na_x \cdot {}_nd_x$

   (open-ended interval: $_\infty L_x = \dfrac{l_x}{_\infty m_x}$)

8. $T_x = \sum\limits_{a=x}^{\infty} {}_nL_a$

9. $e_x^o = \dfrac{T_x}{l_x}$

Example: Austria, males, 1992

Age x	$_nN_x$	$_nD_x$	$_nm_x$	$_na_x$	$_nq_x$	$_np_x$	l_x	$_nd_x$	$_nL_x$	T_x	e_x^o
0	47,925	419	0.008743	0.068	0.008672	0.991328	100,000	867	99,192	7,288,901	72.889
1	189,127	70	0.000370	1.626	0.001479	0.998521	99,133	147	396,183	7,189,709	72.526
5	234,793	36	0.000153	2.500	0.000766	0.999234	98,986	76	494,741	6,793,526	68.631
10	238,790	46	0.000193	3.143	0.000963	0.999037	98,910	95	494,375	6,298,785	63.682
15	254,996	249	0.000976	2.724	0.004872	0.995128	98,815	481	492,980	5,804,410	58.740
20	326,831	420	0.001285	2.520	0.006405	0.993595	98,334	630	490,106	5,311,431	54.014
25	355,086	403	0.001135	2.481	0.005659	0.994341	97,704	553	487,127	4,821,324	49.346
30	324,222	441	0.001360	2.601	0.006779	0.993221	97,151	659	484,175	4,334,198	44.613
35	269,963	508	0.001882	2.701	0.009368	0.990632	96,492	904	480,384	3,850,023	39.900
40	261,971	769	0.002935	2.663	0.014577	0.985423	95,588	1,393	474,686	3,369,639	35.252
45	238,011	1,154	0.004849	2.698	0.023975	0.976025	94,195	2,258	465,777	2,894,953	30.734
50	261,612	1,866	0.007133	2.676	0.035082	0.964918	91,937	3,225	452,188	2,429,176	26.422
55	181,385	2,043	0.011263	2.645	0.054861	0.945139	88,711	4,867	432,096	1,976,988	22.286
60	187,962	3,496	0.018600	2.624	0.089062	0.910938	83,845	7,467	401,480	1,544,893	18.426
65	153,832	4,366	0.028382	2.619	0.132925	0.867075	76,377	10,152	357,713	1,143,412	14.971
70	105,169	4,337	0.041238	2.593	0.187573	0.812427	66,225	12,422	301,224	785,699	11.864
75	73,694	5,279	0.071634	2.518	0.304102	0.695898	53,803	16,362	228,404	484,475	9.005
80	57,512	6,460	0.112324	2.423	0.435548	0.564452	37,441	16,307	145,182	256,070	6.839
85	32,248	6,146	0.190585	5.247	1.000000	0.000000	21,134	21,134	110,889	110,889	5.247

Data source: United Nations, 1994.

b. Adopt a set of $_na_x$ values. For example,

- under 5, use Coale–Demeny equations shown in table 3.3;
- above 5, use values borrowed from another population (e.g. in Keyfitz and Flieger, 1990).

For actuarial application where a great deal of precision is required, graduation procedures will usually be preferred for estimating $_na_x$.

c. Compute $_nq_x$ as:

$$_nq_x = \frac{n \cdot {}_nm_x}{1 + (n - {}_na_x)_n m_x}$$

For the open-ended category, $_\infty q_x = 1.00$

    d. Compute $_n p_x = 1 - {_n q_x}$.

    e. Choose a value of l_0, the "radix" of the life table. This is the Latin term for root; its value will determine most of the remaining values of the life table. The choice of the radix is arbitrary. Values that have been used range from 1 to 1 million; 100,000 is perhaps the most conventional. l_x, $_n d_x$, $_n L_x$, and T_x columns will vary in exact proportion to the radix chosen. Thus the *scale* of a period life table is completely arbitrary and is totally unrelated to the size of the population whose mortality is being described in the table. Failing to grasp this point is a common source of confusion.

    f. Calculate $l_{x+n} = l_x \cdot {_n p_x}$, working sequentially from the youngest age to the oldest, e.g.,

$$l_1 = l_0 \cdot {_1 p_0}$$
$$l_5 = l_1 \cdot {_4 p_1}$$
$$l_{10} = l_5 \cdot {_5 p_5}$$
$$\vdots$$

    g. Derive $_n d_x$ as $l_x - l_{x+n}$ (or as $l_x \cdot {_n q_x}$).

    h. Derive the person-years lived between ages x and $x + n$ as:

$$_n L_x = n \cdot l_{x+n} + {_n a_x} \cdot {_n d_x}$$

This formula was used in deriving the $_n m_x \rightarrow {_n q_x}$ conversion. Once we have selected the $_n a_x$ values for that conversion, we have used up our degrees of freedom in making the conversion from l_x to $_n L_x$. This point is often overlooked. For the open ended interval that begins with age x^*, set

$$_\infty L_{x^*} = \frac{l_{x^*}}{_n m_{x^*}}$$

    i. Derive

$$T_x = \sum_{a=x}^{\infty} {_n L_a}$$

This is simply an instruction to add up the $_n L_x$ column from age x to the final row of the life table, in order to derive person-years lived above age x. This operation starts at the bottom of the life table (i.e., the highest age) and proceeds to the top.

    j. Derive life expectancy at age x as $e_x^o = T_x / l_x$. This formula for e_x^o divides the number of person-years that will be lived above age x by the number of persons who will live them.[2]

    Box 3.1 shows an example of period life table construction using data from Austria.

    A life table in which all age intervals are one year wide is often referred to as a "complete" life table, whereas tables containing larger age intervals, usually 5 years wide, are sometimes referred to as "abridged" life tables. Figures 3.2 and 3.3 show graphically some important columns of life tables. Figure 3.2 presents the $_n m_x$ column for males and females in the US in 1992, and figure 3.3 shows the $_n m_x$, l_x, and $_n d_x$ columns from Swedish female life tables in 1895 and 1995. The age intervals in these life tables are one year wide ($n = 1$).

    Table 3.4 presents estimates of life expectancy at birth in the major regions of the world for a recent period. These life expectancies are obtained by aggregating life expectancies at birth across individual countries. One way to aggregate life expectancies is by merging deaths

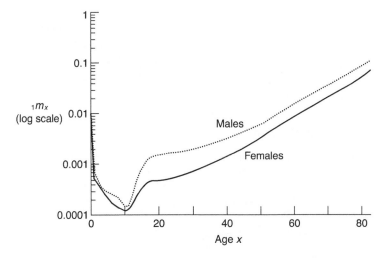

Figure 3.2 Age-specific death rates ($_1m_x$) by age, US, 1992, males and females
Data source: National Center for Health Statistics, 1996.

and population at risk in the larger unit, and recalculating a life table in the conventional way described above using the aggregated age-specific mortality rates. It should be noted than when using the merging procedure, the resulting aggregate life expectancy could under rare circumstances be outside the range of life expectancies in the original populations being merged. A second way is to calculate a weighted average of country-level life expectancies. Because of the conventional interpretation given to life expectancy at birth, one appropriate set of weights to use might be the number of births in the respective regions. Relative population size is perhaps an equally attractive alternative.

The two procedures give similar results when the populations being merged are relatively homogeneous, but the difference can be substantial when aggregating populations that have diverse patterns and levels of mortality. Lutz and Scherbov (1992) recommend using the merging procedure rather than the averaging procedure because it may be more appropriate when dealing with populations open to migration and with changing mortality. The United Nations shifted from the averaging to the merging procedure in 1990, a shift that produced an increase of 2.5 years in their estimate of the global life expectancy at birth for the period 1980–5 (United Nations, 1989, 1991).

3.6 Interpreting the Life Table

A period life table summarizes the mortality experience of a population. Each parameter presented corresponds to a specific age or age interval, e.g. the probability of surviving or of dying between age x and $x + n$ ($_np_x$ and $_nq_x$ respectively), the age-specific death rate between age x and $x + n$ ($_nM_x$), or the life expectancy at age x (e_x^o). The verbal interpretation of each column was provided in table 3.1. Additional information can be gained by combining two or more ages. For example, the ratio l_y/l_x indicates the probability of surviving from age x to age y in the population, i.e., in a hypothetical cohort constructed from data on the population. Box 3.2 illustrates some of the most important interpretations that can be drawn from life table columns.

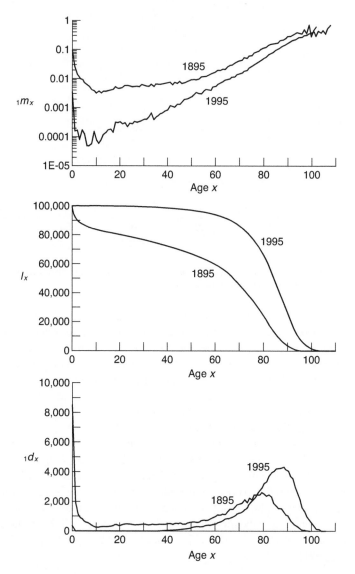

Figure 3.3 Age-specific death rates ($_1m_x$), survivors (l_x), and deaths ($_1d_x$) in Swedish female life tables, 1895 and 1995
Data source: Statistiska Centralbyrån and Berkeley Mortality Database.
http://demog.berkeley.edu/wilmoth/mortality

Assuming that the mortality experience of the population applies to an individual throughout his or her life, i.e., that at every age he or she is subjected to the mortality rates from which the life table is constructed, then the life table also illustrates the expected life experience of the individual. The most salient example is life expectancy. Life expectancy at age x is the average number of *additional* years to be lived by a member of the cohort who survives to age x. If we knew nothing else about an individual except the fact that he or she survived to age x, life

Table 3.4: *Life expectancy at birth, by major areas, 1995–2000*

Major area	Both sexes	Males	Females
Africa	51.4	50.0	52.8
Asia	66.3	64.8	67.9
Europe	73.3	69.2	77.4
Latin America and the Caribbean	69.2	66.1	72.6
Northern America	76.9	73.6	80.2
Oceania	73.8	71.4	76.3

Source: United Nations, 1999.

expectancy at age x would be our best guess about how long that individual would live. Hence, it is an expected value for a randomly-chosen individual.

A useful simplification has gained widespread currency and will be used later in this volume: the probability of surviving from birth to age x is designated $p(x)$ and the cumulative probability of dying between birth and age x is designated $q(x)$. So

$$p(x) = \frac{l_x}{l_0}$$

$$q(x) = 1 - p(x) = 1 - \frac{l_x}{l_0} = \frac{l_0 - l_x}{l_0} = \frac{{}_x d_0}{l_0}$$

3.7 The Life Table Conceived as a Stationary Population

The stationary population is the first of two important population models that are described in this volume. The other model is that of a stable population, developed in chapter 7. In fact, the stationary population model is a special case of the more general stable population model. The concept of a stationary population is independent of the life table apparatus, but it is convenient to develop its features by reference to life table notation.

A stationary population results from the continued operation of three demographic conditions:

1) Age-specific death rates that are constant over time (but usually not constant over age);
2) A flow of births that is constant over time; the same number of newborns are added to the population per unit of time, whether the unit is a year, a month, or a day;
3) Net migration rates that are zero at all ages; in effect, the population is assumed to be closed to migration.[3]

The conversion of a life table into a stationary population model simply requires a little notational sleight-of-hand. If we assume that l_0 is the annual number of births in a population that meets the three conditions of a stationary population, then many of the other columns and elements of a life table take on a new meaning:

l_x is the number of persons who reach age x in any calendar year, $l_x = l_0 \cdot {}_x p_0$;
${}_n L_x$ is the number of persons alive at any point in time between ages x and $x + n$;
T_x is the number of persons alive at any point in time above age x, so that
T_0 is the total size of the population;
${}_n d_x$ is annual number of deaths between ages x and $x + n$;
e_0^o is the mean age at death for persons dying in any particular year.

Box 3.2 *Interpreting the Life Table*

1. The basic columns:

x = Exact age x

l_x = Number of people left alive at age x

$_nd_x$ = Number of people dying between ages x and $x + n$

$_nq_x$ = Probability of dying between ages x and $x + n$

$_np_x$ = Probability of surviving from age x to age $x + n$

$_nL_x$ = Person-years lived between ages x and $x + n$

T_x = Person-years lived above age x

e_x^o = Expectation of life at age x

$_nm_x$ = Age-specific death rate between ages x and $x + n$

$_na_x$ = Average person-years lived between ages x and $x + n$ for persons dying in the interval

---

2. Additional information:

$(l_y)/l_x = {}_{y-x}p_x$	= Probability of surviving from age x to age y
$1 - (l_y)/l_x = {}_{y-x}q_x$	= Probability of dying between ages x and y
$l_x - l_y = {}_{y-x}d_x$	= Number of people dying between ages x and y
$T_x - T_y = {}_{y-x}L_x$	= Number of person-years lived between ages x and y
$(_nd_x)/(l_0)$	= Probability that a newborn will die between ages x and $x + n$
$(l_x - l_y)/l_0$	= Probability that a newborn will experience his death between ages x and y
$(T_x - T_y)/l_0$	= Number of years that a newborn can expect to live between ages x and y

Example: Austria, males, 1992 (data shown in box 3.1)

Life expectancy at birth = 72.889 years

Life expectancy at age 50 = 26.422 years

  (a male who has reached age 50 can expect to live 26.422 additional years)

Probability of surviving from birth to age 40 = l_{40}/l_0 = 95,588/100,000 = .95588

Probability that a person who survived to age 40 would die before age 60

  = $(l_{40} - l_{60})/l_{40} = 1 - l_{60}/l_{40} = 1 - 83,845/95,588 = .12286$

Number of years that a newborn male could expect to live in the age interval 25–50

  = $(T_{25} - T_{50})/l_0 = (4,821,324 - 2,429,176)/100,000 = 23.9$ years

Probability that a newborn will die between ages 70 and 75

  $_5d_{70}/l_0 = 12,422/100,000 = .12422$

Probability that a newborn will die between ages 70 and 85

  = $(l_{70} - l_{85})/l_0 = (66,225 - 21,134)/100,000 = .45091$

The most difficult connection to understand is that involving $_nL_x$. Table 3.5 demonstrates why the person-years lived between ages x and $x + n$ by a cohort of l_0 births, the function that we have previously designated $_nL_x$, must also equal the number of persons alive between ages x and $x + n$ in a stationary population with l_0 annual births. In this table, we assume that a stationary population exists in which there are 365,000 annual births, a process that has extended indefinitely throughout the past. These births are evenly distributed over time so that there are 1,000 births per day. The probability of surviving from birth to various ages (expressed in days) is assumed to be as shown in the $_xp_0$ column. With these assumptions, and no migration, the population size and age structure within the first year of life will be constant

Table 3.5: *Life table and age structure of a stationary population*

Age in days x	Probability of surviving to age x $_x p_0$	Population alive on:							
		Jan. 1	Jan. 2	Jan. 3	Jan. 4	Jan. 5	Jan. 6	.....	Dec. 31
0	1.000	1,000	1,000	1,000	1,000	1,000	1,000	.....	1,000
1	.970		970	970	970	970	970	.....	970
2	.950			950	950	950	950	.....	950
3	.946				946	946	946	.....	946
4	.942					942	942	.....	942
.	.						.	.....	.
.	.							.....	.
364	0.900							.....	900

(hence the name, stationary population). This is readily seen by beginning with the cohort of 1,000 babies born on January 1 and following it forward as illustrated in the rest of the table.

It is clear that the number of persons at any particular age becomes constant over time because it is the product of a constant number of births and constant probabilities of survival. The number of people alive at any point in time (e.g., January 5) between exact ages 0 and 1 is:

$$_1 N_0 = 1000 + 970 + 950 + 946 + 942 + \cdots + 900$$

The number of person-years lived in the first year of life by an annual cohort of births will equal the number of daily cohorts, 365, times the person-years lived by each daily cohort. Each daily cohort lives $1000 \cdot (1/365)$ person-years on January 1, $970 \cdot (1/365)$ on January 2, and so on down to $900 \cdot (1/365)$ on December 31. So the total number of person-years lived in the first year of life by an annual cohort of births is:

$$_1 L_0 = 365 \cdot [1000/365 + 970/365 + 950/365 + \ldots 900/365]$$

$$= 1000 + 970 + 950 + \cdots + 900.$$

Thus, $_1 L_0 = {}_1 N_0$; the number of person-years lived by an annual cohort of births in an age interval will equal the number alive in that interval at any moment of time. Finally, note that both quantities will also equal the number of person-years lived in the age-time bloc jointly circumscribed by ages 0 and 1 and by a calendar year that extends from January 1 to December 31. Since there are $_1 N_0$ persons alive at any point in time between ages 0 and 1, there will be $_1 N_0 \cdot (1/365)$ person-years lived in that age interval on January 1, another $_1 N_0 \cdot (1/365)$ lived on January 2, and altogether $365 \cdot {}_1 N_0 \cdot (1/365) = {}_1 N_0$ over the course of the year.

Using life table notation to describe the functions of a stationary population, the birth rate is equal to the annual number of births divided by the total size of the population, or l_0/T_0. Since life expectancy at birth is T_0/l_0, it must be the case that, in a stationary population:

$$CBR = 1/e_0^o$$

The crude birth rate is the reciprocal of life expectancy at birth. Why this reciprocal relationship exists can perhaps be understood by imagining a population in which no one dies until age 60, at which point everyone dies. Then life expectancy at birth would obviously be 60 years. If annual births are B, then the size of the population must be $60 \cdot B$ and the crude birth rate must be $B/(60 \cdot B) = 1/60$. Each birth lives 60 years; every 60 person-years lived in the population each year produces one birth.

Since a stationary population must be constant in size because the number of persons at each age is constant, then the crude death rate must equal the crude birth rate:

$$CDR = CBR = 1/e_0^o$$

Since the number of persons above age x must also be constant, then the number of persons arriving at age x each year, l_x, must equal the number of persons dying above age x that year. Therefore:

$$_\infty M_x = \frac{l_x}{T_x} = \frac{1}{[T_x/l_x]} = \frac{1}{e_x^o}$$

So in a stationary population, the death rate of any open-ended population segment above age x must equal the reciprocal of the life expectancy at age x.

The proportion of the stationary population that is aged x to $x + 1$ is:

$$_1C_x^S = \frac{_1L_x}{T_0} = \frac{_1L_x}{l_0} \cdot \frac{l_0}{T_0} \simeq \frac{l_{x+0.5}}{l_0} \cdot CBR$$

In developing this final expression, we have assumed that $_1L_x$ is approximately equal to $l_{x+0.5}$, which would be exactly correct if the l_a function were linear in the interval between x and $x + 1$.

Thus, the stationary population model provides explicit expressions that connect the major demographic parameters to one another: life expectancy, birth rates, death rates, and age structure. The explicitness of these relations is one reason why the stationary population has become an important demographic model. The model can be invoked in order to estimate one demographic parameter on the basis of another. For example, an archeologist who encounters a collection of skeletons and assigns ages to them (producing the equivalent of the $_nd_x$ function of a life table) can estimate the birth rate of the population that gave rise to the skeletons as $1/e_0^o$. Or a demographer who encounters the age distribution of the 1881 census of India (equivalent to the $_nL_x$ function of a stationary population) can estimate probabilities of survival from one age interval to the next ($_5L_{x+5}/_5L_x$). In both cases, of course, the assumption of stationarity is required. The fact that, until the eighteenth century, the world population was growing very slowly means that, on average, the assumption of stationarity may not be too distortive in many applications. At least, the direction of bias would be hard to predict.

The fact that every human population has an underlying life table, whether or not it is accurately estimated, means that every population can form the basis of a model stationary population. This model is the population that would eventually emerge if age-specific mortality rates remained constant at values contained in the life table, if births were constant, and if there were no migration. What time span is implied by "eventually?" For full precision, it is equal to the human life span, the maximum age attained by any individual. For other purposes where less than complete precision is required, it could be a shorter period.

As noted earlier, the scale of the life table is set by l_0, the arbitrarily-chosen radix whose value has a proportionate effect on l_x, $_nL_x$, T_x, and $_nd_x$. Because of this arbitrariness, the scale of the life table bears no necessary relationship to the size of the population that produced

---

Box 3.3 *The Life Table Conceived as a Stationary Population*

l_0 = Annual number of births and annual number of deaths
l_x = Number of persons who reach age x in any calendar year
$_nL_x$ = Number of persons alive at any point in time between ages x and $x + n$
T_x = Number of persons alive at any point in time above age x
T_0 = Total size of the population
$_nd_x$ = Annual number of deaths between ages x and $x + n$
e_0^o = Mean age at death for persons dying in any particular year

$$\text{Crude Birth Rate} = \text{Crude Death Rate} = \frac{1}{e_0^o}$$

$$\text{Death Rate above age } x = \frac{l_x}{T_x} = \frac{1}{e_x^o}$$

$$\text{Age Structure} = {}_nC_x^S = \frac{{}_nL_x}{T_0} \simeq \frac{l_{x+n/2}}{l_0} \cdot n \cdot CBR$$

Example: Austria, males, 1992 (data shown in box 3.1)

Number of annual births = l_0 = 100,000
Number of people reaching their 20th birthday in any calendar year = l_{20} = 98,334
Number of people alive between ages 30 and 35 = $_5L_{30}$ = 484,175
Number of people above age 60 = T_{60} = 1,544,893
Total size of the population = T_0 = 7,288,901
Annual number of deaths between ages 50 and 55 = $_5d_{50}$ = 3,225
Mean age at death= e_0^o = 72.889 years
$CBR = CDR = 1/e_0^o = 1/72.889 = .01372$
Death rate above age 60 = $1/e_{60}^o = 1/18.426 = .05427$
Proportion of people aged 25 to 30 = $_5L_{25}/T_0 = 487,127/7,288,901 = .0668$
or

$$_5C_{25}^S \simeq \frac{l_{27.5}}{l_0} \cdot 5 \cdot CBR \simeq \frac{\dfrac{l_{25} + l_{30}}{2}}{l_0} \cdot 5 \cdot CBR = \frac{\dfrac{97,704 + 97,151}{2}}{100,000} \cdot 5 \cdot .01372 = .0668$$

---

it. Likewise, the scale of the model stationary population produced by any life table is also arbitrary and should not be confused with the size of the actual population to which it pertains.

Any population – any collection of individuals meeting some defined criteria for membership in the population – has a set of attrition rates that describe the process of leaving the population. These rates can be arrayed by duration of membership in the population. Hence, any collectivity has a life table that can be converted into a model stationary population. Without making direct reference to the stationary model, analysts often make use of stationary population relations in thinking about these collectivities. For example, a graduate program that matriculates 10 students per year and has a student body of 40 can be assumed to have a mean duration in graduate school of 4 years ($e_0^o = T_0/l_0$). If one million new cases of cancer are diagnosed each year and someone with newly-diagnosed cancer can be expected to live 8 years, then the population of persons with diagnosed cancer numbers 8 million ($T_0 = l_0 \cdot e_0^o$). If persons remain with a firm an average of 5 years, then the annual attrition rate is 0.20 ($CDR = 1/e_0^o$).

In order to be accurate, these inferences require that the population be stationary. In many instances, this is a reasonable approximation. In some instances, especially when mean duration in the population is long, they can be very misleading. The most important demographic example of serious error that can result from a casual invocation of stationary relations involves the relationship between the mean age at death in a population and life expectancy at birth in that population. *In a stationary population*, the mean age of people dying in any particular year is equal to life expectancy at birth in that population. The mean age at death in a *cohort* (life expectancy at birth in the cohort) results from combining age-specific death rates $(_nm_x)$ with the distribution of years lived by the cohort $(_nL_x)$. The mean age at death in the *population* results from combining those same death rates $(_nm_x)$ with the age structure of the population $(_nN_x)$. But we have already seen that, in a stationary population, $_nN_x = {}_nL_x$. So the mean age at death in the population must be the same as that in a cohort.

If the population is *not* stationary, however, the mean age of persons dying in a particular period can be very different from life expectancy at birth. The reason is that a particular set of age-specific death rates, $_nm_x$, are being applied to two age structures that can be very different from one another. The age structure in the life table is, as before, $_nL_x$. But in the absence of stationary conditions, there is no necessary connection between the $_nL_x$ column in the period life table (which is entirely a product of current age-specific death rates) and the $_nN_x$ column, representing the actual age structure of the population. For example, if the annual number of births has been growing over time instead of constant (as assumed in the stationary population model), then the actual age structure of the population will be younger than that implied by the stationary population model. Relative to births 30 years ago, for example, there will have been more births in the past year. So the ratio of persons under age 1 to persons aged 30 in the actual population will be higher than in the stationary population. So will the ratio of 30-year-olds to 60-year-olds.

Because annual births have been growing in most developing countries, this example represents the typical pattern of discrepancy between the age structure of actual populations and the age structure of the stationary population implied by current mortality. For example, males in Colombia in 1964 had a life expectancy at birth (based on vital statistics) of 58.2 years. But the mean age of males dying in Colombia in 1964 was only 26.1 years, less than half as large (Preston, Keyfitz and Schoen, 1972). The mean age of persons dying in 1964 would have been a horribly biased estimator of life expectancy at birth in that year. The reason for the discrepancy is simply that births in Colombia had been growing in the years prior to 1964, rather than constant as assumed in the stationary model.

The stationary model is applicable to the analyses of all populations. Consider the population of US graduate students. The mean duration of time in graduate school spent by persons receiving their Ph.D. in any particular year has been drifting steadily upwards, leading to calls for program reform. But the main reason for the drift is not that progress has been slowed for persons entering graduate school but that the number of entrants has been declining, lengthening the mean duration of persons in the graduate student population at any moment in time regardless of their attrition rates. Since the base populations became "older," the mean duration in graduate school of persons achieving the Ph.D. in any year grew higher.

In these examples, the stationary model helps us understand how common sense can go seriously awry. By understanding the stationary model, we can gain some novel insights; by recognizing when it does not apply, we can identify and avoid some serious errors.

3.8 Mortality as a Continuous Process

By its tabular nature the life table can display mortality functions only at particular ages or for discrete age intervals. But the risk of death surely acts continuously on cohorts; persons in no age interval, no matter how small, are exempt from the risk. Development of the mathematics of this continuous process illuminates some of what has already been discussed and sets the stage for some of what is to come.

Let us consider the dying out of a cohort using life table notation. Since the risk of death acts continuously on members of the cohort, the number left alive at age x, l_x, changes continuously and can be represented by a continuous function, denoted $l(x)$. Mortality also changes continuously rather than by discrete leaps. The number of deaths among members of the cohort between ages x and $x + n$ is:

$$_nd_x = l(x) - l(x+n)$$

and the death rate is, as before, $_nm_x = {_nd_x}/{_nL_x}$. We now let the age interval n identifying the death rate grow shorter and shorter. The key concept in the continuous development is the "force of mortality," denoted $\mu(x)$, and defined as:

$$\mu(x) = \lim_{n \to 0} \frac{_nd_x}{_nL_x} = \lim_{n \to 0} {_nm_x}$$

It is essential to recognize that, by dealing with a tiny interval of age instead of, say, an interval of $n = 1$, we are not altering the scale of $_nm_x$. For example:

$$_1m_{30} = \frac{_1d_{30}}{_1L_{30}} = \frac{\textit{Deaths in a cohort between ages 30 and 31}}{\textit{Person-years lived in the cohort between ages 30 and 31}}$$

and

$$_{0.5}m_{30} = \frac{_{0.5}d_{30}}{_{0.5}L_{30}} = \frac{\textit{Deaths in a cohort between ages 30 and 30.5}}{\textit{Person-years lived in the cohort between ages 30 and 30.5}}$$

By reducing the age interval (n) from one year to half a year, we have reduced both numerator and denominator by approximately one-half, thereby retaining the same approximate level of the $_nm_x$ function. The same result would obtain if we were to have made n equal to 0.25, to 0.10, or to a very tiny value. The force of mortality function retains the character of an annualized rate; it is a death rate per person-year of exposure[4]. Since $_nd_x = l(x) - l(x+n)$, and since $_nL_x = n \cdot l(x)$ for an interval n so small that person-years within the interval are negligibly reduced by death, we can write:

$$\mu(x) = \lim_{n \to 0} {_nm_x} = \lim_{n \to 0} \left[\frac{l(x) - l(x+n)}{n \cdot l(x)} \right] \tag{3.3}$$

By the definition of a derivative, the expression,

$$\lim_{n \to 0} \left[\frac{l(x) - l(x+n)}{n} \right]$$

is simply the derivative of the $l(x)$ function at x multiplied by (-1) (the derivative itself has $l(x + n) - l(x)$ in the numerator). When we divide the derivative of l_x by the value of l_x, we produce the derivative of the natural logarithm of $l(x)$. So:[5]

$$\mu(x) = \lim_{n \to 0} \left[\frac{l(x) - l(x + n)}{n \cdot l(x)} \right] = \frac{-d \ln(l(x))}{dx} \tag{3.4}$$

Let us now take the negative of (3.4) and integrate both sides between two exact ages y and z:

$$- \int_y^z \mu(x)\, dx = \ln l(z) - \ln l(y)$$

Now taking exponentials of both sides we have:

$$e^{-\int_y^z \mu(x)\, dx} = \frac{l(z)}{l(y)} \tag{3.5}$$

Or:

$$l(z) = l(y)e^{-\int_y^z \mu(x)\, dx} \tag{3.6}$$

Equation (3.6) is one of the most important equations in formal demography. It expresses the proportionate change in the size of a cohort between two ages completely in terms of the force of mortality function prevailing between those ages. It says that the proportionate change in cohort size between y and z is a simple function of the sum of the force of mortality function between those ages. The order in which the death rates occur is immaterial; all that matters is their sum. If the younger age is zero and the older is a, then:

$$l(a) = l(0)e^{-\int_0^a \mu(x)\, dx} \tag{3.7}$$

Note the similarity between equation (3.7) and equation (1.5):

$$N(T) = N(0)e^{\int_0^T r(t)\, dt}$$

The latter equation expresses the size of the total population at time T in terms of its size at time zero and the sum of intervening growth rates. Likewise, the size of a cohort at age a can be expressed in terms of its size at age zero and the sum of intervening death rates. The death rate at age x is simply acting as a (in this case, negative) growth rate at age x for the cohort. Because we choose to define death rates ($\mu(x)$ and $_n m_x$) as positively valued functions, the negative sign must appear in equation (3.7) to make the analogy with growth rates complete.

All life table functions can be expressed in terms of $l(x)$ and $\mu(x)$. For instance, the number of person-years in the interval $[x, x + n]$ is:

$$_n L_x = \int_x^{x+n} l(a)\, da \; .$$

Since $_n d_x = {_n L_x} \cdot {_n m_x}$, the number of deaths in a small interval da is $l(a)\mu(a)da$ and the continuous formula for $_n d_x$ is:

$$_n d_x = \int_{x}^{x+n} l(a)\mu(a)\, da$$

Note that, since the number of survivors to any age is equal to the number of deaths above that age, the following relationship must hold:

$$l(x) = \int_{x}^{\infty} l(a)\mu(a)\, da$$

Another internal relationship represents the equivalence of calculating person-years lived above a certain age as the sum over age of the number of survivors versus the sum over survivors of the time lived until death. As noted above, there are $l(a)\mu(a)da$ persons dying in the small interval $[a, a + da]$ and each one lives $(a - x)$ years beyond age x, so:

$$\int_{x}^{\infty} l(a)\, da = \int_{x}^{\infty} l(a)\mu(a)(a - x)\, da$$

Life expectancy can then be written in two equivalent forms, using the two relationships above:

$$e_x^o = \frac{\int_x^\infty l(a)\mu(a)(a - x)\, da}{\int_x^\infty l(a)\mu(a)\, da} = \frac{\int_x^\infty l(a)\, da}{l(x)}$$

The expression on the left corresponds to the definition of life expectancy in terms of ages at death whereas the expression on the right shows that it is also a sum of person-years lived.

Since $l(x)$ itself can be expressed in terms of $l(0)$ and $\mu(x)$ (equation 3.7), all life table functions can further be expressed in terms of $l(0)$ and $\mu(x)$ alone. Such expressions are provided for reference in appendix 3.1, at the end of this chapter.

3.9 Life Table Construction Revisited

From the above expressions for $_n d_x$ and $_n L_x$, we can derive the continuous expression for $_n m_x$ as:

$$_n m_x = \frac{\int_x^{x+n} l(a)\mu(a)\, da}{\int_x^{x+n} l(a)\, da} \tag{3.8}$$

The expression for $_n m_x$ illuminates a feature of life table construction that we have heretofore suppressed. It shows that a cohort's death rate in the interval x to $x + n$ is a weighted average of the force of mortality function between ages x and $x + n$. The weights are supplied by the $l(a)$ function, the number of survivors in the cohort at age a, within the interval x to $x + n$. Now suppose that we are observing the age-specific death rate between ages x and $x + n$ in some population, rather than in a cohort. The population's age-specific death rate is denoted

$_nM_x$. Given a certain underlying force of mortality function in that population, its death rate between ages x and $x + n$ will be:[6]

$$_nM_x = \frac{\int_x^{x+n} N(a)\mu(a)\, da}{\int_x^{x+n} N(a)\, da}$$
(3.9)

where $N(a)da$ = number of persons in the interval of age a to $a + da$. A comparison of 3.8 and 3.9 shows that, even when a cohort and a population have exactly the same $\mu(a)$ function in the interval x to $x+n$, the value of $_nm_x$ for a cohort subject to that force of mortality function may not equal the value of $_nM_x$ for the population subject to that same function. The reason is that the $\mu(a)$ function is being weighted by $l(a)$ in the cohort and by $N(a)$ in the population. There are only two conditions in which we can be certain that $_nm_x = {}_nM_x$:

1) $\mu(a)$ is constant in the interval x to $x + n$: $\mu(a) = \mu^*$, for $x \le a \le x + n$.
   In this case, the constant value comes out of the integral sign in the numerators of (3.8) and (3.9) and: $_nm_x = {}_nM_x = \mu^*$.
   Substituting this constant value into equation (3.5) gives:

$$_nP_x = \frac{l_{x+n}}{l_x} = e^{-_nM_x \cdot n}$$
(3.10)

Equation (3.10) is, in effect, performing the $_nm_x \rightarrow {}_nq_x$ conversion (actually, it is an $_nM_x \rightarrow {}_nq_x$ conversion) when mortality is constant in the interval x to $x + n$. A formula for ascertaining the value of $_na_x$ in this case was presented in section 3.2.4. But the step involving $_na_x$ can be skipped and one can ascertain the value of $_nL_x$ directly from:

$$_nL_x = \frac{n d_x}{_nm_x} = \frac{l_x - l_{x+n}}{_nM_x}$$

2) The other case where $_nM_x$ will always equal $_nm_x$ (providing that the $\mu(a)$ function is the same for the cohort and population) occurs when $N(a)$ is proportional to $l(a)$ throughout the interval x to $x + n$. Substituting $N(a) = k \cdot l(a)$ into (3.9) gives the same expression as (3.8). This proportionality condition applies when the population's age distribution ($N(a)$) is *stationary* in the age interval x to $x + n$. It will be stationary, of course, when the preconditions described above for establishing a stationary population are met (or, possibly, by chance).

   The most commonly observed departure from stationarity is that a population's age distribution is younger than that of the stationary population produced by the same $\mu(a)$ function. Most likely, it is younger because of a history of rising numbers of births or falling mortality, both of which are manifest in positive growth rates. In contrast to the first assumption, that $\mu(a)$ is constant between x and $x + n$, this assumption of stationarity does not automatically supply formulas for calculating all other life table functions, e.g., $_na_x$ and $_nL_x$. One must use one of the procedures described in section 3.2 to complete the life table.

Because neither of these assumptions will apply in many cases, it should not be an automatic choice that the $_nm_x$ function chosen for a period life table simply be the set of $_nM_x$ values observed in the population. Anomalous features of the population's age distribution may render the $_nM_x$ function a poor estimator of $_nm_x$, although within 5-year age intervals the distortions would rarely be large. One could, of course, simply argue that the period life table is *designed* to reproduce the $_nM_x$ function, that $_nM_x$ is how we choose to operationalize period mortality conditions. But a more precise indication of those conditions is given by the $\mu(x)$ function. This function cannot be directly observed because it pertains to infinitesimal intervals of age. But its main features can be inferred from the $_nM_x$ function, particularly if the latter is adjusted for age-distributional disturbances.

Keyfitz (1966, 1968a) has been a principal exponent of adjusting $_nM_x$ before it is incorporated into the life table in the form of $_nm_x$. In particular, his iterative life table system attempts to purge $_nM_x$ of the effects of population growth. When the population is growing, the age distribution of the population within an n-year wide interval will be younger than the age distribution of years lived by a cohort having the same $\mu(a)$ function. For age intervals in which the death rate rises with age (usually, those beyond age 30), $_nm_x$ will exceed $_nM_x$ because the latter is "biased" downwards by the population's youthful age distribution, just as the crude death rate is reduced by a young age distribution. Although Keyfitz's procedure is a useful advance on earlier ones, the difference that it makes for actual life table functions computed from data is, just as for other advances in life table construction, rather small. For this reason we shall not develop it in detail here. However, nonstationarity typically makes a larger difference in the highest, open-ended interval and we defer a discussion of how to deal with it to section 7.8. Table 3.6 shows the relationship between $_nm_x$ and $_nM_x$ and the growth rate of selected age groups in the US in 1985.

Let us now return briefly to the issue of using an $_na_x$ function that is directly observed in a population. We have seen that $_nM_x$ is, in general, biased downwards relative to $_nm_x$ in a growing population. Likewise, it is intuitively clear that $_na_x$, the mean number of years lived in the interval for persons dying in the interval x to $x+n$, is also biased downwards in a growing population relative to the equivalent function in a cohort having the same force of mortality function. Suppose we convert $_nM_x$ into $_nq_x$ using the formula:

$$_nq_x = \frac{n \cdot {_nM_x}}{1 + (n - {_na_x}) \cdot {_nM_x}}.$$

$_nq_x$ will be biased downwards because $_nM_x$ is too low (the proportionate downward bias in the numerator is greater than that in the denominator). Now suppose that we choose a value of $_na_x$ that is directly observed for the same period (e.g., by getting detail on the exact ages at death for persons dying between ages 60 and 65 in 1996). Since $_na_x$ itself will be biased downwards, the denominator will be biased upwards by this choice. The bias in using the observed $_na_x$ values doesn't compensate for the bias in using $_nM_x$, it exaggerates it.

The development of the relations in this section was deterministic. For what is often a more elegant development of some of these relations using probabilistic reasoning, see Mode (1985), Hoem (1972), or Chiang (1968, 1978).

Table 3.6: *Comparison of $_nM_x$ and $_nm_x$, US, females, 1985*

Age	$_nM_x$ (1)	$_nm_x$ (2)	Ratio (2)/(1)	$_nr_x$ (growth rate of age group between 1/1/1985 and 1/1/1986)
15–19	0.000466	0.000466	1.0000	−0.001
70–5	0.025997	0.026048	1.0020	0.011
75–9	0.040951	0.041186	1.0057	0.024

Data source: Keyfitz and Flieger, 1990.

3.10 Decomposing a Difference in Life Expectancies

When analyzing changes in life expectancy at birth or studying differences in life expectancy between two populations, it is sometimes useful to estimate what mortality differences in a specific age group contribute to the total difference in life expectancy. The estimation method involves decomposition procedures that are not as straightforward as those developed in chapter 2. The main reason for complications is the interdependence among age groups in the determination of life expectancy. A change in the death rate between ages 20 and 25 has a direct effect on $_5L_{20}$, but it also has an indirect effect on all the $_nL_x$ above age 25 because of the change in the number of survivors at age 25. This latter change will have a bigger effect on life expectancy at birth when 25-year-olds have a longer life expectancy.

There are two main approaches in decomposing a difference in life expectancies, a continuous approach (Pollard, 1982) and a discrete approach (Arriaga, 1984). Although both procedures are formally identical (Pollard, 1988), Arriaga's formula is easier to apply to traditional life table data. The total effect, $_n\Delta_x$, of a difference in mortality rates between ages x and $x + n$ on the life expectancy at birth can be expressed as:

$$_n\Delta_x = \frac{l_x^1}{l_0^1} \cdot \left(\frac{_nL_x^2}{l_x^2} - \frac{_nL_x^1}{l_x^1} \right) + \frac{T_{x+n}^2}{l_0^1} \cdot \left(\frac{l_x^1}{l_x^2} - \frac{l_{x+n}^1}{l_{x+n}^2} \right) \tag{3.11}$$

where l_x, $_nL_x$ and T_x are conventional functions of the life table and where superscripts 1 and 2 refer to time 1 and 2 or to population 1 and 2.

The first term in the right-hand side of equation (3.11),

$$\frac{l_x^1}{l_0^1} \cdot \left(\frac{_nL_x^2}{l_x^2} - \frac{_nL_x^1}{l_x^1} \right),$$

corresponds to the direct effect of a change in mortality rates between ages x and $x + n$, i.e., the effect that a change in the number of years lived between ages x and $x + n$ produces on the life expectancy at birth. The second term of the equation,

$$\frac{T_{x+n}^2}{l_0^1} \cdot \left(\frac{l_x^1}{l_x^2} - \frac{l_{x+n}^1}{l_{x+n}^2} \right),$$

corresponds to the sum of the indirect and interaction effects, i.e., the contribution resulting from the person-years to be added because additional survivors at age $x + n$ are exposed to new mortality conditions. For the open-ended age interval, there will be only a direct effect, and the following equation applies:

$$_\infty\Delta_x = \frac{l_x^1}{l_0^1} \cdot \left(\frac{T_x^2}{l_x^2} - \frac{T_x^1}{l_x^1} \right) \tag{3.12}$$

It can be demonstrated that $e_0^o(2) - e_0^o(1) = \sum_0^\infty {}_n\Delta_x$.

Equations (3.11) and (3.12) pertain to the decomposition of differences of life expectancy *at birth*. The same equations can be used for decomposing a change in life expectancies at age a, replacing l_0 by l_a and estimating $_n\Delta_x$ for $x \geq a$. Box 3.4 shows an example of the method to decomposing change in e_0^o among American females between 1935 and 1995. In chapter 4, we will examine how we can further decompose differences in life expectancies by calculating the contribution of various causes of death.

Box 3.4 *Age Decomposition of Differences in Life Expectancies at Birth*

$l_x^1, {}_nL_x^1, T_x^1$ = Life table functions at time 1 (or in population 1)

$l_x^2, {}_nL_x^2, T_x^2$ = Life table functions at time 2 (or in population 2)

$${}_n\Delta_x = \frac{l_x^1}{l_0^1} \cdot \left(\frac{{}_nL_x^2}{l_x^2} - \frac{{}_nL_x^1}{l_x^1} \right) + \frac{T_{x+n}^2}{l_0^1} \cdot \left(\frac{l_x^1}{l_x^2} - \frac{l_{x+n}^1}{l_{x+n}^2} \right) = \text{contribution of mortality difference in age group } x$$
$$\text{to } x + n \text{ to differences in life expectancy at birth}$$

$${}_\infty\Delta_x = \frac{l_x^1}{l_0^1} \cdot \left(\frac{T_x^2}{l_x^2} - \frac{T_x^1}{l_x^1} \right) = \text{contribution of mortality difference in open-ended age group to differences}$$
$$\text{in life expectancy at birth}$$

$$e_0^o(2) - e_0^o(1) = \sum_x {}_n\Delta_x$$

Example: US, females, 1935–95

Age x	l_x^{1935}	${}_nL_x^{1935}$	T_x^{1935}	l_x^{1995}	${}_nL_x^{1995}$	T_x^{1995}	${}_n\Delta_x$	Percent
0	100,000	96,354	6,332,064	100,000	99,410	7,900,065	3.06	19.5%
1	95,458	377,877	6,235,709	99,321	396,947	7,800,655	1.11	7.1%
5	93,887	467,474	5,857,833	99,179	495,676	7,403,708	0.46	2.9%
10	93,174	464,534	5,390,358	99,096	495,275	6,908,032	0.32	2.0%
15	92,613	460,915	4,925,823	98,999	494,459	6,412,758	0.45	2.9%
20	91,681	455,193	4,464,909	98,772	493,254	5,918,299	0.64	4.1%
25	90,341	447,783	4,009,717	98,524	491,863	5,425,046	0.69	4.4%
30	88,746	439,466	3,561,935	98,206	489,996	4,933,183	0.65	4.1%
35	86,997	429,742	3,122,468	97,769	487,383	4,443,186	0.69	4.4%
40	84,847	418,269	2,692,726	97,152	483,743	3,955,802	0.67	4.3%
45	82,368	403,859	2,274,456	96,298	478,583	3,472,059	0.78	4.9%
50	79,012	384,356	1,870,596	95,048	470,679	2,993,477	0.84	5.4%
55	74,539	358,766	1,486,241	93,085	458,397	2,522,798	0.87	5.6%
60	68,688	324,494	1,127,475	90,071	439,689	2,064,401	0.95	6.1%
65	60,779	279,761	802,981	85,504	411,580	1,624,711	0.93	6.0%
70	50,757	223,797	523,220	78,775	372,191	1,213,130	0.96	6.1%
75	38,276	155,169	299,422	69,655	318,738	840,940	0.89	5.7%
80	23,930	89,054	144,253	57,275	248,061	522,201	0.48	3.1%
85+	12,281	55,200	55,200	41,424	274,139	274,139	0.26	1.7%
Sum							15.68	100.0%

Total difference: $e_0^o(1995) - e_0^o(1935) = 79.00 - 63.32 = 15.68$ years
Contribution of mortality change before age 1 = 3.06 years (19.5% of total difference)

Data source: Bell, F. C., A. H. Wade, and S. C. Goss, 1992. *Life Tables for the United States Social Security Area: 1900–2080.* Baltimore, Maryland, US Social Security Administration, Office of the Actuary, Actuarial Study No. 107.

3.11 Adaptation of the Life Table for Studying Other Single Decrement Processes

A single decrement process is one in which individuals have only one recognized mode of exit from a defined state. Mortality is one such process. Life tables can be used to study all single decrement processes. In each case, they describe quantitatively the process of attrition from a defined state arrayed by duration in that state. Individuals would always enter the state at duration zero and the cohort entering the state would typically be traced until the last member had exited. In the case of the "classic" life table that we have developed, the defined state is "being alive" and the mode of exit is death. The functions of a classic life table are displayed by age because, in this case, age corresponds exactly to the duration of the state of being alive. Age is used in a life table only when it is a perfect surrogate for duration in the state.

Processes in which there are more than one recognized mode of exit are termed "multiple decrement processes." Empirically, multiple decrement processes are far more common than single decrement processes. In fact, for a real cohort, mortality is the *only* single decrement process. For any state that we can define other than being alive (e.g., being single; living in one's place of birth) one can leave the state by some form of status change (e.g., getting married, migrating to another place) as well as by death. This additional risk of status change exposes a person to multiple decrements. None of these additional risks is able to cancel out the risk of death; a real cohort is always subject to the risk of dying at the same time that it is subject to other risks.

Although the apparatus for studying single decrement processes may appear to be very specific to mortality, there are three circumstances that increase its applicability:

1) The multiple sources of decrement can often be collapsed analytically into one

Even mortality can be considered a multiple decrement process if the analyst chooses to recognize different causes of death. But for many purposes, including the calculation of life expectancy, this complication is often irrelevant. Likewise, the different modes of exit from marriage, from the labor force, or from any other state of interest can under some circumstances be ignored depending on the question asked. For example, we can calculate expected years to be spent in a firm by a new hire from data on entrances and exits without distinguishing among modes of exit.

2) Life histories are often available for surviving members of a cohort

It is very common in surveys to ask questions about events that have occurred in the past. These questions are addressed only to living members of a cohort. Although these persons were subject to the risk of mortality, we can be sure that none of them succumbed to the risk. For these persons, the force of mortality function was, in effect, zero at all prior ages. Therefore, their progress from one state to another need not be studied by multiple decrement processes but can be viewed as a single decrement process, assuming that there is only one remaining mode of leaving a state.

For example, let us define the state we are interested in as "never married." Suppose that we take a survey of 50-year-old women and ask about their marital histories. These women could have left the state of being "never-married" only by getting married. Thus, getting married in their nuptiality table would be analogous to dying in the classic life table. The force of nuptiality function (the rate of first marriage for the never-married population aged x) replaces the force of mortality function. Other obvious translations of life table concepts and notation in this case are the following:

l_x = number of women who are never married at age x.

$_n p_x$ = probability of staying unmarried in the age interval x to $x + n$ for a never-married woman aged x.

Box 3.5 *Application of Life Table Construction to Analysis of Marital Histories*

Example: Bangladesh, cohort of 655 women aged 45–9 in 1993–4, who all married before age 30. State of interest: "never married"

Age x	n	l_x	$_nd_x$	$_nq_x$	$_na_x$	$_nL_x$	T_x	e_x^o
0	5	655	0	0.00000	2.5	3275.0	9202.5	14.05
5	5	655	0	0.00000	2.5	3275.0	5927.5	9.05
10	2	655	119	0.18168	1.0	1191.0	2652.5	4.05
12	3	536	388	0.72388	1.5	1026.0	1461.5	2.73
15	3	148	106	0.71622	1.5	285.0	435.5	2.94
18	2	42	16	0.38095	1.0	68.0	150.5	3.58
20	2	26	13	0.50000	1.0	39.0	82.5	3.17
22	3	13	7	0.53846	1.5	28.5	43.5	3.35
25	5	6	6	1.00000	2.5	15.0	15.0	2.50
30								

Interpretation of the columns:
n = length of interval
l_x = number of women who are never married at age x
$_nd_x$ = first marriages between ages x and $x + n$
$_nq_x$ = probability of having a first marriage between ages x and $x + n$
$_na_x$ = average person-years lived in the never-married state between ages x and $x + n$ by women
      marrying in the interval (assumption: $_na_x = n/2$)
$_nL_x$ = number of person-years lived in the never-married state between ages x and $x + n$
T_x = number of person-years lived in the never-married state above age x
e_x^o = expected number of years to be spent in the never-married state for a never-married person aged
      x. In this case, $e_0^o = 14.05$ can be interpreted as the mean age at marriage for those women.

Data source: Mitra, S. N., et al., 1994. *Bangladesh Demographic and Health Survey,*
1993–1994. Dhaka, Bangladesh, National Institute of Population Research and Training (NIPORT).

$_nL_x$ = person-years lived in the never-married state between ages x and $x + n$.
e_x^o = expected number of years to be spent in the never married state for a never married
      person aged x.[7]

    The natural radix of this nuptiality table, l_0, is simply the number of 50-year-old women who are reporting on their first-marriage histories. It is important to recognize that the experience described in the resulting nuptiality table (or marriage life table) pertains only to the surviving members of the cohort. This experience may not be representative of the full cohort that began life at age zero, or of the cohort members who survived to age 20. If the surviving members of the cohort had, age for age, higher or lower risks of marriage than the members who died, then the experience of the surviving members would clearly differ from that of the full cohort. The biases for many purposes are small and usually must be tolerated because the retrospective information from surviving members of the cohort is the only information available. Box 3.5 presents an example of a life table for first marriage constructed from a retrospective survey.

*3)   Single decrement processes can be modeled for cohorts subject to
      multiple decrements*

Although a real cohort is always subject to mortality in addition to any other decrement that is operating, we can easily perform a thought experiment in which a hypothetical cohort is subject to only one form of decrement. Actuaries, biostatisticians, and demographers have developed techniques to carry out this experiment. These are used to produce what are sometimes called "associated single decrement life tables." The term "associated" conveys that the single decrement table is associated with a multiple decrement process. The methods for constructing associated single decrement tables are developed in the next chapter.

Table 3.7 presents a few examples of the many processes that can be profitably studied by means of a life table. In general, a life table is valuable when the risk of leaving a state depends on the duration of time spent in the state. Without such duration dependence, there is little to be gained by arraying all functions by duration.

The life table apparatus, developed centuries ago, has acquired new salience because of recent statistical developments. These enable researchers to study simultaneously the duration dependence of some risk of attrition and the influence of identifiable characteristics, or covariates, on the level of that risk. These procedures, termed life tables with covariates or proportional hazards procedures, were introduced by Cox (1972) and have been elaborated by many others, including Kalbfleisch and Prentice (1980). A textbook on these procedures is Collett (1994).

Table 3.7: *Examples of single decrement processes that can be studied by means of a life table*[a]

Process	State studied	State entered when. . .	State left when. . .	Vertical dimension of the table
Mortality	Being alive	Born	Die	Duration of life (age)
Nuptiality (first marriage)	Being unmarried	Born	Marry	Duration of single life (age)
Migration from place of birth	Living in place of birth	Born	Move to another place	Duration of residence (age)
Entering the labor force	Having never worked	Born	First enter labor force	Duration of life (age)
Becoming a mother	Having no births	Born	Have first birth	Duration of life (age)
Subsequent childbearing	Not having an additional birth	Have a birth	Have an additional birth	Duration since having a birth
Marital survival	Being in intact marriage	Marry	Marriage ends	Duration of marriage
Unemployment spells	Being unemployed	Become unemployed	Leave state of unemployment	Duration of unemployment
Incarceration	Being in jail	Enter jail	Leave jail	Duration of incarceration

[a] All of these processes can also be conceived as multiple decrement processes. Here we ignore other risks of leaving the state of interest.

Appendix 3.1: Life Table Relationships in Continuous Notation

$$l(x) = l(a)e^{-\int_a^x \mu(y)\,dy} \quad \text{for } x > a$$

$$_np_x = \frac{l(x+n)}{l(x)} = e^{-\int_x^{x+n} \mu(a)\,da}$$

$$_nd_x = \int_x^{x+n} l(a)\mu(a)\,da = \int_x^{x+n} l(x)e^{-\int_x^a \mu(y)\,dy}\mu(a)\,da = l(x)\int_x^{x+n} e^{-\int_x^a \mu(y)\,dy}\mu(a)\,da$$

$$_nq_x = \frac{_nd_x}{l(x)} = \int_x^{x+n} e^{-\int_x^a \mu(y)\,dy}\mu(a)\,da$$

$$_nL_x = \int_x^{x+n} l(a)\,da = \int_x^{x+n} l(x)e^{-\int_x^a \mu(y)\,dy}\,da = l(x)\int_x^{x+n} e^{-\int_x^a \mu(y)\,dy}\,da$$

$$_nm_x = \frac{_nd_x}{_nL_x} = \frac{\int_x^{x+n} l(a)\mu(a)\,da}{\int_x^{x+n} l(a)\,da} = \frac{\int_x^{x+n} e^{-\int_x^a \mu(y)\,dy}\mu(a)\,da}{\int_x^{x+n} e^{-\int_x^a \mu(y)\,dy}\,da}$$

$$_na_x = \frac{\int_x^{x+n} l(a)\mu(a)(a-x)\,da}{\int_x^{x+n} l(a)\mu(a)\,da} = \frac{\int_x^{x+n} e^{-\int_x^a \mu(y)\,dy}\mu(a)(a-x)\,da}{\int_x^{x+n} e^{-\int_x^a \mu(y)\,dy}\mu(a)\,da}$$

$$T_x = \int_x^\infty l(a)\,da = l(x)\int_x^\infty e^{-\int_x^a \mu(y)\,dy}\,da$$

$$e_x^o = \frac{T_x}{l_x} = \frac{\int_x^\infty l(a)\,da}{l(x)} = \int_x^\infty e^{-\int_x^a \mu(y)\,dy}\,da$$

$$= \frac{\int_x^\infty l(a)\mu(a)(a-x)\,da}{\int_x^\infty l(a)\mu(a)\,da}$$

NOTES

1. In the first chapter, we demonstrated the equivalence of two methods for computing person-years, one summing time across individuals, one summing individuals across time (figure 1.1). A similar equivalence exists in computing person-years above age x, either as a sum across age-groups beginning with the age-interval x to $x + n$ or as a sum across individuals. The formula used in table 3.1 computes person-years lived above age x by adding person-years lived within each age-interval above age x. Alternatively, we could compute the person-years lived above age x for each member of the cohort and sum across individuals. For example at age 0, T_0 is also the sum of the age at death of all members of the cohort.

2. Since exposure is here measured in person-years, life expectancy is measured in years. If the time/age dimension of a life table were months, then $_nL_x$ would refer to person-months lived and life expectancy would be measured in months.

3. Actually, the stationary population model can be generalized to include non-zero rates of migration as long as age-specific rates of migration are constant over time. But we will not pursue this elaboration.

4. The argument here parallels the one for $r(t)$ in chapter 1. The annualized growth rate, continuously compounded, refers to an infinitesimal period but is still an annualized rate as long as time is measured in years.

5. Again, note the formal similarity between $\mu(x)$ in equation (3.4) and $r(t)$ in equation (1.3).

6. Actually, the expression for $_nM_x[0, T]$ is slightly more complicated because we can only measure that rate over a discrete period in which $N(a)$ and $\mu(a)$ do not usually remain constant. So what we are really observing is rather:

$$_nM_x[0, T] = \frac{\int_0^T \int_x^{x+n} N(a, t)\mu(a, t)\, da\, dt}{\int_0^T \int_x^{x+n} N(a, t)\, da\, dt}$$

where $N(a, t)$ = number of persons aged a to $a + da$ at time t to $t + dt$, and
$\mu(a, t)$ = death rate in the age interval a to $a + da$ at time t to $t + dt$.

We have simplified this expression by assuming that $N(a, t)$ and $\mu(a, t)$ do not vary over the time interval in which death rates are being measured.

7. In the case where information is available for the cohort of survivors only up to age 50, and if some women remain single at that age, e_x^o must be truncated at that age. So it would be interpreted as the "expected number of years before age 50 to be spent in the never-married state for a never-married person aged x."

4 Multiple Decrement Processes

4.1 Multiple Decrement Tables for a Real Cohort
4.2 Multiple Decrement Life Tables for Periods
4.3 Some Basic Mathematics of Multiple Decrement Processes
4.4 Associated Single Decrement Tables from Period Data
4.5 Cause-specific Decomposition of Differences in Life Expectancies
4.6 Associated Single Decrement Tables from Current Status Data
4.7 Stationary Populations with Multiple Sources of Decrement

In the previous chapter, we defined a single decrement process as one in which individuals have only one mode of exit from a defined state. A multiple decrement process is one in which individuals have more than one mode of exit. As we noted, multiple decrement processes are far more common in demography than are single decrement processes. These situations arise, for example, in fertility analysis when individuals are viewed as being exposed to the risk of pregnancy and to discontinuance of use of contraception; in migration, when individuals are exposed to the risk of moving to different places; in nuptiality, when married persons are exposed to the risks of divorce and widowhood; and in many other circumstances. And as we noted earlier, persons in a particular state in a real cohort are always exposed to the risk of death, in addition to whatever other risks they may have of leaving that state. Multiple decrement processes are sometimes referred to as situations of "competing risks."

4.1 Multiple Decrement Tables for a Real Cohort

Conceptually, the construction of a multiple decrement table for a real cohort is no more challenging than the construction of a single decrement table. It is only necessary to add columns equivalent to other columns in a single decrement life table but which pertain exclusively to particular causes of decrement (i.e., to particular modes of exit from the table). The functions in these columns have a straightforward interpretation:

$_nd_x^i$ = number of decrements from cause i in the age interval x to $x + n$

$_nq_x^i$ = probability of leaving the table from cause i between ages x and $x + n$ for someone who reached age x

$= {_nd_x^i}/l_x$

$_nm_x^i$ = rate of decrement from cause i in the age interval x to $x+n$

$$= {_nd_x^i}/{_nL_x}$$

l_x^i = number of persons reaching age x who will eventually succumb to cause i

$$= \sum_{a=x}^{\infty} {_nd_a^i}$$

The l_x values in these formulas pertain to the number of cohort members who reach age x, i.e., who have survived *all* causes of decrement before age x. Likewise, the $_nL_x$ column pertains to all person-years lived between x and $x+n$ by the cohort members who have survived all causes of decrement. All of the columns customarily found in a single decrement table are also found in a multiple decrement table, where they refer to "all causes of decrement combined." Although we are using age x as the basic dimension of the multiple decrement table for illustrative purposes, it is representing the more general dimension of duration since entry into the state.

Note that we have not defined columns for $_nL_x^i$, T_x^i, $_na_x^i$, or e_x^i. The reason is that e_x^i (for which the other columns are needed as input) does not admit to a straightforward interpretation. In one sense, it could be "the life expectancy at age x for persons who will succumb to cause i." But those who will later succumb to i cannot be identified at age x. They will only be identifiable at later stages as the competing risks work themselves out. It is pointless to compute an expectation for unidentifiable people. A similar problem of interpretation arises in regard to l_x^i, the number of persons aged x who will eventually exit from cause i. But this is a useful column because it can be used to calculate l_x^i/l_x, the proportion of persons aged x who will eventually leave the table from cause i. One of its major uses, for example, is to calculate the probability that a marriage will end in a divorce. The *base* of this proportion is l_x, all persons surviving to age x, and this number is indeed identifiable by age x. It is when l_x^i is made the base of a probability or expectation that conceptual difficulties become intractable.

Added up over all causes i, the decrements must sum to the total number leaving the defined state:

$$\sum_i {_nd_x^i} = {_nd_x}$$

By our formulas for $_nm_x^i$ and $_nq_x^i$, these must also sum to the equivalent function in the life table for all causes combined:

$$\sum_i {_nm_x^i} = \sum_i \frac{_nd_x^i}{_nL_x} = \frac{_nd_x}{_nL_x} = {_nm_x}$$

and

$$\sum_i {_nq_x^i} = \sum_i \frac{_nd_x^i}{l_x} = \frac{_nd_x}{l_x} = {_nq_x}$$

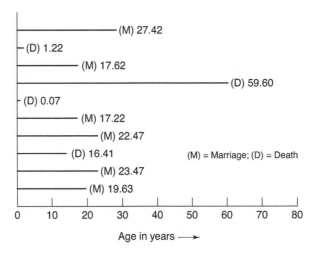

Figure 4.1 Life-lines in the single state for a hypothetical cohort of 10 births; date of birth, January 1, 1800

Also, since

$$l_x^i = \sum_{a=x}^{\infty} {}_nd_a^i,$$

$$\sum_i l_x^i = \sum_i \sum_{a=x}^{\infty} {}_nd_a^i = \sum_{a=x}^{\infty} {}_nd_a = l_x \tag{4.1}$$

The relation in (4.1) simply says that all of the survivors to age x in the cohort must leave the defined state from one or another recognized cause of decrement above that age.

Figure 4.1 presents life-lines for a cohort of 10 individuals each of whom was born on January 1, 1800. The state of interest is being single, i.e., never-married. Exits from the state are to marriage and death, as indicated on the figure. The life lines are converted into certain columns of a multiple decrement life table in table 4.1.

4.2 Multiple Decrement Life Tables for Periods

Constructing a multiple decrement table for real cohorts involves preparing a basic life table for all causes of decrement combined, and then adding the columns that pertain to decrements from the individual causes. This latter task is simply a matter of recording what has happened. But very often the analyst wants to draw forth the implications of the intensities of a multiple decrement process that are recorded during some specific period of time. Almost always, these intensities will be represented by sets of decrement rates from various causes, ${}_nM_x^i$. So the basic problem is one of converting these observed rates into the probabilities of exiting the table from various causes.

Table 4.1: Life table in the single state for a hypothetical cohort of 10 births shown in figure 4.1

Age	Number remaining in single state at age x	Number dying between ages x and x+n while in single state	Number marrying between ages x and x+n	Number leaving single state between ages x and x+n	Probability of dying between ages x and x+n while in single state	Probability of marrying between ages x and x+n	Probability of leaving single state between ages x and x+n	Number reaching age x who will eventually die while in single state	Number reaching age x who will eventually marry	Person-years lived in single state between ages x and x+n
x	l_x	$_n d_x^D$	$_n d_x^M$	$_n d_x = {_n d_x^D} + {_n d_x^M}$	$_n q_x^D$	$_n q_x^M$	$_n q_x = {_n q_x^D} + {_n q_x^M}$	l_x^D	l_x^M	$_n L_x$
0	10	1	0	1	1/10	0	1/10	4	6	9.07
1	9	1	0	1	1/9	0	1/9	3	6	32.22
5	8	0	0	0	0	0	0	2	6	40.00
10	8	1	3	4	1/8	3/8	4/8	2	6	70.88
20	4	0	3	3	0	3/4	3/4	1	3	23.36
30	1	0	0	0	0	0	0	1	0	10.00
40	1	0	0	0	0	0	0	1	0	10.00
50	1	1	0	1	1/1	0	1/1	1	0	9.60
60	0							0	0	

In order to make this conversion, refer back to the relation between rates of decrement and probabilities of decrement for a cohort:

$$_nm_x^i = \frac{_nd_x^i}{_nL_x}$$

and

$$_nq_x^i = \frac{_nd_x^i}{l_x}$$

Note that, just as in the basic life table of chapter 3, the numerators of $_nm_x^i$ and $_nq_x^i$ are the same whereas the denominators of the former is $_nL_x$ and of the latter, l_x. So we can use the relation between l_x and $_nL_x$ derived in chapter 3 to develop a conversion formula. Substituting $(_nL_x + (n - _na_x)_nd_x)/n$ for l_x in the expression for $_nq_x^i$ gives:

$$_nq_x^i = \frac{n \cdot _nm_x^i}{1 + (n - _na_x)_nm_x} \tag{4.2}$$

This formula for $_nq_x^i$ is very similar to formula (3.1) for $_nq_x$. The denominators are identical; the only difference between the formulas is that (4.2) has $_nm_x^i$ in the numerator where (3.1) has $_nm_x$. The values of $_na_x$ and $_nm_x$ in the denominator of (4.2) are *not* specific to cause i but are the values pertaining to all causes of decrement combined.

It is common to write the rate of decrement from causes other than i in the age interval x to $x + n$ as $_nm_x^{-i}$. So $_nm_x = _nm_x^i + _nm_x^{-i}$. Inserting this relation in formula (4.2) gives:

$$_nq_x^i = \frac{n \cdot _nm_x^i}{1 + (n - _na_x)(_nm_x^i + _nm_x^{-i})} \tag{4.3}$$

Now the competing nature of the multiple decrements comes into full view. Holding constant $_nm_x^i$, the higher is $_nm_x^{-i}$ in (4.3), the lower will be $_nq_x^i$. In other words, given a certain death rate from cancer in the age interval 65–9, for example, the proportion of 65-year-olds who die from cancer between ages 65 and 70 will be lower the higher are death rates from other causes. The reason for this dependence is that, when $_nm_x^{-i}$ is higher, more of the potential victims of cancer will be carried off by other causes in the age interval. Because of this dependence, $_nq_x^i$ is commonly referred to as a "dependent probability."

Does this dependence mean that when the death rate from other causes declines the death rate from cancer must rise? Not at all. This common confusion results from a mistaken view that the rates of decrement are necessarily dependent on one another, that "people must die of something, after all." But nothing requires that the *rate* of cancer death *per person-year* of exposure be increased when other causes decline. What is clear is that the number of person-years of exposure to the risk of cancer deaths will increase when other causes decline, so that the *number* of cancer deaths will increase. Given the same number starting out an age interval (l_x), the number of deaths from cancer, and hence the probability of cancer death, will be increased in the interval. The necessary relationship that governs the multiple decrement process relates *not to the rates but to the probabilities*; all persons starting life must die of something, and if the probability of exiting from one cause declines, the probability of exiting from some other cause(s) must increase.

Formula (4.2) for $_nq_x^i$ will provide a straightforward way of converting $_nm_x^i$ to $_nq_x^i$ and thereby completing the multiple decrement life table. However, it is unnecessarily tedious to implement. Note that, by dividing $_nq_x^i$ by $_nq_x$, we get:

$$\frac{_nq_x^i}{_nq_x} = \frac{_nd_x^i}{_nd_x} = \frac{_nm_x^i}{_nm_x}$$

So:

$$_nq_x^i = _nq_x \cdot \frac{_nd_x^i}{_nd_x} = _nq_x \cdot \frac{_nm_x^i}{_nm_x}$$

Once we have computed the life table for all causes combined, we can simply take the $_nq_x$ series from that table and apportion it to various causes of decrement according to their relative rates of decrement, since the probabilities are in the same ratio as the rates, or the recorded decrements, themselves.

So the steps for constructing a period multiple decrement life table are the following:

a) Compute a life table for all causes of decrement combined. The basic ingredient in this table is

$$_nm_x = \sum_i {_nm_x^i},$$

the rate of decrement from all causes combined in the age interval x to $x + n$. The usual procedure consists of assuming for each cause that $_nM_x^i = _nm_x^i$ (which also implies $_nM_x = _nm_x$), where $_nM_x^i$ is the observed decrement rate from cause i between ages x and $x + n$ in the population. This must be converted to $_nq_x$, as described in chapter 3.

b) Compute the probability of exit from cause i in the age interval x to $x + n$ as:

$$_nq_x^i = _nq_x \cdot \frac{_nm_x^i}{_nm_x}$$

Note that if we have accepted $_nM_x^i = _nm_x^i$, then the relationship becomes:

$$_nq_x^i = _nq_x \cdot \frac{_nM_x^i}{_nM_x} = _nq_x \cdot \frac{_nD_x^i}{_nD_x}$$

where $_nD_x^i$ is the observed number of decrements from cause i between ages x and $x + n$ in the population and $_nD_x$ is the observed number of decrements from all causes combined in the interval.

c) Compute the number of decrements from cause i in the age interval x to $x + n$ as:

$$_nd_x^i = _nq_x^i \cdot l_x$$

d) Compute the number of persons aged x^* who will eventually leave the table from cause i as:

$$l_{x^*}^i = \sum_{x=x^*}^{\infty} {_nd_x^i}$$

Box 4.1 *Multiple Decrement Life Table*

1. $_nq_x^i = {}_nq_x \cdot \dfrac{_nD_x^i}{_nD_x}$

2. $_nd_x^i = {}_nq_x^i \cdot l_x$

3. $l_x^i = \displaystyle\sum_{a=x}^{\infty} {}_nd_a^i$

Example: US, females, 1991. Cause i = death from neoplasms, l_x = "master" US life table for 1991, females, for all causes combined

Age x	$_nD_x$ All deaths	$_nD_x^i$ Deaths from neoplasms	l_x	$_nq_x$	$_nq_x^i$	$_nd_x^i$	l_x^i
0	15,758	63	100,000	0.00783	0.00003	3	21,205
1	3,169	275	99,217	0.00168	0.00015	14	21,201
5	1,634	268	99,050	0.00092	0.00015	15	21,187
10	1,573	217	98,959	0.00090	0.00012	12	21,172
15	3,955	318	98,870	0.00236	0.00019	19	21,160
20	4,948	467	98,637	0.00262	0.00025	24	21,141
25	6,491	856	98,379	0.00314	0.00041	41	21,117
30	9,428	1,924	98,070	0.00425	0.00087	85	21,076
35	12,027	3,532	97,653	0.00584	0.00171	167	20,991
40	15,543	5,958	97,083	0.00818	0.00314	304	20,823
45	19,264	8,434	96,289	0.01330	0.00582	561	20,519
50	25,384	11,673	95,008	0.02095	0.00963	915	19,958
55	37,211	17,078	93,018	0.03371	0.01547	1,439	19,043
60	59,431	25,263	89,882	0.05155	0.02191	1,969	17,604
65	88,087	33,534	85,249	0.07669	0.02920	2,489	15,634
70	114,693	36,695	78,711	0.11552	0.03696	2,909	13,145
75	143,554	36,571	69,618	0.17427	0.04439	3,091	10,236
80	164,986	30,220	57,486	0.27363	0.05012	2,881	7,146
85	320,578	32,739	41,756	1.00000	0.10212	4,264	4,264
All	1,047,714	246,085				21,205	

Proportion of female newborns that will eventually die from neoplasms under the US age-cause-specific death rates of 1991: $21,205/100,000 = 21.2\%$
Proportion of females who survive to age 75 that will die from neoplasms: $10,236/69,618 = 14.7\%$

Data source: National Center for Health Statistics, 1996.

Box 4.1 presents several columns for a multiple decrement life table for US females in 1991, using the l_x and $_nq_x$ columns for the "master" life table in the US in 1991. The state of interest is being alive and decrements from that state are attributed to neoplasms (cancer) and all other causes of death. The chance that a newborn would die from neoplasms is 0.212 (21,205/100,000).

4.3   Some Basic Mathematics of Multiple Decrement Processes

Recall that in chapter 3 we defined the force of mortality as:

$$\mu(x) = \lim_{n \to 0} {}_n m_x$$

We can correspondingly define the force of decrement from cause i as:

$$\mu^i(x) = \lim_{n \to 0} {}_n m_x^i$$

The force of decrement from cause i at age x is simply the rate at which persons are leaving the defined state from cause i in the tiny interval of age from x to $x + dx$. It is an annualized rate because its units are number of events (i.e., decrements) per person-year of exposure.

Since, with k causes of decrement,

$$_n m_x^1 + {}_n m_x^2 + \cdots + {}_n m_x^k = {}_n m_x,$$

as we take the limit of both sides as n approaches zero we must have

$$\mu^1(x) + \mu^2(x) + \cdots + \mu^k(x) = \mu(x)$$

where $\mu(x)$ is the "force of decrement from all causes combined." The force of decrement functions from various causes are additive and their sum equals the force of decrement from all causes combined as long as we define the set of decrements to be mutually exclusive and exhaustive (i.e., we haven't left any out and we haven't counted any decrements twice).

We asserted in chapter 3 that one of the most important relations in demography is:

$$_n p_x = e^{- \int_x^{x+n} \mu(y)\, dy}$$

In a multiple decrement process we can express $\mu(y)$ as the sum of $\mu^i(y)$ over all i, so that:

$$_n p_x = e^{- \int_x^{x+n} [\mu^1(y) + \mu^2(y) + \cdots + \mu^k(y)]\, dy}$$

$$= e^{- \int_x^{x+n} \mu^1(y)\, dy} \cdot e^{- \int_x^{x+n} \mu^2(y)\, dy} \cdots \cdots e^{- \int_x^{x+n} \mu^k(y)\, dy}$$

or,

$$_n p_x = {}_n^* p_x^1 \cdot {}_n^* p_x^2 \cdots \cdots {}_n^* p_x^k$$

where

$$_n^* p_x^i = e^{- \int_x^{x+n} \mu^i(y)\, dy} \tag{4.4}$$

is the probability of remaining in the defined state during the interval x to $x + n$ if *only* decrement i were operating.

Equation (4.4) says that the probability of remaining in the defined state between x and $x + n$ when many causes are operating (i.e. the probability of surviving all decrements) is the product of each of the probabilities of remaining in that state if individual decrements were acting alone. The analogy to coin-tossing is obvious. If we define an event as tossing a head, then the probability that no event will occur in three tosses is the product of the probabilities than no head will appear on each of the three tosses: $0.5 \cdot 0.5 \cdot 0.5$. This multiplicative property pertains only when the outcomes of the three tosses are statistically independent: when one outcome does not depend on the others. Clearly, the assumption of independence has also slipped into our derivation of (4.4). It entered at the point where we defined members of the set of decrements to be mutually exclusive and exhaustive. That is, the process of *assignment* of a cause to each particular decrement created a set of wholly separate and "independent" entities. That these statistical entities are independent – admit no overlap or combinations or synergistic relations – does not mean that the underlying processes that they represent are independent. For example, it is very likely that an increase in the incidence of influenza in a population will raise death rates from certain cardiovascular diseases as well as from influenza. But whatever this synergistic relation among *disease processes*, the data will always come to the analyst in a set of cause-of-death assignments in which influenza and cardiovascular diseases are tidily separated; equation (4.4) will continue to hold.

Other functions in the life table from all decrements combined can be similarly expressed in terms of the various force of decrement functions by substituting $\mu^1(x) + \mu^2(x) + \cdots + \mu^k(x)$ for $\mu(x)$ in the corresponding continuous notation formula (see appendix 3.1). For example:

$$e_0^o = \int_0^\infty e^{-\int_0^x \mu(a)\,da}\,dx = \int_0^\infty e^{-\int_0^x [\mu^1(a)+\mu^2(a)+\cdots+\mu^k(a)]\,da}\,dx$$

In addition, functions from single decrement i can be derived by noting that deaths from cause i over a small age interval da are $l(a)\mu^i(a)\,da$. Then:

$$_nq_x^i = \frac{_nd_x^i}{l(x)} = \frac{\int_x^{x+n} l(a)\mu^i(a)\,da}{l(x)} = \int_x^{x+n} e^{-\int_x^a \mu(y)\,dy}\mu^i(a)\,da$$

$$= \int_x^{x+n} e^{-\int_x^a [\mu^1(y)+\mu^2(y)+\cdots+\mu^k(y)]\,dy}\mu^i(a)\,da$$

$$_nm_x^i = \frac{_nd_x^i}{_nL_x} = \frac{\int_x^{x+n} e^{-\int_x^a \mu(y)dy}\mu^i(a)da}{\int_x^{x+n} e^{-\int_x^a \mu(y)dy}\,da}$$

$$= \frac{\int_x^{x+n} e^{-\int_x^a [\mu^1(y)+\mu^2(y)+\cdots+\mu^k(y)]\,dy}\mu^i(a)\,da}{\int_x^{x+n} e^{-\int_x^a [\mu^1(y)+\mu^2(y)+\cdots+\mu^k(y)]\,dy}\,da}$$

The formula for $_nq_x^i$ shows again why the probability of succumbing to cause i in a discrete age interval depends upon the value of other decrements; the higher is any other force of decrement, the lower will be $_nq_x^i$.

The formula for $_nm_x^i$ shows that its value is also "dependent" on the force of decrement from causes other than i. However, the direction of this dependence is not predictable, since both numerator and denominator include these terms.

In a cohort, the age composition of person-years lived in the age interval x to $x+n$ will depend only on the $l(a)$ function in that interval, i.e. on $\mu^1(a)+\mu^2(a)+\cdots+\mu^k(a)$ for $x \leq a \leq x+n$.

For a population at a moment in time, the age composition, $N(a)$, depends not only on those force of decrement functions but also on the preexisting age composition of the population. So the mortality rate from decrement i between age x and $x + n$ observed in the population, $_nM_x^i$, will be:

$$_nM_x^i = \frac{\int_x^{x+n} N(a)\mu^i(a)\, da}{\int_x^{x+n} N(a)\, da} = \int\limits_x^{x+n} c(a)\mu^i(a)\, da \qquad (4.5)$$

where $c(a)$ is the proportion of the population aged a to $a + da$ within the age group x to $x + n$. As in the case of the basic life table, it need not be the case that $_nM_x^i$ in a population equal $_nm_x^i$ in a cohort with the same force of decrement functions from i and $-i$. But, as in the case of the basic life table, it is common to assume that the life table $_nm_x^i$ in a population equal $_nM_x^i$ in the population (for an exception, see Preston, Keyfitz, and Schoen, 1972).

4.4 Associated Single Decrement Tables from Period Data

Associated with each decrement i in a multiple decrement process is a force of decrement function, $\mu^i(x)$. Very often the analyst is interested in knowing what a life table would look like if *only* that cause of decrement were operating to diminish a cohort. The life table that results from asking this question is called an associated single decrement life table (ASDT). The decrement we are interested in may equally well be $-i$ (all decrements other than i). If a table is constructed based on $\mu^{-i}(x)$, it is sometimes called a "cause-deleted" table, since cause i has been arbitrarily deleted from the set of multiple decrements. Such a table would still be considered an associated single decrement table since cause $-i$ can be considered one of two decrements – along with i – in a multiple decrement process.

Almost always, the activity of a particular decrement i will be observed as it works itself out within a multiple decrement process. Normally, we don't observe directly associated single decrement processes: processes in which one decrement alone is operating. The construction of an associated single decrement table therefore involves a thought experiment in which we ask "what would happen if ... " In an associated single decrement table for a period, this feature involves an additional layer of hypothesizing beyond that involved in constructing a hypothetical cohort.

We denote all functions of an associated single decrement table with a "*" as a superscript on the left. It is easy to specify what the functions in an associated single decrement table should be in terms of $\mu^i(x)$. They are the same functions defined for the basic life table in chapter 3. The formulas of appendix 3.1 can readily be adapted for these functions, by replacing $\mu(x)$ by $\mu^i(x)$. Equation (4.4) expresses the formula for $_n^*p_x^i$, the probability of surviving from age x to $x + n$ in an associated single decrement life table where cause i is the only decrement.

It is not necessary to repeat all these formulae but it might be useful to review the three types of functions encountered so far. Functions involving all decrements combined are obtained by computing both survivors and deaths with $\mu(x) = \mu^1(x) + \cdots + \mu^k(x)$. Similarly, associated single decrement functions are obtained by computing both survivors and deaths with $\mu^i(x)$ alone. Functions referring to one of the decrements in a multiple decrement life table have a "mixed" structure since survivors to any age must be computed with the $\mu(x)$ functions whereas deaths from cause i must be computed using $\mu^i(x)$. For example, compare:

$$_nd_x = l(x) \int_x^{x+n} e^{-\int_x^a \mu(y)\,dy} \mu(a)\,da$$

$$_n^*d_x^i = {}^* l^i(x) \int_x^{x+n} e^{-\int_x^a \mu^i(y)\,dy} \mu^i(a)\,da$$

$$_nd_x^i = l(x) \int_x^{x+n} e^{-\int_x^a \mu(y)\,dy} \mu^i(a)\,da$$

Although we can readily define associated single decrement functions in terms of $\mu^i(x)$, we cannot directly observe $\mu^i(x)$. We can observe $_nm_x^i$ in a cohort (or $_nM_x^i$ in a population). But it is important to note that the value of $_nM_x^i$ we observe when multiple decrements are operating to generate the observation would not typically be the same value we would observe if only decrement i were operating. We observe $_nm_x^i$ in a cohort but we need $_n^*m_x^i$ for the ASDT:

$$_n^*m_x^i = \frac{\int_x^{x+n} e^{-\int_x^a \mu^i(y)\,dy} \mu^i(a)\,da}{\int_x^{x+n} e^{-\int_x^a \mu^i(y)\,dy}\,da} \qquad \text{whereas} \qquad _nm_x^i = \frac{\int_x^{x+n} e^{-\int_x^a \mu(y)\,dy} \mu^i(a)\,da}{\int_x^{x+n} e^{-\int_x^a \mu(y)\,dy}\,da}$$

In general, the rate of decrement from $\mu^i(x)$ if i were the *only* decrement ($_n^*m_x^i$) differs from what it would be if i were working in the presence of other decrements ($_nm_x^i$). Since at all ages $\mu(a) > \mu^i(a)$, the age-distribution of person-years lived in the interval is older when a single decrement is operating than when multiple decrements are operating. This weighting differential raises $_n^*m_x^i$ relative to $_nm_x^i$ if $\mu^i(x)$ is rising in the interval. If we use conventional procedures, we will already have accepted the $_nM_x^i$ function to estimate $_nm_x^i$ in the multiple decrement table. How can we then turn around and say that we want to reproduce that same $_nM_x^i$ function in the associated single decrement table to estimate $_n^*m_x^i$? But if we don't start with $_nM_x^i$, where do we begin?

There are several solutions to this dilemma, none of them completely satisfactory:

(a) Ignore the disparity between $_n^*m_x^i$ and $_nm_x^i$. The disparity is produced by a process exactly analogous to the age distributional disturbances that can produce a disparity between $_nm_x$ and $_nM_x$ even when the force of mortality functions are the same in a cohort as in a population. We have generally ignored this latter disparity in producing a basic life table, so we might do the same in moving from a multiple decrement table to an ASDT. In this case we would proceed as in chapter 3 for the basic life table. The $_nm_x \to _nq_x$ conversion would be:

$$_n^*m_x^i = {}_nM_x^i = {}_nm_x^i$$

and

$$_n^*q_x^i = \frac{n \cdot {}_nm_x^i}{1 + (n - {}_n^*a_x^i) {}_nm_x^i}$$

The remaining problem of life table construction is then to adopt a set of $_n^*a_x^i$ values, a problem which could be solved by procedures similar to those outlined in chapter 3. Graduation procedures become relatively more attractive since "borrowing" $_n a_x^i$ functions from other populations is difficult (practically none are published) and hazardous.

Procedure (a) risks committing relatively large errors in some circumstances. In cause-of-death life tables at high ages (say, above 65), mortality is high from many causes and is rising rapidly with age. The changes in age structure induced through the thought experiment performed in producing an ASDT can be relatively large if the causes deleted have high death rates. So fairly substantial changes can be induced in the death rates from remaining causes.

However, when the causes deleted in the ASDT are relatively minor, this approach should work quite well because the age structural changes induced by the deletion within 5-year-wide intervals could not be very large.

(b) A second solution is to make the assumption that the force of decrement function for i is constant at some value γ in the interval x to $x + n$. By substituting γ for the $\mu^i(x)$ function in the expressions for $_n^* m_x^i$ and $_n m_x^i$ we find that $_n^* m_x^i$ and $_n m_x^i$ are both also equal to γ. So in this case, $_n m_x^i = {}_n^* m_x^i = {}_n M_x^i$. If the force of mortality function is constant with age in the interval, then the rate of decrement is undisturbed by any age distributional changes induced by deleting a cause. Also, if the force of mortality function is constant in the age interval at $_n m_x^i$, then:

$$_n^* p_x^i = e^{-\int_x^{x+n} {}_n m_x^i \, dx} = e^{-n \cdot {}_n M_x^i}$$

$$_n^* L_x^i = \frac{{}^* l_x^i - {}^* l_{x+n}^i}{{}_n M_x^i}$$

and the rest of the table can be readily completed.

This procedure is logically consistent and simple to apply. When the assumption is tenable, it is the preferred approach. But the assumption is rarely very satisfactory unless the age interval is small.

(c) A third approach is proposed by Chiang (1968). Assume that the force of decrement function from cause i is proportional to the force of decrement function from all causes combined in the age interval x to $x + n$:

$$\mu^i(a) = R^i \cdot \mu(a) \quad \text{for } x \le a \le x + n,$$

where R^i is the constant of proportionality for decrement i in the interval. This assumption, of course, means that $\mu^i(a)$ and $\mu^{-i}(a)$ have exactly the same shape between ages x and $x + n$, although their levels will generally differ. Since, by assumption,

$$_n^* p_x^i = e^{-\int_x^{x+n} \mu^i(a) \, da} = e^{-\int_x^{x+n} R^i \cdot \mu(a) \, da}$$

then

$$_n^* p_x^i = e^{-R^i \cdot \int_x^{x+n} \mu(a) \, da} = \left[e^{-\int_x^{x+n} \mu(a) \, da} \right]^{R_i}$$

$$= [_n p_x]^{R^i}$$

So in this case, the $_n p_x$ function in the ASDT bears a simple relation to the $_n p_x$ function in the "parent" life table for all causes combined. It is equal to the $_n p_x$ in the parent life table raised to the power R_i.

Furthermore, by the assumption of proportionality, the value of R_i in the interval will simply equal the ratio of the observed decrements from cause i to the decrements for all causes combined:

$$\frac{{}_nD_x^i}{{}_nD_x} = \frac{\int_x^{x+n} N(a)R^i\mu(a)\,da}{\int_x^{x+n} N(a)\mu(a)\,da} = R^i$$

So making this substitution for R^i gives:

$${}_n^*p_x^i = {}_np_x^{\left(\frac{{}_nD_x^i}{{}_nD_x}\right)}$$

This ingenious device solves the ${}_nm_x \rightarrow {}_nq_x$ conversion problem in producing the ASDT. However, it does not tell us what value of ${}^*{}_nm_x^i$ should be used in the life table or, what amounts to the same thing, what value of ${}_n^*a_x^i$ should be used. Nor is there any obvious solution to this problem. In the official US cause-of-death life tables of 1959–61 (NCHS, 1968), which used this approach, the values of ${}_n^*a_x^i$ were set equal for all i to ${}_na_x$ in the parent life table. But a moment's thought suggests that, with the same shape of the force of mortality functions as for all causes combined, a life table that reflects the operation of a decrement with higher values of $\mu^i(a)$ in the interval will have a younger age distribution of person-years lived and hence a lower value of ${}_na_x$. In fact, by the Chiang assumption, the ${}_na_x$ value in the parent life table must fall short of the ${}_n^*a_x^i$ values for all i.

The most satisfactory approach to estimating ${}_n^*a_x^i$ is probably to graduate the ${}_n^*q_x^i$ function in successive intervals and infer the value of ${}_n^*a_x^i$ from the general conformation of this schedule, similar to an approach suggested for all causes (section 3.2.2). If we assume that the distribution of deaths from cause i follows a quadratic function over the age interval $x - 5$ to $x + 10$, then the simple graduation formula for data tabulated in 5-year age or duration intervals is:

$${}_5^*a_x^i = \frac{-\frac{5}{24}{}_5^*d_{x-5}^i + 2.5{}_5^*d_x^i + \frac{5}{24}{}_5^*d_{x+5}^i}{{}_5^*d_x^i} \tag{4.6}$$

No iteration is required in this case because the ${}_n^*d_x^i$ function is directly calculable without knowing ${}_5^*a_x^i$.

An approach that is adaptable to intervals of irregular length is to approximate the value of ${}_n^*a_x$ by interpolation between two extreme situations. The first one is when there are no deaths from cause i in that age interval. The average number of years lived in the interval by those dying from cause i, ${}_n^*a_x^i$, is then undetermined, but clearly the number of years lived in the interval by those alive at the beginning of the interval must be n. The other extreme situation is when all deaths in the age interval are from cause i. Then, the average number of years lived in the interval by those alive at the beginning of the interval must be the same in the ASDT and in the parent life table. Since R^i represents the proportion of deaths in the age interval due to cause i, the two extreme situations correspond to $R^i = 0$ and $R^i = 1$ respectively. In the intermediate cases, we can interpolate between these extremes:

$$\frac{{}_n^*L_x^i}{{}^*l^i(x)} = n - R^i\left(n - \frac{{}_nL_x}{l(x)}\right) \tag{4.7}$$

In both the ASDT and the parent life table the following relationship must hold:

$$\frac{{}_nL_x}{l(x)} = n \cdot {}_np_x + {}_na_x \cdot {}_nq_x$$

$$= n - (n - {}_na_x) \cdot {}_nq_x$$

So equation (4.7) can be written as:

$$\overset{*}{}_na_x^i = n + R^i \frac{{}_nq_x}{\overset{*}{}_nq_x^i}({}_na_x - n) \tag{4.8}$$

This equation can also be derived through a Taylor expansion.

Which of the general approaches to constructing an ASDT should be used in any particular application obviously depends upon the nature of the data and tenability of assumptions. Elandt-Johnson and Johnson (1980) have compared several of these approaches and concluded that results are not very sensitive to the procedure used, as should have been anticipated on the basis of the discussion in chapter 3. If the interval n is short, approach (b) is best since it is completely consistent and fully developed. If one is constructing cause-deleted tables in which relatively small causes of decrement are deleted, then approach (c) is best because the assumption of proportionality must be very good (the decrements that remain are a very high proportion of total decrements to which they are assumed proportional). In other situations, convenience may dictate the approach selected.

Box 4.2 presents an associated single decrement table for causes of deaths other than neoplasms. It is based upon the data for US females in 1991 that were presented in box 4.1. The table is constructed by Chiang's method (approach c), with the $\overset{*}{}_na_x^{-i}$ values developed by graduation (equation 4.6) for $x = 10$ to 75, and using equation (4.8) for $x = 0, 1, 5,$ and 80. For the last age group, we use here the assumption that $\overset{*}{}_nm_x^i = {}_nm_x^i$, in which case $\overset{*}{}_\infty a_{85}^{-i}$ is simply e_{85}^o/R^{-i}. In chapter 7, we will investigate how to obtain a better estimate of $\overset{*}{}_\infty a_{85}^{-i}$. The table shows that, in absence of neoplasms, life expectancy at birth would have been 82.46 years, a gain of 3.54 years relative to the life table with all causes present.

4.5   Cause-specific Decomposition of Differences in Life Expectancies

In section 3.10, we presented a method for estimating the contribution of age-specific mortality differences to differences between two life expectancies. This method can be easily extended to estimate the contribution of differences in cause-specific death rates by assuming that the distribution of deaths by cause is constant within each age group in each population. Under this assumption, the contribution of differences in all-cause mortality in a specific age group can be distributed proportionately to the difference in cause-specific mortality in the corresponding age group (Arriaga, 1989). The specific contribution of differences in mortality rates from cause i between ages x and $x + n$, ${}_n\Delta_x^i$, can be estimated with the following equation:

$$_n\Delta_x^i = {}_n\Delta_x \cdot \frac{{}_nm_x^i(2) - {}_nm_x^i(1)}{{}_nm_x(2) - {}_nm_x(1)}$$

$$= {}_n\Delta_x \cdot \frac{{}_nR_x^i(2) \cdot {}_nm_x(2) - {}_nR_x^i(1) \cdot {}_nm_x(1)}{{}_nm_x(2) - {}_nm_x(1)} \tag{4.9}$$

Box 4.2 *Associated Single Decrement Life Table for Causes of Death other than Neoplasms (via approach c)*

$$R^{-i} = \frac{{}_nD_x - {}_nD_x^i}{{}_nD_x}$$

$l_x, {}_np_x, {}_na_x, e_x^o =$ functions in the master life table

$${}_n^*p_x^{-i} = [{}_np_x]^{R^{-i}}$$

$${}^*l_{x+n}^{-i} = {}^*l_x^{-i} \cdot {}_n^*p_x^{-i}$$

${}_n^*a_x^{-i}$: calculated from equation (4.8) for $x = 0, 1, 5, 80$
   from equation (4.6) for $x = 10$ to 75

$${}_\infty^*a_{85}^{-i} = {}^*e_{85}^{-i} = \frac{e_{85}^o}{R^{-i}}$$

Example: US, females, 1991; cause i = neoplasms

Age x	R^{-i}	l_x	${}_np_x$	${}_na_x$	e_x^o	${}_n^*p_x^{-i}$	${}^*l_x^{-i}$	${}_n^*a_x^{-i}$	${}^*e_x^{-i}$
0	0.99600	100,000	0.99217	0.152	78.92	0.99220	100,000	0.152	82.46
1	0.91322	99,217	0.99832	1.605	78.54	0.99846	99,220	1.605	82.10
5	0.83599	99,050	0.99908	2.275	74.67	0.99923	99,068	2.275	78.23
10	0.86205	98,959	0.99910	2.843	69.74	0.99922	98,992	2.875	73.29
15	0.91960	98,870	0.99764	2.657	64.80	0.99783	98,915	2.653	68.34
20	0.90562	98,637	0.99738	2.547	59.95	0.99763	98,700	2.548	63.48
25	0.86813	98,379	0.99686	2.550	55.10	0.99727	98,467	2.577	58.63
30	0.79593	98,070	0.99575	2.616	50.26	0.99661	98,198	2.585	53.78
35	0.70633	97,653	0.99416	2.677	45.46	0.99587	97,866	2.582	48.96
40	0.61668	97,083	0.99182	2.685	40.72	0.99495	97,462	2.637	44.15
45	0.56219	96,289	0.98670	2.681	36.03	0.99250	96,969	2.672	39.36
50	0.54014	95,008	0.97905	2.655	31.48	0.98863	96,242	2.695	34.64
55	0.54105	93,018	0.96629	2.647	27.10	0.98162	95,148	2.703	30.00
60	0.57492	89,882	0.94845	2.646	22.95	0.97003	93,399	2.695	25.51
65	0.61931	85,249	0.92331	2.631	19.05	0.95178	90,600	2.696	21.22
70	0.68006	78,711	0.88448	2.628	15.42	0.91991	86,231	2.686	17.16
75	0.74525	69,618	0.82573	2.618	12.09	0.86701	79,325	2.676	13.42
80	0.81683	57,486	0.72637	2.570	9.08	0.77017	68,776	2.637	10.07
85	0.89788	41,756	0.00000	6.539	6.54	0.00000	52,969	7.283	7.28

Probability of surviving to age 85 for all causes combined: 0.42
Probability of surviving to age 85 in the absence of neoplasms: 0.53
Life expectancy at birth for all cause combined: 78.92 years.
Life expectancy at birth in the absence of neoplasms: 82.46 years.

Data source: National Center for Health Statistics, 1996.

where

$_nR_x^i(j)$ = proportion of deaths from cause i in age group x to $x + n$ $(_nD_x^i/_nD_x)$ in population j (or at time j), and

$_n\Delta_x$ = contribution of all-cause mortality differences in age group x to $x + n$ to differences in life expectancies, as expressed in equation (3.11)

It can be easily shown that

$$_n\Delta_x = \sum_i {_n\Delta_x^i}, \quad \text{and} \quad e_0^o(2) - e_0^o(1) = \sum_x {_n\Delta_x} = \sum_x \sum_i {_n\Delta_x^i}$$

The age- and cause-specific contribution to differences in life expectancies can thus be presented in a two-by-two table where the elementary contributions add up to the total difference in life expectancies. Box 4.3 presents an application of the age and cause decomposition method to analyzing the difference in male life expectancies at birth between China and India in 1990. It shows that about 68 percent of the 8.2 additional years of life expectancy at birth in China is attributable to lower rates of communicable diseases below age 5 in this country. However, the total difference in e_0^o is reduced by about one year due to lower rates of noncommunicable diseases in India in 1990.

4.6 Associated Single Decrement Tables from Current Status Data

We noted in chapter 3 that a restricted associated single decrement process can be directly observed when cohorts are asked about their event histories. Since the members of the cohort who respond in the survey have clearly had a force of mortality function of zero, we need not view them as subject to a multiple decrement process. Therefore, it is possible to proceed directly to the construction of an ASDT for the process under investigation. The only restriction on the kind of functions that can be displayed will result from limitations in the data. For example, a question might be asked on "what was your marital status five years ago," rather than the more complex set of questions needed to construct a complete marital history. From the 5-year question, it will be possible to estimate $_5^*p_x^M$, the probability that a person who was aged x five years earlier (i.e. who is aged $x + 5$ at the time of survey) will have remained single to the time of the survey. But no information will be available on $_5^*a_x^M$. It should be reiterated that tables constructed from such data will pertain only to the surviving members of the cohort who did not emigrate. Their force of decrement function may differ from that of the original members of the cohort.

Such applications require retrospective questions. John Hajnal (1953) was apparently the first to recognize that certain ASDT's could also be constructed from current status data. In particular, he proposed that an associated single decrement table for first marriages be constructed from data on the current marital status of the population, without any resort to retrospective questions. In our example, the proportion never-married at age x, which can be obtained by question on current status in a survey, is closely related to the l_x column of the birth cohort's ASDT. Under the assumption that there is no differential mortality or migration by first-marriage status, the l_x column of the cohort's ASDT (with a radix of one) will exactly equal the proportion single at age x.

To see this more formally, let us assume the population to be closed to migration. Then the force of decrement from all causes combined for the single population at age x will be:

$$\mu^s(x) = \mu^{Ds}(x) + \mu^M(x),$$

Box 4.3 *Age and Cause Decomposition of Difference in Life Expectancies at Birth*

$_nm_x(1), _nm_x(2)$ = all-cause mortality rate between ages x and $x + n$ at time 1 and time 2 (or in population 1 and 2)

$_nR_x^i(1), _nR_x^i(2)$ = proportion of deaths from cause i between ages x and $x + n$ at time 1 and time 2 (or in population 1 and 2)

$_n\Delta_x$ = contribution of all-cause mortality differences in age group x to $x + n$ to differences in e_0^o (from equation 3.11)

$$_n\Delta_x^i = _n\Delta_x \cdot \frac{_nR_x^i(2) \cdot _nm_x(2) - _nR_x^i(1) \cdot _nm_x(1)}{_nm_x(2) - _nm_x(1)}$$

Example: India and China, males, 1990*

Age x	India				China				$_n\Delta_x$	$_n\Delta_x^1$	$_n\Delta_x^2$	$_n\Delta_x^3$
	$_nm_x$	$_nR_x^1$	$_nR_x^2$	$_nR_x^3$	$_nm_x$	$_nR_x^1$	$_nR_x^2$	$_nR_x^3$				
0	0.0267	0.882	0.073	0.046	0.0084	0.677	0.174	0.149	5.6	5.5	0.1	−0.0
5	0.0025	0.504	0.188	0.309	0.0009	0.174	0.337	0.488	0.8	0.6	0.1	0.2
15	0.0021	0.382	0.223	0.394	0.0015	0.068	0.380	0.552	0.3	0.4	−0.1	−0.0
30	0.0043	0.429	0.315	0.257	0.0028	0.101	0.573	0.326	0.6	0.6	−0.1	0.1
45	0.0139	0.304	0.592	0.104	0.0102	0.095	0.796	0.109	0.8	0.7	0.0	0.1
60	0.0388	0.248	0.722	0.030	0.0342	0.070	0.879	0.051	0.3	0.5	−0.1	−0.0
70	0.0929	0.247	0.728	0.025	0.1003	0.084	0.877	0.039	−0.3	0.7	−0.9	−0.1
Sum									8.2	9.0	−1.0	0.2

*In this example:

Cause 1 = Communicable diseases, maternal, perinatal and nutritional conditions;

Cause 2 = Noncommunicable diseases;

Cause 3 = Injuries.

Total Difference = e_0^o(China) − e_0^o(India) = 66.5 − 58.3 = 8.2 years= $\sum_{x=0}^{70} \sum_{i=1}^{3} {}_n\Delta_x^i$

Data source: Murray, C. J. and A. D. Lopez, 1996. *The Global Burden of Disease: A Comprehensive Assessment of Mortality and Disability from Diseases, Injuries, and Risk Factors in 1990 and Projected to 2020*. Boston, Harvard University, School of Public Health.

where $\mu^{Ds}(x)$ is the force of mortality at age x for the single population and $\mu^M(x)$ is the force of first marriage (defined of course only for the never-married population). By relations developed above, the number of single persons in a cohort at age x, $S(x)$, will be found by cumulating the forces of decrement:

$$S(x) = S(0) \cdot {}_xp_0 = S(0) \cdot e^{-\int_0^x \mu^s(a)\,da}$$

$$= S(0) \cdot e^{-\int_0^x [\mu^{Ds}(a) + \mu^M(a)]\,da}$$

where $S(0)$ is the number who were single in the cohort at birth.

The total population aged x in the cohort, $N(x)$, can be similarly derived as:

$$N(x) = N(0)e^{-\int_0^x \mu^{DT}(a)\,da}$$

where $\mu^{DT}(a)$ is the force of mortality function for the total population at age a. Now form the ratio of the single to the total population at age x:

$$\frac{S(x)}{N(x)} = \frac{S(0) \cdot e^{-\int_0^x \left[\mu^{Ds}(a)+\mu^M(a)\right]da}}{N(0) \cdot e^{-\int_0^x \mu^{DT}(a)\,da}}$$

$$= e^{-\int_0^x \left[\mu^M(a)+(\mu^{Ds}(a)-\mu^{DT}(a))\right]da} \tag{4.10}$$

since $S(0) = N(0)$. This expression includes a term in $[\mu^{Ds}(a) - \mu^{DT}(a)]$, the difference between the force of mortality functions for the single and total populations. If we assume that this difference is zero at all ages – there is no differential mortality by marital status – then:

$$\frac{S(x)}{N(x)} = e^{-\int_0^x \mu^M(a)\,da} = {}_x^* p_0^M \tag{4.11}$$

where ${}_x^* p_0^M$ is the probability of remaining in the single state between ages 0 and x in the cohort's ASDT, based on the force of first marriage alone. So we see a very simple connection between an observed proportion single for a cohort at age x, $S(x)/N(x)$, and the ASDT for that cohort.

If the assumption of no differential mortality by marital status is wrong, then $S(x)/N(x)$ is biased as an estimator of the cohort's ${}_x^* p_0^M$. Suppose that the death rate for the single population exceeds that of the total population at some or all ages. Then $S(x)/N(x)$ will be biased as an estimate of ${}_x^* p_0^M$ by the factor:

$$\exp\left(-\int_0^x \left[\mu^{Ds}(a) - \mu^{DT}(a)\right] da\right).$$

The proportion single at x will underestimate the probability of remaining single in the cohort ASDT because single persons have higher mortality; a smaller fraction of them will have survived to report their marital status in the survey. Nevertheless, $S(x)/N(x)$ is an unbiased estimate of ${}_x^* p_0^M$ for the cohort members who survived.

A single-round survey asking about current marital status thus yields one piece of information about the ASDT for each cohort interviewed. But suppose we can assume that the force of nuptiality has been constant over time. Then each cohort would trace out the same history as every other cohort and features of that history could be inferred by comparisons across cohorts. This is the logic of Hajnal's procedure.

Hajnal's method is typically applied in 5-year age intervals. Define the proportion single (i.e., never married) at ages x to $x+5$ as:

$$_5\Pi_x = \frac{_5S_x}{_5N_x}.$$

The person-years lived in the single state below age 50 could then be estimated by adding up successive values of $_5\Pi_x$ and multiplying by 5, the number of years the cohort will spend in each age interval:

$$PY^S(0, 50) = 5 \cdot \sum_{x=0,5}^{45} {}_5\Pi_x$$

This value could serve as an estimate of the mean age at marriage for the hypothetical cohort except that not all members of the cohort will have married by age 50. Hajnal estimates the proportion who will not marry by age 50 as:

$$\Pi(50) = \frac{1}{2}({}_5\Pi_{45} + {}_5\Pi_{50})$$

He then calculates the mean age at marriage over the base of those who do in fact marry by age 50:

$$SMAM = \frac{5 \cdot \sum_{x=0,5}^{45} {}_5\Pi_x - 50 \cdot \Pi(50)}{1 - \Pi(50)}$$

Those not marrying are excluded from the denominator and their person-years lived in the single state below age 50 are excluded from the numerator. *SMAM* is called "the singulate mean age at marriage," because it refers only to marriage occurring to the single population. Box 4.4 illustrates the computation of *SMAM* for Turkish males in 1990.

The value of *SMAM* is the mean age at first marriage for a cohort of women (or men) who marry by age 50. Its computation from current-status data in a single census or survey assumes that first marriage rates have been constant over time and that differences in mortality or migration rates by marital status are negligible. If rates have been changing, the value of *SMAM* is a hodge-podge of rates in the recent and distant past. Nevertheless, because it requires only a census tabulation of marital status by age, it is the only measure of marriage age available in many historic populations.

Although we have illustrated the concept of deriving ASDTs from current-status data with examples drawn from first marriage, the procedure can be applied to a wide range of processes. Among these are the process of becoming a mother, of moving from place of birth, of ever using contraception, of becoming sterilized, entering school, entering the work force, and other processes. The proportion of a cohort who have remained in a state is clearly a product of its cumulative rates of leaving the state, as shown in equations (4.10) and (4.11). Current-status data are not as informative about the timing of events as vital statistics or retrospective survey data. But they can be informative if interpreted correctly, and sometimes they are the only data available.

4.7 Stationary Populations with Multiple Sources of Decrement

In section 7 of chapter 3, we introduced one of the two most basic models in demography, the stationary population model. Recall that a stationary population would result from the maintenance of three conditions: a constant flow of births per unit of time; a constant set of age-specific mortality rates; and zero net migration rates at all ages. Let us now extend the assumption about mortality rates to include constancy of age-specific risks from each of the multiple sources of decrement. Since we have already shown that a stationary population with

Box 4.4 *Associated Single Decrement Tables from Current-status Data: Calculation of Singulate Mean Age at Marriage*

$_5N_x$ = Total population aged x to $x + n$

$_5S_x$ = Number of single persons aged x to $x + n$

$_5\Pi_x$ = $\dfrac{_5S_x}{_5N_x}$ = proportion single at ages x to $x + n$

$\Pi(50) = \dfrac{_5\Pi_{45} + _5\Pi_{50}}{2}$

$SMAM = \dfrac{5 \cdot \sum_{x=0}^{45} {_5\Pi_x} - 50 \cdot \Pi(50)}{1 - \Pi(50)}$

Example: Turkey, males, 1990

Age x	$_5N_x$	$_5S_x$	$_5\Pi_x$
0	3,052,255	3,052,255	1.000
5	3,541,409	3,541,409	1.000
10	3,560,900	3,560,900	1.000
15	3,165,061	3,030,203	0.957
20	2,581,153	1,853,222	0.718
25	2,435,765	629,077	0.258
30	2,096,899	180,767	0.086
35	1,784,121	77,134	0.043
40	1,418,784	43,412	0.031
45	1,111,113	28,627	0.026
50	980,115	22,527	0.023

$\sum_{x=0}^{45} {_5\Pi_x} = 5.119$

$\Pi(50) = \dfrac{.026 + .023}{2} = .0245$

$SMAM = \dfrac{5 \cdot 5.119 - 50 \cdot .0245}{1 - .0245} = 25.0 \; years$

Data source: Turkey. Basbakanlik Devlet Istatistik Enstitusu. *Statistical Yearbook of Turkey*, 1995. [*Turkiye istatistik yilligi*, 1995.] Ankara, Turkey, Basbakanlik Devlet Istatistik Enstitusu, 1996.

l_0 annual births would have $_nL_x$ persons at each age (where each function pertains to the same life table), it must also be the case that each year it would have $_nL_x \cdot {_nm_x^i} = {_nd_x^i}$ deaths from cause i at age x to $x + n$. Thus, the sum of annual deaths from cause i over all ages must be equal to l_0^i, the number of persons in an annual cohort of births who will eventually succumb to cause i.

In other words, in a stationary population the probability that a newborn will eventually die from cause i is equal to the annual number of deaths from cause i divided by the annual number of births (or of deaths from all causes, since the annual number of births must equal the annual number of deaths). Likewise, the probability that someone aged x will eventually die of cause i is equal to the proportion of annual deaths at ages $x+$ that are attributable to cause i.

These relations have wide applicability in populations that can be assumed to be stationary:

1. The probability that a marriage will end in divorce could be estimated by the ratio of annual divorces to annual marriages.
2. The probability that someone entering graduate school will eventually receive a Ph.D. could be found by dividing the annual number of Ph.D.s by the number of entrants to graduate school.
3. The probability that a newborn will be diagnosed with cancer at some point in his or her life will be equal to the number of annual cancer diagnoses divided by the annual number of births.
4. The probability that someone with newly diagnosed cancer will eventually die from cancer would equal the ratio of cancer deaths to cancer diagnoses. This probability is typically called a "case-fatality ratio" in epidemiology and its value is often estimated by resorting to stationary population assumptions.
5. The expected number of years spent with morbidity from a newly-diagnosed disease would equal the number of persons suffering from the disease at a moment in time divided by the annual number of new diagnoses of that disease. This is equivalent to life expectancy at birth being equal to population size divided by the annual number of births.
6. The "incidence" of a disease can be defined as the ratio of new cases of the disease diagnosed in a particular period divided by the person-years lived in the population during that period. The "prevalence" of a disease can be defined as the proportion of the population having the disease at a moment in time. If the number having the disease at a moment in time is H and the annual number of new diagnoses of the disease is I^H, then in a stationary population

$$\underset{\text{prevalence}}{\frac{H}{T_0}} = \underset{\text{incidence}}{\frac{I^H}{T_0}} \cdot \underset{\text{expected duration of the disease}}{\frac{H}{I^H}}.$$

5 Fertility and Reproduction

Mortality refers to the decrement process by which living members of a population gradually die out. Fertility refers to the increment process by which living members of a population produce live births, that is, new living members of the population. Although often associated with fertility, the term "reproduction" in demographic parlance refers to the process by which new members of a population replace outgoing members, a process that may comprise mortality as well as fertility.

Fertility analysis is more complex than mortality analysis in several respects. First, human fertility involves two individuals of opposite sexes. The difficulties are typically skirted in demography by relating births to one individual only, traditionally the mother. This tradition may reflect the fact that data on births are more often available for the mother than for the father. In this volume, we follow this tradition, although the measures described here for women could be readily transposed to men.

Fertility analysis must also take into account that, as opposed to the risk of mortality, fertility – or the "risk" of producing a live birth – is not universal in the female population. First, every member of the population is not necessarily capable of producing a live birth. In demography, fecundity refers to this biological component of fertility (the definitions of fertility and fecundity are reversed in biology).[1] Fecund women may experience some temporary infecundity, whereas the term "sterility" refers to a woman's or a man's permanent inability to conceive under any circumstances. Lifetime sterility is usually called "primary sterility," while sterility that develops during the reproductive years is termed "secondary sterility." Among nonsterile individuals, fecundity varies with age. In particular, fecundity is restricted to the period between two age-dependent processes, menarche and menopause, a period referred to as the reproductive span. Age is thus, as in mortality analysis, an important dimension of fertility analysis.

Among fecund individuals, the risk of giving birth depends on their behaviors and foremost on their sexual activity. The fact that sexuality is socially regulated and often limited to visible social structures partly alleviates the difficulty from a demographer's point of view. In some settings, marriage delineates the members of the society at risk of giving birth and in these cases only the behavior of married women needs to be considered. Even if there is some out-of-wedlock childbearing, the fertility rates of married women and unmarried women typically differ so that fertility analysis is usually made more precise by considering separately in-wedlock and out-of-wedlock births.

Fertility rates also depend on whether sexual partners attempt to influence the likelihood that their sexual activity will result in a live birth. Behaviors intended to reduce the chance of conception are referred to as contraceptive, whereas behaviors intended to increase the chance are sometimes referred to as proceptive. A conception may not produce a birth but may instead be terminated by an abortion.[2] Abortions may be spontaneous or may be induced in order to prevent a birth.

These multiple aspects of the process of giving birth complicate fertility analysis, but the main conceptual difference between fertility and mortality is that giving birth is a repeatable event. Therefore, fertility must be analyzed not only as a multidimensional process but also as a cumulative one: giving birth may be experienced more than once and only temporarily removes a woman from the risk of giving birth.

Given these various degrees of complexity, fertility analysis often begins by defining sub-groups of the female population according to characteristics affecting the exposure to the risk of giving birth, such as age, marital status, or parity (the cumulative number of a woman's live births). Once the population is divided into subgroups, a common analytic strategy is to show how subgroup behavior combines with population composition by subgroup to produce some aggregate measure of fertility. Some of these approaches rely on the standardization and decompositional methods introduced in chapter 2. More complex methods are invoked to study the biomedical determinants of fertility.

5.1 Period Fertility Rates

Fertility rates relate the number of births in a population during a period of time to some measure of exposure. In chapter 1, we defined the period Crude Birth Rate (CBR), as the number of births in a particular period divided by the number of person-years lived in the population during the same period:

$$CBR[0, T] = \frac{\text{Births in the period 0 to } T}{\text{Person-years lived in the population between time 0 and } T}$$

The CBR only loosely approximates an occurrence/exposure fertility rate because only women in their reproductive ages can actually give birth. The length of the reproductive life span varies from one woman to another but, in most settings, the vast majority of births occurs to women aged 15 to 50. This refinement of exposure gives rise to the General Fertility Rate (GFR):

$$GFR[0, T] = \frac{\text{Births in the period 0 to } T}{\text{Person-years lived in the period 0 to } T \text{ by women aged 15 to 50}}$$

The CBR remains, however, a more frequently used measure of fertility, in part because it is easier to calculate than the GFR, which requires that population be tabulated by age and sex. In addition, the CBR indicates how much births are contributing to population growth: it is the rate at which the population is growing by virtue of the arrival of newborns. Clearly the CBR and the GFR are related by:

$$CBR[0, T] = GFR[0, T] \cdot {}_{35}C^F_{15}[0, T] \tag{5.1}$$

Table 5.1: *Comparison of crude birth rates and general fertility rates in selected countries, 1985–90*

Country	Total population (thousands)	Number of women aged 15–49 (thousands)	Proportion of women aged 15–49	Annual births (thousands)	Crude birth rate	General fertility rate	rank CBR	rank GFR
Zaire	34,569	7,601	0.220	1,652	0.0478	0.2173	1	2
Kenya	21,747	4,522	0.208	1,002	0.0461	0.2216	2	1
Senegal	6,851	1,530	0.223	312	0.0455	0.2039	3	3
South Africa	35,055	8,401	0.240	1,153	0.0329	0.1372	4	4
India	809,412	191,970	0.237	25,339	0.0313	0.1320	5	5
Tunisia	7,671	1,865	0.243	228	0.0297	0.1223	6	6
Indonesia	175,072	44,325	0.253	4,974	0.0284	0.1122	7	7
Lebanon	2,612	674	0.258	73	0.0279	0.1083	8	8
Argentina	31,436	7,469	0.238	686	0.0218	0.0918	9	9
USA	244,195	64,203	0.263	3,900	0.0160	0.0607	10	10
Australia	16,265	4,243	0.261	246	0.0151	0.0580	11	11
France	55,944	13,801	0.247	772	0.0138	0.0559	12	12
Japan	122,187	31,111	0.255	1,321	0.0108	0.0425	13	13

Data source: United Nations, 1995.

where $_{35}C_{15}^F[0, T]$ is the proportion of person-years lived in the population that are lived by females between the exact ages 15 and 50. Although the GFR seems to approximate better an occurrence/exposure rate than the CBR, the quantity $_{35}$ C_{15}^F varies relatively little across populations, even with quite different demographic regimes. Comparing GFRs across populations often provides little additional insight relative to a comparison of CBRs, a measure more readily available. Such a comparison is shown in table 5.1.

Despite the multiplicity of demographic influences on fertility, many of the measures of fertility are based exclusively on age. Fertility varies by age because biological fecundity varies with age but also because social, behavioral, or motivational determinants vary with age. As opposed to the relative size of the age group 15–49 in the population, the age structure within the age range of 15 to 50 years may vary substantially across populations, which justifies the computation of age-specific rates.

Age-specific fertility rates are defined in a way exactly analogous to age-specific mortality rates. The numerator restricts births to those occurring to mothers of a certain age interval and the denominator consists of person-years lived by women in that age interval:

$$_n F_x[0, T] = \frac{\text{Births in the period 0 to } T \text{ to women aged } x \text{ to } x + n}{\text{Person-years lived in the period 0 to } T \text{ by women aged } x \text{ to } x + n}$$

As in the case of age-specific mortality rates, age-specific fertility rates can be defined for very short age intervals as n tends toward zero. The age pattern of fertility can then be represented by a continuous density function, $f(a)$.

To compare fertility across populations in a way that removes the influence of differences in age and sex structures, one could use the technique of standardization introduced in chapter 2. Breaking the reproductive life span into I age intervals, and using a standard age and sex distribution, C_i^S, an age and sex standardized crude birth rate can be defined as:

$$ASCBR[0, T] = \sum_{i=1}^{I} F_i \cdot C_i^S$$

where C_i^S is the proportion of the total population (male and female) that consists of women in age group i, and F_i is the age-specific fertility rate for women in the ith age interval. The population age structure is functioning as a proxy for the person-years lived in different age intervals.

If we wish to limit the analysis to the female population, then the birth rate and F_i schedule would count only female births and C_i^S would refer to the proportion of the female population that consists of women in age group i.

In chapter 2, we showed that the choice of a standard is crucial in comparing age-standardized rates. The need for this choice introduces an unfortunate element of arbitrariness into the rates. Fertility analysis has avoided this arbitrariness by settling on a different means of combining age-specific fertility rates in the form of a measure called the Total Fertility Rate (TFR).

In discrete notation, the total fertility rate (TFR) can be written as:

$$TFR[0, T] = n \cdot \sum_{x=\alpha}^{\beta-n} {}_nF_x[0, T] \tag{5.2}$$

where α and β are the minimum and maximum ages at childbearing. The TFR is the single most important indicator of fertility. It achieves this status not merely because it is one of the many possible age-standardized measures of fertility, but also because it has a powerful interpretation: the TFR is the average number of children a woman would bear if she survived through the end of the reproductive age span and experienced at each age a particular set of age-specific fertility rates. These rates may pertain either to a birth cohort of women passing through life or, more commonly, to the set of age-specific fertility rates of a particular period. The period TFR measures the average number of children who would be born to a hypothetical cohort of women who survive to the end of their reproductive period and who bear children at each age at the rate observed during a particular period. The term, n, appears as a multiplier of age-specific rates in formula (5.2) because a woman spends n years in (each) n-year-wide age interval, during which she is bearing children at annual rate ${}_nF_x$. The cohort TFR is further described below, but we will refer to the period TFR unless otherwise specified. Box 5.1 illustrates the calculation of age-specific fertility rates and the Total Fertility Rate for the US in 1992, and table 5.2 presents estimates of TFRs in major regions of the world in recent years.

Note that, in most populations, the number of persons alive between ages 15 and 49 declines with age. Therefore, the CBR, a weighted average of the age-specific fertility rates using the actual population distribution as weights, gives more importance to younger age groups than does the TFR, which gives equal weight to all ages. The CBR would, in general, be more responsive to a postponement of marriage or of first birth than would the TFR, whereas the TFR would be more responsive than the CBR to fertility changes later in the reproductive span.

Although not as popular as age-specific rates, other fertility rates are sometimes constructed based on characteristics such as marital status, parity (a women's number of previous live births), or contraceptive method used. Any restriction must be consistently applied to both the

Box 5.1 *Example of Computation of Age-specific Fertility Rates and the Total Fertility Rate*

$_nW_x$ = Mid-year number of women aged x to $x + n$

$_nB_x$ = Number of births to women aged x to $x + n$ during the year

$_nF_x = \dfrac{_nB_x}{_nW_x}$ = Age-specific fertility rate for age interval x to $x + n$

$$TFR = n \cdot \sum_{x=\alpha,n}^{\beta-n} {_nF_x}$$

Example: US, 1992

Age x	$_5W_x$	$_5B_x$	$_5F_x$
10	8,831,206	12,220	0.0014
15	8,324,273	505,415	0.0607
20	9,344,413	1,070,490	0.1146
25	10,047,198	1,179,264	0.1174
30	11,165,144	895,271	0.0802
35	10,619,275	344,644	0.0325
40	9,519,450	55,702	0.0059
45	7,820,172	2,008	0.0003
Sum			0.4128

$$\sum_{x=10,5}^{45} {_5F_x} = .4128$$

$TFR = 5 \cdot .4128 = 2.064$ *children per woman*

Data source: National Center for Health Statistics, 1996.

Table 5.2: *Total fertility rate, by major areas,* 1995–2000

Major area	TFR
Africa	5.06
Eastern Asia	1.77
South-central Asia	3.36
South-eastern Asia	2.69
Western Asia	3.77
Europe	1.42
Latin America and the Caribbean	2.70
North America	1.94
Oceania	2.38

Source: United Nations, 1999.

numerator and denominator of the rate. For instance, one can define a parity-specific fertility rate as:

$$F_p[0, T] = \frac{\text{Births in the period 0 to } T \text{ to women at parity } p}{\text{Person-years lived in the period 0 to } T \text{ by women at parity } p}$$

Combining age and marital status specific rates, age-specific marital fertility rates are defined as:

$$_n F_x^L[0, T] = \frac{\text{Births in the period 0 to } T \text{ to married women aged } x \text{ to } x + n}{\text{Person-years lived in the period 0 to } T \text{ by married women aged } x \text{ to } x + n}$$

Summing this latter rate over all age groups, one can derive a total marital fertility rate (TMFR) that is analogous to the TFR. The comparison of the TMFR and the TFR indicates the contribution of a given nuptiality pattern to the level of fertility. The force of the comparison is diminished by out-of-wedlock conceptions, which can artificially inflate marital fertility rates if they are quickly followed by marriage, or render marital status less relevant if they are not. If there are no out-of-wedlock births, then $_n F_x = {_n F_x^L} \cdot {_n \Phi_x}$, where $_n \Phi_x$ is the proportion of women who are married at ages x to $x + n$. In this case, the ratio of the TFR to the TFMR is

$$\frac{TFR}{TMFR} = \frac{n \cdot \sum_{x=\alpha}^{\beta} {_n F_x^L} \cdot {_n \Phi_x}}{n \cdot \sum_{x=\alpha}^{\beta} {_n F_x^L}}$$

$$= \sum_{x=\alpha}^{\beta} \left(\frac{_n F_x^L}{\sum_{x=\alpha}^{\beta} {_n F_x^L}} \right) \cdot {_n \Phi_x} \tag{5.3}$$

The ratio, TFR/TMFR, appears as a weighted average of the proportion married in each age interval, the weights being the contribution of an age group to the total marital fertility rate. The ratio is thus a fertility-weighted average of proportions married by age. The comparison of fertility rates standardized on two dimensions (age and marital status in the TMFR) and on one of these dimensions (age only in the TFR) provides an assessment of the impact of the other dimension (marriage) on fertility.

In order to compare fertility levels in historical European populations for which births were not always tabulated by age of the mother and thus did not allow computation of age-specific fertility rates, Coale (1969) proposed a similar standardization to evaluate the contribution of the nuptiality pattern to fertility levels. The procedure requires data on the age distribution of the female population, W_i. Using the observed marital fertility rates of the Hutterites, a well-documented and highly fertile population living in the United States and Canada, the number of births in the population was compared to the number of births that would occur if the women in each age-group had the same fertility rates as the marital fertility rates observed for the Hutterites,[3] H_i. This age-standardized index of general fertility is thus:

$$I_f = \frac{B}{\sum_{i=1}^{I} H_i \cdot W_i} = \frac{\sum_{i=1}^{I} F_i \cdot W_i}{\sum_{i=1}^{I} H_i \cdot W_i}$$

If we assume again that births only occur within marriage and denote W_i^L the number of married women in age group i, then

$$\sum_{i=1}^{I} F_i \cdot W_i = B = B^L = \sum_{i=1}^{I} F_i^L \cdot W_i^L,$$

where F_i^L is rate of childbearing among married women in the ith age interval.

Now we can write I_f as:

$$I_f = \frac{\sum_{i=1}^{I} F_i^L \cdot W_i^L}{\sum_{i=1}^{I} H_i \cdot W_i^L} \cdot \frac{\sum_{i=1}^{I} H_i \cdot W_i^L}{\sum_{i=1}^{I} H_i \cdot W_i}$$

$$= I_g \cdot I_m$$

The first term of the product, denoted I_g and called the index of marital fertility, is the ratio of the number of marital births to the number that would occur if all married women had Hutterite fertility. Although the numerator is written with rates to illustrate the standardization procedure, computation of the rates is unnecessary since the sum in the numerator is simply the observed number of births. The second term, denoted I_m and called the index of proportions married, indicates the impact of the nuptiality pattern on the standardized index of fertility I_f. Although the weights are different in the two cases, I_m has a structure similar to the TFR/TMFR ratio in equation (5.3). In both relationships, the point is to decompose an age-standardized measure of fertility into an age- and marriage-standardized measure of fertility (TMFR or I_g) and an index of the contribution of nuptiality to fertility (TFR/TMFR or I_m). Box 5.2 shows an application of Coale's fertility indexes to data from a French village at the beginning of the nineteenth century.

When there is substantial out-of-wedlock childbearing, the double standardization on age and marriage is slightly more complicated but follows the same structure. In this case, Coale's index of general fertility can be decomposed as:

$$I_f = I_m \cdot I_g + (1 - I_m) \cdot I_h$$

where I_h is the ratio of the number of out-of-wedlock births to the number that would occur if all unmarried women bore children at the Hutterite rate:

$$I_h = \frac{B - B^L}{\sum_{i=1}^{I} H_i \cdot (W_i - W_i^L)} \tag{5.4}$$

The second term in the more elaborate equation for I_f decomposes illegitimate births[4] into the index of the proportion unmarried and an index of illegitimate fertility. In many historical European populations where out-of-wedlock births are infrequent, this component of total fertility can be ignored. Comparison between different fertility levels could be based on the index of marital fertility and the index of the proportion married alone. In many contemporary Western countries, however, nonmarital fertility has become an important component of total fertility. In the United States, 33 percent of childbearing occurred outside marriage in 1995 (National Center for Health Statistics, 1996). The proportion is even higher in parts of Northern Europe. In some populations, the distinction between marital and nonmarital births is

Box 5.2 *Computation of Coale's Fertility Indexes I_m, I_f, I_g (with assumption of no illegitimacy)*

W_i^L = Number of married women in age group i

W_i = Number of women in age group i

H_i = Marital fertility rates of the Hutterites

B = Actual number of births during the considered year

$$I_f = \frac{B}{\sum_{i=1}^{7} H_i \cdot W_i} = \text{Index of fertility.} \quad I_g = \frac{B}{\sum_{i=1}^{7} H_i \cdot W_i^L} = \text{Index of marital fertility}$$

$$I_m = \frac{\sum_{i=1}^{7} H_i \cdot W_i^L}{\sum_{i=1}^{7} H_i \cdot W_i} = \text{index of proportions married}$$

$$I_f = I_g \cdot I_m$$

Example: Tourouvre-au-Perche (France), 1801

Age group i	Age	W_i^L	W_i	H_i	$H_i \cdot W_i^L$	$H_i \cdot W_i$
1	15–19	1	73	0.300	0.3	21.9
2	20–4	19	87	0.550	10.5	47.9
3	25–9	33	49	0.502	16.6	24.6
4	30–4	58	66	0.447	25.9	29.5
5	35–9	48	56	0.406	19.5	22.7
6	40–4	42	56	0.222	9.3	12.4
7	45–9	37	51	0.061	2.3	3.1
Sum					84.3	162.1

Estimated total births in 1801: B = 59

$I_f = 59/162.1 = 0.364$
$I_g = 59/84.3 = 0.700$
$I_m = 84.3/162.1 = 0.520$

Data source: Charbonneau, Hubert, 1970. *Tourouvre-au-Perche aux XVIIe et XVIIIe siècles.* Paris, PUF.

clouded by frequent nonmarital conceptions that are later legitimated by marriage, introducing important imprecision into Coale's measures.

5.2 Decomposition of Period Fertility

To attribute differences in period fertility to the various dimensions of the process, demographers have decomposed overall fertility in a number of different ways. For instance, in their analysis of the early phase of the postwar baby boom, Grabill, Kiser, and Whelpton (1958) suggested the following decomposition of the number of births in year T:

$$B(T) = W(T) \cdot \frac{M(T)}{W(T)} \cdot \frac{O(T)}{M(T)} \cdot \frac{B(T)}{O(T)} \qquad \textbf{(5.5)}$$

where

$B(T)$ = number of births in year T;
$W(T)$ = number of women aged 15 to 49 in year T;
$M(T)$ = number of married women aged 15 to 49 in year T;
$O(T)$ = number of mothers (women of parity one or more) aged 15 to 49 in year T.[5]

The number of births then appears as the product of:

- the number of women aged 15 to 49;
- the proportion of women aged 15 to 49 who are married;
- the proportion of married women who are mothers (i.e. who have ever given birth);
- the average number of births per mother.

There have been many other decompositions of numbers of births or of standardized fertility rates. We mentioned Coale's decomposition of a index of general fertility into an index of marital fertility and an index of the proportion married. Bongaarts (1978) has developed a decompositional model of fertility that begins with the TFR/TMFR ratio but introduces measures designed to reflect other bio-behavioral influences on fertility.

In Bongaart's scheme, the total fertility rate is first expressed as an identity involving ratios of different factors that cancel out:

$$TFR = \frac{TFR}{TMFR} \cdot \frac{TMFR}{TNFR} \cdot \frac{TNFR}{MTFR} \cdot MTFR$$

where TNFR is the total natural fertility rate and MTFR is the maximum potential fertility rate. These various ratios are then made operational in a series of indexes:

$$TFR = \frac{TFR}{TMFR} \cdot \frac{TMFR}{TNFR} \cdot \frac{TNFR}{MTFR} \cdot MTFR$$

$$= C_m \cdot (C_c \cdot C_a) \cdot C_i \cdot 15.3 \tag{5.6}$$

where 15.3 is the assumed value of maximum potential fertility, MTFR, and the ratio, TMFR/TNFR, is expressed in the form of a product of two indexes, $C_c \cdot C_a$. The three ratios are thus related to four indexes, each one representing a set of fertility determinants, often called "proximate determinants" of fertility. C_i first compares the maximum potential fertility to the natural fertility level (TNFR) by reflecting breastfeeding behavior which affects the length of postpartum nonsusceptible period. Natural fertility is further related to the total marital fertility rate (TMFR) by contraceptive use and induced abortion, each represented by an index, C_c and C_a respectively. Lastly, total marital fertility is related to total fertility by the index C_m. The index C_m is simply the TFR/TMFR shown in equation (5.3). As noted above, this decomposition implicitly assumes that there is no out-of-wedlock childbearing or that unions are broadly defined to cover all sexual relationships.

The relationships between the proximate determinants and the four indexes were empirically estimated. For example, the index of fertility reduction due to contraception is estimated as:

$$C_c = 1 - 1.08 \cdot u \cdot e \tag{5.7}$$

where u is the proportion of women using contraception and e is the average use-effectiveness of contraception. The average use-effectiveness is defined as the proportionate reduction in the monthly probability of conception that results from the use of contraception (Trussell et al., 1993). The estimation of contraceptive use-effectiveness is based on life table techniques described in chapter 4. More specifically, it requires the derivation of an associated single decrement life table to separate conception from other potential reasons to discontinue contraceptive use (a hypothetical example is provided in box 5.3). The coefficient 1.08 in equation (5.7) is added to account for the fact that sterile couples may not use contraception knowing that they are not at risk of conception. The index should thus reach zero with less than 100 percent effective contraceptive use.

The index of proportionate reduction in TFR due to abortion, C_a, is estimated as:

$$C_a = \frac{TFR}{TFR + 0.4(1 + u)TA} \tag{5.8}$$

where TA is the total abortion rate (the sum of age-specific abortion rates that is equivalent in its computational design to the Total Fertility Rate). The coefficient $.4(1 + u)$ represents the number of births prevented by one abortion. This number is smaller than one because an abortion "uses up" less of a woman's reproductive life than does a live birth. Bongaarts' relation suggests that, with no contraception, an abortion prevents 0.4 births, and that if all women are contracepting, an abortion prevents 0.8 births.

Finally, C_i is the index of reduction due to postpartum infecundity. The index is estimated as:

$$C_i = \frac{20}{18.5 + i} \tag{5.9}$$

where i is the length of postpartum infecundity in months. If i is 1.5 months, then there is no reduction to the maximum natural fertility regime. When a direct estimate of i is not available, it can be approximated from the mean months of breast-feeding, $\overline{BF}$ (Bongaarts, 1982: 188):

$$i = 1.753 \exp\left(.1396\,\overline{BF} - .001872\,\overline{BF}^2\right) \tag{5.10}$$

The maximum potential fertility is estimated at 15.3. This figure suggests that in a population without contraception, without induced abortion, with a minimum nonsusceptible period of 1.5 months, and in which all women marry at 15 and remain married to age 50, the total fertility rate would be 15.3. This figure is higher than that observed in any known high-fertility population, including the Hutterites. No population pulls out all of the stops in order to maximize fertility.

Stover (1998) reviews the performance of the Bongaarts model in more than a hundred applications and suggests some modifications of the indexes. Perhaps the most significant modification is the use of sexual activity rather than marriage to indicate exposure to pregnancy.

5.3 Cohort Fertility

Like mortality analysis, fertility analysis can benefit from a cohort perspective. In fertility analysis, however, the cohort approach gains additional relevance from the fact that total fertility is a cumulative process and that a woman's past birth history may affect her future fertility. In chapter 2, we defined cohort age-specific rates. Cohort age-specific fertility rates can be summed to give the cohort's total fertility rate. The cohort TFR is the average number of children who would be born to an actual birth cohort of women if they had all survived to

Box 5.3 *Contraceptive Failure Rates using Associated Single Decrement Life Tables (with assumption of a constant failure risk within each interval)*

x = Duration since beginning of contraceptive use (in months)

l_x = Number using contraception at the beginning of the interval

$_n d_x^P$ = Number becoming pregnant during the interval

$_n d_x^D$ = Number discontinuing use during the interval

$_n L_x = \dfrac{(l_{x+n} - l_x) \cdot n}{\ln(l_{x+n}/l_x)}$ = Person-months of use during the interval, assuming constant failure rate

$_n M_x^P = \dfrac{_n d_x^P}{_n L_x}$ = Contraceptive failure rate in the interval x to $x + n$

$_n^* p_x^P = e^{-n \cdot _n M_x^P}$ = Probability of survival in the interval if contraceptive failure was the only reason to discontinue contraceptive use

$^* l_x^P$ = number using contraception at the beginning of the interval if contraceptive failure was the only reason to discontinue contraceptive use

Theoretical example

x	l_x	$_n d_x^P$	$_n d_x^D$	$_n L_x$	$_n M_x^P$	$_n^* p_x^P$	$^* l_x^P$
0	100	5	15	268.89	0.0186	0.9457	1,000
3	80	4	6	224.67	0.0178	0.9480	946
6	70	5	5	194.61	0.0257	0.9258	897
9	60	2	2	173.93	0.0115	0.9661	830
12	56						802

Probability of survival in first year of use = $\dfrac{^* l_{12}^P}{^* l_0^P} = .802$

Probability of contraceptive failure in first year of use = $1 - \dfrac{^* l_{12}^P}{^* l_0^P} = .198 = 19.8\%$

the end of their reproductive period, and born children at each age at the rate observed for the surviving members of the cohort at each age. If cohort members who died had the same rate of childbearing at each age as the women who survived, then the cohort's total fertility rate would be identical to the mean number of children ever born to women in that cohort who survived to the end of childbearing.

The cohort TFR can only be calculated when all surviving women in the birth cohort have reached the end of their reproductive years. If demographic rates at every age are constant over time, there would be no difference between the longitudinal (cohort) and cross-sectional (period) measures. In some situations, however, period measures may provide a misleading indicator of the behavior of any real cohort. Henry (1953), in France, and Ryder (1965 and 1986), in the United States, have contributed most to the discussion of relations between period measures of fertility and cohort measures. Cohort measures and period measures of fertility will differ even when the cohort total fertility rate is constant over time if the age-pattern of fertility is changing. Imagine a population in which women normally have 5 births, one in each of the age-intervals 15–19, 20–4, 25–9, 30–4, and 35–9. But because of extraordinary conditions there are no births in a certain 5-year period. Woman experiencing this "lost birth" are assumed to "catch up" by having one additional birth between age 40 and 44. In this case, as shown in table 5.3, the period TFR would fluctuate between 0 and 6 whereas the cohort TFR – identifiable by tracking a cohort diagonally down the table – would remain unchanged at 5.0.

A simple way to analyze the effect of changing fertility schedule from one cohort to another is to decompose the period TFR, TFR^P , into a timing component and a volume component:

$$TFR^P = \sum_{i=1}^{I} F_i^P = \sum_{i=1}^{I} \frac{F_i^P}{TFR^{Ci}} \cdot TFR^{Ci}$$

$$= \sum_{i=1}^{I} p_i^P \cdot TFR^{Ci}$$

where TFR^{Ci} is the cohort TFR of the cohort C_i which occupied age interval i in the period P. Thus p_i^P can be interpreted as the proportion of the total number of children born (TFR) in cohort C_i that actually occurred in period P (i.e., in the age interval i). This expression thus shows explicitly how the period TFR depends on the volume of childbearing achieved by the cohorts bearing children during that period (TFR^{Ci}) and a timing component, p_i^P, representing the fraction of those children who were born during the period.

To compare the actual period TFR to a hypothetical period TFR devoid of timing effects, one could compute a timing-standardized period TFR using a standard distribution, p_i^s, of the cohort fertility distribution over the lifetime of the cohort. Kiser, Grabill, and Campbell (1968: 255–64) use this approach to show that, in the United States, this standardization of timing factors would sharply reduce the amount of fluctuation in period TFRs. In other words, timing factors have reinforced volume factors in the cohort TFR, making the period TFR more volatile than the cohort TFR. Periods of high fertility had both a high volume of fertility among cohorts then bearing children (i.e., a large completed family size) and an unusually high concentration of fertility in such periods. During the postwar baby boom in the US, the period TFR peaked at 3.7 whereas no cohort then bearing children achieved a value higher than 3.3.

Table 5.3: *Illustration of the distinction between period and cohort total fertility rates*

Age				*Age-specific fertility rates*					
	Period								
	1930–4	1935–9	1940–4	1945–9	1950–4	1955–9	1960–4	1965–9	1970–4
15–19	.2	.2	0	.2	.2	.2	.2	.2	.2
20–4	.2	.2	0	.2	.2	.2	.2	.2	.2
25–9	.2	.2	0	.2	.2	.2	.2	.2	.2
30–4	.2	.2	0	.2	.2	.2	.2	.2	.2
35–9	.2	.2	0	.2	.2	.2	.2	.2	.2
40–4	0	0	0	.2	.2	.2	.2	.2	0
Period TFR	5.0	5.0	0	6.0	6.0	6.0	6.0	6.0	5.0

The approach just described requires completed fertility histories to implement. It does not address an issue of great current interest: to what extent the very low fertility in parts of the industrialized world are attributable to timing factors – the stretching out of births through time as the mean age of childbearing increases – or to volume factors. Bongaarts and Feeney (1998) have developed a procedure designed to purge period TFRs of timing fluctuations, but assumptions required to implement it limit its applicability (Kim and Schoen, 2000).

Attention to the differences between period measures and cohort measures of fertility is required in the interpretation of fertility measures derived from period data. Whether period or cohort age-standardized fertility rates are more appropriate is not a measurement issue but depends on the relative importance of period and cohort influences on fertility. There is no consensus on this conceptual issue in demography (Bhrolchain, 1992).

A cohort's total fertility rate can be readily estimated through a census or survey question about parity, the number of live births a woman has had. The mean parity, or mean number of children ever born, of a cohort of women who have completed childbearing, is equal to the cohort's total fertility rate if reporting is accurate and if there are no differentials in mortality or migration by parity. (The role of mortality or migration differentials can be studied using the same logic that produced equation (4.10).)

The fertility process can be represented not only through a woman's movement from one age to the next but also by her movement from one parity to the next. This latter movement can be represented by parity progression ratios, introduced by Henry (1953: 22). A woman's parity is the number of her live births, so the parity progression ratio from parity i to parity $i + 1$ is the proportion of a cohort who had at least i live births who went on to have at least one more:

$$PPR_{(i,i+1)} = \frac{\text{Number of women at parity } i + 1 \text{ or more}}{\text{Number of women at parity } i \text{ or more}} = \frac{P_{i+1}}{P_i}$$

This cohort measure is usually calculated only for cohorts who have completed their child-bearing. From a survey of 50-year-old women, the cohort total fertility rate is retrospectively estimated as the total number of births among women in the cohort divided by the number of women in the cohort. These can be added across age groups, as in the conventional TFR, but they can also be added across birth orders of the children (first births, second births, etc.). If we denote as P_i the number of women at parity i or more and W as the total number of women, then the number of first births will equal P_1, of second births P_2, etc., and

$$\begin{aligned}
TFR^C &= \frac{P_1}{W} + \frac{P_2}{W} + \frac{P_3}{W} + \cdots \\
&= \frac{P_1}{W} + \frac{P_1}{W} \cdot \frac{P_2}{P_1} + \frac{P_1}{W} \cdot \frac{P_2}{P_1} \cdot \frac{P_3}{P_2} + \cdots \\
&= PPR_{(0,1)} + PPR_{(0,1)} \cdot PPR_{(1,2)} + PPR_{(0,1)} \cdot PPR_{(1,2)} \cdot PPR_{(2,3)} + \cdots
\end{aligned} \quad \text{(5.11)}$$

A cohort's total fertility rate can in this fashion be derived entirely from its set of parity progression ratios. Parity progression ratios are especially useful in studying the patterns of fertility-limiting behavior in a population, which are often keyed to the number of children a woman has already born (Henry, 1961a; Feeney and Feng, 1993). An application of the parity progression ratio methodology is presented in box 5.4.

It is interesting to note that the volume of fertility often looks different from a child's perspective than from a woman's perspective. The average number of children born to a child's

Box 5.4 *Calculation of Parity Progression Ratios for a Cohort that has Completed Childbearing*

W_i = number of women at parity i. $P_i = \sum_{a=i}^{I} W_a$ = number of women at parity i or greater

B_i = number of births of parity $i = P_i$ (for all $i > 0$)

$$PPR_{(i,i+1)} = \frac{P_{i+1}}{P_i} = \frac{B_{i+1}}{B_i} \qquad PPR_{(0,i)} = \frac{P_i}{P_0} = \prod_{a=0}^{i-1} PPR_{(a,a+1)}$$

$$TFR = \frac{B}{W} = \frac{\sum_{i=1}^{I} B_i}{W} = \sum_{i=1}^{I} PPR_{(0,i)}$$

Example: 903 ever-married Egyptian women aged 45 or more in 1980, asked about their number of children ever born

Parity i	W_i	P_i	B_i	$PPR_{(i,i+1)}$	$PPR_{(0,i)}$
0	33	903		0.9635	
1	37	870	870	0.9575	0.9635
2	38	833	833	0.9544	0.9225
3	33	795	795	0.9585	0.8804
4	65	762	762	0.9147	0.8439
5	85	697	697	0.8780	0.7719
6	91	612	612	0.8513	0.6777
7	117	521	521	0.7754	0.5770
8	108	404	404	0.7327	0.4474
9	101	296	296	0.6588	0.3278
10	91	195	195	0.5333	0.2159
11	41	104	104	0.6058	0.1152
12	37	63	63	0.4127	0.0698
13	12	26	26	0.5385	0.0288
14	9	14	14	0.3571	0.0155
15	2	5	5	0.6000	0.0055
16	2	3	3	0.3333	0.0033
17	1	1	1	0.0000	0.0011
18	0	0	0		0.0000
Sum	903		6,201		6.867

$$W = \sum_{i=0}^{18} W_i = 903. \quad B = \sum_{i=1}^{18} B_i = 6{,}201. \quad \sum_{i=1}^{18} PPR_{(0,i)} = 6.867.$$

$$TFR = \frac{B}{W} = \sum_{i=1}^{18} PPR_{(0,i)} = \frac{6{,}201}{903} = 6.867 \; children \; per \; woman$$

Data source: Egypt. Central Agency for Public Mobilisation and Statistics; World Fertility Survey [WFS]. *The Egyptian Fertility Survey, 1980.* Cairo, Central Agency for Public Mobilisation and Statistics, 1983.

mother, $\overline{C}$, depends not only upon the mean parity of women, $\overline{P}$, but also upon how children are distributed across women. When half of a cohort of women bear 5 children and half bear 1 child, the mean parity of women is obviously 3 but the mean number of siblings (including ego) per child is

$$\frac{(.5)5(5) + (.5)1(1)}{(.5)5 + (.5)1} = \frac{13}{3} = 4.33$$

The reason for the disparity is that the children from 5-parity women are over-represented (by a factor of 5) among offspring relative to children of 1-parity women. The disparity between the two means is often great. For example, among Depression-era American mothers – women aged 45–9 in 1950 – the mean parity was 2.29, but the children born to these women were born to mothers with a mean parity of 4.91 (Preston, 1976b). In general, the relation between the two means is

$$\overline{C} = \overline{P} + \frac{\sigma^2}{\overline{P}},$$

where σ^2 is the variance in parity among women (ibid.). Only if all women had the same number of children would the two means be equal. Clearly, one should not commit the (fairly common) mistake of estimating fertility in the past directly from reports from offspring about their mother's parity.

5.4 Birth Interval Analysis

The analysis of birth intervals explicitly recognizes the distinct renewable nature of the fertility process. Elegant mathematical representations of lifetime fertility have been developed, in particular by Sheps and Menken (1973) in the United States and by Henry (1957 and 1961b) in France. Instead of computing total fertility by summing age-specific rates, birth interval analysis considers the progression from one birth to the next in the course of a woman's reproductive life. It rests on the principle that, because the female reproductive span is limited in extent, a woman's total fertility can be profitably viewed in terms of the interval between her first exposure to the risk of giving birth and her first birth, and then in terms of the average interval between subsequent births. If all birth intervals had the same length in the population, the average total fertility rate in the population would be equal to the length of the reproductive span from beginning of first interval to end of last divided by the length of the interval.

The birth interval itself can be decomposed into a nonsusceptible period, including pregnancy and an additional anovulatory period after birth whose length depends mostly on the length of breast-feeding; a waiting period, W, during which a fecund woman is exposed to the risk of conception and the length of which depends on her readiness to conceive and use of contraception; and some additional time to account for the risk that a conception would not yield a live birth.

The length of a birth interval can be studied by the life table techniques discussed in chapters 3 and 4. Giving birth is equivalent to "death," and the time dimension is no longer age but duration in the birth interval, that is, the length of time since last giving birth (or the length of time since marriage in the case of a first birth). Duration is often referred to as "waiting time" when the table applies to women trying to conceive. As in nuptiality analysis, the risk of giving birth is always accompanied by the risk of death, so multiple decrement life tables and associated single decrement life tables are appropriate devices. However, mortality is typically low during the reproductive ages, and the assumption of no mortality at these ages is generally acceptable in order to facilitate the calculations.

An important biological determinant of birth interval length is fecundability, defined by Gini (1924) as the monthly probability of conception in the absence of contraception and of temporary nonsusceptibility. Mean fecundability can be estimated by following a cohort of newly married, nonpregnant, noncontracepting women. For example, Pearl (1933) suggested dividing the number of pregnancies observed among such women by the number of woman-months of exposure, a proxy for the number of discrete ovulatory "trials."

Problems with using this approach to estimate fecundability arise when a population is heterogeneous, consisting of subgroups with differing levels of fecundability. To illustrate, assume that the female population is made of two subgroups of the same size but different fecundability, 0.1 and 0.3 respectively. The average fecundability is thus 0.2. A duration life table of birth following marriage, in the absence of contraception, is shown in table 5.4.[6] Usually, a study of fecundability is truncated after some duration (typically 6 months or 12 months) and the estimated fecundability is computed for that duration. But when the population is heterogeneous, estimated fecundability will decline with the duration over which its value is calculated. In our example, its value after one month of observation will be:

$$p(1) = (400/2,000) = .200, \text{ a correct estimate for the cohort}$$

But after three months it is:

$$p(3) = [(400 + 300 + 228)/(2,000 + 1,600 + 1,300)] = .189$$

After the first six months its value is:

$$p(6) = [(400 + \cdots + 109)/(2,000 + \cdots + 758)] = .178$$

The estimate declines with duration because the low fecundability group becomes a larger and larger proportion of the nonpregnant. Only in the first month does its value provide an unbiased estimate of fecundability in the population as a whole. The estimate would be consistent at different durations within each group only when fecundability is the same for every woman. Unfortunately, fecundability usually varies among women. Henry (1961b and 1964)

Table 5.4: *Waiting time to conception by fecundability*

Duration since marriage (months)	Group I l_x	Group I $_n d_x$	Group II l_x	Group II $_n d_x$	Total l_x	Total $_n d_x$
0	1,000	100	1,000	300	2,000	400
1	900	90	700	210	1,600	300
2	810	81	490	147	1,300	228
3	729	73	343	103	1,072	176
4	656	66	240	72	896	138
5	590	59	168	50	758	109
6	531	53	118	35	649	88

suggested that fecundability across individuals in the population can be represented by a Pearson distribution:

$$f(p) = \frac{p^{a-1} q^{b-1}}{\int_0^1 p^{a-1} q^{b-1} \, dp}$$

where $q = 1 - p$ and a and b are parameters to be determined.[7]

Once fecundability is estimated, the average waiting period, W, can be estimated. W is the "life expectancy at birth" in the birth-interval life table. If fecundability is assumed to be constant in the reproductive age interval and across women, then the average waiting period in the interval is the reciprocal of fecundability ($1/p$). The probability of waiting n months is the probability of conceiving during that month, p, times the probability of not having conceived during the previous $n - 1$ months, $(1 - p)^{n-1}$. So

$$P[W = n] = p(1 - p)^{n-1}$$

The mean waiting time (the expected value of W) is then:

$$E[W] = \sum_{n=1}^{\infty} n \cdot P[W = n] = \sum_{n=1}^{\infty} n \cdot p \cdot (1 - p)^{n-1}$$

Since it can be shown that

$$\sum_{n=1}^{\infty} n x^{n-1} = \frac{1}{(1 - x)^2},$$

the average waiting period is thus:

$$E[W] = p \cdot \frac{1}{[1 - (1 - p)]^2} = \frac{1}{p}$$

Note that this is the same reciprocal relationship that prevails in a stationary population between life expectancy at birth and the crude death rate.

We have just demonstrated that, if all women have the same fecundability, p, then the expected interval between first exposure and first conception is $1/p$. On the other hand, if women are heterogeneous and $f(p)$ is the proportion of women whose fecundability is p, then the mean waiting time is the harmonic mean of $f(p)$:

$$E[W] = \int_0^1 \frac{1}{p} f(p) \, dp$$

The expected length of time between one birth and the next will be higher than the length of time between marriage and first birth because it will include 9 months of pregnancy plus the nonsusceptible period after a birth, s_b. Assuming fecundability p to be constant across women between the ages α and β and zero outside that interval, the expected interval between conceptions will be $(1/p) + 9 + s_b$. On average, assuming no fetal loss, a birth will thus occur $[(1/p) + 9]$ months after marriage and then every $[(1/p) + 9 + s_b]$ months thereafter.

By dividing the time left after the first birth by the average birth interval and adding the first birth, the TMFR appears as:

$$TMFR = 1 + \frac{\beta - \alpha - \left(\frac{1}{p} + 9\right)}{\frac{1}{p} + 9 + s_b}$$

$$= \frac{\beta - \alpha + s_b}{\frac{1}{p} + 9 + s_b}$$

If we assume that every woman "marries" (i.e., begin her exposure to the risk of conception) at age α_m (measured in months; $\alpha_m > \alpha$) and that there is no divorce nor out-of-wedlock childbearing, then the TFR is similarly:

$$TFR = \frac{\beta - \alpha_m + s_b}{I_b} \tag{5.12}$$

$$\text{with } I_b = \frac{1}{p} + 9 + s_b$$

Let us finally distinguish between conceptions leading to a live birth and other conceptions. Assume that the length of the nonsusceptible period (pregnancy plus anovulatory aftermath) associated with such conceptions is s_w. The interval between live births is then increased by $(1/p) + s_w$ for each spontaneous fetal loss. If the probability that a conception does not end in a live birth is ω, then the interval between live births increases by $(1/p) + s_w$ for a proportion ω of the births, and by another $(1/p) + s_w$ for a proportion ω^2 of the births (two successive pregnancies ended by spontaneous fetal wastage), and so on. The mean interval between live births is then:

$$I_b = \frac{1}{p} + 9 + s_b + \omega \left(\frac{1}{p} + s_w\right) + \cdots + \omega^n \left(\frac{1}{p} + s_w\right) + \cdots$$

$$= \frac{1}{p} + 9 + s_b + \frac{\omega}{1 - \omega} \left(\frac{1}{p} + s_w\right)$$

$$= \frac{1}{p(1 - \omega)} + 9 + s_b + \frac{s_w \omega}{1 - \omega} \tag{5.13}$$

Fetal wastage adds the same average length of time to the interval between marriage and first birth, so formula (5.12) for the TFR is still applicable with I_b now as in (5.13).

Let us now illustrate some applications of this model, in the process linking it to the Bongaarts model. Assume that fecundability is 0.2 for every woman between ages 15 and 45, and that the nonsusceptible period following a live birth is 7.5 months. In the absence of fetal wastage, women will have their first live birth after 14 months (5 months of average waiting time and 9 months of pregnancy) and then a live birth every 21.5 months thereafter. If the probability of fetal wastage is 0.2 and the corresponding nonsusceptible period s_w is 5 months, each mean interval (between marriage and first birth and between higher order births) is increased by $(.2/.8)(5 + 5) = 2.5$ months. The interval between marriage and first birth becomes

16.5 months and the interval between births 24 months. If we assume that women all marry at age 15, then the TFR is (from (5.12)):

$$TFR = TMFR = [30 + (7.5/12)]/2 = 15.3$$

This is the value of the maximum total fertility rate used in Bongaarts' decompositional model. If all women married at age 25, then the TFR would be 10.3.

Contraception efficiency, e, is defined as the proportionate reduction in the monthly probability of conception that results from the use of contraception. If the probability is p in the absence of contraception, then it is $p(1 - e)$ in the presence of contraception. Formula (5.12) for the TFR is unchanged by the addition of contraception to the model, but the birth interval is now:

$$I_b = \frac{1}{p(1 - e)(1 - \omega)} + 9 + s_b + \frac{s_w \omega}{1 - \omega} \qquad (5.14)$$

Let's suppose that contraceptive efficiency is 0.9. Then the monthly probability of conception drops to 0.02. The mean birth interval is now $62.5 + 9 + 7.5 + 1.25 = 80.25$ months, or 6.6875 years. If all women marry at age 25, then

$$TFR = [20 + (7.5/12)]/6.6875 = 3.08$$

It is important to note that contraception reduced the monthly probability of conception by a factor of 10 but "only" reduced TFR from 10.3 to 3.08. The reason is that the waiting time to pregnancy is the only component of the birth interval to be affected by contraception. The length of pregnancy, of postpartum nonsusceptibility, and of the sterile period associated with fetal wastage are unchanged. A change in any component of the birth interval will result in a less than proportional change of the entire birth interval.

Another useful application of the model is to study the effect of abortion on the TFR. An abortion (spontaneous or induced) adds $(1/p[1 - e]) + s_w$ to a birth interval and will thus reduce the TFR in absolute amount by:

$$\frac{\dfrac{1}{p(1 - e)} + s_w}{\dfrac{1}{p(1 - e)(1 - \omega)} + 9 + s_b + \dfrac{s_w \omega}{1 - \omega}} \qquad (5.15)$$

This expression is less than unity; one abortion prevents fewer than one live birth because a woman is restored more quickly to the susceptible state when a conception is terminated by an abortion than when it ends in birth. Using our earlier parameters, in the absence of contraception, an additional abortion increases a birth interval from 24 months to 34 (since $[1/p] + s_w = 5 + 5 = 10$) and prevents $10/24 = 0.435$ births. With 90 percent effective contraception, an additional abortion increases a birth interval from 80.25 months to 135.25 months ($[1/p(1 - e)] + s_w = 50 + 5 = 55$) and prevents $55/80.25 = 0.685$ births. When contraception is very effective (e.g., 99 percent), a birth interval with one abortion is virtually equal to twice a birth interval without abortion, so one abortion effectively "prevents" one birth. The reason is that, with highly effective contraception, the waiting time to pregnancy dominates the interbirth interval and is the same following an abortion as following a live birth. Induced abortion can be formally included in the model for TFR by replacing the probability of spontaneous abortion, ω, by a probability including both types of abortion.

This simple model permits us to gain some understanding of the potential impact of changes in the determinants of fertility. Obviously, the model omits some potentially significant phenomena such as marital disruption. It assumes that reproductive parameters are constant through reproductive life. It also applies mean values to each woman and thus does not account for population heterogeneity. Microsimulation techniques allow both more complex modeling of the reproductive process and the introduction of heterogeneity (Menken, 1977). The process leading to a live birth can be represented by a Markovian renewal process with each woman being exposed to risks of transition between different statuses in which fecundability varies (marriage, divorce, widowhood, remarriage, postpartum nonsusceptibility), and with probabilities of possible outcomes (spontaneous abortion, live birth, still birth) being applied to conceptions.

The effect of population heterogeneity can be illustrated by a numerical application of our simple model. Let's assume that fecundability is 0.2 for all women but half of them use contraception with 90 percent effectiveness so that their effective fecundability is 0.02. We also assume that half of the women breastfeed for a year so s_b is 13.5, whereas the other half does not breastfeed at all and s_b is 1.5. Finally, we assume that half of the women marry at age 20 and the other half at age 30. Other values are as above and the same for every woman within a group.

If breastfeeding, marriage, and contraception are independent, we have defined 8 groups of women of equal size. The TFR for each group is shown in table 5.5. The bottom line shows the average TFR that would be computed from the arithmetic mean values of each group's fecundability and nonsusceptible period. From the mean parameter values, we would compute a population TFR of 8.50, whereas the actual TFR in this population is the average of the TFRs in each of the eight equal-sized subpopulations, or 7.01 ($= [16.75 + 10.08 + \cdots + 2.24]/8$).

The complexity of the birth interval models, the restrictiveness of their assumptions, and their sensitivity to distributional influences undermine their use in measuring total fertility. In many settings, there is also insufficient data on the models' parameters. But as illustrated in the few examples above, they have proved quite useful analytical tools to understand the determinants of fertility and how they interact.

In working with data on birth intervals from cross-sectional surveys, it is important to distinguish between "closed" and "open" birth intervals. A closed interval is an interval between two observed events, e.g., between time of birth and time of death in a classical mortality life

Table 5.5: *TFR in a heterogeneous population*

Contraception	Breastfeeding	Birth interval (1)	Age at marriage	TFR (2)
	No	18	20	16.75
No	$s_b = 1.5$		30	10.08
$p = .2$	Yes	30	20	10.45
	$s_b = 13.5$		30	6.45
	No	74.25	20	4.06
Yes	$s_b = 1.5$		30	2.44
$p(1 - e) = .02$	Yes	86.25	20	3.63
	$s_b = 13.5$		30	2.24
Mean Prob.	$s_b = 7.5$	29.11	25	8.50
$p(1 - e_m) = .11$				

(1) Birth interval is computed from equation (5.14) with $s_w = 5$ and $\omega = 0.2$.
(2) TFR is computed from equation (5.12) with birth interval as in (5.14) and $\beta = 45$.

table or between two births in a woman's fertility history. At the time of a retrospective survey, there will also be open intervals, i.e. intervals for which the closing events has not yet been experienced because the interval was "censored" at the time of the survey. One's age (time since birth) is such an open interval in mortality analysis; time since last birth is an open interval in fertility analysis.

It may be intuitively clear that, when all closed intervals have the same length, an average (randomly selected) open interval in a survey would be half the length of the closed intervals. For example, if all women have a birth every 24 months and women are randomly distributed with respect to their time since last birth, then the mean length of time since last birth would be 12 months. But if some closed intervals are shorter than others, then the situation is more complex. If half of the women in the population have a birth every 12 months and half of the women have a birth every 36 months, and women are randomly distributed with respect to their time since last birth, then the mean length of time since last birth among women would still be 12 months. It will be 6 months for the first group of women, and 18 months for the second group, and since the two groups are equally large, the population mean "open" interval is still 12 months. On the other hand, women with shorter closed intervals will have birth more frequently than others, so in any given period there will be more births after 12 months than after 36 months. If we used a birth-weighted measure of the length of the closed interval (measuring intervals based upon births during a particular period rather than upon a random sample of women), then the mean length of the closed interval would be less than 24 months. In this example, the short-interval group of women will have three times as many births in any period as long-interval women. Thus the birth-weighted mean length of the closed interval (whether measured backwards to the preceding birth or forward to the subsequent birth) is:

$$.75(12) + .25(36) = 18 \text{ months}$$

The value is clearly less than double the value of the mean length of the open interval, 12 months. Pressat (1972) shows that the mean length of an open interval, L_o, is:

$$L_o = \frac{L_c + \frac{\sigma^2}{L_c}}{2} \qquad\qquad (5.16)$$

where L_c and σ are the birth-weighted mean and standard deviation of closed intervals.[8] In the example, we are using:

$$12 = [18 + (108/18)]/2$$

This relation is pertinent not only to the analysis of birth interval from retrospective surveys. It can also be applied to a conventional stationary population represented by a mortality life table. In this case, the mean age at death in the distribution of deaths (the closed interval) is simply life expectancy at birth in the stationary population. The mean age of the population (the length of the open interval between birth and death) can thus be expressed as:

$$\overline{A} = \frac{e_0 + \frac{\sigma^2}{e_0}}{2}$$

Note that when the rate of decrement is the same at all durations, the number of decrements (deaths) is always proportional to the number of persons at risk (alive), so that the mean age of persons alive (the open interval) would be equal to the mean age at death (the closed interval). On the other hand, if everyone died at the same age, i.e., at the age equal to life expectancy at birth, then $\sigma^2 = 0$ and the mean age of the stationary population would be exactly half of the value of life expectancy at birth.

5.5 Reproduction Measures

Fertility and mortality processes combine to determine the natural growth of population. In chapter 1, we described population growth rates and developed one way to look at the joint contribution of fertility and mortality: the difference between the crude birth rate and the crude death rate is the period rate of natural increase. Another way to look at the growth of the population is to compare the size of successive generations. The TFR measures the number of children a woman would give birth to if she survived through her reproductive life span. If we limit births to female births, we get an indication of the number of daughters born to the average woman, which is closer to a measure of whether childbearing women are "reproducing themselves" in number. Let us define the age-specific rate of having a female birth as:

$$_nF_x^F[0, T] = \frac{\text{Female births in the period 0 to } T \text{ to women aged } x \text{ to } x + n}{\text{Person-years lived in the period 0 to } T \text{ by women aged } x \text{ to } x + n}$$

When they cannot be confused with the life table notation for age-specific mortality rates, these rates are often denoted $_nm_x$ for maternity rates, their continuous equivalent being the maternity function of age, $m(a)$.

The Gross Reproduction Rate (GRR) is equivalent to the TFR, but it uses maternity rates instead of fertility rates:

$$GRR[0, T] = n \cdot \sum_{x=\alpha}^{\beta-n} {_nF_x^F[0, T]} \tag{5.17}$$

The GRR represents the number of female births an average woman would have if she lived through the end of her reproductive span. It is a gross measure of reproduction, because it does not account for mortality.

A realistic measure of reproduction must take mortality into account. This is accomplished by introducing the $_nL_x$ column of a life table. Since the value $_nL_x$ represents the number of person-years lived between age x and age $x + n$ in a cohort of l_0 births, the number of years lived in each age interval by an average female subjected to the period mortality conditions through her reproductive life span is $_nL_x^F/l_0$. The Net Reproduction Rate is then defined as:

$$NRR[0, T] = \sum_{x=\alpha}^{\beta-n} {_nF_x^F[0, T]} \cdot \frac{_nL_x^F}{l_0} \tag{5.18}$$

The NRR can be interpreted as the average number of daughters that female members of a birth cohort would bear during their reproductive life span if they were subject to the observed age-specific maternity rates $(_nF_x^F)$ and mortality rates (embodied in $_nL_x^F$) throughout their lifetimes. If the NRR is greater than 1.00, then a cohort of girl babies will leave behind a larger cohort of daughters than they themselves represented. Box 5.5 shows the calculation of period gross and net reproduction rates for the US in 1991.

Note that if all women survived until age β, $_nL_x^F/l_0$ would be n and the GRR and the NRR would be equal. In general, the NRR must be smaller. Coale (1972) has derived a convenient

Box 5.5 *Calculation of Period Gross and Net Reproduction Rates*

$_nW_x$ = Mid-year number of women aged x to $x+n$

$_nB_x^F$ = Number of female births during the year to women aged x to $x+n$

$_nL_x^F$ = Number of person-years lived between ages x and $x+n$ by a hypothetical cohort of l_0 births in the period life table for females

$$_nF_x^F = \frac{_nB_x^F}{_nW_x} = \text{Age-specific maternity rate}$$

$$GRR = n \cdot \sum_{x=\alpha}^{\beta-n} {}_nF_x^F \qquad NRR = \frac{1}{l_0} \cdot \sum_{x=\alpha}^{\beta-n} {}_nF_x^F \cdot {}_nL_x^F$$

Example: US, 1991; $l_0 = 100,000$

Age x	$_5W_x$	$_nB_x^F$	$_nL_x^F$	$_nF_x^F$	$_nF_x^F \cdot {}_nL_x^F$
10	8,620,000	5,816	494,603	0.0007	333.71
15	8,371,000	253,979	493,804	0.0303	14,982.18
20	9,419,000	532,712	492,552	0.0566	27,857.35
25	10,325,000	596,823	491,138	0.0578	28,389.58
30	11,125,000	431,694	489,356	0.0388	18,988.95
35	10,344,000	162,005	486,941	0.0157	7,626.34
40	9,496,000	25,531	483,577	0.0027	1,300.15
45	7,188,000	829	478,475	0.0001	55.18
Sum				0.2026	99,533.45

$GRR = 5 \cdot 0.2026 = 1.013$ daughter per woman

$NRR = 99,533.45/100,000 = 0.995$ daughter per woman

Data source: National Center for Health Statistics, 1996.

approximate relationship between GRR and NRR. This relationship is easiest to derive in continuous notation. The NRR is the sum of the product of the maternity function, $m(a)$, and the probability of surviving to age a, $p(a)$:

$$NRR = \int_\alpha^\beta m(a)p(a)\,da \qquad (5.19)$$

So:

$$NRR = \frac{\int_\alpha^\beta m(a)p(a)\,da}{\int_\alpha^\beta m(a)\,da} \cdot \int_\alpha^\beta m(a)\,da$$

The second term is simply the GRR. The first term is a weighted average of the survivorship function, $p(a)$, between ages α and β, the weights being provided by the maternity function.

By the mean value theorem, there exists an age γ in the interval $[\alpha, \beta]$ such that the weighted average is simply $p(\gamma)$, so $NRR = p(\gamma) \cdot GRR$. If the $p(a)$ function is linear between ages α and β, then $p(a)$ can be written as $\alpha_0 + \alpha_1 a$, and:

$$\frac{\int_\alpha^\beta m(a) \cdot p(a)\, da}{\int_\alpha^\beta m(a)\, da} = \frac{\int_\alpha^\beta m(a) \cdot (\alpha_0 + \alpha_1 \cdot a)\, da}{\int_\alpha^\beta m(a)\, da}$$

$$= \alpha_0 + \alpha_1 \cdot \frac{\int_\alpha^\beta m(a) \cdot a\, da}{\int_\alpha^\beta m(a)\, da} = p(A_M)$$

where $p(A_M)$ is the probability of surviving to the mean age of the maternity function. Thus:

$$NRR \simeq p(A_M) \cdot GRR \tag{5.20}$$

This relation between NRR and GRR is exact when survivorship is linear in the reproductive interval and is a good approximation in most conditions. In discrete notation, A_M can be computed as:

$$A_M = \frac{\int_\alpha^\beta m(a) \cdot a\, da}{\int_\alpha^\beta m(a)\, da} = \frac{\sum_{x=\alpha}^{\beta-n} {}_n F_x^F \cdot \left(x + \frac{n}{2}\right)}{\sum_{x=\alpha}^{\beta-n} {}_n F_x^F} \tag{5.21}$$

It is often satisfactory to assume that the ratio of male to female births (commonly called sex ratio at birth, SRB) does not vary with age. Since the age-specific maternity rates are the product of the age-specific fertility rates and of the ratio of female to total births, if the latter ratio is the same at all ages, we can derive another approximation:

$$TFR = (1 + SRB) \cdot GRR = \frac{(1 + SRB)}{p(A_M)} \cdot NRR \tag{5.22}$$

A NRR of 1 implies that a female population permanently subjected to the $m(a)$ and $p(a)$ age schedules would exactly replace itself. Fertility rates that correspond to an NRR of 1.00 are often referred to as *replacement level* fertility, although there are an infinite number of $m(a)$ schedules that can combine with $p(a)$ to produce an NRR = 1. The replacement level of fertility corresponds to a GRR $\simeq 1/p(A_M)$ and a TFR $\simeq (1 + SRB)/p(A_M)$. In populations with low levels of mortality, as in most developed countries, the replacement level of TFR is about 2.1. In populations with higher mortality, in particular high childhood mortality, the probability of reaching the age A_M can be much lower and the replacement level of TFR can be as high as 3.5 or 4.0.

These measures of reproduction indicate whether the female population is "reproducing" itself, rather than whether the entire population of both sexes is. If calculated for the male population, reproduction measures would often differ slightly from female-based reproductive measures, a classic problem of demography referred to as the two-sex problem (Karmel, 1947; Henry, 1969). Differences are typically slight and analysis of female reproduction will usually provide a satisfactory description of how fertility and mortality regimes combine to determine population dynamics.

When NRR > 1, each generation is larger than the previous generation, so the population will grow from natural increase across the generations. But the NRR does not indicate how fast the population will grow on an annual basis. Achieving an NRR > 1 only means that newborn females will produce, on average, more than one daughter during their lifetime. How fast the population grows from year to year also depends on when the births occur in that lifetime. The shape and location of the maternity schedule is not summarized in the NRR. The link between the growth rate and measures of reproduction is described in chapter 7, in the context of populations subjected to constant mortality and fertility processes. The link between fertility, reproduction, and growth can also be analyzed empirically through population projections that are described in the next chapter.

NOTES

1. They are also reversed from the French terminology: *fécondité* means fertility whereas *fertilité* means fecundity.
2. According to the definition of the World Health Organization, a birth showing any sign of life is to be classified as a live birth as opposed to a stillbirth. The duration of gestation (28 weeks) is used to classify stillbirths and abortions. The distinction between live births and stillbirths is not always well recorded and even less well remembered in retrospective surveys. Conceptions are even more difficult to record because they are often unrecognized, e.g., when they are terminated very early and spontaneously.
3. The marital fertility schedule of the Hutterites, for the marriage cohorts of 1921 to 1930, is the following (Henry, 1961a: 84):

20–4	25–9	30–4	35–9	40–4	45–9
.550	.502	.447	.406	.222	.061

    Knodel (1988) suggests using a value of 0.300 for Hutterite marital fertility rates at ages 15–19.
4. Illegitimate births are defined as births to unmarried mothers.
5. More precise definitions of $W(T)$, $M(T)$, and $O(T)$ respectively would be the number of person-years lived in year T by women aged 15 to 49, by married women aged 15 to 49, and by mothers aged 15 to 49.
6. In the following table, the risk of mortality is assumed to be zero. We also assume that all pregnancies occur exactly at the end of the month. The number of pregnancies in the interval x to $x + n$ is denoted $_n d_x$.
7. See Leridon (1977) on how to estimate the values of the distribution parameters.
8. Sheps and Menken (1973: 154) show a more general relationship:

$$E(x^r) = \frac{m^{(r+1)}}{(r+1)m}$$

where x is the time since last event, $E(x^r)$ is the expected value in the population, and $m^{(n)}$ is the nth moment of the distribution of events, $f(x)$, i.e.:

$$m^{(r)} = \int_0^\infty x^r f(x)\, dx$$

When $r = 1$, the expected time since last event in the population is equivalent to the average length of the open interval (time since last event in the population), whereas the first moment is equivalent to the average length of closed intervals in the distribution of births, so:

$$E(x) = \frac{m^{(2)}}{2m} = \frac{m^2 + \sigma^2}{2m}$$

6 Population Projection

Population projection is probably the demographic technique that is most frequently requested by demography's "clients." Governments seek projections of future demographic parameters in order to anticipate demands of all kinds: for roads, schools, medical personnel, and national parks. Private businesses seek population projections in order to estimate the potential size of their future "market." Population projection has been elevated to one of the most important tools for determining US tax and expenditure policies: the US Social Security Trust Fund is required to be in actuarial balance over a projected 75-year period, and population projections are the most central factor in determining whether it is.

In addition to satisfying the needs of clients, demographers also use population projections more abstractly to analyze the implications of a certain set of demographic parameters for population size, composition, and growth. Projections illustrate the implications of certain demographic characteristics (the model's user-selected inputs) on population parameters over time (the model's outputs). Although most population projections concentrate on the consequences of a set of fertility, mortality, and migration assumptions, projections can also be designed to demonstrate the consequences of marriage patterns, contraceptive use regimes, and many other demographic processes.

6.1 Projections and Forecasts

Population projections are calculations which show the future development of a population when certain assumptions are made about the future course of fertility, mortality, and migration. They are in general purely formal calculations, developing the implications of the assumptions that are made. A population forecast is a projection in which the assumptions are considered to yield a realistic picture of the probable future development of a population. (United Nations, 1958: 45)

By this definition, the quality of projections is determined by their internal validity, i.e. whether they accurately and consistently model relations among demographic variables. The gauge of a forecast, on the other hand, is its external validity, i.e. how well predictions correspond to subsequent events. Demographers take it as an article of faith that projections having a higher degree of internal validity are also likely to have a higher degree of external validity.

Unlike forecasts, population projections can be made for the past as well as for the future. Projection parameters need not bear any resemblance to those of any real population. Population projections can be used to address purely hypothetical situations and to answer questions of the "what if?" type. For example, we may want to calculate characteristics of the present US population *if* mortality had remained at its 1900 level, even though in reality mortality has declined substantially (White and Preston, 1996). We may want to calculate what the population size of a high fertility country would become if fertility remained constant, say, for the next 50 years. In a famous example, Coale (1974) computed that if world population growth was to remain constant at its level at that time (2 percent annually):

> In less than 200 years there would be one person for every square foot on the surface of the earth, in less than 1,200 years the human population would outweigh the earth, in less than 6,000 years the mass of humanity would form a sphere expanding at the speed of light. (Coale, 1974: 51)

Clearly, this calculation implies no belief that population growth would actually remain constant but, on the contrary, is intended to show that such a rapid growth is not sustainable.

But most users of population projections want to know what the actual demographic parameters at some future date are likely to be. Most projections derive their utility from their relative success as forecasts. Because the future is inevitably uncertain, population projections using several alternative scenarios are frequently prepared. The demographer, however, is most often pressed to prepare a central or most likely scenario corresponding to his or her best assessment of what the future will be like. This scenario will typically be used as a forecast (Keyfitz, 1972). Recent promising developments in projection methodology provide useful information about the confidence bands that can be placed around a central forecast.

6.2 Population Projection Methodology

Since the accuracy of population forecasts can only be evaluated *ex post*, projection methodologies must be selected using other criteria. The most obvious criterion for choosing a method is that it should have internal validity, i.e., obey the demographic accounting relations that have been developed in this volume. We should also select a model that incorporates as many relevant facts and relationships as possible. Knowing how well a method has worked to produce accurate forecasts in the past is also useful, although some successes may be a result of pure luck and some failures a consequence of unforeseeable events.

The choice of a projection methodology also implies a set of necessary projection inputs and achievable projection outputs. One should select a projection methodology that will provide the desired level of detail in the output. One must also select a model whose data requirements can be met. This criterion might conflict with the goal of incorporating relevant relationships. More sophisticated projection methodologies will typically be more demanding of data. The gain from using a more realistic model of population dynamics might sometimes be outweighed by the loss introduced by error in the additional data required.

Let us start with the simplest projection need: assume that we know total population size at time 0 and want to estimate total population size at time T. In chapter 1, we have seen that the two quantities are related by:

$$N(T) = N(0)e^{\int_0^T r(t)\,dt} = N(0)e^{\bar{r}[0,T]\cdot T}$$

where $\bar{r}[0, T]$ is the mean annualized growth rate between times 0 and T.

This equation can serve as a projection methodology: if we are able to correctly estimate $N(0)$ and make an accurate assumption about the mean growth rate over the period 0 to T, then we can accurately project $N(T)$. In the absence of information about population growth, the simplest forecast would be to assume that population size will remain constant in the future. Since in most populations, the absolute annual growth rate is a few percent or less, this assumption will often provide a fair approximation for very short periods, say a year or less. The assumption amounts to saying that, in the short term, the main "component" of future population size is the size of the population already alive at a previous date.

If we have an estimate of the growth rate, r, the next simplest projection method is to assume that population growth rate will remain constant over time, so that population size at any other time T is given by:

$$N(T) = N(0)e^{r\cdot T} \tag{6.1}$$

Early population forecasters, e.g., Bonynge (1852), used such exponential extrapolation. Bonynge predicted the United States population in year 2000 at 703 million inhabitants.

Other models using only population size have been developed, especially in early forecasting attempts, such as polynomial models (Pritchett, 1891) or logistic functions (Verhulst, 1838 and Pearl and Reed, 1920). We refer interested readers to Dorn (1950) for a description and assessment of early population forecasts.

In chapter 1, we saw that we could express the crude growth rate in terms of the crude birth rate, crude death rate, crude in-migration rate, and crude out-migration rate (equation 1.2). This elaboration suggests the possibility of doing projections that explicitly account for fertility, mortality, and migration. In turn, in chapter 2, we have shown the considerable extent to which crude rates are affected by age compositional effects. A constant exponential growth model (equation 6.1) is thus a sensible model when fertility, mortality, and migration conditions can be assumed not to vary much over the projection period *and* when the age distribution can be assumed to remain constant. But the age distribution itself is produced by fertility, mortality, and migration conditions: it is endogenous to the process of population change. So an improved prediction model ought to take into account age distributional effects by modeling the age distribution over time as a product of fertility, mortality, and migration conditions. This insight is the basis of more modern approaches to population projection. An additional reason for explicitly treating the age distribution in population projection is that it is one of the most valuable outputs of the process.

6.3 The Cohort Component Method

The method most commonly used that does account for age distribution is called the "cohort component" method. The approach can be traced back to Cannan (1895) but the method was independently developed by Whelpton (1928 and 1936) (Smith and Keyfitz, 1977: 193–4). It is now nearly the only method used for population projections, representing a rare consensus for the social sciences. The approach consists of segmenting the population into different subgroups differentially exposed to the "risks" of fertility, mortality, and migration and separately computing the changes over time in each group. In any population, exposure varies by age and sex so at a minimum the method segregates the population by age and sex. Other differentiation may recognize race, nationality, location (region, urban/rural), educational attainment, or religion.

As opposed to continuous-time models based on mathematical functions discussed in section 6.2, the cohort-component model is a discrete-time model of population dynamics. Population characteristics are only calculated at certain moments of time separated by lengthy time intervals. The projection period is usually divided into time intervals of the same length as the age intervals that are employed. Projection is then carried out one projection interval at a time. For each projection interval, the method basically consists of three steps:

1) Project forward the population in each subgroup at the beginning of the time interval in order to estimate the number still alive at the beginning of the next interval;

2) Compute the number of births for each subgroup over the time interval, add them across groups, and compute the number of those births who survive to the beginning of the next interval;

3) Add immigrants and subtract emigrants in each subgroup during the interval; compute the number of births to these migrants during the interval; and project forward the number of migrants and the number of their births that will survive to the beginning of the next interval.

If the population is only segregated by age and sex, the first step is technically straightforward: use a single decrement life table for each sex to survive forward the population alive at the baseline. Survival probabilities are required for each subgroup and the survivors are assigned to the same sex and next age group (since time and age intervals are congruent). If the population is also divided across individual characteristics that change over time, such as marital status, a more detailed life table must be used to represent the survivors' transitions between subgroups. As discussed in chapter 12, such life tables are called increment–decrement life tables because they represent both entries in a subgroup and multiple ways to exit the subgroup. The corresponding projections are called multistate projections (Rogers, 1995b).

The second step is more complicated since every birth is produced by two individuals. Ideally, births would be attributed to sexual unions and the creation and dissolution of such unions would be treated explicitly in the projection framework. In practice, the normal strategy is to pretend that births are produced by women only. The number of births can then be estimated by applying fertility rates to women only: this is called a "female-dominant" model. When projections recognize more subgroups than those defined by age and sex, a second difficulty is to allocate births to a subgroup. Following the logic of the female-dominant projection, a simple approach is often to assume that the birth will belong to the same segment of the population as the mother.

The third step adds some practical difficulty to the projection as one needs to project not only the total number of migrants in each projection interval but also the timing of migration within the interval, since exposure to birth and death depends on when migrants enter or leave the population.

Let us first present the cohort component method for a closed female population. The population is only broken down by age; it is (initially) assumed to be closed to migration; and the number of males is assumed to be irrelevant to rates of childbearing. The logic of projection is best illustrated by reference to this simplified population. Additional complexities can be incorporated to make the model more realistic; those will complicate the specification of the model without altering the logic of the projection.

6.3.1 Projection of a closed female population

To project forward a closed female population by the cohort component method, we need an estimate of the number of females in each age group at baseline. Age groups need to be of the same length, except for the last, open-ended, age group. The projection period should be broken down into projection intervals of the same length as the age groups. The *method* is identical for each projection interval, although different parameters may be used in different periods. The projected female population from one projection interval becomes the baseline population for projection over the next interval. For each projection interval, we need both a life table representing age-specific mortality conditions assumed to prevail during the interval *and* a set of age-specific fertility rates assumed to prevail in the interval. Age intervals used in the life table and fertility rates must be the same as those used in the population estimates. The construction of age group information may require merging some age groups, for example age groups 0–1 and 1–5 in the life table.

We will develop the basic projection method for 5-year age groups and 5-year projection intervals. We will denote the number of females aged x to $x + 5$ at the beginning and the end of the projection interval as $_5N_x^F(t)$ and $_5N_x^F(t + 5)$ respectively.

Step 1, the projection forward of women still alive five years later, proceeds by applying survivorship ratios to each age group. For any age group except for the youngest and oldest, the basic formula is:

$$_5N_x^F(t + 5) = {_5N_{x-5}^F}(t) \cdot \frac{_5L_x}{_5L_{x-5}} \tag{6.2}$$

The survivorship ratio used, $_5L_x/_5L_{x-5}$, is the proportion of the person aged $x - 5$ to x that will be alive 5 years later in a stationary population subject to the appropriate life table. Assuming that we have got mortality conditions right in the form of the $\mu(x)$ function, then this survivorship ratio would be exactly correct if the age distribution of the population *within* the interval $x - 5$ to x were the same as the age distribution within that age interval in the stationary population subject to the same life table. The distributional disturbances created by nonstationarity within 5-year age groups are not likely to be very distortive.[1]

For the open-ended age group, we need to combine survivors from two previous age groups:

$$_\infty N_x^F(t + 5) = \left({_5N_{x-5}^F}(t) \cdot \frac{_5L_x}{_5L_{x-5}} \right) + \left({_\infty N_x^F}(t) \cdot \frac{T_{x+5}}{T_x} \right)$$

The first product is the number of surviving women who were in the 5-year age group immediately before the open-ended age group at time t. The second product is the number of survivors among women already in the open-ended age group at the beginning of the projection interval. The survivorship ratio is again borrowed from a stationary population as the ratio of the number of person-years lived above age $x + 5$ to the number of person-years lived above age x. Note that this procedure requires the open-ended age group in the life table to begin at an age that is 5 years older than that used in the population. If this additional detail is not available, then we must use:

$$\infty N_x^F (t+5) = \left({}_5N_{x-5}^F(t) + \infty N_x^F(t) \right) \cdot \frac{T_x}{T_{x-5}}$$

This formula assumes that the population age structure is stationary beginning at age $x - 5$.

Lastly, we need to estimate the number of surviving females in the first age group, 0–4. For this purpose, we need to project the number of births during the projection period using age-specific fertility rates. During the projection interval t to $t + 5$, the normal procedure is to derive the number of births to women aged x to $x + n$ as:

$$_5F_x \cdot 5 \cdot \left[\frac{{}_5N_x^F (t) + {}_5N_x^F (t+5)}{2} \right] = {}_5F_x \cdot 5 \cdot \left[\frac{{}_5N_x^F (t) + {}_5N_{x-5}^F(t) \cdot \frac{{}_5L_x}{{}_5L_{x-5}}}{2} \right] \qquad (6.3)$$

The number of births to women in the age group is obtained by multiplying the period age-specific fertility rate, ${}_5F_x$, by the number of person-years lived by women in the age group during the projection interval. The left-hand side of equation (6.3) approximates person-years lived at ages x to $x + n$ in the projection interval as the length of the time interval multiplied by the average number of women alive at the beginning and at the end of the period.[2] The latter number can be derived as a function of the population at the beginning of the interval and survival through the interval, as shown on the right-hand side of equation (6.3).

The total number of births during the period is then obtained by summing births across age groups of the mother:

$$B[t, t+5] = \sum_{x=\alpha}^{\beta-5} \frac{5}{2} \cdot {}_5F_x \cdot \left({}_5N_x^F (t) + {}_5N_{x-5}^F(t) \cdot \frac{{}_5L_x}{{}_5L_{x-5}} \right) \qquad (6.4)$$

where α and β are the lower and upper bounds of the childbearing ages. The number of female births is then normally obtained by applying the ratio of male to female births (SRB):

$$B^F [t, t+5] = \frac{1}{1 + SRB} \cdot B[t, t+5] \qquad (6.5)$$

This formula is correct when the sex ratio at birth does not vary with the age of the mother, an assumption that is seldom problematic. Alternatively, one can use age-specific maternity rates, ${}_5F_x^F$, instead of fertility rates, ${}_5F_x$, if age-specific fertility rates are available by sex of the child.

Finally, the number of females aged 0 to 4 at the end of the projection interval is obtained by surviving female births through time $t + 5$. If births are assumed to be distributed evenly during the period t to $t + 5$, then the relations of a stationary population can be invoked. In a stationary population, the ratio of the number of persons aged 0–4 to the number of births in the preceding 5-year period is ${}_5L_0/(5 \cdot l_0)$. Thus,

$$_5N_0(t+5) = \frac{B[t, t+5] \cdot {}_5L_0}{5 \cdot l_0} \qquad (6.6)$$

The number of females aged 0 to 4 can thus be derived by replacing births by female births in equation (6.6). Replacing female births by its expression in (6.4) and (6.5) yields:

$$_5N_0^F(t+5) = B^F[t, t+5] \cdot \frac{_5L_0}{5 \cdot l_0}$$

$$= \frac{_5L_0}{2 \cdot l_0} \cdot \frac{1}{1+SRB} \cdot \sum_{x=\alpha}^{\beta-5} {_5F_x} \cdot \left(_5N_x^F(t) + {_5N_{x-5}^F}(t) \cdot \frac{_5L_x}{_5L_{x-5}} \right)$$

Note that 5s have canceled out of the numerator and denominator in this expression.

6.3.2 Projection of a two-sex closed population

The male population could be projected in a similar manner using a male life table for survivorship ratios and male fertility rates. A problem with this approach is that independently projected male and female births would not necessarily produce a plausible sex ratio at birth. The easiest way to address this concern is to derive the total number of births (male and female) from female fertility rates and to derive the number of male births by applying a sex ratio at birth to the total number of female births. This procedure is that of a female-dominant projection.

The steps for deriving the male population in a female-dominant projection are, first, to survive the male population forward as in equation (6.2):

$$_5N_x^M(t+5) = {_5N_{x-5}^M}(t) \cdot \frac{_5L_x^M}{_5L_{x-5}^M}$$

and, for the open-ended age group:

$$_\infty N_x^M(t+5) = \left(_5N_{x-5}^M(t) \cdot \frac{_5L_x^M}{_5L_{x-5}^M} \right) + \left(_\infty N_x^M(t) \cdot \frac{T_{x+5}^M}{T_x^M} \right)$$

The number of male births is obtained from the total number of births in (6.4):

$$B^M[t, t+5] = \frac{SRB}{1+SRB} \cdot B[t, t+5]$$

The number of males in the first age group is then obtained by surviving the male births using the appropriate survivorship ratio for the male life table:

$$_5N_0^M(t+5) = B^M[t, t+5] \cdot \frac{_5L_0^M}{5 \cdot l_0}$$

Of course, it is possible to calculate a male-dominant projection in which the total number of births (male and female) would be derived from male fertility rates and the male age distribution. The two approaches may, as noted, yield different projections, which is another aspect of the two-sex problem mentioned in chapter 5. Box 6.1 presents an example of female-dominant projection.

Box 6.1 (part 1) *Cohort Component Female-dominant Projection in a Population Closed to Migration*

1. Females

$_5N_x^F(t) =$ number of women aged x to $x + 5$ at time t

$_5L_x^F =$ number of person-years lived by women from age x to $x + 5$ (from the life table)

$_5F_x =$ age-specific fertility rate in interval x to $x + 5$

$$_5N_x^F(t+5) = {}_5N_{x-5}^F(t) \cdot \frac{_5L_x^F}{_5L_{x-5}^F}; \qquad _\infty N_{85}^F(t+5) = \left(_5N_{80}^F(t) + {}_\infty N_{85}^F(t) \right) \cdot \frac{T_{85}^F}{T_{80}^F}$$

$$_5B_x[t, t+5] = 5 \cdot {}_5F_x \cdot \frac{_5N_x^F(t) + {}_5N_x^F(t+5)}{2}$$

$$= \text{births to women aged } x \text{ to } x + 5 \text{ between time } t \text{ and time } t + 5$$

$$B[t, t+5] = \sum_{x=\alpha}^{\beta-5} {}_5B_x[t, t+5] = \text{total births between } t \text{ and } t + 5$$

$$B^F[t, t+5] = B[t, t+5] \cdot \frac{1}{1 + 1.05}$$

$$= \text{number of females births between } t \text{ and } t + 5 \text{ (with SRB} = 1.05)$$

$$_5N_0^F(t+5) = B^F[t, t+5] \cdot \frac{_5L_0^F}{5 \cdot l_0}$$

2. Males

$_5N_x^M =$ number of men aged x to $x + 5$ at time t

$_5L_x^M =$ number of person-years lived by men from age x to $x + 5$ (from the life table)

$$_5N_x^M(t+5) = {}_5N_{x-5}^M(t) \cdot \frac{_5L_x^M}{_5L_{x-5}^M} \qquad _\infty N_{85}^M(t+5) = \left(_5N_{80}^M(t) + {}_\infty N_{85}^M(t) \right) \cdot \frac{T_{85}^M}{T_{80}^M}$$

$$B^M[t, t+5] = B[t, t+5] \cdot \frac{1.05}{1 + 1.05} = \text{number of males births between } t \text{ and } t + 5$$

$$_5N_0^M(t+5) = B^M[t, t+5] \cdot \frac{_5L_0^M}{5 \cdot l_0}$$

6.3.3 Projection of an open population

It is fairly easy to adapt this projection methodology to take into account emigration. Since emigration is a decrement from the population of interest, we could compute emigration rates by age and sex, then derive a two-decrement life table combining the risks of death and emigration. We would then use the corresponding survivorship ratios from the multiple decrement life table for the projection. This method is entirely appropriate for populations in which the dominant migration flow is emigration. We will not develop it further here, assuming that the reader can construct a multiple decrement life table through methods described in chapter 4.

Box 6.1 (part 2)

Example: Sweden, baseline 1993 (females); $l_o = 100,000$

Age x	$_5N_x^F$ (1993.0)	$_5L_x^F$	$_5F_x$	$_5N_x^F$ (1998.0)	$_5B_x$ [1993.0, 1998.0]	$_5N_x^F$ (2003.0)	$_5B_x$ [1998.0, 2003.0]
0	293,395	497,487		293,574		280,121	
5	248,369	497,138		293,189		293,368	
10	240,012	496,901		248,251		293,049	
15	261,346	496,531	0.0120	239,833	15,035	248,066	14,637
20	285,209	495,902	0.0908	261,015	123,993	239,529	113,624
25	314,388	495,168	0.1499	284,787	224,541	260,629	204,394
30	281,290	494,213	0.1125	313,782	167,364	284,238	168,193
35	286,923	492,760	0.0441	280,463	62,554	312,859	65,414
40	304,108	490,447	0.0074	285,576	10,909	279,147	10,447
45	324,946	486,613	0.0003	301,731	470	283,344	439
50	247,613	480,665		320,974		298,043	
55	211,351	471,786		243,039		315,045	
60	215,140	457,852		205,109		235,861	
65	221,764	436,153		204,944		195,388	
70	223,506	402,775		204,793		189,260	
75	183,654	350,358		194,419		178,141	
80	141,990	271,512		142,324		150,666	
85+	112,424	291,707		131,768		141,960	
Sum	4,397,428			4,449,570	604,866	4,478,712	577,148

B [1993.0, 1998.0] = 604,866 B [1998.0, 2003.0] = 577,148
B^F [1993.0, 1998.0] = 295,057 B^F [1998.0, 2003.0] = 281,536
B^M [1993.0, 1998.0] = 309,810 B^M [1998.0, 2003.0] = 295,612

Dealing with immigration is more difficult. People already in the population are not at risk of immigrating into it and relating immigration flows to the population by age and sex does not provide the same advantages as it does for mortality or fertility. Immigration is typically affected by immigration policies that are more often set in terms of maximum numbers and flows than in terms of rates.

For these reasons, migration assumptions are more often formulated in the form of absolute numbers than of rates. The formal difficulty of integrating migration in projection is that migration continuously affects the population at risk both of dying and of giving birth. If migration were taking place by discrete leaps exactly at the end of each projection interval, we would only need to add or subtract migrants at the right ages. But more realistically, some migrants will not survive until the end of the interval and some may bear children who will survive until the end of the interval.

One convenient approach to modeling the continuous migration process is to divide the number of migrants during the interval into two discrete quantities, and to assume that half of the migrants moved exactly at the beginning of the projection interval and the other half moved exactly at the end of the interval. Let's denote as $_5I_x^F[t, t+5]$ the net flow of immigrants during the projection period in the age interval x to $x + 5$ (the number can be negative if the migration

Box 6.1 (part 3)

Example: Sweden, baseline 1993 (males)

Age x	$_5N_x^M$ (1993.0)	$_5L_x^M$	$_5N_x^M$ (1998.0)	$_5N_x^M$ (2003.0)
0	310,189	496,754	307,798	293,693
5	261,963	496,297	309,904	307,515
10	252,046	495,989	261,800	309,711
15	274,711	495,113	251,601	261,338
20	296,679	493,460	273,794	250,761
25	333,726	491,475	295,486	272,692
30	296,774	489,325	332,266	294,193
35	299,391	486,487	295,053	330,339
40	314,295	482,392	296,871	292,569
45	338,709	476,532	310,477	293,265
50	256,066	467,568	332,338	304,637
55	208,841	452,941	248,055	321,941
60	199,996	428,556	197,598	234,701
65	197,282	390,707	182,333	180,146
70	184,234	336,027	169,672	156,815
75	133,856	261,507	143,377	132,044
80	86,732	172,333	88,211	94,485
85+	49,095	128,631	58,052	62,512
Sum	4,294,585		4,354,685	4,393,358
Total population size	8,692,013		8,804,255	8,872,071

Note: This example assumes that mortality and fertility stay constant at their 1993 levels during the projection period.

Data source: United Nations, *1993 Demographic Yearbook. 45th*. New York, United Nations, Department for Economic and Social Information and Policy Analysis, Statistical Division, 1995.

balance in the age group is negative). There are thus two additional terms in the number of survivors at the end of any projection interval for the age group x to $x + n$:

- half of the increments between the age x and $x + 5$ are added directly at the end of the interval;
- half of the increments between the age $x - 5$ and x are added at the beginning of the interval and survived to age x to $x + 5$.

Surviving the population forward (step 1), equation (6.2) becomes:

$$_5N_x^F(t+5) = \left[\left(_5N_{x-5}^F(t) + \frac{_5I_{x-5}^F[t, t+5]}{2}\right) \cdot \frac{_5L_x}{_5L_{x-5}}\right] + \frac{_5I_x^F[t, t+5]}{2} \qquad \textbf{(6.7)}$$

A similar adjustment should be made to the number of survivors in the open-ended age group and to male survivors.

The number of births in the period must also be adjusted. Increments at the end of the interval do not contribute to the number of births in the population during the interval. Increments at the beginning of the interval are usually assumed to bear children at the same rate as the population they are joining so births are obtained by equation (6.4) where $_5N_x^F(t)$ should be replaced by $_5N_x^F(t) + [_5I_x^F[t, t+5]/2]$. In other words, the following quantity represents the additional number of births due to migration:

$$\Delta B[t, t+5] = \sum_{x=\alpha}^{\beta-5} \frac{5}{4} \cdot {_5F_x} \cdot \left({_5I_x^F(t)} + {_5I_{x-5}^F(t)} \cdot \frac{_5L_x}{_5L_{x-5}} \right) \tag{6.8}$$

Note that the quantity will be negative if net out-migration is occurring. The negative value reflects the number of births that would have occurred but which were lost to the population through the emigration of potential mothers. Finally, these births are divided by sex based on a sex ratio at birth and survived forward using the life table to obtain the migration "correction" to the 0–4 age group. Since half of the migration at 0–4 is also to be added at the end of the interval, the equation for the first age group becomes:

$$_5N_0^F(t+5) = B^F[t, t+5] \cdot \frac{_5L_0}{5 \cdot l_0} + \frac{_5I_0^F[t, t+5]}{2} \tag{6.9}$$

These approximations for migration effects allow us to adapt formulas for a closed population without having to turn to a more complex methodology. The approximations are highly accurate if migration is relatively evenly distributed in the interval and does not vary dramatically from one 5-year age interval to the next. For expositional clarity, we discussed migration last. To implement the projection, the simplest procedure is to add half of the projected migration flow to each subgroup before beginning step one, and to add the second half at the very end. An example is provided in box 6.2.

The adjustments were presented for net increments, i.e. those combining in- and out-migration. This approach makes presentation easier because it avoids repeating similar adjustments for immigrants and emigrants. However, it is analytically disconcerting. Emigration and immigration need not have the same causes and constraints. As mentioned, emigration is better handled, when possible, through a multiple decrement life table, whereas immigration can be handled in the manner just described. Even when both in- and out-migration are handled as flows, we may want to apply different mortality and fertility rates to immigrants and emigrants. Emigration can be selective on variables related to mortality and fertility, and immigrants' behavior and risks in their new location need not mirror those for longstanding residents.

6.3.4 Further disaggregation

The essence of the cohort-component method is the recognition of different age groups. Because mortality often varies substantially between males and females, and because fertility rates are most often available only for females, it is desirable to divide the population by age and sex. Further disaggregation may be desired if information is sought on subpopulations or if the rates vary among subpopulations so that disaggregation allows a more accurate projection of the total population.[3] The cohort-component method allows further disaggregation by

Box 6.2 *Cohort-component Female-dominant Projection with Migration*

$_5I_x^F(t, t+5) =$ Number of net female migrants between t and $t+5$

$$_5N_x^F(t+5) = \left(_5N_{x-5}^F(t) + \frac{_5I_{x-5}^F[t, t+5]}{2}\right) \cdot \frac{_5L_x^F}{_5L_{x-5}^F} + \frac{_5I_x^F[t, t+5]}{2}$$

$$_\infty N_{85}^F(t+5) = \left(_5N_{80}^F(t) + _\infty N_{85}^F(t) + \frac{_5I_{80}^F[t, t+5] + _\infty I_{85}^F[t, t+5]}{2}\right) \cdot \frac{T_{85}^F}{T_{80}^F} + \frac{_\infty I_{85}^F[t, t+5]}{2}$$

$$_5B_x[t, t+5] = 5 \cdot _5F_x \cdot \frac{_5N_x^F(t) + _5I_x^F[t, t+5]/2 + _5N_x^F(t+5)}{2}$$

$$_5N_0^F(t+5) = B^F[t, t+5] \cdot \frac{_5L_0^F}{5 \cdot l_0} + \frac{_5I_0^F[t, t+5]}{2}$$

Example: Sweden, females, baseline 1993 (see Box 6.1)

Age x	$_5N_x^F$ (1993.0)	$_5L_x^F$	$_5F_x$	$_5I_x^F$ [1993.0, 1998.0]	$_5N_x^F$ (1998.0)	$_5B_x$ [1993.0, 1998.0]
0	293,395	497,487		6,840	302,392	
5	248,369	497,138		4,150	298,682	
10	240,012	496,901		3,365	252,007	
15	261,346	496,531	0.0120	5,270	244,150	15,244
20	285,209	495,902	0.0908	9,240	268,267	126,688
25	314,388	495,168	0.1499	8,230	293,515	229,354
30	281,290	494,213	0.1125	5,470	320,624	170,057
35	286,923	492,760	0.0441	3,155	284,767	63,203
40	304,108	490,447	0.0074	1,770	288,031	10,971
45	324,946	486,613	0.0003	1,115	303,166	472
50	247,613	480,665		1,075	322,062	
55	211,351	471,786		845	243,989	
60	215,140	457,852		645	205,841	
65	221,764	436,153		530	205,516	
70	223,506	402,775		465	205,270	
75	183,654	350,358		300	194,771	
80	141,990	271,512		250	142,565	
85+	112,424	291,707		175	131,966	
Sum	4,397,428				4,507,581	615,988

B [1993.0, 1998.0] = 615,988
B^F [1993.0, 1998.0] = 300,482
Total number of females in 1998 with migration = 4,507,581
Total number of females in 1998 without migration (Box 6.1) = 4,449,570

Source: United Nations, *Demographic Yearbook* (various years).

characteristics established at birth (e.g., race). Cohort-component projections can be prepared for males and females of each subpopulation as described above, with the addition of a rule to allocate births. The simplest rule when doing a female-dominant projection is to assume that births belong to the same subpopulation as the mother and to use a sex ratio at birth to divide them between males and females. Real situations are often too complex for this approach to be very satisfactory, e.g., when the classification of a child's race is more likely to be associated with the father's race than with the mother's.

The cohort-component method cannot be simply adjusted to project population by characteristics that are changing during the life course. Transitions among subpopulations are best handled by a multistate methodology that explicitly recognizes patterns of transition by age and sex (see chapter 12). But when the characteristic of interest varies in the course of life with some sort of regularity, it may be possible to approximate the multistate projections by simply projecting the population by age and sex and then applying to it an age pattern of the characteristic. Assuming an age pattern is simpler than making assumptions about the transfer rates into and out of each age group. Input data can be supplied by a single cross-section, whereas the estimation of transition rates typically requires longitudinal data.

6.4 Projections in Matrix Notation

The mechanics of cohort component projections can be compactly written in matrix notation as has been gradually established by Bernardelli (1941), Lewis (1942) and, especially, Leslie (1945) (Smith and Keyfitz, 1977: 193–4, 215–38). This rewriting often facilitates computer applications and also allows the use of matrix algebra to establish important relations in population dynamics. In this section, we provide a simplified illustration of the use of matrix notation. No additional concepts are developed in this section and readers unfamiliar with matrix algebra can skip to the next section.

To illustrate how to summarize the cohort component projection methodology using matrix notation, we will divide the population into five age groups only (0–14, 15–29, 30–44, 45–59, 60+) and refer to those as groups 1 to 5 (6 in T_6 will refer to age 75+). For a closed female-only population (denoted W), surviving the population at time t fifteen years forward implies, for $i = 2, 3, 4$:

$$W_i(t + 15) = W_{i-1}(t) \cdot \frac{L_i}{L_{i-1}}$$

and for $i = 5$:

$$W_5(t + 15) = \left(W_4(t) \cdot \frac{L_5}{L_4} \right) + \left(W_5(t) \cdot \frac{T_6}{T_5} \right)$$

If we assume that fertility is limited to ages 15 to 45, then equation (6.4) becomes:

$$B[t, t + 15] = \frac{15}{2} \cdot F_2 \cdot \left(W_2(t) + W_1(t) \cdot \frac{L_2}{L_1} \right)$$

$$+ \frac{15}{2} \cdot F_3 \cdot \left(W_3(t) + W_2(t) \cdot \frac{L_3}{L_2} \right)$$

so the first age group 15 years forward is:

$$W_1(t + 15) = B[t, t + 15] \cdot \frac{1}{1 + SRB} \cdot \frac{L_1}{15 \cdot l_0}$$

$$= k \cdot \left(F_2 \cdot \frac{L_2}{L_1} \cdot W_1(t) + \left[F_2 + F_3 \cdot \frac{L_3}{L_2} \right] \cdot W_2(t) + F_3 \cdot W_3(t) \right)$$

with $k = (1/(1 + SRB))(L_1/(2 \cdot l_0))$.

So in matrix notation:

$$
\begin{pmatrix} W_1(t + 15) \\ W_2(t + 15) \\ W_3(t + 15) \\ W_4(t + 15) \\ W_5(t + 15) \end{pmatrix} =
\begin{pmatrix}
k \cdot F_2 \cdot \dfrac{L_2}{L_1} & k \cdot \left[F_2 + F_3 \cdot \dfrac{L_3}{L_2} \right] & k \cdot F_3 & 0 & 0 \\[2mm]
\dfrac{L_2}{L_1} & 0 & 0 & 0 & 0 \\[2mm]
0 & \dfrac{L_3}{L_2} & 0 & 0 & 0 \\[2mm]
0 & 0 & \dfrac{L_4}{L_3} & 0 & 0 \\[2mm]
0 & 0 & 0 & \dfrac{L_5}{L_4} & \dfrac{T_6}{T_5}
\end{pmatrix}
\cdot
\begin{pmatrix} W_1(t) \\ W_2(t) \\ W_3(t) \\ W_4(t) \\ W_5(t) \end{pmatrix}
$$

$$(6.10)$$

By denoting as $\mathbf{W}(t)$ the column vector of population by age group at time t and $\mathbf{L}[t, t + 15]$ the projection matrix between time t and $t + 15$ (the Leslie matrix), the projection is thus of the following format:

$$\mathbf{W}(t + 15) = \mathbf{L}[t, t + 15] \cdot \mathbf{W}(t)$$

If we assume that the same projection matrix can be applied to a projection period of n successive 15-year intervals, then:

$$\mathbf{W}(t + 15 \cdot n) = \mathbf{L}^n \cdot \mathbf{W}(t)$$

A remarkable finding is that, under assumptions that are nearly always satisfied by human populations, when the matrix $\mathbf{L}$ is raised to a high enough power n, the population age structure of $\mathbf{W}(t+15 \cdot n)$ becomes constant and the population growth rate during each projection interval becomes constant. This result is related to the stable population theorem presented in the next chapter. Matrix algebra offers an elegant way to derive the constant age distribution and the constant growth rate. When a population has reached the stable state, it must satisfy for any subsequent projection interval:

$$\mathbf{W}^S(t + 15) = \mathbf{L} \cdot \mathbf{W}^S(t) = \lambda \cdot \mathbf{W}^S(t)$$

so the 15 years' growth, λ, is the largest real eigenvalue and the stable population distribution, $\mathbf{W}^S(t)$, the corresponding eigenvector of the matrix equation:

$$(\mathbf{L} - \lambda \cdot \mathbf{I}) \cdot \mathbf{W}^S(t) = 0$$

where $\mathbf{I}$ is the identity matrix and 0 is a column-vector of zeros.

Table 6.1: *Population by major areas in* 2000, 2020, *and* 2050 *(thousands)*

Area	2000	2020	2050
World	6,055,049	7,501,521	8,909,095
Africa	784,445	1,187,424	1,766,082
Asia	3,682,550	4,545,249	5,268,451
Europe	728,887	711,909	627,691
Latin America and the Caribbean	519,143	665,093	808,910
Northern America	309,631	353,904	391,781
Oceania	30,393	37,943	46,180

Source: United Nations, 1999. Medium variant.

6.5 Population Forecasts

Simulating constant mortality and fertility conditions is a good example of the use of population projections but does not represent a likely scenario for most populations. The essence of population forecasting by the cohort-component method is defining a set of age-specific mortality and fertility rates and a set of immigrants and emigrants by age and sex for each projection interval. If the projection is further disaggregated, these data are required for each subpopulation. In this section, we describe how such assumptions are typically prepared by the United Nations, the principal agency preparing demographic projections for most countries in the world (United Nations, 1999). Table 6.1 presents results from the UN medium variant global projection up to year 2050. In the next section, we describe a specific population projection for the United States as prepared by the United States Bureau of the Census (Day, 1996).

These two agencies use the cohort-component projection method and produce several demographic scenarios. Before its revision in 1999, the United Nations recognized 17 age groups (from age 0–4 to 80 and above) for each sex, so the formulation of a complete demographic scenario theoretically required, for each projection interval, 36 specific survivorship ratios (18 for each sex, including that from birth to the first age group), 6 age-specific fertility rates (from age 15–19 to age 40–4), 1 sex ratio at birth and 34 specific numbers of emigrants and immigrants (one each for each age/sex group). Each projection interval of 5 years thus requires defining 111 demographic parameters. This task is simplified by the use of model age patterns (see chapter 9), which also ensure some consistency in the specific rates used for different age groups. The analyst needs then to stipulate the level and type of model age pattern that each demographic phenomenon is assumed to follow in each projection interval. Leaving the considerations about appropriate patterns for chapter 9, we concentrate in this chapter on the assumptions about future levels of fertility, mortality, and migration. The assumptions made by most official agencies are fairly mechanical and attempt to take advantage of past regularities, mainly the secular decline in mortality and the fertility transition.

Coale (1981) has characterized the rise in life expectancy over time in many populations by postulating a linear relationship between the annual rate of increase in e_0^o and its level. Using this relation for future periods, future gains in life expectancy are assumed to be faster when recent gains were fast, but slower when life expectancy is already at a high level. The United Nations (United Nations, 1995: 144–5) uses a similar approach. Future life expectancy gains from one projection interval to the next depend on the level of life expectancy and follow three improvement patterns (slow, medium, and fast) among which one is selected based on recent

Table 6.2: *United Nations estimates and projections of mortality levels*

Countries	Life expectancy at birth (females)		
	1995–2000	2015–20	2040–50
Nigeria	51.5	57.7	70.2
India	62.9	70.3	76.6
Brazil	71.0	75.6	79.7
China	72.0	76.9	81.0
Germany	80.2	82.2	84.5
USA	80.1	82.1	84.4
Japan	82.9	84.5	86.7

Source: United Nations, 1999. Medium variant.

performance.[4] Table 6.2 presents United Nations estimates of and assumptions about female life expectancy for selected countries.

The linear relationship in Coale's model implies that populations will reach a maximum life expectancy. United Nations guidelines also anticipate that life expectancy improvements will slow down as limits to human life span are approached. The existence of such a limit, however, is questionable (Le Bras, 1976; Vaupel, 1997; Wachter and Finch, 1997). Recent gains in countries already at low levels of mortality have exhibited little sign of slowing down. Lee and Carter (1992) fit the following function to the past United States mortality rates:

$$\ln[M(x, t)] = a_x + K(t) \cdot b_x$$

where $M(x, t)$ is the death rate at age x, time t, a_x and b_x represent the fixed age effects and age pattern of mortality change, respectively, and $K(t)$ the level of mortality at time t. Their important analysis reveals that the value of $K(t)$ was declining linearly at a remarkably steady pace throughout the twentieth century.

Similarly, fertility assumptions typically stipulate a fertility age-schedule and a fertility level indicator, usually the total fertility rate. Changes in fertility are thought to be less predictable than changes in mortality because fertility trends have been far less uniform than mortality trends. At high fertility levels, fertility has been falling in most of Latin America and Asia whereas it has remained about constant in much of sub-Saharan Africa and parts of western Asia. Fertility trends at low levels of fertility are equally disparate. The most systematic trend is that of countries in the midst of the "fertility transition", where a linear extrapolation of the trend has been a reasonable assumption until fertility approaches the replacement level. For countries in which fertility has remained almost constant at a high level, the United Nations fertility assumptions are based on an expectation of the date when a fertility decline would begin, a target date when the replacement level should be reached, and a linear decline in between. For the more developed countries, United Nations fertility assumptions are based on national projections prepared by national statistical offices and typically assume that fertility will either remain constant or tend toward the replacement level. Table 6.3 presents some estimates of and assumptions about total fertility rates for selected countries. The National Research Council (2000) has thoughtfully reviewed the procedures and performance of United Nations world population projections since 1950.

Table 6.3: *United Nations estimates and projections of fertility levels*

Countries	Total fertility rate		
	1995–2000	2015–20	2040–50
Nigeria	5.15	3.52	2.10
India	3.13	2.10	2.10
Brazil	2.27	2.10	2.10
USA	1.99	1.90	1.90
China	1.80	1.90	1.90
Japan	1.43	1.68	1.75
Germany	1.30	1.51	1.64

Source: United Nations, 1999. Medium variant.

In spite of the difficulties of projecting mortality and fertility, many demographers would consider migration to be the most difficult demographic component to predict. Migration is often viewed as an exogenous factor of population change as it depends on international immigration policies and on unpredictable upheavals or crises. This position seems to result less from empirical evidence than from a lack of understanding of the determinants of migration which has not yet benefitted from as much attention as mortality and fertility in the demographic community. If migration trends are often irregular because they are, in part, responding to temporary situations, e.g., refugee movements, migration also depends on more predictable demographic factors. For instance, the large immigration flows to many West European countries in the 1970s corresponded to the small birth cohorts of the war years entering the labor force and to the resulting labor shortage. Immigration policies are thus not fully exogenous factors and their changes often reflect changing demographic conditions. Similarly, emigration flows are partly spurred by domestic labor force growth in excess of domestic employment growth. Although such instances of links between demographic conditions and migration can be identified, migration assumptions are seldom based on an analysis of their determinants and their implications. More often, persistent, structural migration flows are conservatively assumed to continue at the same level whereas more recent or idiosyncratic ones are assumed to diminish (United Nations, 1995: 150–1).

6.6 The USBOC Projection of the United States Population

The United States Bureau of the Census projections for the United States make three different assumptions regarding future mortality levels, three different assumptions regarding fertility, and four different assumptions about migration. Among the possible combinations of these assumptions, 10 combinations are retained for population projections. Assumptions are described as low, middle, and high, depending on their impact on future population size; the fourth migration assumption is no migration. The middle series for each of the three variables produces the middle population projection. The assumptions of high fertility, high life expectancy (low mortality), and high migration (since migration is dominated by immigration) produce the highest projected population; likewise, the low assumptions produce the lowest projection. Combined with the middle assumption of the other two components, high and low

Table 6.4: *US Bureau of the Census projection assumptions*

Parameter	1995 (estimate)	2050 level (assumption)		
		Low	Middle	High
TFR	2.055	1.910	2.245	2.580
e_0	75.9	74.8	82.0	89.4
Migration	820	300	820	1370

(Migration figures are net immigrants per year in thousands.)
Source: Day, 1996.

fertility, high and low mortality, high, low, and no migration scenarios are also displayed. Table 6.4 summarizes the assumptions of recent projections (Day, 1996).

These assumptions are in line with the ones described for developed countries in the previous section. The medium fertility assumption is that fertility levels by race will more or less stay at their current levels, while mortality assumptions are based on different paces of mortality decline (note that in the low variant, the projected decline is more overweighted by a projected spread of the HIV/AIDS epidemic). The middle migration assumption is a constant absolute migration flow but quite different migration assumptions are also simulated. This range is due in part to the potential volatility of immigration, discussed in the previous section, and also to the importance of immigration in future population growth. In the middle projections series, immigrants between 1995 and 2050 amount to 25 percent of 2050 total population and contribute about 60 percent of the population growth over the period.

The difference in the 2050 population size between the high and low projections is 102 million for fertility, 48 million for mortality, and 87 million for migration. Population projections illustrate how seemingly small variations of fertility have important consequences for future population size. Variations in mortality have a more modest impact on the total population size but affect substantially population composition. In this projection, the mortality component has the largest impact on the ratio of 65+/25–64 in 2050, a ratio of obvious economic importance.

6.7 Alternative Forecasting Methods

As mentioned, the cohort-component methodology is practically unchallenged as the methodology for population projections and/or forecasts. As a projection device, it has a high degree of internal validity because the basic demographic accounting relations are preserved. The assumptions introduced for computational convenience – stationarity within age intervals, person-years computed by using the average of beginning and ending population, fixed sex ratio at birth – have negligible effects on results. An exception to this claim is that the assumption of stationarity in the open-ended age interval at the highest ages biases projected numbers downward where growth rates are positive at these ages, so that choosing too low an age to begin the open-ended interval can introduce important error.

As a forecasting tool, examination of past performances provides less support than the almost exclusive resort to the cohort component projection methodology would suggest (Rogers, 1995a). In the United States at least, it seems that the age-standardized series of age-specific fertility rates (TFR or GRR) have historically exhibited more variability than the crude birth rates. As shown in chapter 5, the crude birth rate and the age-specific rates are related by:

$$CBR[t, t+5] = \sum_{x=\alpha}^{\beta-5} {}_5F_x[t, t+5] \cdot {}_5C_x^F[t, t+5]$$

where ${}_5C_x^F[t, t+5]$ is the ratio of person-years lived in the interval by females aged x to $x+5$ to the person-years lived by the total population. Variation in the crude birth rates might be more regular or smoother than those in the series of age-specific fertility rates if variations of the latter are compensated by variations in the proportion of women in reproductive age groups (i.e., if a negative correlation exists between the ${}_5C_x^F$ and ${}_5F_x$ time series). Such a phenomenon has in fact been observed in the United States over the period 1900–90. There are several possible explanations. First, Easterlin (1980) argues that members of large birth cohorts achieve lower relative economic status which, in turn, tends to reduce their fertility. A second possible explanation relates to the marriage market. When the population of reproductive ages is growing rapidly, there is often a surplus of females in the marriage market because females typically enter the marriage market at a younger age than males. This surplus may translate into a lower propensity to marry and lower fertility rates. Finally, it is possible that the negative correlation between the number of women and their fertility is purely a result of chance.

Most models of population dynamics are based on individuals, but larger units such as households can also be used (van Imhoff and Keilman, 1991). A related possibility is to use a two-sex model in which people of opposite sex form unions and children are ascribed to unions. The formation of unions could be modeled as (Schoen, 1988):

$$U_{ij} = \alpha_{ij} \cdot \frac{M_i W_j}{M_i + W_j}$$

where α_{ij} is the force of attraction between men from subpopulation i and women from subpopulation j. The dissolution of unions could then be modeled using rates of widowhood and divorce, so population projections would include simultaneous projections of the unmarried population and of the number of unions. In this more realistic model, fertility rates are applied to unions, not to individuals, and depend on the ages of each member of the union.

6.8 Accuracy and Uncertainty

The accuracy of population forecasts can only be assessed after the fact. The most immediate indicator of the accuracy of a forecast of the total population size is the difference between the forecasted size and the actual one, or the difference as a proportion of the projected size. This relative difference still misses the temporal dimension of a forecast; a 10 percent error indicates different forecast qualities when it refers to a long-term projection as opposed to a short-term one.

A better gauge of the quality of the forecast of population is the following measure of relative error:

$$E = \frac{N(T) - N^P(T)}{N(T) - N(0)}$$

where $N^P(T)$ is the predicted population size at time T, while $N(0)$ and $N(T)$ are the actual population size at time 0 and T. Time 0 can be chosen as the latest population estimate that was available when the forecast was prepared. The measure does not directly control for the length of the forecast but rather for the actual population change. Similar measures comparing the error of the forecast to the error of other basic forecast methodology can be designed. For example, $N(0)$ can be replaced by the forecast obtained by projecting constant population growth (Keyfitz, 1985: 230–3).

Another way to evaluate forecast quality is by comparing the actual growth rate to the projected growth rate (Stoto, 1983)[5]:

$$\varepsilon = \bar{r}^P[0, T] - \bar{r}[0, T]$$

$$= \frac{\ln\left(\dfrac{N^P(T)}{N(T)}\right)}{T}$$

Note that when T is measured in years, this ratio is an annualized measure of the forecast error.

These measures of forecasting error and the analysis of past performances allow one to consider confidence intervals for forecasts (Keyfitz, 1981; Stoto, 1983). The most promising method for developing confidence intervals is to treat demographic rates as stochastic processes and estimate their time-trend and variance around it using time series analysis. The estimation also allows one to extend the time-trend to the future instead of relying either on "expert" judgment for the future or on measures of error derived from past forecasts (Lee, 1998). We mentioned a convincing example above by Lee and Carter (1992) with respect to mortality. Lee (1993), and Lee and Tuljapurkar (1994) extended this approach, adding a similar estimation of the trend in fertility rates. Among the products are confidence intervals for features of the age distribution, which are especially valuable for estimating the fiscal viability of Social Security and Medicare (Tuljapurkar, 1992; Lee and Tuljapurkar, 1998). For a more complete discussion of uncertainty in forecasts, the reader is referred to National Research Council (2000: chapter 7) and Alho (1998).

6.9 Other Uses of Population Projections

Although forecasting is the most common use of population projections, the set of interrelations among demographic variables embodied in the cohort-component method can also serve important analytical purposes. One practical use is to show how the existing population age structure conditions future population growth, a phenomenon referred to as demographic "momentum." In its narrowest formulation, the term refers to the fact that a closed population may continue to grow even when fertility is at the "replacement" level (see section 7.7). More generally, population growth depends not only on current fertility and current mortality but also on the age structure which, in turn, is a legacy of past fertility and mortality (see chapter 8). Bourgeois-Pichat and Taleb (1970) illustrated this phenomenon by showing, using data from Mexico, that the goal of a zero-growth rate for the year 2000 was unrealistic because its age structure was too conducive to positive growth. Only dramatic changes of fertility, ones that might actually have detrimental long-term consequences, would have produced such a decrease in the growth rate. Bongaarts (1994) used World Bank long-term projections to divide future world population growth into three components: demographic momentum (growth that would occur even if fertility were to stabilize universally and immediately at the replacement level); the additional growth due to desired fertility above replacement level; and the additional growth due to additional "undesired" fertility. (The distinction between desired and undesired fertility is of course not clear-cut.) Because it clarified the future sources of growth at a time when population policies were being reconsidered on a global scale, Bongaarts' article is one of the most influential ever written in demography.

Finally, population projections can serve theoretical purposes. We mentioned earlier that population projection can be used to show that a closed population exposed to fixed conditions of fertility and mortality converges toward a stable state. Such a result, and the properties of populations having reached the stable state, can be derived analytically and are described in the next chapter. The approaches are complementary: although the analytical approach allows one to grasp stable populations in all their generality, population projections allow one to simulate and illustrate more readily how and how fast a particular population actually approaches this state.

NOTES

1. If mortality increases with age during the interval and the population distribution within the interval is younger than that of the stationary population produced by the same $\mu(x)$ function, then the life table survivorship ratio is too low by (typically) a very small amount. The maximum bias introduced by distributional disturbances can be assessed by comparing $_5L_x/_5L_{x-5}$ and l_x/l_{x-5}, which would be the survivorship ratio with the youngest possible age distribution within the age group (i.e., everyone between age x and $x + 5$ is of exact age x).

2. As discussed in chapter 1, this approximation would be exact if the number of women in this age interval were changing linearly during the period. If the growth rate in the interval is constant (the population is changing exponentially rather than linearly), then we would estimate person-years as:

$$[_5N_x^F(t + 5) - _5N_x^F(t)] \cdot 5/\ln[_5N_x^F(t + 5)/_5N_x^F(t)]$$

The reason for not using the exponential estimation for period person-years here is not substantive but formal. Having expressed $_5N_x^F(t + 5)$ as a function of $_5N_{x-5}^F(t)$, the number of births in (6.4) appears as a linear combination of population by age-group at the beginning of the interval. This allows the use of more compact notation and matrix algebra (see section 6.4, below).

3. Note for example that an aggregate population is projected to grow less rapidly than the sum of its components projected separately when one component is growing faster than the rest of the population. Intuitively, the fastest growing segment of the population gradually represents a larger share of the total population, thus pulling the aggregate growth upward. This tendency is obscured by a projection of the aggregate population that implicitly "freezes" population composition at its initial level (for a formal proof, see Keyfitz, 1985: 14–17).

4. Note that some adjustments to this general pattern of mortality decline were necessary in some countries to account for the projected toll of AIDS (see United Nations, 1995: 145–6).

5. Stoto's measure includes an additional term, the ratio of the estimated to the actual population at time 0 (*ex ante* error).

7 The Stable Population Model

In chapters 3 and 4 we encountered a model that is sometimes used to study population processes, the stationary population model. A stationary population will result from the indefinite continuation of a constant number of births (constant per day, month, and year), a constant life table, and zero migration at all ages. Such a population will have a constant age structure and certain simplified relationships among demographic parameters. For example, the birth rate of a stationary population is the reciprocal of life expectancy at birth. In a stationary population, short-cut methods of demographic accounting can often be employed.

In this chapter, we encounter the second major demographic model, the stable population model. It is closely related to the stationary population model; in fact, a stationary population is a special case of a stable population. The stable model is used by demographers to demonstrate the long-term implications of maintaining short-term demographic patterns and to identify the effects of change in one parameter on the value of others. It is the device that demographers use most frequently to study how the different components of population structure and processes are connected to one another. It has also been used to estimate the value of demographic parameters in populations that can be assumed to be stable.

7.1 A Simplified Example of a Stable Population

Suppose that the life table of a population is constant over time and that there is zero net migration at every age. These same two assumptions are used in the creation of a stationary population. However, let us modify the third and final assumption of the stationary population model, the constancy of births. Let us assume instead that births are growing "exponentially," i.e., at a constant (annualized) growth rate:

$$B(t) = B(0) \cdot e^{rt}$$

For purposes of illustration, we will assume that the life table in this (nonhuman) population is such that everyone dies before age 5. The hypothetical life table values are:

Exact age (a)	l_a	l_a/l_0
0	100,000	1.000
1	60,000	0.600
2	40,000	0.400
3	20,000	0.200
4	5,000	0.050
5	0	0.000

Finally, assume that there were 1,000 births in this population on January 1, 1800. Therefore, there will be 600 individuals ($1{,}000 \times 0.600$) at exact age 1 on January 1, 1801, 400 individuals at exact age 2 on January 1, 1802, and so on. The progress of the cohort born on Jan. 1, 1800 is shown on the left-most diagonal of table 7.1. Since the number of births is growing at annual rate r, we know that there will be $1000 \cdot e^r$ births on January 1, 1801. Following this birth cohort through life, there will be $1000 \cdot e^r \cdot (0.600)$ one-year-olds on Jan. 1, 1802, $1000 \cdot e^r \cdot (0.400)$ two-year-olds on Jan. 1, 1803, and so on down the second diagonal in table 7.1. The next cohort, born Jan. 1, 1802, will number $1000 \cdot e^{2r}$ at birth and will proceed through life along the third diagonal. And so on.

Compare the numbers of persons by age on Jan. 1, 1805 and Jan.1, 1806. At every age, there are more people in 1806 by the factor e^r. The two age distributions are proportional to one another. The proportionate age distribution – often referred to as the "age composition" of the population – is constant over time. It is clear that, as long as births continue to grow at a constant rate and the life table is constant, the age composition of the population will also be constant in years beyond 1806. Filling in the rest of the calendar year with births that are growing at annual rate r (e.g., births on Jan. 2, 1800 will number

$$1000 \cdot e^{r \cdot (1/365)})$$

does not alter this result but simply produces a smoother age distribution of the population surface. The most useful way to think about this type of population is that the number of births is changing continuously at an annualized rate of r.

Table 7.1: *Population by age on January 1, years 1800 to 1806*

Age	1/1/1800	1/1/1801	1/1/1802	1/1/1803	1/1/1804	1/1/1805	1/1/1806
0	1000	$1000 \cdot e^r$	$1000 \cdot e^{2r}$	$1000 \cdot e^{3r}$	$1000 \cdot e^{4r}$	$1000 \cdot e^{5r}$	$1000 \cdot e^{6r}$
1		600	$600 \cdot e^r$	$600 \cdot e^{2r}$	$600 \cdot e^{3r}$	$600 \cdot e^{4r}$	$600 \cdot e^{5r}$
2			400	$400 \cdot e^r$	$400 \cdot e^{2r}$	$400 \cdot e^{3r}$	$400 \cdot e^{4r}$
3				200	$200 \cdot e^r$	$200 \cdot e^{2r}$	$200 \cdot e^{3r}$
4					50	$50 \cdot e^r$	$50 \cdot e^{2r}$
5						0	0

Since births are growing at annual rate r and the total population is growing at this same rate after 1805, then the crude birth rate must be constant after this date. And since the crude birth rate and the growth rate are constant, the crude death rate (the difference between the crude birth rate and the growth rate) must also be constant. The constancy of the crude death rate also follows from the fact that both age-specific death rates (embodied in the life table) and the age composition of the population are constant.

The population depicted in table 7.1 is, starting in 1805, a stable population. Despite the fact that the population is growing, it has a constant birth rate, death rate, growth rate, and age composition. The population in each age interval is growing at the same rate, the rate at which the annual number of births is growing. This set of attributes will be maintained until the population is "destabilized" by a change in the growth rate of births or in the prevailing life table.

The age composition of the stable population is determined by two factors: the prevailing life table and the growth rate in the annual number of births. To see this more clearly, we express the ratio of population numbers in various age intervals on Jan. 1, 1805 to the number of births on Jan. 1, 1805 as:

$$\frac{N(1)}{B} = e^{-r} p(1)$$

$$\frac{N(2)}{B} = e^{-2r} p(2)$$

The number of one-year-olds is smaller than the number of births not only because some births die before reaching age one (expressed as a $p(1)$ term that is less than 1.000), but also because the one-year-olds derived from the 1804 birth cohort that was smaller at birth than the 1805 birth cohort by the factor e^{-r} (assuming that r is positive). The number of two-year-olds in 1805 is even smaller than the number of births in 1805 because more births die before reaching age two and the cohort born in 1803 is smaller than the cohort born in 1805 by the factor e^{-2r}.

Continuing with this example, the ratio of the number of two-year-olds to the number of one-year-olds in 1805 is:

$$\frac{N(2)}{N(1)} = e^{-r} \, {}_1p_1$$

since $p(2) = p(1)_1p_1$. Again, the younger cohort is larger than the older cohort not only because some have died between the younger and the older ages but also because the younger cohort was larger at birth. This growth factor, and not higher mortality, is the principal reason why age distributions in developing countries are much younger than age distributions in developed countries.

Beyond 1804, we can express the number of a-year-olds at time t in terms of the number of births at time t:

$$N(a, t) = B(t) \cdot e^{-ra} \cdot p(a)$$

Dividing both sides by $N(t)$, the total population size at time t, gives an expression for the proportion of the population that is aged a at time t, denoted $c(a, t)$:

$$c(a, t) = b(t) \cdot e^{-ra} \cdot p(a)$$

where $b(t)$ is the birth rate at time t. But we have already seen that the birth rate will be constant beyond 1804, so $b(t) = b$ and:

$$c(a, t) = b \cdot e^{-ra} \cdot p(a) = c(a)$$

The age composition will be constant and can be expressed in terms of the birth rate, growth rate, and life table survival function. If a population is stable, there are clearly useful connections among demographic processes that can be compactly expressed. That was also true of the stationary population model, but that model was less general because it restricted the growth rate in the number of births to be zero. A stationary population is a special case of a stable population that arises when $r = 0$.

7.2 Lotka's Demonstration of Conditions Producing a Stable Population

We have seen in a nonrigorous fashion that a stable population will emerge if three conditions prevail for a long enough period:

1) the growth rate in the annual number of births is constant,
2) age-specific death rates (i.e., the life table) are constant,
3) age-specific rates of net migration are zero.

For a population to be "stable" in all parts of the age distribution, these conditions must prevail for a period as long as the maximum age to which anyone survives.

In one of the most important developments in demography, Alfred Lotka (1939) showed that a stable population would be produced by another set of conditions. He demonstrated that maintaining a constant set of age-specific fertility rates would, in combination with conditions 2 and 3, eventually produce a constant growth rate in the annual number of births. In effect, he showed that condition 1 above could be replaced by:

1*) age-specific fertility rates are constant.

He also showed how the age-specific fertility rates and mortality rates combine to produce the growth rate in the annual number of births, hence the growth rate of the entire population.

This demonstration has powerful implications. For one thing, it means that populations with unchanging vital rates – which must be a reasonable macroscopic approximation over long sweeps of human history – would be stable. In turn, the accounting relationships of a stable population can be invoked to investigate their demographic properties. For another thing, it means that every population's set of age-specific fertility and mortality rates implied an underlying stable population that would emerge if those rates remained unchanged. This underlying "model" population, usually termed the "stable equivalent" population, provides a detailed indication of what current demographic parameters imply for demographic prospects. Finally, the relations established by Lotka provide a means for investigating how changes in one demographic parameter affect all others.

Lotka's achievement is important enough that an outline of his proof is appropriate. Assume that:

1) Age-specific fertility rates are constant over time,
2) Age-specific mortality rates are constant over time,
3) Net migration rates are zero at all ages.

Note that Lotka dealt with a one-sex population and did not explicitly incorporate the other sex into reproduction. He examined the birth sequence in such a population beginning at time 0, when these conditions were first imposed:

$$B(t) = \int_0^t N(a, t)m(a)da + G(t) \tag{7.1}$$

where

$B(t)$ = the number of births at time t,
$N(a, t)$ = the number of persons aged a at time t,
$m(a)$ = rate of bearing female children for women aged a,
$G(t)$ = births at time t to women alive at time 0.

These functions all have the form of a statistical density function. That is, the number of births in the tiny interval of time from t to $t + dt$ (as $dt \rightarrow 0$) is $B(t)dt$. As always, dt and hence the density functions are defined in terms of years.

The $N(a, t)$ function for women born after time 0 can be expressed in terms of the number of births into their cohort and the probability of surviving to age a, $p(a)$:

$$N(a, t) = B(t - a) \cdot p(a) \quad t > 0$$

Making this substitution in (7.1) gives:

$$B(t) = \int_0^t B(t - a)p(a)m(a)da + G(t) \tag{7.2}$$

Eventually, the value of $G(t)$ will be zero. After 50 years, none of the people alive at time 0 will be giving birth. Hence, the birth sequence can eventually be expressed as:

$$B(t) = \int_0^t B(t - a)p(a)m(a)da \quad t > 50 \tag{7.3}$$

Equation (7.3) is called a homogeneous integral equation. It is an integral equation because it involves a function, $B(t)$, and the integral of that function. It is homogeneous because it does not include a constant term. Integral equations can be solved by a process of trial and error. The equation is solved when an expression for $B(t)$ can be found that, when substituted into equation (7.3), succeeds in equating the left-hand side and the right-hand side. Lotka showed that an exponential birth series solved the equation, as illustrated in figure 7.1:

$$B(t) = B \cdot e^{\rho t} \tag{7.4}$$

Substituting the trial solution (7.4) into (7.3) gives:

$$B \cdot e^{\rho t} = \int_0^t B \cdot e^{\rho(t-a)} p(a)m(a)da \quad t > 50$$

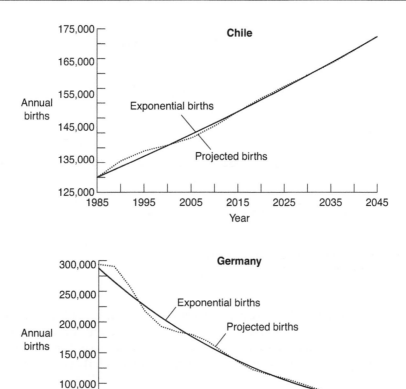

Figure 7.1   Births trajectories in two populations subject to constant vital rates
Data source: Keyfitz and Flieger, 1990.

Canceling the $B \cdot e^{\rho t}$ term from both sides gives:

$$1 = \int_0^t e^{-\rho a} p(a)m(a)da \quad t > 50 \tag{7.5}$$

So (7.4) is a solution to the homogeneous integral equation if a value of ρ can be found that makes the right-hand side of equation (7.5) equal to 1. If we consider (7.5) as an equation with a single unknown ρ, it appears that a value of ρ can always be found that makes the right-hand side equal to 1. Since $p(a)$ and $m(a)$ are always positive-valued functions, the right-hand side of 7.5 is a continuous, strictly decreasing function of ρ, $y(\rho)$. If $\rho = -\infty$, the value of the right-hand side will always be $+\infty$. If $\rho = +\infty$, the value of the right-hand side will always be equal to zero. When ρ takes all the values between $-\infty$ and $+\infty$, the right-hand side will take all the value between $+\infty$ and 0 (assuming continuity of $m(a)$ and $p(a)$). In particular, there will be a unique value of ρ, denoted r, such that $y(r)$ is exactly equal to 1, as illustrated on figure 7.2. That value of r is the growth rate in the annual number of births needed in (7.4) and thus

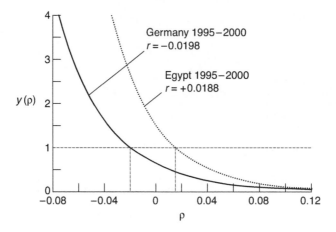

Figure 7.2 $y(\rho)$ function in Germany and Egypt
Source: United Nations, 1994, 1995.

becomes the growth rate of the stable population itself. It is usually called the "intrinsic growth rate" – the population growth rate that is intrinsic to the $m(a)$ and $p(a)$ schedules that produced it. Its value is determined by equation (7.5). If α is the minimum age at childbearing and β is the maximum age (hence $m(a) = 0$ at all other ages), equation (7.5) can be rewritten as:

$$1 = \int_{\alpha}^{\beta} e^{-ra} p(a)m(a)da \tag{7.6}$$

The rest of Lotka's proof consists of showing that the trial solution (7.4) is eventually (i.e., as t gets larger) the only pertinent solution to the equation; all other solutions become numerically irrelevant. For a more detailed discussion of Lotka's proof, with useful elaborations, see Keyfitz (1968b: ch. 5). The proof can also be done using matrix algebra and discrete time and age intervals (McFarland, 1969; Keyfitz, 1968b: ch. 3; Parlett, 1970).

7.3 The Equations Characterizing a Stable Population

As we have just seen, a stable population has an exponential birth series: $B(t) = B \cdot e^{rt}$. The value of r in a particular application is the value that, given the $m(a)$ and $p(a)$ schedules, satisfies (7.6). The number of persons aged a at time t will equal the number of births $t - a$ years earlier times the probability of surviving from birth to age a: $N(a, t) = B(t - a) \cdot p(a)$. Substituting this former formula into the latter gives:

$$N(a, t) = B \cdot e^{r(t-a)} \cdot p(a) = B \cdot e^{rt} \cdot e^{-ra} \cdot p(a)$$

$$= B(t) \cdot e^{-ra} \cdot p(a) \tag{7.7}$$

We now integrate both sides of (7.7) from age 0 to ω, the highest age attained in the population, and rearrange:

$$\int_0^\omega N(a,t)da = B(t) \int_0^\omega e^{-ra} p(a)da,$$

or

$$\frac{B(t)}{\int_0^\omega N(a,t)da} = \frac{B(t)}{N(t)} = b(t) = \frac{1}{\int_0^\omega e^{-ra} p(a)da} = b \qquad (7.8)$$

Equation (7.8) expresses the crude birth rate of a stable population, b, in terms of the growth rate and survival schedule of the population. It is constant over time.

Returning to equation (7.7), we divide both sides by $N(t)$, the total population size at time t, and derive an expression for the proportionate age distribution of the population, $c(a,t)$:

$$c(a,t) = \frac{N(a,t)}{N(t)} = \frac{B(t)}{N(t)} e^{-ra} p(a)$$

$$= be^{-ra} p(a) = c(a) \qquad (7.9)$$

The proportionate age distribution of the population is also constant. One interpretation of (7.9) that may clarify the role of its components is the following. When it was born, the cohort aged a represented the proportion b (the birth rate) of the population. Subsequent to birth, mortality reduced its size by the factor $p(a)$. Meanwhile, the entire population was growing by the factor e^{ra}, so that the cohort aged a was reduced by the factor e^{-ra} relative to the rest of the population. These three factors combine to determine the relative size of the cohort at age a.

To reconnect these expressions with the fertility rates and complete the circle, we multiply both sides of (7.9) by $m(a)$ and integrate over the ages of childbearing, α to β. After these operations, the right-hand side is simply the crude birth rate of the population, $\int_\alpha^\beta c(a)m(a)\,da$, which cancels out with b on the left-hand side, giving:

$$\int_\alpha^\beta e^{-ra} p(a)m(a)da = 1 \qquad (7.10)$$

Equation (7.10) just repeats (7.6), but derives it from age distributional considerations. The term inside the integral sign in (7.10) is the proportionate age distribution of women at childbirth in the stable population; that is why it must sum to unity across the ages of childbearing.

The age distribution, birth rate, death rate, and growth rate of a stable population are entirely determined by the $m(a)$ and $p(a)$ schedules. Whatever the features of the population on which those $m(a)$ and $p(a)$ schedules are imposed, the population will eventually attain the characteristics "intrinsic" to those schedules. If we applied the same set of schedules to Italy and Nigeria, the demographic features of those two populations would eventually become identical to one another (apart from their size), as illustrated on figure 7.3. The populations

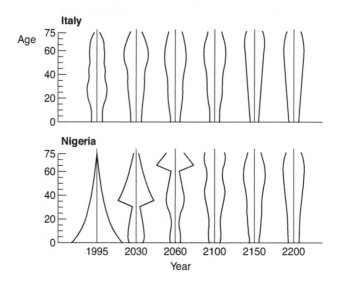

Figure 7.3 Relative age distributions of Italy and Nigeria, both projected with the 1995 vital rates of Italy
Data source: United Nations, 1995, 1996.

"forget their past," a property known as *ergodicity*; they take on features entirely determined by the regime of vital rates to which they have been exposed. Alvaro Lopez (1961) proved that this property of ergodicity applied even if the $m(a)$ and $p(a)$ schedules were changing.[1] Italy and Nigeria would eventually look alike even if they were subject to continuously changing vital rates, as long as the sequence of rates were the same for each.

How long will it take for a population to "stabilize" after a constant set of $m(a)$ and $p(a)$ schedules is imposed? There is no precise answer to this question. The answer depends in part on how much precision the analyst requires. It also depends on the difference between the age distributions of the population on which they are imposed and that of the ultimate stable population that will emerge. The bigger the difference, in general, the longer the time to stability. If the differences are very large and the application demands a high degree of accuracy, stability could take longer than a century to achieve. For most practical purposes, a period of 70 years often serves as a convenient rule of thumb. Fortunately, the ready availability of procedures for population projection means that the question need not be answered in the abstract.

Lotka developed the stable population model by assuming that age-specific net migration rates are zero at all ages, or that the population is "closed" to migration. In fact, this is an unnecessarily restrictive assumption. A stable population would also result if the schedule of age-specific net migration rates were constant over time. To see this, it is only necessary to recognize that the $p(a)$ schedule represents the proportionate change in cohort size between birth and age a. That schedule could be expanded to include the effects of migration as well as of mortality on the cohort's size. If both net migration rates and mortality rates were constant, then the expanded $p(a)$ schedule would also be constant and the population would stabilize.

The interpretation of the parameters would, of course, also need to be expanded to include migration.

7.4 The "Stable Equivalent" Population

Since every population has a set of fertility and mortality rates ($m(a)$ and $p(a)$), every population has an underlying stable population that would emerge if those rates were to continue indefinitely. This underlying model stable population is often referred to as the "stable equivalent" population. For example, the United States in 1996 has a "stable equivalent" population. To determine its characteristics, one would use equations (7.8)–(7.10) in the previous section and solve for the relevant parameters, beginning with the solution for r in equation (7.10). Of course, one would use the $m(a)$ and $p(a)$ schedules of the US in 1996. The growth rate, birth rate, death rate, and age distribution of this model population are termed "intrinsic"; they are intrinsic to the $m(a)$ and $p(a)$ schedules and are not influenced by the actual age distribution of the US in 1996, which is highly irregular.

The model population that would result from applying these equations to the $m(a)$ and $p(a)$ schedules of the US in 1996 should be identical to the population that would eventually emerge from projecting the US population of 1996 forward by the constant set of fertility and mortality rates of 1996, using the projection procedures developed in the previous chapter.[2] Note that, for this result to apply, the baseline population to which the constant rates are applied in forward projection need not be the US of 1996 or any other year; the ergodic property of population trajectories ensures the equivalence between the model stable population and the ultimate projected population regardless of the baseline population to which the constant rates of fertility and mortality are applied.

If age-specific vital rates have been constant in an actual population for a long period, then that population will be stable. In this case, the "stable equivalent" population will be identical to the actual population in its crude birth rate, death rate, growth rate, and age structure. If fertility or mortality rates have been changing, then the actual population will almost certainly differ in some or all of these features from the stable equivalent population. The test of whether an actual population is stable is developed below. In short, it is stable (and equations 7.8–7.10 apply to it) if age-specific growth rates are constant with age. This determination will normally require having two censuses and making a comparison of their age distributions. Constancy of age-specific growth rates means that the age composition (i.e., the proportionate age distribution) of the population is unchanging.

Identifying the features of the stable equivalent population requires that we adapt equations (7.8)–(7.10) to the discrete age intervals in which demographic data are normally presented. In one-year-wide age intervals, the expressions equivalent to (7.8)–(7.10) are:

$$b = \frac{1}{\sum_{a=0,1}^{\omega} e^{-r(a+0.5)} \frac{{}_1L_a}{l_0}} \qquad (7.8a)$$

$$_1c_a = b e^{-r(a+0.5)} \frac{{}_1L_a}{l_0} \qquad (7.9a)$$

$$1 = \sum_{a=\alpha,1}^{\beta-1} e^{-r(a+0.5)} \frac{{}_1L_a}{l_0} \, {}_1m_a \qquad (7.10a)$$

In 5-year age intervals, the equivalent expressions are:

$$b = \frac{1}{\sum_{a=0,5}^{\omega} e^{-r(a+2.5)} \frac{5L_a}{l_0}}$$

(7.8b)

$$_5c_a = b e^{-r(a+2.5)} \frac{5L_a}{l_0}$$

(7.9b)

$$1 = \sum_{a=\alpha,5}^{\beta-5} e^{-r(a+2.5)} \frac{5L_a}{l_0} \, _5m_a$$

(7.10b)

10-year-wide age intervals are too wide to provide reliable information.

Identifying the features of the stable equivalent population begins with the identification of r, the intrinsic growth rate. This is a process of trial and error using (in the conventional case of 5-year-wide age intervals) equation (7.10b). Coale (1957) has provided a useful strategy for quickly identifying the value of r. Treating the value of the integral in (7.10) as a function $y(\rho)$:

$$y(\rho) = \int_{\alpha}^{\beta} e^{-\rho a} p(a) m(a) da$$

he shows that the derivative of $y(\rho)$ with respect to ρ is:

$$\frac{dy(\rho)}{d\rho} = -A_B y(\rho),$$

or

$$d\rho = -\frac{dy(\rho)}{y(\rho) A_B}$$

(7.11)

where $A_B = \int_{\alpha}^{\beta} e^{-ra} p(a) a m(a) \, da$, the mean age of childbearing in the stable population.[3]

Equation (7.11) shows the connection between an error in the estimated value of r and the value of y that is produced. Suppose we choose an arbitrary value of r_0 and evaluate $y(r_0)$ using that value. If the trial value of $y(r_0)$ is 1.10, then the proportionate error in y is $+0.10$, since its true value should be 1.000. Equation (7.11) says that we have chosen too low a value of r, since an error in r produces an error in $y(r)$ (i.e., a deviation from 1.000) in the opposite direction. Our next trial value of r, r_1, should be raised by $0.10/A_B$. A value of A_B of 27 is reasonable to use for this purpose and will eventually get us to the right answer; we can't know the true value of A_B until we have solved for r. This process continues for a second and possibly a third round until the new value of r_n produces a value of $y(r_n)$ that is tolerably close to 1.000. In the next section, we will justify the procedure for choosing the initial value of $r_0 = \ln(NRR)/27$; again, any value will do if we are willing to endure a large enough number of steps in the iteration. Box 7.1 shows an example of the estimation of the intrinsic growth rate using Coale's iterative procedure. Box 7.2 presents a detailed example of the construction of a stable-equivalent population for the US in 1991. Both the actual and intrinsic age distributions are shown on figure 7.4.

Table 7.2 shows the value of the intrinsic growth rate, the crude rate of natural increase, and the net reproduction rate for a number of populations. For populations in Europe and North America, there is obviously a large discrepancy between the intrinsic growth rate and

Box 7.1 *Identification of the Intrinsic Growth Rate*

$_5L_a$ = Number of person-years lived between ages a and $a + 5$ (from female period life table with $l_0 = 1$)

$_5m_a$ = Rate of bearing female children between ages a and $a + 5$

$$r_0 = \frac{\ln NRR}{27} = \frac{\ln\left(\sum_{a=15,5}^{45} {_5L_a} \cdot {_5m_a}\right)}{27}$$

$$y(r_n) = \sum_{a=15,5}^{45} e^{-r_n(a+2.5)} {_5L_a} \cdot {_5m_a}$$

$$r_{n+1} = r_n + \frac{y(r_n) - 1}{27}$$

Example: Egypt, 1997

Age a	$_5L_a$	$_5m_a$	$_5L_a \cdot _5 m_a$	$r_0 =$ 0.01569	$r_1 =$ 0.01415	$r_2 =$ 0.01425	$r_3 =$ 0.01424
				\multicolumn{4}{c}{$e^{-r_n(a+2.5)} {_5L_a} \cdot _5 m_a$}			
15	4.66740	0.00567	0.02648	0.02012	0.02067	0.02063	0.02064
20	4.63097	0.06627	0.30687	0.21561	0.22322	0.22268	0.22273
25	4.58518	0.11204	0.51371	0.33371	0.34816	0.34714	0.34723
30	4.53206	0.07889	0.35751	0.21472	0.22575	0.22497	0.22504
35	4.46912	0.05075	0.22681	0.12595	0.13344	0.13291	0.13296
40	4.39135	0.01590	0.06982	0.03585	0.03828	0.03810	0.03812
45	4.28969	0.00610	0.02616	0.01242	0.01336	0.01329	0.01330
Sum			1.53	0.95838	1.00289	0.99973	1.00002

$NRR = 1.53$ daughters per woman

$r_0 = \ln(1.53)/27 = .01569$ $y(r_0) = .95838$

$r_1 = .01569 + (.95838 - 1)/27 = .01415$ $y(r_1) = 1.00289$

$r_2 = .01415 + (1.00289 - 1)/27 = .01425$ $y(r_2) = .99973$

$r_3 = .01425 + (.99973 - 1)/27 = .01424$ $y(r_3) = 1.00002$

After three iterations, we obtain .01424 for the intrinsic growth rate of Egypt in 1997.

Data source: United Nations, 1995.

the crude rate of natural increase; the rate of natural increase would fall if the fertility and mortality conditions were maintained. The disparity between the two rates indicates that large changes in fertility and/or mortality have occurred in the histories of these populations. For other countries, the disparity between the two rates is smaller, indicating that past changes in fertility and mortality had not seriously "destabilized" these population structures.

Box 7.2 *Construction of a Stable-equivalent Population*

$$_5C_a^{actual} = \frac{_5W_a}{\sum_{x=0}^{85} {_5W_a}} = \text{actual age structure of the population}$$

$$b = \frac{1}{\sum_{a=0.5}^{80} e^{-r(a+2.5)}\frac{_5L_a}{l_0}}$$

$$_5C_a^{stable} = be^{-r(a+2.5)}\frac{_5L_a}{l_0} = \text{stable-equivalent age structure of the population}$$

For age interval 85+: T_{85} is used instead of $_5L_{85}$; the age to which the e^{-ra} function is applied is $(85 + e_{85}^o)$, not 87.5.

Example: US, females, 1991; $l_0 = 100,000$

Age a	$_5C_a^{actual}$	$_5L_a$	$_5m_a$	$e^{-r(a+2.5)}\frac{_5L_a}{l_0}$	$_5C_a^{stable}$
0	0.0726	495,804		4.9603	0.0624
5	0.0689	495,002		4.9567	0.0623
10	0.0667	494,603	0.0007	4.9572	0.0623
15	0.0648	493,804	0.0303	4.9536	0.0623
20	0.0729	492,552	0.0566	4.9455	0.0622
25	0.0799	491,138	0.0578	4.9358	0.0621
30	0.0861	489,356	0.0388	4.9223	0.0619
35	0.0801	486,941	0.0157	4.9024	0.0617
40	0.0735	483,577	0.0027	4.8729	0.0613
45	0.0556	478,475	0.0001	4.8258	0.0607
50	0.0464	470,374		4.7484	0.0597
55	0.0421	457,712		4.6247	0.0582
60	0.0436	438,502		4.4346	0.0558
65	0.0429	410,756		4.1578	0.0523
70	0.0365	371,990		3.7688	0.0474
75	0.0294	319,192		3.2368	0.0407
80	0.0203	249,203		2.5293	0.0318
85+	0.0176	273,044		2.7759	0.0349
Sum	1.0000			79.5087	1.0000

$r = -.00018$ (See Box 7.1 for identification procedure)

$b = 1/79.5087 = .01258$

$d = b - r = .01258 - (-.00018) = .01276$

Note: in this example, $e_{85}^o = 6.79$.
Data source: National Center for Health Statistics, 1996.

7.5   The Relation between the Intrinsic Growth Rate and the Net Reproduction Rate

Calculation of the intrinsic growth rate and the net reproduction rate require exactly the same ingredients, $m(a)$ and $p(a)$ schedules for a particular population. And both measures are

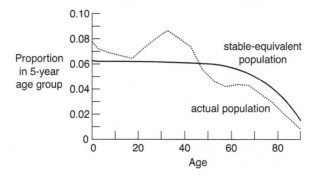

Figure 7.4 Comparison of actual and stable-equivalent age distribution, US, females, 1991.
Data source: National Center for Health Statistics, 1996.

Table 7.2: *Population parameters compared with stable-equivalent population parameters*

Country, year	NRR	Intrinsic rates (females)			Crude rates (females)		
		r	*b*	*d*	*CRNI*	*CBR*	*CDR*
United States, 1970–4	1.00	.0000	.0133	.0133	.0073	.0154	.0081
United States, 1978	0.86	−.0057	.0103	.0159	.0067	.0145	.0078
Belgium, 1978	0.80	−.0083	.0094	.0177	.0010	.0119	.0109
Fed. Rep. Germany, 1978	0.65	−.0145	.0066	.0211	−.0015	.0126	.0141
Sweden, 1975–9	0.81	−.0080	.0091	.0171	.0017	.0114	.0097
United States, 1975	0.88	−.0048	.0104	.0152	.0069	.0150	.0081
Panama, 1960–4	2.45	.0333	.0411	.0077	.0333	.0406	.0073
Venezuela, 1964	2.79	.0369	.0441	.0072	.0362	.0431	.0069
Malaysia, 1966–9	2.29	.0290	.0361	.0073	.0285	.0351	.0066
Sri Lanka, 1965	2.09	.0256	.0341	.0085	.0261	.0339	.0078
Taiwan, 1985	0.89	−.0042	.0111	.0153	.0141	.0180	.0039

Data source: Population Index, vol. 47, no. 2. (Summer 1981): pp. 402–15; Keyfitz and Flieger, 1990.

indicators of long-term growth prospects, one referring to an annual growth rate that will eventually apply if rates remain constant and the other to the growth factor between generations. It would be surprising if the two were not closely connected analytically. And they are.

Recall from chapter 5 that the formula for the net reproduction rate (5.19) is:

$$NRR = \int_{\alpha}^{\beta} p(a)m(a)da$$

The integral of $p(a)m(a)$ also "appears" inside formula (7.10), the formula that determines the value of the intrinsic growth rate. However, in this case $p(a)m(a)$ is being multiplied by e^{-ra} before it is summed across ages. The value of e^{-ra} will exceed 1.000 at all ages if r is negative, fall short of 1.000 if r is positive, and equal 1.000 if $r = 0$. Since the entire function in equation (7.10) must integrate to 1.000, it is necessarily true that:

If $NRR > 1.000$, then $r > 0$,
If $NRR < 1.000$, then $r < 0$,
If $NRR = 1.000$, then $r = 0$.

This relation between NRR and r only stands to reason: if the $p(a)$ and $m(a)$ schedules are such that a population will grow each generation (NRR exceeds 1.000), then it is logical that it would also be growing each year (r exceeds 0). Table 7.2 demonstrates these relations for actual populations.

The relation between the intrinsic growth rate and the net reproduction rate was formulated by Alfred Lotka in the following way:

$$NRR = e^{rT} \tag{7.12}$$

where T is termed the mean length of generation. T has no existence apart from this equation; the equation defines T. In particular, T is the length of time (in years) that it will take for a population growing at rate r to increase by the factor NRR. For example, if NRR is 2.000 and r is .025, T will be $\ln(2)/.025 = 27.73$. It will take the stable population 27.73 years to grow by the factor of intergenerational increase given by the NRR.

Although equation (7.12) defines T, it is intuitively clear that its value will depend in some way on the ages at which women bear children. In fact, the value of T is to a close approximation equal to the average of the mean age at childbearing in the stable population (A_B defined above) and the mean age of childbearing in a cohort subject to the $m(a)$ and $p(a)$ schedules (μ defined below) (Coale, 1972: 19):

$$A_B = \frac{\int_\alpha^\beta e^{-ra} p(a) a m(a) da}{\int_\alpha^\beta e^{-ra} p(a) m(a) da} \qquad \left(= \int_\alpha^\beta e^{-ra} p(a) a m(a) da \right)$$

$$\mu = \frac{\int_\alpha^\beta p(a) a m(a) da}{\int_\alpha^\beta p(a) m(a) da}$$

$$T \simeq \frac{A_B + \mu}{2}$$

Its value almost always lies between 26 and 33, with a mode around 27–8. For a tabulation of empirical T values, see Keyfitz and Flieger (1990).

Visualizing T to be something concrete related to the mean age of childbearing enables us to use equation (7.12) to illuminate the factors that determine long-term population growth rates. Rearranging the equation and taking natural logs of both sides gives:

$$r = \frac{\ln(NRR)}{T} \tag{7.13}$$

Let us now introduce Coale's useful approximation from chapter 5:

$$NRR = GRR \cdot p(A_M) \tag{7.14}$$

where *GRR* is the gross reproduction rate, i.e., the mean number of daughters that would be born to a cohort of women subject to the $m(a)$ schedule

$$GRR = \int_0^\infty m(a)da,$$

and $p(A_M)$ is the probability of surviving from birth to the mean age of childbearing,

$$A_M = \frac{\int_\alpha^\beta m(a)ada}{\int_\alpha^\beta m(a)da}.$$

If the proportion of births that are female is constant at S across ages of mothers, which is another very good approximation, then equation (7.14) becomes

$$NRR = TFR \cdot S \cdot p(A_M) \tag{7.15}$$

where *TFR* is the total fertility rate.

Finally, substituting the expression for *NRR* in equation (7.15) into the formula for *r* (equation 7.13) gives:

$$r = \frac{\ln TFR + \ln S + \ln p(A_M)}{T} \tag{7.16}$$

Equation (7.16) contains a number of valuable lessons. For one thing, it indicates that mortality and fertility levels have essentially separable influences on the intrinsic growth rate. That is to say, the mortality term and the fertility term in the numerator of (7.16) are additive in their effects on *r* rather than related to one another in some more complex fashion. To predict the effect of a change in fertility on the intrinsic growth rate of a population, one doesn't need to know the level of mortality.[4]

Second, the equation shows that the intrinsic growth rate is an additive function of the *log* of the total fertility rate, rather than of the rate itself. This feature of the equation has received little if any comment despite the fact that it has powerful implications for long-term population growth.

Suppose that we compare the intrinsic growth rates before and after a decline in the total fertility rate, and keep values of S, $p(A_M)$, and T constant. Then the change in the intrinsic growth rate resulting from a reduction in the TFR will simply be

$$\Delta r = \frac{\ln \left(\frac{TFR(2)}{TFR(1)} \right)}{T} \tag{7.17}$$

where $TFR(1)$ and $TFR(2)$ refer to the total fertility rates at times 1 and 2, before and after the change in fertility.

Thus, the effect on the intrinsic growth rate depends only on the proportionate decline in the TFR and not on the absolute decline. A decline in the TFR from 3 to 2 will have exactly the same impact as a decline from 6 to 4. A decline from 7 to 3.5 will have the same effect as a decline from 3.5 to 1.75. In terms of its impact on long-term growth rates, fertility reduction clearly has increasing returns.

This result simply reflects the fact that the long-term growth rate of a population depends on how large one generation is relative to the previous generation. If the factor of growth from one generation to the next is multiplied by 1.5 – whether it results from an increase in the TFR from 2 to 3 or from 4 to 6 – then the effect is to raise the growth rate by approximately $\ln(1.5)/27.5 = 0.015$, where 27.5 is used as the value of T.

Table 7.3 shows the effect of a decline of the TFR by one child on the intrinsic growth rate of different regions of the world during 1995–2000. Clearly, the effect is smallest in Africa, where fertility rates are the highest, and greatest in Europe, where they are lowest. A decline of one child per woman in Europe would reduce the TFR of this region by more than 50 percent and lead to extremely rapid population decline at a rate of 0.056 per year. The rate of population decline would be much faster than the rate of population growth in any region during any substantial period of the twentieth century.

On the other hand, for those programs aimed at reducing rates of population growth in developing countries, equation (7.16) represents good news. Even though the process of fertility reduction may slow down as lower levels of fertility are achieved, the impact of any particular decline on the long-term growth rate will increase. Bongaarts (e.g., 1982) and others have usefully demonstrated how the biosocial components of the TFR typically change with its average level across populations. In order to understand the growth implications of changes in biosocial components, one must also recognize that changes in TFR induce quite different impacts on rates of population growth across these levels.

Finally, equation (7.16) shows that the value of T may have an important effect on the intrinsic growth rate. Coale and Tye (1961) discussed the case of growing populations, showing that if r is positive, then increasing the ages of reproduction will reduce r even if the TFR stays constant; the factor of growth across generations will be stretched out across more years because the mean length of generation is increased. Increasing T from 28 to 32 would multiply the intrinsic growth rate by the factor of 0.875. Analogously, and perhaps more surprisingly, when the intrinsic growth rate is negative, as in contemporary Europe, increasing T by delaying childbearing

Table 7.3: *Effect of a decline of the TFR by one child on the intrinsic growth rate of various regions*

Region	Level 1995–2000			
	TFR	NRR	r	Δr
Africa	5.31	2.03	.026	−.008
Eastern Asia	1.78	.80	−.008	−.030
South-central Asia	3.42	1.43	.013	−.013
Southeastern Asia	2.86	1.27	.009	−.016
Western Asia	3.82	1.70	.019	−.011
Europe	1.45	.69	−.013	−.043
Latin America and Carribean	2.65	1.22	.007	−.017
Northern America	1.93	.93	−.003	−.027

Data source: United Nations, 1997.
Assumption: $T = 27.5$.

would actually raise the intrinsic growth rate, i.e., make it less negative. The factor of decline from one generation to the next would be stretched over a longer period of years between generations. The intrinsic (stable-equivalent) age distribution would have more women towards the end of their childbearing years than towards the beginning. Thus, delaying childbearing in the lifetimes of women, e.g., by sliding the age-specific fertility schedule upwards along the age axis, would actually increase the birth rate by raising fertility among the more numerous older women.[5]

The impact of generational length on population growth has been recognized in population policies that attempt to delay childbearing to older ages, as in China's policy of "later, longer, fewer." For an explicit consideration of how much change in population growth would be produced by shifts in Chinese ages of childbearing, see Bongaarts and Greenhalgh (1985).

In the previous section, we discussed how to solve for the intrinsic growth rate given age-specific rates of fertility and mortality, but did not justify how to choose an initial trial value for r_0 to begin the iteration process. Equation (7.13) provides a simple strategy: first calculate the net reproduction rate, using the procedure in chapter 5, and then divide by some number like 27 or 29 as an estimate of T. Again, we cannot know T exactly until we have solved for r, but the narrow range of values that T assumes provides a useful tactic for identifying r.

7.6 The Effects of Changes in Fertility and Mortality on Age Structure, Growth Rates, Birth Rates, and Death Rates

The single most important lesson of the stable population model is that, if fertility and mortality rates have been constant over a long enough period (say, 70 years), then the age structure of the population will also be constant. This result means that the *levels* of fertility and mortality are irrelevant to whether a population is aging or growing younger; only *changes* in fertility or mortality can produce *changes* in population age structure.

The stable model is a convenient vehicle for studying the long-term impact of changes in fertility and mortality on the age structure and other demographic features of a population. The standard approach is what economists call "comparative statics." This approach compares two stable populations that differ from one another in some specifiable feature of fertility or mortality conditions. The exercise is equivalent to asking what would eventually happen to a previously stable population if a change in fertility or mortality were imposed. The structure of the post-change population is examined after the population has come to rest at the new stable equilibrium. That structure is then compared to the structure of the stable population before the change. The dynamics of transition to the new equilibrium are ignored; the stable population theorem assures us that a new equilibrium will be achieved.

A related question is sometimes asked but cannot be answered: what is the effect of a change in the rate of population growth on a population's age structure? This question cannot be answered because the rate of population growth is itself an outcome of fertility and mortality rates. Changes in fertility and mortality rates have radically different impacts on a population's age structure, as we shall see, so we would have to know the source of the change in growth rates before we could begin to address the question posed. It is far more precise to view the population growth rate and age structure as joint products of fertility and mortality conditions.

For handy reference, let us reprint here the three basic equations that characterize a stable population:

$$b = \frac{1}{\int_0^\omega e^{-ra} p(a)da} \tag{7.8}$$

$$c(a) = be^{-ra} p(a) \tag{7.9}$$

$$1 = \int_\alpha^\beta e^{-ra} p(a)m(a)da \tag{7.10}$$

7.6.1 Effect of changes in fertility

Let us consider more explicitly than in section 5 what will happen to a stable population in which the life table remains constant but fertility increases at all ages. The increase in $m(a)$ values would cause an imbalance in equation (7.10) unless there were a compensating change in r (since $p(a)$ is assumed to be fixed). To keep the left-hand side of this equation equal to 1.000, r must increase so that the value of e^{-ra} decreases at all ages. Therefore, in the long run, an increase in fertility levels will raise the rate of population growth. This result is hardly surprising and simply confirms intuition.

What effect will the increase in fertility and r have on the birth rate? In (7.8), the denominator of the expression for the birth rate will decrease, so that the birth rate will increase. Again, hardly surprising.

The effect on the age structure of a fertility-induced increase in r can be found by differentiating the logarithm of the expression for the proportionate age distribution in (7.9) with respect to r (Lotka, 1939; Keyfitz, 1985: 186):

$$\frac{d \ln[c(a)]}{dr} = \frac{d\{(-ra) + \ln[p(a)] - \ln[\int_0^\omega e^{-ra} p(a)da]\}}{dr}$$

$$= -a + \frac{\int_0^\omega ae^{-ra} p(a)da}{\int_0^\omega e^{-ra} p(a)da}$$

This last expression is the mean age of the stable population,

$$A_P = \frac{\int_0^\omega c(a)ada}{\int_0^\omega c(a)da}$$

So:

$$\frac{d \ln[c(a)]}{dr} = A_P - a \tag{7.18}$$

(7.18) is sheer poetry. It says in one compact and elegant expression that when fertility increases, the new stable population will have a larger proportion at ages below the mean age of the population (where the derivative is positive) and a smaller proportion at all ages above the mean age (where it is negative). The old and new proportionate age distributions will cross at the mean age (remember that derivatives involve infinitesimal changes, so that the mean age

Table 7.4: *Effect of a 20 percent fertility increase on the intrinsic demographic rates of the United States in 1991*

	Before fertility increase	After fertility increase
NRR	0.99560	1.19472
Intrinsic growth rate	−0.00018	0.00675
Intrinsic birth rate	0.01258	0.01650
Intrinsic death rate	0.01276	0.00975

Data source: National Center for Health Statistics, 1996.

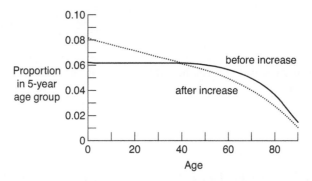

Figure 7.5 Effect of a 20 percent fertility increase on the stable-equivalent age distribution of the United States in 1991
Data source: National Center for Health Statistics, 1996.

will change infinitesimally). The proportion will change more the further an age is from the mean age. For non-infinitesimal changes, the crossing will occur at (approximately) the mean of the two mean ages of the stable populations. Table 7.4 shows the effect of a 20 percent fertility increase on the intrinsic demographic rates of the United States in 1991, and the effect on the stable-equivalent age distribution is shown on figure 7.5.

The effect of a change in fertility on the death rate can be derived in a similar way. Express the death rate as:

$$d = \int_0^\omega c(a)\mu(a)da = \int_0^\omega be^{-ra}p(a)\mu(a)da = b \cdot \int_0^\omega e^{-ra}p(a)\mu(a)da$$

Taking the logarithm and its derivative with respect to r, gives:

$$\frac{d\ln(d)}{dr} = \frac{d\ln(b)}{dr} + \frac{\frac{d}{dr}\int_0^\omega e^{-ra}p(a)\mu(a)da}{\int_0^\omega e^{-ra}p(a)\mu(a)da}$$

The first term can be obtained by computing the derivative of

$$-\ln\left(\int_0^\omega e^{-ra}p(a)da\right)$$

Alternatively, we can use equation (7.18) when age equals 0, so:

$$\frac{d\ln(b)}{dr} = A_P$$

The second term is:

$$-\frac{\int_0^\omega ae^{-ra}p(a)\mu(a)da}{\int_0^\omega e^{-ra}p(a)\mu(a)da} = -\frac{\int_0^\omega be^{-ra}p(a)\mu(a)ada}{\int_0^\omega be^{-ra}p(a)\mu(a)da}$$

$$= -\frac{\int_0^\omega c(a)\mu(a)ada}{\int_0^\omega c(a)\mu(a)da} = -A_D$$

where A_D is the mean age at death in the stable population. The derivative of the logarithm of the death rate is then:

$$\frac{d\ln(d)}{dr} = A_P - A_D \tag{7.19}$$

This expression shows that the death rate will fall when fertility rises if the mean age at death exceeds the mean age of the population, i.e., if deaths are skewed towards the higher ages. This will be the case in most populations but not all. Young populations with high mortality may have a mean age at death below the mean age of the population, so that an increase in fertility actually raises the death rate by giving more weight to the high mortality rates at very young ages. No populations in the contemporary world, but many in the past, have the required configuration. Today, increases in fertility will invariably reduce the crude death rate in the long run (Preston, 1972).

7.6.2 Effects of changes in mortality

The consequences of a change in mortality cannot be expressed so compactly because they depend upon the ages at which mortality changes. A decline in the age-specific death rate at age x will raise the $p(a)$ values at all ages above x. Equation (7.10) shows that an increase in the $p(a)$ function at some or all ages below β will, other things equal, change the value of the integral. An increase in the growth rate must occur to restore the equality. So as intuition suggests, a decline in mortality will speed long-term population growth.

There is, however, one exception. If the only declines in mortality occur above age β, the highest age of childbearing, then there will be no effect on the intrinsic growth rate. The reason is that a change in mortality beyond the ages of childbearing will have no effect on the annual flow of births, whose rate of growth ultimately determines the growth rate of the stable population. The new population will be larger than the old population after postreproductive mortality is reduced, but it will eventually be growing at the same rate in the steady state.

A simple expression for the impact of mortality change on the intrinsic growth rate can be derived from equation (7.13) by assuming that all childbearing occurs at one age, A^o. Then

A_M and T will both equal A^o and the equation simplifies to:

$$r = \frac{\ln[p(A^o)] + \ln[GRR]}{A^o}$$

$$= \frac{-\int_0^{A^o} \mu(a)da + \ln[GRR]}{A^o}$$

$$= -\bar{\mu}(0, A^o) + \frac{\ln[GRR]}{A^o} \qquad \text{(7.20)}$$

where $\bar{\mu}(0, A^o)$ is the (unweighted) mean death rate in the age interval 0 to A^o. When mortality falls, the increase in the growth rate will equal the decline in the mean age-specific death rate between birth and the age of childbearing. What may be surprising is that all ages below A^o receive equal weight in this expression; mortality changes at age 12 have the same impact as changes in infancy. The reason is that they have the same effect on the probability of surviving to the age of reproduction and hence on the annual flow of births.

The effect of mortality decline on the stable age distribution is more complex to analyze. As a general rule, the effects are not large. In one instance, termed a "neutral" mortality change, there will be no effect whatsoever. A neutral mortality change is produced by an equal absolute decline in death rates at all ages:

$$\mu'(a) = \mu(a) - k \quad \text{for } a \geq 0$$

The prime identifies the age-specific death rate after the change in mortality. In this case, mortality has declined by an annualized amount k at all ages. When $\mu(a)$ changes in this fashion, the effect on the $p(a)$ function will be:

$$p'(a) = e^{-\int_0^a [\mu(x)-k]dx}$$

$$= p(a)e^{ka}$$

The effect on r of a neutral decline in mortality of amount k will be an increase in the growth rate of amount k. This result is seen by equating the prechange and postchange versions of (7.10) to one another, which follows from the fact that they must both equal 1.000:

$$1 = \int_\alpha^\beta e^{-ra} p(a)m(a)da = \int_\alpha^\beta e^{-r'a} p(a)e^{ka}m(a)da$$

These last two integrals can only equal one another if $r' = r + k$. Finally, let's examine the effect on the age distribution, given by (7.9):

$$c'(a) = \frac{e^{-r'a}p'(a)}{\int_0^\omega e^{-r'x}p'(x)dx} = \frac{e^{-(r+k)a}p(a)e^{ka}}{\int_0^\omega e^{-(r+k)x}p(x)e^{kx}dx}$$

$$= \frac{e^{-ra}p(a)}{\int_0^\omega e^{-rx}p(x)dx} = c(a)$$

So a neutral mortality change has no effect on the age distribution. Accordingly, it will have no effect on the birth rate, since age-specific fertility rates are unchanged. The death rate will fall by amount k to keep the balancing equation in balance.

That a mortality reduction may have no effect on the age distribution comes as a shock to many people. A mortality reduction will increase life expectancy and result in greater survivorship to older ages. Why doesn't this make the population older? This kind of common-sense reasoning, focusing on a cohort life cycle, fails to account for the fact that cohorts bear children. Reduced mortality will increase the flow of births. In the case of a neutral mortality reduction in amount k, each 1-year survival probability will increase by the factor e^k. Therefore, the number of people one year after the mortality decline will grow by the same factor at each age. With constant fertility, the number of births will also grow by this factor and the age distribution will be undisturbed.

A neutral mortality decline becomes the standard against which actual mortality declines must be compared. Declines that are uniform by age except for larger declines in infancy will make a population younger; declines that are uniform by age except for unusually large decline at older ages (say, above 50) will make a population older. A (nonneutral) decline concentrated in infancy will have the same effect on age structure as an increase in fertility because an age distribution can't tell the difference between children who die in early infancy and births that never occurred. Analogous to the fertility increase analyzed in the previous section, a mortality decline in infancy alone will pivot the stable age distribution about its mean age.

Knowing the effect of an actual decline in mortality on the stable age distribution thus becomes a question of identifying the ages at which declines are exceptionally large. As shown above, what matters is the absolute decline in age-specific death rates and not the relative or proportionate decline. Empirically, the typical pattern of mortality decline shows unusually large declines below age 5 and above age 45. As shown in figure 7.6, the left leg dominates the right leg; the largest declines occur in infancy.

As a result, mortality declines have, throughout human history, tended to make populations younger. Once a population reaches a life expectancy of approximately 65 years, subsequent mortality declines tend to produce an older population. Because they typically induce a mild decline in the proportion of the population of childbearing ages, mortality declines have exerted a slight depressing effect on the crude birth rate. Table 7.5 shows the effect of mortality decline

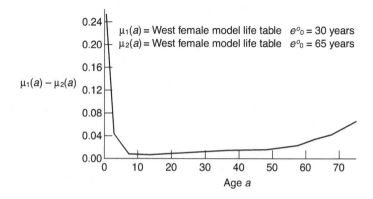

Figure 7.6 Typical pattern of mortality decline
Source: Coale (1972: 35)

Table 7.5: *Effect of mortality decline on intrinsic growth and age structure*

Change in life expectancy at birth	Corresponding absolute change in:			
	Intrinsic growth rate	Mean age of the population	Proportion aged 0 to 14 years	Proportion aged 65 and over
from 40 to 50 years	+0.0068	−0.83	+1.98%	−0.01%
from 50 to 60 years	+0.0054	−0.71	+1.62%	−0.12%
from 60 to 70 years	+0.0040	−0.34	+1.03%	+0.14%
from 70 to 80 years	+0.0021	+0.60	−0.10%	+1.20%

Data source: Coale and Demeny (1983) West model female life table, combined with a GRR of 2.

on the intrinsic growth rate and the intrisic age-structure of a theoretical population with a GRR of 2 and a model age pattern of mortality (see section 9.1). For more details, see Coale (1972) or Preston (1974).

The stable model provides information about the long-term effects of changes in fertility and mortality on the age distribution. Understanding the short-term effects does not require this elegant machinery. When a permanent fertility increase is initiated at time t, the number of persons below age 1 will be higher at time $t + 1$, the number of persons below age 2 will be higher at $t + 2$, and so on. Eventually, the additional births begin to have births themselves and the stable model becomes increasingly instructive. Likewise, a permanent reduction in death rates at age x at time t will increase the number of persons aged x to $x + 1$ at time $t + 1$, the numbers aged x to $x + 2$ at time $t + 2$, and so on. The stable model provides a means of investigating the ultimate impact of such a change (Keyfitz, 1972).

7.7 The Momentum of Population Growth

One valuable application of the stable population model by Keyfitz (1971) relates to population size rather than to age composition or vital rates. Keyfitz asked what would happen to the size of a previously growing stable population if its fertility rates were immediately reduced to the replacement level (NRR = 1.000) and maintained thereafter at the new level until the new stable equilibrium is attained. In this case, the new equilibrium is a stationary population of fixed size. The manner in which replacement-level fertility is achieved is by having all age-specific fertility rates reduced proportionally by the factor 1/NRR, where NRR refers to the pre-decline net reproduction rate. The answer is that these populations would continue to grow, often by sizable amounts. This demonstration proved influential in policy circles because it demonstrated how difficult it would be to halt population growth even after fertility had fallen to replacement levels.

The original Keyfitz formulation had several limitations. First, it required that the initial population on which replacement-level fertility was imposed be "stable," i.e., that it have had constant fertility and mortality conditions for the preceding 70–100 years. Few contemporary populations come close to meeting this criterion. Second, he required that replacement-level fertility be achieved by applying a scalar multiple to the fertility rates in the initial population. However, the shape of the age-profile of fertility typically changes as levels of fertility change. Third, the expression developed for population momentum was cumbersome and did not make intuitively clear the factors on which momentum is based.

Keyfitz himself provided the basis for a more general expression (Keyfitz, 1985: 155–7). Using Lotka's integral equation for the birth trajectory in a population subject to constant vital rates, Keyfitz showed that, when replacement fertility rates, $m^*(a)$, are imposed on a closed population whose age distribution is $N(a)$ and survival function $p(a)$, the annual number of births in the eventual stationary population will be:[6]

$$B_S = \frac{\int_0^\beta N(a) \int_a^\beta \frac{p(y)}{p(a)} m^*(y)\, dy\, da}{A^*},$$

where A^* is the mean age at birth in the stationary population. By expressing the function $\int_a^\beta p(y)m^*(y)dy/A^*$ as $w(a)$ and rearranging, we can simplify this expression to:

$$B_S = \int_0^\beta \frac{N(a)}{p(a)} \cdot w(a)da$$

The eventual size of the stationary population is:

$$N_S = B_S \cdot e_0^o = \int_0^\beta \frac{N(a)}{p(a)} \cdot w(a)da \cdot e_0^o$$

Now dividing N_S by the initial population size gives the expression for population momentum in any closed population (Preston and Guillot, 1997):

$$M = \frac{N_S}{N} = \int_0^\beta \frac{N(a)}{N} \cdot \frac{e_0^o}{p(a)} \cdot w(a)da$$

or

$$M = \int_0^\beta \frac{c(a)}{c_S(a)} \cdot w(a)da \qquad\qquad \textbf{(7.21)}$$

Equation (7.21) involves three distributions, each of which sums across age intervals to 1.000. One, $c(a)$, is the proportionate age distribution of the population at the time when replacement-level fertility is imposed; the second, $c_S(a)$, is the proportionate age distribution of the stationary population that will eventually emerge after replacement-level fertility has been in place for many years. This latter age distribution is completely a function of the population's life table or survival function, $p(a)$. Because this survival function inevitably declines from age to age, so does the stationary population age distribution; there are more people at age 0 than at any other age.

The third distribution in equation (7.21), $w(a)$, is less familiar. The numerator is the expected lifetime births that will occur above age a in the replacement-level fertility regime,

$$\int_a^\beta p(y)m^*(y)dy.$$

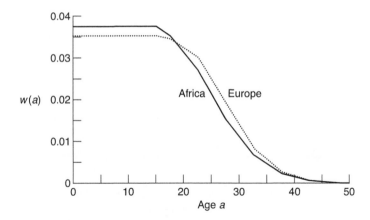

Figure 7.7 $w(a)$ functions in Africa and Europe
Data source: United Nations, 1994, 1997; Coale and Demeny, 1983.

The denominator is the (unweighted) sum of those expected births over all ages, which is equal to A^*, the mean age at birth in the stationary population.[7] The shape of the $w(a)$ function will be very similar from population to population. It has a maximum value of $1/A^*$ at all ages from 0 to 15, presuming that 15 is the earliest age of childbearing. It then descends steadily to a value of 0 at age 50, assumed to be the maximum age of childbearing. Figure 7.7 shows the estimated $w(a)$ functions in Africa and Europe, using United Nations estimates of regional mortality and a "late" replacement-level fertility pattern in Europe and a "medium" replacement-level fertility pattern in Africa (United Nations, 1995: 150). Clearly, the patterns of $w(a)$ are similar in shape despite the regional differences in the age patterns of mortality and fertility that they embody.

So equation (7.21) shows that the momentum of a population is a relatively simple function of disparities between its actual age distribution and the eventual stationary age distribution. If the proportions are higher in the actual population than in the stationary population at ages where $w(a)$ is high, i.e., below age 15, 20, or 25, then the momentum factor will exceed 1.00 (see also Kim et al., 1991). If the proportions are lower in the actual population than in the stationary population at these ages, then momentum will be less than unity and population size will fall after replacement-level fertility is imposed. If the initial age distribution is already stationary ($c(a) = c_S(a)$ at all ages), then of course $M = 1.00$.

Equation (7.21) helps show why the momentum factor has typically exceeded 1.00 in developing countries. Because population growth has been positive, the proportion of young people is higher than in the eventual stationary population. As we showed earlier in this chapter, a growing stable population will have a higher proportion at all ages below the mean age of the population than a stationary population with the same mortality level, and the proportionate disparity will grow as the distance from the mean age increases (Keyfitz, 1968b). On the other hand, a stable population with a negative growth rate will have smaller proportions at young ages than in the eventual stationary population. Figure 7.8 presents the $c(a)/c_S(a)$ ratio for initially stable populations with life expectancies of 70 years and growth rates of $+.02$ and $-.02$.

Table 7.6 shows the value of population momentum for the major regions of the world in 1997, and for several countries with low fertility. If fertility were to decline to the replacement

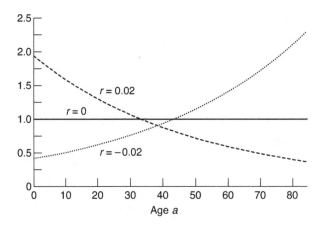

Figure 7.8 $c(a)/c_s(a)$ ratio for initially stable populations with life expectancy at birth of 70 years
Data source: Coale and Demeny, 1983.

Table 7.6: *Value of population momentum for the major regions of the world and selected countries*

Region or country	Population momentum
Africa	1.56
Eastern Asia	1.22
South-central Asia	1.47
Southeastern Asia	1.48
Western Asia	1.56
Europe	.98
Latin America and Carribean	1.48
Northern America	1.10
Austria	.96
Russia	.94
Italy	.91
Germany	.88
World total	1.35

Source: Preston and Guillot, 1997.

level in 1997, the populations of Africa and Western Asia would grow by the largest factor, 1.56. This growth simply reflects the youthfulness of the current population age structures in these regions. The population of Europe would decline by 2 percent. The momentum factor of 0.98 for Europe is an average across countries some of whom have factors greater than one and others of whom are below 1.00. Russia, Austria, Italy, and Germany have momentum factors below 1.00, with Germany occupying the lower limb of the distribution at 0.88. Clearly, there can be a momentum to population decline as well as to population growth. The details of the procedure needed to estimate population momentum with actual discrete data are shown in box 7.3.

Box 7.3 (part 1) *Estimation of Population Momentum*

1. Data

$_5N_a^F$ = number of women aged a to $a + 5$ in the actual population

$_5L_a^F$ = person-years lived between ages a and $a + 5$ in the actual female life table with a radix of unity

N_F = total number of females in the population

N_M = total number of males in the population

e_0^{oF} = female life expectancy at birth

e_0^{oM} = male life expectancy at birth

2. Estimation of replacement-level fertility rates in the studied population

$_5m_a$ = actual age-specific maternity rates

$$NRR = \sum_{a=15}^{45} {_5m_a} \cdot {_5L_a^F} = \text{actual Net Reproduction Rate}$$

$$_5m_a^* = \frac{_5m_a}{NRR} = \text{replacement-level age-specific maternity rates}$$

3. Estimation of the ultimate number of females births in the stationary population

$$A^* = \sum_{a=15}^{45} (a + 2.5) \cdot {_5m_a^*} \cdot {_5L_a^F} = \text{mean age at birth in the stationary population}$$

$$_5w_a = \frac{\left(\frac{_5L_a^F}{2} \cdot {_5m_a^*} + \sum_{y=a+5}^{45} {_5L_y^F} \cdot {_5m_a^*} \right)}{A^*}$$

$$B_S^F = \sum_{a=0}^{45} \frac{_5N_a^F}{_5L_a^F/5} \cdot {_5w_a}$$

4. Estimation of ultimate population and momentum

$N_S^F = B_S^F \cdot e_0^{oF}$ = number of females in the ultimate population

$N_S^M = B_S^F \cdot SRB \cdot e_0^{oM}$ = number of males in the ultimate population (SRB = sex ratio at birth)

$$\text{Population momentum} = M = \frac{N_S^F + N_S^M}{N^F + N^M}$$

Population momentum is one of the most widely misunderstood phenomena in demography. Typically, a momentum factor larger than 1.00 is said to reflect the youthful age structure of the population on which replacement-level fertility is imposed. As we have seen, this is a correct intuition. Ironically, it owes nothing to Keyfitz's (1971) original formula for momentum, which had no term directly characterizing the age structure.

But then most commentators go on to say that the momentum of population growth reflects the large numbers of persons who must still pass through the childbearing interval, implying an enormity of reproductive potential. This implication is perhaps too vague to be called incorrect, but it is certainly misleading. After replacement-level fertility is imposed, the youthful cohorts already born will simply replace themselves; they will not give rise to an unprecedented number of births. In fact, if mortality has been constant, the annual number of births

Box 7.3 (part 2)

Example: Western Asia, 1995–2000

Age a	$_5N_a^F$ (thousands)	$_5L_a^F$	$_5m_a$	$_5m_a \cdot {}_5L_a^F$	$_5m_a^*$	$_5m_a^* \cdot {}_5L_a^F$	$(a+2.5) \cdot {}_5m_a^* \cdot {}_5L_a^F$	$_5w_a$	$\frac{_5N_a^F}{_5L_a^F/5} \cdot {}_5w_a$
0	12,023	4.834						.03759	468
5	11,027	4.803						.03759	432
10	9,856	4.789						.03759	387
15	8,614	4.773	0.043	0.205	0.025	0.121	2.11	.03533	319
20	7,694	4.748	0.112	0.532	0.066	0.312	7.03	.02719	220
25	6,893	4.716	0.112	0.528	0.066	0.310	8.53	.01549	113
30	6,135	4.678	0.058	0.271	0.034	0.159	5.18	.00667	44
35	5,318	4.631	0.029	0.134	0.017	0.079	2.96	.00219	13
40	4,376	4.570	0.007	0.032	0.004	0.019	0.80	.00035	2
45	3,510	4.483	0.000	0.000	0.000	0.000	0.00	.00000	0
Sum				1.703		1.000	26.60		1,996

$$N_F = 87{,}176; \quad e_0^{oF} = 70.30 \text{ years}$$

$$N_M = 91{,}845; \quad e_0^{oM} = 65.90 \text{ years}$$

$$\text{Actual NRR} = 1.703; \quad A^* = 26.60 \text{ years}$$

$$B_S^F = 1{,}996$$

$$N_S^F = 1{,}996 \cdot 70.30 = 140{,}332$$

$$N_S^M = 1{,}996 \cdot 1.05 \cdot 65.90 = 138{,}126$$

$$M = \frac{140{,}332 + 138{,}126}{87{,}176 + 91{,}845} = 1.56$$

Data source: United Nations, 1994, 1995.

after replacement-level fertility is imposed will simply be a weighted average of the annual number of births *before* replacement-level fertility is imposed (Preston, 1988). Immediately after replacement-level fertility is first imposed, the weighting function determining the annual number of births will be precisely the $w(a)$ function identified above, where $w(a)$ is the weight to be applied to the number of births occurring a years earlier (Preston, 1988). If mortality has been improving, then the annual number of births immediately after replacement fertility is achieved is initially *below* this weighted average of births.

The suggestion that births will grow after replacement-level fertility is imposed is correct not for a before/after comparison but only for an after/after comparison. Once replacement-level fertility is in place, the number of births will increase for a generation or so in a previously-growing population as the population of reproductive age grows. But there will be no more births in the post-replacement population than in the population *before* replacement-level fertility is achieved. The change in the number of post-replacement births from year to year reflects shifts in the weighting function applied to the time series of births.

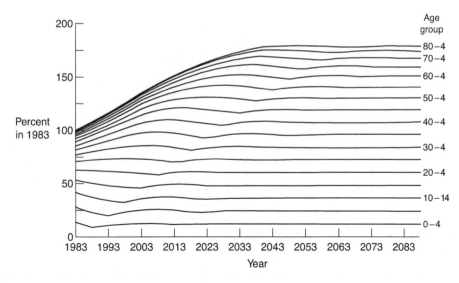

Figure 7.9 Momentum and evolution of age-groups, Mexico, 1983
Source: Keyfitz and Flieger, 1990; Kim et al., 1991.

In rapidly growing populations, population momentum results from the fact the cohorts at older ages at the time when replacement-level fertility is imposed were much smaller at birth than the cohorts who will subsequently age into the older years. As they are replaced at older ages by later-born cohorts, the population at these ages will grow. So population momentum in a previously growing population is coincident with population aging, as illustrated on figure 7.9. Preston (1986) shows that all of the growth in population after replacement-level fertility is achieved typically occurs above some age near the middle of the childbearing interval. Kim et al. (1991) and Kim and Schoen (1993) provide more precise expressions for identifying this age. Some explicit connections between momentum and aging are developed by Kim and Schoen (1997).

If fertility were below the replacement level at the time when replacement-level fertility is imposed, the situation would be reversed; populations may grow younger after replacement-level fertility is achieved. This would surely happen if the initial population were stable with a negative growth rate, as shown in figure 7.8. However, there are no empirical examples of such a population (although Japanese fertility has been below the replacement level for 40 years). In all empirical cases, below-replacement fertility has been achieved by declines from above-replacement fertility in the lifetime of cohorts still alive. In this case, age distributional changes resulting from the imposition of replacement-level fertility will be more complex. Figure 7.10 compares the age distribution of Europe's population in 1997 to that of the stationary population implied by Europe's life table of 1997.

7.8   Uses of the Stable Population Model in Demographic Estimation

If a population is demographically stable – its age composition is constant – then all of the equations of a stable population will apply. This statement may be confusing in light of the demonstration in the previous section that a neutral change in mortality will have no impact on

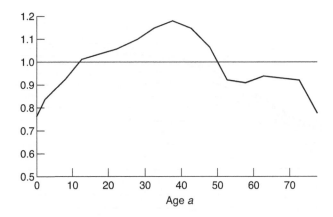

Figure 7.10 $c(a)/c_s(a)$ function in Europe in 1997
Data source: United Nations, 1994, 1997.

the age distribution, while at the same time it clearly violates one of the conditions creating a stable population. This is an instance (the only such instance) in which a stable population is subject to a demographic perturbation and instantaneously achieves a new stable equilibrium at the new vital rates. Equations based on the old rates will apply before the change, and equations based on the new rates will apply immediately after the change. More generally, historical patterns of mortality change have had much less impact on age structure than have patterns of fertility change, and stable equations have sometimes been applied without introducing major distortions even in instances where sizable mortality change has occurred.

Until 1950 or so, most populations in Asia, Africa, and Latin America were, to a close approximation, demographically stable. While they had typically experienced some mortality decline, the declines were not such as to invalidate the applicability of the stable equations. Demographers often used stable population methods to investigate the properties of such populations. The permutations were many. The most influential and valuable procedures were developed by Coale and Demeny (United Nations, 1967). These invariably started with a census age distribution. One other piece of information was required, usually an intercensal growth rate. Coale and Demeny also developed a set of "model" life tables for use in such applications (see section 9.1). These tables showed the typical pattern of age-specific death rates and other life table functions for populations at a particular level of mortality, as indexed by life expectancy at birth. One application of the stable equations combined with model life tables was made by Arriaga (1968), who rewrote equation (7.9) as:

$$\ln[c(a)/p(a)] = \ln[b] - r \cdot a$$

He then used trial and error to find the $p(a)$ function in a set of model life tables that produced a slope of $\ln[c(a)/p(a)]$ that was closest to the observed intercensal growth rate, r. The procedure also supplies an estimate of the stable birth rate as the intercept (in log form) of this equation; another estimate can be obtained from equation (7.8). Arriaga produced life tables for historic populations in Latin America using this method. Coale and Demeny recommended a procedure based upon the cumulative age distribution rather than upon $c(a)$ itself, since the cumulative distribution is less sensitive to errors in age reporting.

The stable population model can also be used for demographic estimation at older ages when information for these ages is aggregated into one single, open-ended age interval. In chapter 3, we estimated the life expectancy at the age starting the open-ended age interval by taking the reciprocal of the death rate in that interval. Specifically, for an open-ended age interval starting at age a, we estimated e_a^o by simply taking $1/{}_\infty M_a$. This formula would be correct if the population in that interval were stationary, in which case ${}_\infty M_a = {}_\infty m_a$. In most populations, however, this assumption is not valid. Mortality at older ages has been declining, and as a result, the older population has been growing rather than stationary. This growing older population will produce a death rate, ${}_\infty M_a$, that typically underestimates ${}_\infty m_a$, the death rate that would be observed if the population were stationary and had the actual $\mu(x)$ function. The estimated e_a^o using $1/{}_\infty M_a$ would thus overestimate the true e_a^o. For example, in Sweden in 1995, ${}_\infty M_{85}$ was equal to 0.1528, which produces a life expectancy of 6.54 at age 85. This overestimates the true e_{85}^o, estimated by more accurate methods, by 0.44 years.

The use of the stable population model permits one to improve the accuracy of the estimated value of e_a^o when detailed data at older ages is not available. With the assumptions that the force of mortality above age a follows a Gompertz curve (see section 9.1 for a definition of the Gompertz curve) and that the population above that age a follows a stable distribution, Horiuchi and Coale (1982) derived an equation for e_a^o that requires information on the growth rate of the last age group $({}_\infty r_a)$ in addition to ${}_\infty M_a$, the death rate in that age group:

$$e_a^o = \frac{1}{{}_\infty M_a} \cdot \exp\{-.0951 \cdot {}_\infty r_a \cdot ({}_\infty M_a)^{-1.4}\}, \quad \text{for } a \geq 65 \qquad \textbf{(7.22)}$$

When used for Sweden with ${}_\infty M_{85} = .152807$ and ${}_\infty r_{85} = .0347$ in 1995, equation (7.22) gives a life expectancy at age 85 of 6.25 years, which is only 0.15 years above the true value. This equation can be used for open-ended age intervals starting at any age above and including 65.

Horiuchi and Coale's equation can also be adapted for estimating ${}^*e_a^{-i}$, the life expectancy at age a in the absence of cause i. In chapter 4, we used the traditional method which assumes that ${}^*_\infty m_a^{-i} = {}_\infty m_a^{-i}$ (and $= {}_\infty M_a^{-i}$ if no official "master" life table is available). Horiuchi and Coale's formula allows us to refine the estimate of ${}^*e_a^{-i}$ with the same assumptions used for equation (7.22). We must recognize that the operation of "other" causes of death on the actual age distribution (that is, the causes other than the one whose implications we are attempting to model) is analogous to the operation of the growth process. Both population growth and the presence of extraneous causes serve to make the actual distribution younger than the stationary distribution that would result from the operation of a particular decrement alone. This suggests that we treat the death rate from cause i exactly analogously to the growth rate in attempting to model the implications of the operation of cause $(-i)$ alone. The analogy would be exact if the death rate from cause i were constant at ages a and above, a constancy that is also assumed for the growth rate. Thus,

$$*e_a^{-i} = \frac{1}{{}_\infty M_a^{-i}} \cdot \exp\{-.0951 \cdot ({}_\infty r_a + {}_\infty M_a^i) \cdot ({}_\infty M_a^{-i})^{-1.4}\}, \quad \text{for } a \geq 65 \qquad \textbf{(7.23)}$$

When applied to data from Sweden in 1995, equation (7.23) gives an estimate of ${}^*e_a^{-i} = 6.74$ years with $R^{-i} = .90$. This estimate is only 0.18 year higher than an estimate of ${}^*e_{85}^{-i}$ using a Gompertz model in the cause-deleted life table. This is an improvement relative to the simple formula, $1/({}_\infty M_{85} \cdot R^{-i})$, which in this example gives an estimate of ${}^*e_{85}^{-i} = 7.27$ years, i.e., 0.71 years higher than the Gompertz reference.

These methods and others related to them typically require an age distribution and a growth rate in order to apply the stable equations. The growth rate is almost always supplied by a comparison of population size in two census enumerations. But if two enumerations are available, another set of techniques can be employed that does not require the assumption of population stability. These are developed in the next chapter.

NOTES

1. This property is sometimes referred to as "weak ergodicity" in opposition to the strong ergodicity of stable population.
2. Population projection has the added advantage of giving the total population size at future dates, as well as the value of other population parameters during the transition to stability.
3. For A_B to appear as a mean age, it should be written as

$$A_B = \frac{\int_\alpha^\beta e^{-ra} p(a)m(a)a\,da}{\int_\alpha^\beta e^{-ra} p(a)m(a)\,da},$$

    but the denominator is 1 from the stable population property 7.6.
4. This claim ignores the generally minor effect that a change in mortality or fertility would induce in the value of T. See Coale (1972: 18–21) or Keyfitz (1968b: 124–6).
5. Sliding the age-schedule of fertility upwards on the age axis in a below-replacement population would not increase the growth rate (make it less negative) if mortality were sufficiently high that many fewer women were surviving to a particular phase of the fertility schedule. That is not likely to be the case for low-fertility human populations (where mortality during the reproductive years is also typically very low), but it may not be uncommon in the rest of the animal kingdom. See Hoogendyk and Estabrook (1984).
6. If applied to a female population, the numerator of this expression corresponds to the total number of female births that will be born to women alive at the time when replacement fertility is imposed. For each woman aged a at that time, the expected number of births depends on her probability of reaching age y (i.e., $p(y)/p(a)$), and on the maternity rate at age y, $m^*(y)$.
7. The relation between $\int_a^\beta p(y)m^*(y)\,dy$ and A^* is the same as that between e_0^o and $p(a)$. $p(a)$ expresses the expected number of deaths per newborn that will occur after age a and e_0^o, derived by integrating the $p(a)$ function, is the expected age at death. $\int_a^\beta p(y)m^*(y)\,dy$ expresses the expected number of births per newborn that will occur after age a and A^*, derived by integrating the $\int_a^\beta p(y)m^*(y)\,dy$ function, is the expected age at giving birth. In both cases, the relation is established by integrating an expression for the mean age by parts.

8 Demographic Relations in Nonstable Populations

In the last chapter, we saw that the stationary population, introduced in chapter 3, was a special case of a stable population. In this chapter, we show that the stable population represents, in turn, a special case of a set of relations that prevail in any population. These relations connect all major demographic functions for a particular period to one another. The connection is made by means of a single, widely observable function, the set of age-specific growth rates. In effect, the use of this function to provide a "growth correction" enables all of the relationships of a stationary population to be reestablished. These more general expressions cast light on population dynamics and provide useful devices for demographic estimation.

8.1 An Illustration

Formally establishing these relationships requires the calculus of several variables. But an understanding of where they come from and how they can be used does not. Let us first define the growth rate at ages x to $x + n$ over the period $[0, T]$ in the conventional fashion as:

$$_nr_x[0, T] = \frac{\ln\left[\frac{_nN_x(T)}{_nN_x(0)}\right]}{T}$$

Note that the sources of change in the size of the population aged x to $x + n$ include death, migration, the attainment of the xth birthday (representing an increment to the size of the group, equivalent to the "birth rate" in the age segment starting with x), and the attainment of the $(x + n)$th birthday, a source of decrement.

Suppose that we are interested in the period from January 1, 1995 to January 1, 1996. The number of persons aged 10 last birthday on January 1, 1996 can be expressed in terms of the number in the same age interval on January 1, 1995 and the growth rate of this age segment over the year:[1]

$$_1N_{10}(1996) = {}_1N_{10}(1995)\, e^{{}_1r_{10}},$$

or

$$_1N_{10}(1995) = {}_1N_{10}(1996)\, e^{-{}_1r_{10}}$$

An alternative expression for the number aged 10 on January 1, 1996 relates it to the size of the same cohort in 1995 and cohort survival experience over the year:

$$_1N_{10}(1996) = {}_1N_9(1995)\, \frac{{}_1L_{10}}{{}_1L_9}$$

This latter expression assumes that the population is closed to migration, an assumption that we will later relax. Substituting this latter expression into the former gives:

$$_1N_{10}(1995) = {}_1N_9(1995)\, e^{-{}_1r_{10}}\, \frac{{}_1L_{10}}{{}_1L_9}$$

Note that this expression relates the number of persons at two successive ages in 1995 to one another in terms of a growth rate and a survival probability over the succeeding year. Using this same approach, we can relate the number of 11-year-olds to the number of 10-year-olds in 1995 by:

$$_1N_{11}(1995) = {}_1N_{10}(1995)\, e^{-{}_1r_{11}}\, \frac{{}_1L_{11}}{{}_1L_{10}}$$

Combining the last two expressions gives:

$$_1N_{11}(1995) = {}_1N_9(1995)\, e^{-{}_1r_{10}}\, e^{-{}_1r_{11}}\, \frac{{}_1L_{10}}{{}_1L_9}\, \frac{{}_1L_{11}}{{}_1L_{10}},$$

or

$$_1N_{11}(1995) = {}_1N_9(1995)\, e^{-\sum_{x=10,1}^{11} {}_1r_x}\, \frac{{}_1L_{11}}{{}_1L_9}$$

Now we have an expression that relates the number of 11-year-olds to the number of 9-year-olds in terms of survival probabilities between 9 and 11 and two age-specific growth rates. More generally:

$$_1N_x(1995) = {}_1N_y(1995)\, e^{-\sum_{a=y+1,1}^{x} {}_1r_a}\, \frac{{}_1L_x}{{}_1L_y} \quad \text{for } x > y$$

8.2   Relations in Continuous Age and Time

What happens as we let the age intervals and time interval in this last expression get smaller and smaller? Using the calculus of several variables, Bennett and Horiuchi (1981) showed that:

$$N(x,t) = N(y,t)\, e^{-\int_y^x r(a,t)\, da}\, \frac{l_x}{l_y} \tag{8.1}$$

where $N(x,t)$ is the number of persons aged x to $x + dx$ at time t to $t + dt$, $r(a,t)$ is the growth rate of the population in the age interval a to $a + da$ during the interval t to $t + dt$, and

l_x / l_y is the probability of surviving from age y to age x in the period life table prevailing in the time period t to $t + dt$.

Equation (8.1) is the fundamental building block for the set of relations developed in this chapter. Preston and Coale (1982) showed that it could be expanded to accommodate migration by adding an additional term:

$$N(x, t) = N(y, t) e^{-\int_y^x [r(a,t) - i(a,t)] da} \frac{l_x}{l_y} \tag{8.2}$$

where $i(a, t)$ is the net immigration rate (immigrants minus out-migrants divided by person-years lived) at ages a to $a + da$ in the time interval t to $t + dt$. For expositional simplicity, we will deal primarily with populations closed to migration throughout this chapter; the relations can be "opened" to migration simply by adding the migration term wherever $r(a)$ appears.

Suppose that the younger age, y, in expression (8.1) is age 0 and designate $N(0, t)$ as $B(t)$ to reflect the fact that the persons at exact age 0 are new births. Then:

$$N(x, t) = B(t) e^{-\int_0^x r(a,t) da} p(x, t) \tag{8.3}$$

where $p(x, t)$ is the probability of survival from birth to age x in the period life table that prevails at time t. Equation (8.3) shows that we can now express the number of people at any age at time t to $t + dt$ in terms of the number of births in that period, the period life table, and the period set of age-specific growth rates. Figure 8.1 presents the different components of equation (8.3) for Japan between 1995 and 2000. It illustrates the fact that the relative difference between $N(x)$ and $e^{-\int_0^x r(a) da}$ corresponds to the $p(x)$ function. In the case of a very smooth $p(x)$, as in this example for Japan between 1995 and 2000, the two functions $N(x)$ and $e^{-\int_0^x r(a) da}$ have a similar shape but increasingly diverge at older ages.

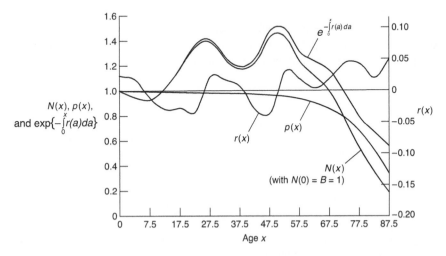

Figure 8.1 Relationship between $N(x)$, $r(x)$, and $p(x)$, Japan, 1995–2000
Data source: Japan Aging Research Center (JARC), 1996. *Statistical Abstracts of Aging in Japan,* Tokyo, JARC.

Preston and Coale (1982) showed how the new expressions could be used to generalize the set of relationships previously established for stable populations.[2] To simplify the development, let us drop the t identifier, recognizing that all functions pertain to the period t to $t + dt$. First, divide both sides of equation (8.3) by N, the size of the total population at time t (or, more precisely, person-years lived in the interval t to $t + dt$):

$$\frac{N(x)}{N} = \frac{B}{N} e^{-\int_0^x r(a)\, da}\, p(x),$$

or

$$c(x) = b\, e^{-\int_0^x r(a)\, da}\, p(x) \tag{8.4}$$

Equation (8.4) bears a striking resemblance to the equivalent expression for the age distribution of a stable population, equation (7.9) of chapter 7:

$$c(x) = b e^{-rx} p(x)$$

In particular, when all age-specific growth rates are constant ($r(a) = r$ at all a), $e^{-\int_0^x r(a)\, da}$ equals e^{-rx} because $\int_0^x r\, da = rx$. In this case, equation (8.4) simplifies to equation (7.9). This equivalence (and others to be established) demonstrates that the appropriate test of whether a population is stable, i.e. whether the relations of a stable population are applicable, is whether the set of age-specific growth rates are constant. If they are constant, regardless of the history of mortality and fertility, then the population is stable and all stable relations pertain. Figure 8.2 presents the $N(x), r(x)$, and $p(x)$ functions in the stable-equivalent population computed from the vital rates for Japan in 1995–2000. In this figure, the relationship between $N(x), r(x)$, and $p(x)$ specified in equation (8.3) applies as well. The difference is that the age-specific growth rates are here constant over age: $r(x) = r(= -.011$ in this example). As a result, the function

$$e^{-\int_0^x r(a)\, da}$$

is equal to e^{-rx}, a simple exponential function.

To develop a general expression for the birth rate, we integrate both sides of equation (8.4) from ages 0 to ∞. The proportionate age distribution summed across all ages must equal unity, so:

$$1 = \int_0^\infty b e^{-\int_0^x r(a)\, da} p(x)\, dx,$$

or

$$b = \frac{1}{\int_0^\infty e^{-\int_0^x r(a)\, da} p(x)\, dx} \tag{8.5}$$

If all age-specific growth rates are constant at r, then equation (8.5) simplifies to the formula for the birth rate of a stable population, equation (7.8) in the previous chapter:

$$b = \frac{1}{\int_0^\infty e^{-rx} p(x)\, dx}$$

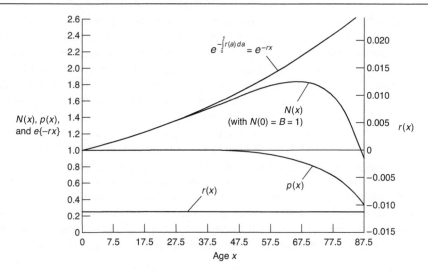

Figure 8.2   Relationship between N(x), r(x), and p(x) in a stable-equivalent population, Japan, 1995–2000
Data source: Japan Aging Research Center (JARC), 1996. *Statistical Abstracts of Aging in Japan*, Tokyo, JARC.

Let us finally express the birth rate in terms of the age distribution and the age-specific maternity rates prevailing in the time interval t to $t + dt$, $m(x)$:

$$b = \int_{\alpha}^{\beta} c(x)m(x)\,dx$$

Substituting the expression for $c(x)$ in equation (8.4) into this last expression gives:[3]

$$b = \int_{\alpha}^{\beta} be^{-\int_0^x r(a)\,da} p(x)m(x)\,dx,$$

or

$$1 = \int_{\alpha}^{\beta} e^{-\int_0^x r(a)\,da} p(x)m(x)\,dx \qquad \textbf{(8.6)}$$

Once again, if age-specific growth rates are constant at r, equation (8.6) simplifies to the equivalent formula for a stable population, equation (7.10):

$$1 = \int_{\alpha}^{\beta} e^{-rx} p(x)m(x)\,dx$$

Thus, the three basic expressions characteristic of a stable population have analogs in any closed population. By adding a migration term, they can be extended to open populations as well. Note that, whereas the stable population relations were developed for only one sex, the more general expressions are equally applicable to one-sex or combined-sex populations.

One feature of these expressions may appear particularly puzzling. It is intuitively obvious, and confirmed in earlier chapters, that the age distribution of a population is a product of its history of mortality, fertility, and migration. How, then, can the age distribution be expressed in terms of contemporaneous values of the birth rate, life table, and age-specific growth rate function? The answer must be that all of the pertinent history is contained in the age-specific growth rate function. It captures in one set of rates, readily estimable whenever two censuses are available, all of the historical information required to relate contemporary fertility, mortality, and age distributions to one another. If mortality were higher in the past, for example, then the subsequent decline in mortality would have raised the size of at least one cohort relative to what it would have been and hence left a permanent mark on the growth rate. The connection between past history and present growth rates is developed more explicitly below.

8.3 Extensions of the Basic Relations

Relations involving growth rates that vary with age, sometimes called variable-r relations, are not confined to analogs of the classic stable population relations. The period net reproduction rate can be expressed in terms of age-specific growth rates in the following way. For the one-sex population of females, designate as $v(x)$ the proportionate distribution of mothers' ages at childbirth, $B(x)/B$. Since $B(x) = N(x)m(x)$, using equation (8.3) to substitute for $N(x)$ gives:

$$v(x) = \frac{Be^{-\int_0^x r(a)\,da} p(x)m(x)}{B}$$

$$= e^{-\int_0^x r(a)\,da} p(x)m(x)$$

Rearranging, we have:

$$v(x)e^{\int_0^x r(a)\,da} = p(x)m(x)$$

Integrating both sides of this last expression over the ages of childbearing, α to β, gives the expression for the net reproduction rate, NRR, on the right-hand side:

$$\int_\alpha^\beta v(x)e^{\int_0^x r(a)\,da}\,dx = NRR \tag{8.7}$$

This rather odd expression shows that the net reproduction rate can be recaptured without any reference to underlying fertility or mortality rates. It is only necessary to observe age-specific growth rates and the proportionate age distribution of mothers at childbirth, two functions that are widely available from censuses and surveys in developing countries. Application of the formula to very good Swedish data for individual years from 1973 to 1977 produced an error of less than 1 percent in each year compared to the NRR computed from age-specific fertility and mortality rates (Preston and Coale, 1982). The equation shows that, if the age-specific growth rates are all equal to zero below age β, then the NRR must equal 1. These relations would obviously prevail in a stationary population. Likewise, any fertility regime above the replacement level must be reflected in positive age-specific growth rates at some or all ages below β. Table 8.1 presents an application of the variable-r method for estimating the NRR to data from Japan between 1995 and 2000, and compares the variable-r method to the traditional method. Using equation (8.7) gives NRR $= .7416$ for Japan in 1995–2000. If one uses the intercensal survivorship ratios to compute $_5L_x$ for the period 1995–2000, the traditional method for computing the NRR produces the exact same value. Differences between the two methods arise when the $_5L_x$ series used in the traditional method differs from the $_5L_x$ computed from the survivorship ratios.

Useful expressions involving the number of decrements, rather than the rate of decrement, can be established by multiplying both sides of equation (8.3) by $\mu(x)$, the death rate at age x:

$$N(x)\mu(x) = Be^{-\int_0^x r(a)\,da}p(x)\mu(x)$$

The left-hand side of this expression is $D(x)$, the actual number of deaths at age x during the interval t to $t + dt$. (More precisely, $D(x)$ is a density function; the number of deaths in the age interval x to $x + dx$ is $D(x)dx$.) The expression, $p(x)\mu(x)$, on the right-hand side is the probability that a newborn will die at age x according to the period life table. It must sum to unity across all ages. Hence, rearranging the last equation and integrating from 0 to ∞, we have:

$$B = \int_0^\infty D(x)e^{\int_0^x r(a)\,da}\,dx \qquad (8.8)$$

This expression provides a direct link between the number of births and the number of deaths in any population. It indicates that the number of births can be inferred directly from the number of deaths, provided that the latter function is growth-adjusted by the $r(a)$ function. In a stationary population, $r(a) = 0$ at all ages, hence

$$B = \int_0^\infty D(x)\,dx.$$

The number of births will equal the number of deaths summed across all ages. If the growth rate is positive at all ages, then the number of births must exceed the number of deaths.

The equivalent expression for the population at any age y in terms of the number of deaths above age y is:

$$N(y) = \int_y^\infty D(x)e^{\int_y^x r(a)\,da}\,dx \qquad (8.9)$$

Equation (8.9) is generalized to multiple sources of increment and decrement in Preston and Coale (1982). Bennett and Horiuchi (1981) use this expression to investigate the completeness of death registration in several populations. The number of deaths above age y, combined with age-specific growth rates, implies a certain census count at age y; an implied count that is too low suggests that deaths above age y are under-registered (or, what is less likely, that the population count is inflated).

Even if deaths are undercounted, the underlying life table can be accurately recaptured using variable-r relations. Since $p(x)\mu(x) = d(x)$, the number of deaths at age x in the period life

Table 8.1: *Comparison of two methods for computing NRR; Japan, females, 1995–2000*

Method 1 (variable-r):
S_x = cumulation of $_5r_x$ to midpoint of interval
$_5v_x = {}_5B_x/B$
NRR $= \sum {}_5v_x \cdot \exp(S_x)$

Method 2 (traditional):
NRR $= \sum {}_5m_x \cdot {}_5L_x$

Age x	$_5N_x$ (1995)	$_5N_x$ (2000)	Intercensal births $_5B_x$	Variable-r method $_5r_x$	$\exp(S_x)$	$_5v_x = {}_5B_x/B$	$_5v_x \cdot \exp(S_x)$	Traditional method $_5L_x$	$_5m_x$	$_5m_x \cdot {}_5L_x$
0	2,988	3,280		0.0186	1.0477			4.9787		
5	3,160	2,976		−0.0120	1.0653			4.9588		
10	3,647	3,157		−0.0289	0.9619			4.9540		
15	4,156	3,641	39	−0.0265	0.8376	0.0118	0.0099	4.9459	0.0020	0.0099
20	4,874	4,140	482	−0.0326	0.7226	0.1463	0.1057	4.9269	0.0215	0.1057
25	4,335	4,862	1,453	0.0229	0.7053	0.4411	0.3111	4.9147	0.0633	0.3111
30	3,998	4,329	1,033	0.0159	0.7772	0.3136	0.2437	4.9079	0.0497	0.2437
35	3,860	3,988	258	0.0065	0.8220	0.0783	0.0644	4.8956	0.0132	0.0644
40	4,470	3,846	28	−0.0301	0.7750	0.0086	0.0066	4.8779	0.0014	0.0066
45	5,284	4,443	1	−0.0347	0.6592	0.0003	0.0002	4.8484	0.0000	0.0002
Sum			B = 3,294			1.0000	NRR = 0.7416			NRR = 0.7416

Data source: Japan Aging Research Center, 1996. *Statistical Abstracts of Aging in Japan*, Tokyo: JARC.

table with a radix of unity, it must be the case that:

$$D(x) = Be^{-\int_0^x r(a)\,da}\, d(x), \quad \text{or}$$

$$\frac{d(y)}{d(x)} = \frac{D(y)}{D(x)} e^{\int_x^y r(a)\,da} \quad y > x \tag{8.10}$$

Applying a growth correction to the observed number of deaths by age in the actual population permits the analyst to infer the age distribution of deaths in the underlying life table. From there, he or she can complete the remaining columns of the life table in the manner described in chapter 3. If recorded deaths are all deficient in the same proportion, then the $D(y)/D(x)$ ratios will be undisturbed and the life table can be reconstructed via a growth correction. Preston et al. (1996) use this procedure to estimate African American mortality rates at advanced ages.

A final application of these relations is to a situation where multiple sources of decrement are recognized. Suppose that we multiply both sides of equation (8.3) by $\mu^i(x)$, the period rate of decrement from cause i, rather than by the rate of decrement from all causes combined. The left-hand side is $D^i(x)$, the observed number of decrements from cause i in the period. The expression, $p(x)\mu^i(x)$, on the right-hand side is the probability that a newborn will succumb to cause i at age x. Integrated over all ages, it gives the probability that a newborn will ever succumb to cause i, one of the basic outputs from a multiple decrement life table. Using the previous notation for this probability, l_0^i/l_0, we have:

$$\frac{l_0^i}{l_0} = \frac{\int_0^\infty D^i(x) e^{\int_0^x r(a)\,da}\, dx}{B} \tag{8.11}$$

Equation (8.11) shows that the probability of eventually succumbing to cause i can be inferred from a growth-corrected number of decrements from i divided by the number of births. (If the number of births is not available, it can be inferred from all decrements combined by using equation (8.8).) If a population is stationary ($r(a) = 0$ at all a), then equation (8.11) shows that the probability of succumbing to a cause can be simply inferred from the ratio of the total number of decrements from that cause to the total number of births, which is also equal to the total number of decrements from all causes. In a growing population in which all age-specific growth rates are positive, the equation shows that the ratio of decrements to births will always underestimate the underlying probability. For example, the ratio of divorces to marriages in a particular period will always understate the probability in the period life table that a marriage will end in divorce when $r(a) > 0$ at all a (i.e., when the growth rate in the number of marriages at duration a is always positive).

One application of (8.11) occurs in epidemiology (Preston, 1987b). The "case-fatality ratio" (or proportion) is the probability that someone who has contracted a disease will die from it. The two recognized sources of decrement are thus death from the disease and death from all others causes combined. One enters the defined state at the point of being diagnosed with the disease, and x in equation (8.11) becomes duration since diagnosis. Thus, B is the number of new diagnoses in a period and $D^i(x)$ is the number of deaths from the cause in question among persons diagnosed x years ago. In a stationary population, the case-fatality ratio can be estimated simply as the ratio of annual deaths from the cause to annual diagnoses. In a growing population, this ratio will always understate the case-fatality ratio.

Table 8.2 shows an application of the growth-correction method to estimate the case-fatality ratio in an artificial population. In this example, where the population of cases is growing ($_1r_x$ greater than 0 at each duration), the observed deaths/diagnoses ratio (47.54 percent)

Table 8.2: *Estimation of the case-fatality ratio in a hypothetical nonstable population*

$_1N_x(t)$	$=$ Number of cases at time t at duration x to $x + 1$
$_1D_x^i[t, t+1]$	$=$ Number of deaths from cause i between t and $t + 1$
$_1r_x$	$=$ duration-specific growth rate in the numbers of cases
S_x	$=$ cumulation of duration-specific growth rates to midpoint of interval
$_1D_x^i \cdot \exp(S_x)$	$=$ growth-corrected deaths from cause i, or deaths from cause i in the period life table

Duration x	$_1N_x(t)$	$_1N_x(t+1)$	$_1D_x^i[t, t+1]$	$_1r_x$	$\exp(S_x)$	$_1D_x^i \cdot \exp(S_x)$
0	1,619	1,804	185	0.108	1.056	195
1	1,048	1,265	271	0.188	1.224	332
2	599	668	245	0.109	1.420	348
3	265	287	163	0.080	1.561	254
4	57	68	63	0.176	1.774	112
Sum			927			1,241
New diagnoses $[t, t+1]$			1,950			1,950
Deaths/diagnoses ratio			47.54%			63.65%

underestimates the true case-fatality ratio (63.65 percent), estimated using the growth correction. If the population was decreasing, the growth-correction factor $\exp(S_x)$ would be less than one at different ages, and the case-fatality ratio would be lower than the observed deaths/diagnoses ratio.

8.4 Deconstructing the Age-specific Growth Rate

How the age-specific growth rate function works its magic may be better understood by identifying its constituents. Let us go back to the example with which we began this chapter, the growth of the population aged 10 last birthday between January 1, 1995 and January 1, 1996. Assume that the population is closed to migration. The number of persons aged 10 on January 1, 1995, is equal to the number of births in 1984, $B(1984)$, times the probability that a birth in this cohort will survive to the beginning of 1995, at which point it is, on average, approximately aged 10.5 in exact years. Designate this survival probability for the cohort as $p(10.5, 1984c)$, where 1984c identifies the birth cohort of 1984. Likewise, the number of 10-year-olds at the beginning of 1996 is $B(1985) \cdot p(10.5, 1985c)$. The growth rate of the population aged 10 last birthday is:

$$_1r_{10}[1995, 1996] = \ln\left[\frac{_1N_{10}(1996)}{_1N_{10}(1995)}\right] = \ln\left[\frac{B(1985)\,p(10.5, 1985c)}{B(1984)\,p(10.5, 1984c)}\right]$$

$$= \ln\left[\frac{B(1985)}{B(1984)}\right] + \ln\left[\frac{p(10.5, 1985c)}{p(10.5, 1984c)}\right]$$

$$= r_B - \int_0^{10.5} \Delta\mu(a)\,da \tag{8.12}$$

where r_B is the growth rate in the annual number of births between 1984 and 1985 and $\Delta\mu(a)$ is the change in death rates at age a between the 1984 cohort and the 1985 cohort $[\mu(a, 1985c) - \mu(a, 1984c)]$. Thus, the growth rate in a particular age interval reflects the growth rate in the number of births into the two cohorts who inhabit that interval and cumulative differences between their age-specific death rates. If the population is experiencing migration, then an additional term is required, $[i(a, 1985c) - i(a, 1984c)]$, where $i(a, 1985c)$ is the net immigration rate at age a for the 1985 birth cohort. This equation is derived more formally in Horiuchi and Preston (1988). The general expression including migration for the growth rate at age a at time t is:

$$r(a, t) = r_B(t - a) - \int_0^a \Delta\mu(y, t)\, dy + \int_0^a \Delta i(y, t)\, dy \qquad \textbf{(8.13)}$$

where $r_B(t - a)$ is the growth rate in the number of births at time $t - a$; $\Delta\mu(y, t)$ is the difference in death rate at age y between the cohort aged a at time t and the cohort aged $a + da$ at time t; and $\Delta i(y, t)$ is the difference in net rate of immigration at age y between the cohort aged a at time t and the cohort aged $a + da$ at time t.

We saw in chapter 7 that a stable population has a constant age distribution so that age-specific growth rates are constant by age. Suppose that, in an otherwise stable population, there had been 70 years earlier a sharp increase in the number of births. Previous conditions were then reestablished and maintained to the present. Then today there would be a "bump" in the actual age distribution at age 70, as shown on figure 8.3, which illustrates this hypothetical example. There would also be a disturbance in the age-specific growth rate function; this function would also have a bump at age 70, preceded by a trough just before age 70 where the unusually large cohort is evacuating the age interval. In terms of equation (8.12), the trough was created by a decrease in the growth rate of births, r_B, when the lower fertility conditions were reestablished.

So there is a one-to-one correspondence between peculiarities in the age distribution and peculiarities in the age-specific growth rate function. That is how equation (8.4) is able to

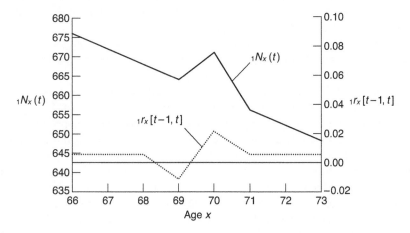

Figure 8.3 $_1N_x$ and $_1r_x$ functions in a destabilized hypothetical population

establish a simple relation between the current age distribution and the current values of the birth rate, life table, and age-specific growth rate function.

The age-specific growth rate function immediately registers changes in fertility and mortality rates. Equation (8.6) shows the relation that must be maintained between growth rates and fertility and mortality rates. A change in the death rate at age x will be immediately registered in the growth rate at age x. A change in fertility rates at any age will be immediately registered in the growth rate at age zero. As a result, the net reproduction rate can be inferred from careful observation of age-specific growth rates, as in equation (8.7).

8.5   Age Structural Dynamics

The stable population model establishes that longstanding conditions of fertility, mortality, and migration will produce a constant age structure. Thus, *changes* in the age distribution cannot be attributable to *levels* of fertility, mortality, or migration. Changes in the age distribution must be produced by changes in demographic conditions. The stable model was helpful in establishing the long-term effect of changes in fertility and mortality on the age distribution. We used it to compare stable age distributions before and after a change in demographic conditions, without any attention to the intervening pathway from one equilibrium to the other. The age-specific growth rate function is a useful bridge between the two. More generally, it can illuminate influences on the age distribution in nonstable populations.

Any changes in the proportionate age distribution of a population must occur via growth rates that are differentiated by age. Suppose that we begin with a previously stable population and impose a persistent decline in fertility rates. It is obvious that the growth rate of the number of births, r_B, will fall. If all age-specific fertility rates decline by 1 percent per year, then for the first 15 years the growth rate in the number of births will be $r_B = r - .01$ rather than r, the growth rate of the previous stable population. After 15 years, the age-specific growth rate function will be flat at r above age 15 (since no cohorts above age 15 have been affected) and flat at $r - .01$ below age 15. Beyond that time, the growth rate in the number of births will fall below $r - .01$ as the growth rate in the number of persons of childbearing age falls below r and fertility rates continue to drop. Thus, the age profile of growth rates approaches one that is continuously rising in age. The population will grow older throughout this process because growth rates at higher ages exceed those at lower ages. As long as the fertility reduction continues, the population will continue aging.

What happens if we impose a persistent mortality decline on a previously stable population, holding fertility constant? As in chapter 7, the answer depends upon the age pattern of mortality decline. If we use the typical pattern of mortality decline described by Coale (1972) and displayed in chapter 7, then the reductions in age-specific death rates will be greatest at ages below 5 and above 50. These age groups will thus begin growing unusually rapidly as soon as the mortality reduction begins. Equation (8.12) shows that the age-specific growth rate is a function of the cumulative change in age-specific mortality rates from one cohort to the next. Thus, the mortality changes accumulate in the age-specific growth rate function and the age profile of growth rates rises over time, maintaining a roughly U-shaped pattern in age. The left-hand side of the U is much less distinct than the right-hand side because each cohort receives an early boost in size relative to its predecessor by virtue of mortality declines below age 5. If $\Delta\mu(y)$ is roughly constant from cohort to cohort, then the age profile of growth rates at younger ages will be flat, a pattern that spreads quickly through the age span until those "saved" by the mortality reduction begin to reproduce. At older ages, on the other hand, the mortality

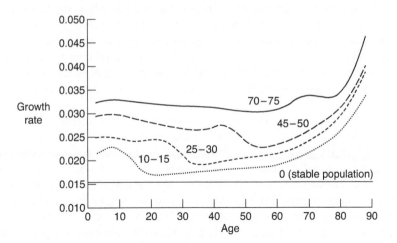

Figure 8.4 Age-specific growth rates by years since mortality decline began: moderate decline
Source: Horiuchi and Preston, 1988: 433.

improvements simply continue to cumulate in the lifetime of cohorts, creating a sharp upward slope in the age profile of growth rates. Figure 8.4 illustrates the pattern of age-specific growth rates when persistent mortality declines are imposed upon an initially stable population.

The effects of migration on the age structure of a population can also be more clearly comprehended through the age-specific growth rate function. It might be thought that the "unnatural" process of migration invariably changes the age structure of a population. But equation (8.13) shows that the growth rate at a particular age is a function of *changes* in the rate of migration, not of the level of migration itself. If there have been no changes in migration rates in the lifetime of relevant cohorts, then migration literally contributes nothing, zero, to the age-specific growth rate. In other words, if each cohort's size changes by the same factor as a result of migration between birth and age a, then the only source of change in their relative size at age a is their relative size at birth (assuming that mortality rates are also constant). If, on the other hand, net immigration rates rise at some set of ages, then the age-specific growth rate will increase at those ages – and at higher ages in subsequent years.

The combined effects of births, mortality, and migration on age structural dynamics can be viewed through the prism of the mean age of a population. The mean age of a population at time t is defined as:

$$A_p(t) = \frac{\int_0^\infty N(a,t)a\,da}{\int_0^\infty N(a,t)\,da} \tag{8.14}$$

Differentiating this expression with respect to time and combining and simplifying terms gives:

$$\frac{dA_p(t)}{dt} = \int_0^\infty c(a,t)r(a,t)[a - A_p]\,da \tag{8.15}$$

where $c(a,t)$ is the proportion of the population at time t who are exact age a.

The right-hand side of equation (8.15) is perhaps recognizable as the covariance between age and age-specific growth rates (Preston, Himes, and Eggers, 1989). When there is a positive covariance (or correlation) between age and age-specific growth rates, the mean age of a population will be rising; when the covariance or correlation is negative, the mean age will be falling. Thus, this equation provides a relatively simple answer to the question, "When will a population grow older?": when age-specific growth rates are positively correlated with age.

By substituting for $r(a, t)$ the three terms involving births, mortality, and migration in equation (8.13), one can decompose the covariance in (8.15) into three covariance terms. Preston, Himes, and Eggers (1989) use this approach to show that the major factor contributing to the rising mean age in the United States and Sweden in the 1980s was their history of mortality decline, captured in the covariance term between age and cumulative changes in mortality. In Sweden, the history of migration – the reduction in out-migration rates earlier in the century, reflected in high growth rates at older ages in the 1980s – was nearly as important.

Finally, age-specific growth rates provide insight into the phenomenon of population momentum addressed in the previous chapter. The term "momentum" refers to the tendency for a previously growing population to continue growing after replacement-level fertility is imposed. Replacement-level fertility means that the net reproduction rate is 1.000. Equation (8.7) provides a link between the net reproduction rate and age-specific growth rates. In particular, it shows that, when NRR $= 1.000$, the (weighted) mean value of the

$$\exp\left[\int_0^x r(a)\, da\right]$$

function must also be 1.000 in the childbearing interval. (The weights are supplied by the ages of mothers at childbearing.) The value of this function is 1.000 when the cumulative sum of growth rates is 0.000.

Therefore, after replacement-level fertility is imposed, the sum of age-specific growth rates must average approximately zero throughout the childbearing interval. By the mean value theorem, there must be some age within the childbearing interval below which age-specific growth rates sum to zero. Preston (1986) uses simulations to show that, in previously stable populations, the population below age T, the mean length of generation, is nearly fixed in size after an NRR of 1.000 is imposed. The reason is that each cohort beyond this time simply replaces itself in size. Thus, essentially all of the population growth beyond the time when replacement-level fertility is achieved occurs in the age bloc beginning with age T. The momentum of population growth is confined to more advanced ages. (See also Kim and Schoen, 1997.)

8.6 Uses of Variable-r Methods in Demographic Estimation

The set of equations developed above has proven useful in demographic estimation. Typically, they work by showing how to apply a growth adjustment that enables the relations in a hypothetical stationary population to be established.

Demographic rates pertain to discrete time intervals rather than to a point in time. Therefore, it is necessary to adapt the equations presented above to discrete time intervals. There are several ways to proceed. The simplest is the following. Since the basic building-block equation (8.1) applies at any time t, it must apply at times t_1 and t_2:

$$N(x, t_1) = N(y, t_1)e^{-\int_y^x r(a,t_1)\, da}\,_{x-y}P_y(t_1)$$

$$N(x, t_2) = N(y, t_2)e^{-\int_y^x r(a,t_2)\, da}\,_{x-y}P_y(t_2)$$

Multiplying these equations by one another and taking the square root of each side gives:

$$N^*(x) = N^*(y)e^{-\int_y^x \frac{[r(a,t_1)+r(a,t_2)]}{2}\, da}\,_{x-y}P_y^*$$

where $N^*(x) = \sqrt{N(x, t_1) \cdot N(x, t_2)}$ and $_{x-y}P_y^* = \sqrt{_{x-y}P_y(t_1) \cdot _{x-y}P_y(t_2)}$. Thus, equation (8.1) also applies to the geometric mean of quantities pertaining at two points in time. Suppose that these points are the beginning and the end of an observational interval, say, two census dates. The growth rate term that satisfies the equation is the average of the growth rates at the beginning and the end of the interval. A convenient assumption is that the growth rate term changed linearly during the time interval, in which case the mean of the growth rates at the beginning and the end of the interval would equal the mean growth rate over the entire interval:

$$\frac{r(a, t_1) + r(a, t_2)}{2} = \frac{\ln\left(\dfrac{N(a, t_2)}{N(a, t_1)}\right)}{t_2 - t_1} = \bar{r}(a)$$

In this case:

$$N^*(x) = N^*(y)e^{-\int_y^x \bar{r}(a)\, da}\,_{x-y}P_y^* \tag{8.16}$$

Using the geometric mean of population counts at the beginning and end of the period and the mean growth rate during the period solves the problem. The equality in (8.16) may not hold, however, if the growth rate function is highly irregular during the interval. Note that the survival experience in this equation is the geometric mean of survival conditions at the beginning and end of the period. Usually, these will be very similar to the mean survival conditions over the entire interval. The correspondence will be exact if the $\mu(a, t)$ function is constant or changes linearly at all ages during the period.

Using this approximation, equation (8.3) will be:

$$N^*(x) = B^*e^{-\int_0^x \bar{r}(a)\, da}p^*(x) \tag{8.17}$$

where B^* can be estimated by summing the births over the interval and dividing by the length of the interval.

A second problem is converting the equations for exact ages into equations for the age intervals in which data are normally found (an exception is the number of births, for which counts are often provided). When data come in 5-year age intervals, a convenient solution to this problem is to assume that the values in (8.17) at the midpoint of an age interval can be approximated by the sum of values in the 5-year interval divided by 5. Hence:

$$_5N_x^* = B^*e^{-S_x}\,_5L_x^* \tag{8.18}$$

where: $S_x = 5 \cdot \sum_{a=0,5}^{x-5} {}_5\bar{r}_a + 2.5\,_5\bar{r}_x$

In view of the need to introduce these approximations, it is reassuring to observe that they will exactly reproduce cohort survival experience when the observational schema enables cohort survival to be directly observed. When data come in 5-year age intervals and observations are separated by 5 years, then the procedure entailed in applying (8.18) will equate $_5L^*_{x+5}/_5L^*_x$ and $_5N_{x+5}(t+5)/_5N_x(t)$ (Preston, 1987a: 61).

Equation (8.18) can be used to investigate any single decrement survival process. Its virtue is that survival conditions can be "indirectly" inferred from the numbers of persons alive in the defined state at two different points in time. If the age intervals and time interval are identical in length, then the equation offers no advantages, as noted in the previous paragraph. When age intervals and time intervals differ, then the equation provides a convenient way of proceeding. It has been used to study the intercensal survival of a population (Preston and Bennett, 1983; United Nations, 1983: 218–22), the survivorship of marriages from all forms of decrement (Preston, 1987a), and the survival of persons diagnosed with cancer (Preston, 1987b). It can also be used to study survival from a single decrement in a multiple decrement situation. Using Hajnal's assumption of no differential mortality between the single and the ever-married population, Preston and Strong (1986) used equation (8.18) to investigate survival in the single state based upon intercensal experience. This approach avoids the need to assume constant nuptiality conditions in the past and provides more timely measures of nuptiality conditions than the one-census approach of Hajnal (1953) developed in section 4.6.

Box 8.1 presents an example that applies the approach to the survival of American marriages during the period 1975–80. The number of intact marriages by duration was observed in 1975 and 1980. The radix of the life table that is constructed is the number of new marriages between these years. Often, the radix will not be available, in which case the life table must begin at a higher age. When data are available in 5-year-wide age (or duration) intervals, then the l_x column cannot begin until age 5. l_x, the number of persons achieving age (or duration) x in the life table that pertains during the period, can be estimated by assuming that the l_x function is linear in the 10-year-wide age interval centered on x. Hence:

$$l_x \cong \frac{(_5L_x + _5L_{x-5})}{10}$$

An alternative approach was developed by Ansley Coale to estimating survival conditions from two observations of a population arrayed by age or duration in a state. This approach uses iterative interpolation to infer survival rates. An example is provided in chapter 11. When data are available in detailed age breakdowns and are quite accurate, the alternative approach will typically provide more accurate estimates than the approach just described. When data are in broader age groups or are seriously inaccurate, there is less to choose between the approaches and the method described above may be preferred for its simplicity.

There is no alternative to several other applications of variable-r procedures. These are instances in which the number of decrements is explicitly recorded. In dealing with a single-decrement process, equation (8.10) shows how a simple growth correction can be applied to convert the number of deaths recorded in a population into the number of deaths in the period life table. This approach would be useful if deaths were incompletely recorded or were based upon a sample of the population. It may also be useful if population data are subject to large distortions from persistent age misreporting. Even though the population age distribution may be too inaccurate to permit construction of a conventional life table, the set of age-specific growth

Box 8.1 *Estimation of Marital Survival Using Variable-r*

$_nN_x(t_1)$ = number of females married once by duration, at time t_1

$_nN_x(t_2)$ = number of females married once by duration, at time t_2

$_nN_x^*$ = $[_nN_x(t_1) \cdot {_n}N_x(t_2)]^{1/2}$ = geometric mean of number of females between t_1 and t_2

$$_nr_x[t_1, t_2] = \frac{\ln\left(\dfrac{_nN_x(t_2)}{_nN_x(t_1)}\right)}{(t_2 - t_1)} = \text{duration-specific growth rate}$$

S_x = cumulation of duration-specific growth rates to midpoint of interval

$_nL_x$ = $_nN_x^* \cdot e^{S_x}$ = person-years lived by marriages in duration interval

l_x = $\frac{1}{2 \cdot n} \cdot (_nL_x + {_n}L_{x-n})$ = number of marriages surviving to duration x

l_0 = radix of the table = mean annual number of first marriages between t_1 and t_2

T_x = person-years lived in marriage above duration x

e_x^o = life expectancy of a marriage surviving to duration x

Example: United States, females, life table for first marriages corresponding to divorce and mortality rates in 1975–80; $l_0 = 1{,}534$

Duration x	$_nN_x(1975)$	$_nN_x(1980)$	$_nN_x^*$	$_nr_x$	S_x	$_nL_x$	l_x	T_x	e_x^o
0	1,428	1,395	1,411	−0.00468	−0.00234	1,408	1,534	43,216	28.17
1	1,448	1,432	1,440	−0.00222	−0.00579	1,432	1,420	41,808	29.44
2	1,457	1,411	1,434	−0.00642	−0.01011	1,419	1,426	40,377	28.32
3	1,436	1,246	1,338	−0.02838	−0.02751	1,301	1,360	38,957	28.64
4	1,315	1,288	1,301	−0.00415	−0.04377	1,246	1,274	37,656	29.57
5	1,462	1,242	1,348	−0.03262	−0.06216	1,266	1,256	36,410	28.99
6	1,383	1,180	1,277	−0.03175	−0.09434	1,162	1,214	35,144	28.94
7	1,258	1,317	1,287	0.00917	−0.10563	1,158	1,160	33,981	29.29
8	1,104	1,217	1,159	0.01949	−0.09130	1,058	1,108	32,823	29.62
9	1,020	1,161	1,088	0.02590	−0.06861	1,016	1,037	31,765	30.63
10	1,039	1,143	1,090	0.01908	−0.04612	1,041	1,028	30,749	29.90
11	975	1,118	1,044	0.02737	−0.02290	1,020	1,031	29,709	28.83
12	943	1,071	1,005	0.02546	0.00352	1,009	1,014	28,688	28.28
13	943	908	925	−0.00756	0.01246	937	973	27,680	28.46
14	954	1,022	987	0.01377	0.01557	1,003	970	26,743	27.57
15	4,477	4,477	4,477	0.00000	0.02245	4,579	988	25,740	26.04
20	4,424	4,200	4,311	−0.01039	−0.00353	4,295	887	21,161	23.85
25	4,712	3,984	4,333	−0.03357	−0.11342	3,868	816	16,866	20.66
30	6,475	7,553	6,993	0.03080	−0.04334	6,697	767	12,998	16.95
40	3,277	3,621	3,445	0.01996	0.21048	4,252	547	6,301	11.51
50	1,351	1,343	1,347	−0.00119	0.30436	1,826	304	2,049	6.74
60	170	167	168	−0.00356	0.28062	223	102	223	2.18

Source: Preston, 1987a.

Box 8.2 *Application of the Death-based Variable-r Method for Estimating Mortality*

$_nN_x(t_1)$ = population aged x to $x + n$ at time t_1

$_nN_x(t_2)$ = population aged x to $x + n$ at time t_2

$_nD_x^*$ = average annual deaths between t_1 and t_2

$$_nr_x[t_1, t_2] = \frac{\ln\left(\dfrac{_nN_x(t_2)}{_nN_x(t_1)}\right)}{(t_2 - t_1)} = \text{age-specific growth rate between } t_1 \text{ and } t_2$$

$$\frac{_nd_x}{_nd_{x-n}} = \frac{_nD_x}{_nD_{x-n}} \cdot e^{n \cdot \left(\frac{_nr_{x-n} + _nr_x}{2}\right)}$$

$$_nd_x = _nd_{x-n} \cdot \frac{_nd_x}{_nd_{x-n}}. \text{ For the first age group, assume that } _nd_0 = _nD_0$$

Example: Vietnam, 1979–89

Age x	$_nN_x$ (1979.75)	$_nN_x$ (1989.25)	$_nD_x^*$	$_nr_x$	$\dfrac{_nD_x}{_nD_{x-n}}$	$\dfrac{_nd_x}{_nd_{x-n}}$	$_nd_x$	l_x	T_x	e_x^o
0	3,946,224	4,668,915	48,580	0.0177	—	—	48,580	556,269	34,014,619	61.15
5	3,928,795	4,403,654	8,029	0.0120	0.1653	0.1780	8,648	507,689	31,438,282	61.92
10	3,632,555	3,884,561	3,928	0.0071	0.4892	0.5131	4,437	499,041	28,921,458	57.95
15	2,954,333	3,402,000	3,783	0.0149	0.9631	1.0173	4,514	494,603	26,437,347	53.45
20	2,281,171	2,935,087	3,856	0.0265	1.0193	1.1304	5,103	490,089	23,975,617	48.92
25	1,742,277	2,764,189	3,469	0.0486	0.8996	1.0855	5,539	484,986	21,537,929	44.41
30	1,177,320	2,280,903	3,053	0.0696	0.8801	1.1826	6,551	479,447	19,126,847	39.89
35	966,580	1,564,740	3,093	0.0507	1.0131	1.3686	8,966	472,896	16,745,991	35.41
40	919,291	1,041,388	3,345	0.0131	1.0815	1.2686	11,374	463,930	14,403,926	31.05
45	994,602	883,098	4,836	−0.0125	1.4457	1.4479	16,469	452,556	12,112,711	26.77
50	825,356	864,699	6,215	0.0049	1.2852	1.2609	20,766	436,087	9,891,104	22.68
55	680,996	904,734	9,138	0.0299	1.4703	1.6040	33,308	415,321	7,762,585	18.69
60	540,920	714,534	12,070	0.0293	1.3209	1.5316	51,014	382,012	5,769,252	15.10
65	419,164	527,053	13,645	0.0241	1.1305	1.2920	65,909	330,998	3,986,726	12.04
70	284,003	326,747	14,310	0.0148	1.0487	1.1558	76,175	265,089	2,496,509	9.42
75	183,222	213,768	14,357	0.0162	1.0033	1.0841	82,582	188,914	1,361,503	7.21
80	64,153	95,528	7,560	0.0419	0.5266	0.6090	50,288	106,332	623,389	5.86
85	39,620	47,662	7,227	0.0195	0.9560	1.1144	56,044	56,044	217,450	3.88

Note: the $_nL_x$ column (not shown here) is calculated with a $_na_x$ of 2.5 at all ages, except for $_0n_5 = .78$ and $_\infty n_{85} = 3.88$.
Data Source: Vietnam General Statistical Office, 1983. *1979 Vietnam Census Report;* Vietnam Census Steering Committee, 1994. *Vietnam Population Census – 1989;* Merli, 1998.

rates may still be usable when patterns of misreporting are similar at the two observations. Box 8.2 presents Giovanna Merli's (1998) application of this method to intercensal survival experience in Vietnam, 1979–89.

The procedures can also be used to estimate certain features of a period multiple decrement life table. Equation (8.11) shows how the probability of succumbing to a particular cause of decrement can be inferred by growth-correcting the observed number of decrements from that cause in a population. No information is needed on the number of decrements from other

Box 8.3 *Computation of the Probability that a Marriage will End in Divorce*

$_nr_x$	$=$ duration-specific growth rate in number of intact marriages (any order) between t_1 and t_2
$_nD_x^i$	$=$ total number of divorces by duration of marriage between t_1 and t_2
S_x	$=$ sum of growth rates from duration 0 to midpoint of interval

$$\frac{_nd_x^i}{l_o} = \frac{_nD_x^i \cdot e^{S_x}}{N(0)} = \text{probability that a marriage just contracted will end in divorce between durations } x \text{ and } x+n.$$

$N(0)$ is the total number of marriages between t_1 and t_2

$$\sum_{x=0,n}^{\infty} \frac{_nd_x^i}{l_o} = \text{probability that a marriage will eventually end in divorce}$$

Example: United States, 1975–80; $N(0) = 11{,}218{,}240$

Duration x	$_nr_x$	$_nD_x^i$	S_x	$\dfrac{_nd_x^i}{l_o}$
0	0.00603	251,888	0.00302	0.0225
1	0.01270	458,995	0.01238	0.0414
2	0.00558	506,574	0.02152	0.0461
3	−0.01319	506,574	0.01772	0.0460
4	0.01300	464,592	0.01762	0.0422
5	−0.02505	405,819	0.01159	0.0366
6	−0.01454	352,642	−0.00820	0.0312
7	0.01799	323,460	−0.00648	0.0286
8	0.02607	265,881	0.01555	0.0241
9	0.01948	229,497	0.03833	0.0213
10	0.01649	766,858	0.08930	0.0747
15	−0.00164	442,202	0.12642	0.0447
20	−0.01092	299,466	0.09502	0.0294
25	−0.03556	179,120	−0.02118	0.0156
30	0.02494	156,730	0.13932	0.0161
Sum				0.5205

Source: Preston, 1987a.

causes; they are inferred from patterns of change in population size, as revealed in age-specific growth rates. This feature is a special advantage in estimating the probability that a marriage will end in divorce. The obvious dimension to use in a multiple decrement life table of marital survival is duration of marriage, but no nation tabulates data on death rates by duration of marriage. Fortunately, such data are not necessary when using variable-r methods. Box 8.3 presents an application of the method to marital survival in the United States.

Other applications of variable-r methods involve the use of model age patterns of mortality. These are introduced in the next chapter, following which we describe other methods of indirectly estimating demographic measures.

NOTES

1. For expositional simplicity, we will drop the time reference in the age-specific growth rate, i.e., $_1r_{10}$ is implicitly $_1r_{10}$ [1995, 1996].
2. For an alternative and complementary demonstration, see Arthur and Vaupel (1984).
3. To be consistent with earlier definitions, we must at this point shift to one-sex notation. For a population of both sexes combined, the "maternity" function in equation (8.6) could be defined in a variety of ways that retain the identity. Perhaps the most straightforward is to assign each birth to an age of father and an age of mother, producing a series of births by age of father, $B^M(x)$, and a series of births by age of mother, $B^F(x)$. Then we can assign half of each birth to the age of father and half to the age of mother, producing a fertility rate at age x of

$$m(x) = \frac{\frac{1}{2}B^M(x) + \frac{1}{2}B^F(x)}{N^M(x) + N^F(x)},$$

where $N^M(x)$ and $N^F(x)$ are the numbers of males and females, respectively, at age x. Another option is to assign male births to the age of father and female births to the age of mother.

9 Modeling Age Patterns of Vital Events

> 9.1 Model Age Patterns of Mortality
> 9.2 Age Patterns of Nuptiality
> 9.3 Age Patterns of Fertility
> 9.4 Model Age Patterns of Migration

Throughout this volume, we have emphasized that the intensity of demographic events varies sharply with age. To describe the mortality rates faced by a population, for example, the analyst will often need to break down the population into age groups within which the death rate is more homogeneous. In an abridged life table, for example, the mortality force is typically described by 19 age-specific mortality rates, for the ages under 1, 1 to 4, five-year intervals up to age 85, and the open age interval, 85+.

Although disaggregation provides a more precise representation of the phenomenon under study, a large set of numbers is cumbersome. Demographers have thus searched for more parsimonious representations of the age variation of demographic events. They study documented age patterns to identify regularities that would allow them to derive a relatively precise description of demographic rates at different ages with a small number of parameters. These parsimonious representations, or model age patterns, serve many purposes in demographic analysis.

1) The models represent a standard or normal pattern because they incorporate the experience of many populations with good data. Thus, a comparison of actual data with a model helps one to identify idiosyncracies in the actual data, including those caused by data error. Significant deviations from existing models are suspicious unless caused by known idiosyncratic conditions. Irregular data can be smoothed and incomplete data completed by referring to the closest, best fitting, model.

2) Age models can simplify the task of preparing demographic projections. As seen in chapter 6, cohort-component projections require age-specific mortality, fertility, and migration rates for each sex and age group, and for each time interval of the projection span. Instead of preparing separate assumptions for each rate, using model age patterns the analyst can make assumptions about the trend in a much smaller number of model parameters and derive the full set of age-specific rates from these parameters.

3) Models allow one to "indirectly" estimate demographic parameters. By assuming that a model pattern pertains, one can often solve for the value of one or two parameters rather than estimating a much larger set of parameters. Some of these indirect estimation techniques are presented in chapter 11.

4)   Although the models are intended to be descriptive only, the discovery of empirical reg-
     ularities across many populations makes it tempting to search for determinants of age
     variations, and to attribute variation to specific biological or behavioral factors that vary
     across populations. Some parameters have a direct behavioral interpretation. Identifying
     the parameter values for which the model best fits the age pattern in a population may
     provide some insight into behavior in the population.

Model age patterns come in three variants. The first approach summarizes age variation by
formulating the risk as a mathematical function of which age is the argument. The second one
presents full tables of age-specific rates that are indexed by some summary measure of intensity,
for example, life expectancy at birth. The third approach combines both the mathematical and
tabular approaches. One or two complete sets of tabulated age-specific rates form a "standard."
A mathematical function is then used to relate the standard rates to estimated or predicted rates
in the population being studied.

In this chapter, we describe model age patterns of mortality, fertility, nuptiality, and migration. Age patterns of mortality have the longest tradition and model age patterns of other vital
events have been largely inspired by these efforts in mortality analysis. Model age patterns of
mortality are discussed first and most extensively.

9.1 Model Age Patterns of Mortality

9.1.1 Mathematical representations

The relation between mortality and age is the oldest topic in demography. The efforts to study
it marked the emergence of demography as a specific field. The pioneering work of Graunt
(1662), Halley (1693), and Deparcieux (1746) established the life table as an essential descriptive and analytical tool. The search for a mathematical model of age variation in mortality risks
("mortality law") also has a long history. The shape of the mortality curve (figure 3.2) suggests that representing mortality risks at all ages would involve many parameters. Past middle
adult ages, however, the mortality curve displays a more regular, nearly exponential, increase.
Gompertz (1825) first noticed that a "law of geometric progression pervades," after a certain
age, in many populations and suggested representing the mortality risk (with the notation of
the present volume) as:

$$\mu(x) = \alpha \cdot e^{\beta x} \tag{9.1}$$

Thus, $\ln[\mu(x)] = \ln(\alpha) + \beta x$; the log of the death rate is a linear function of age. This function
was actually meant to represent only "underlying" mortality, i.e. mortality purged of accidental
or infectious causes. In order to include these two sets of mortality causes which are assumed
to act independently of age, Makeham (1860) suggested adding a constant to Gompertz's
specification:

$$\mu(x) = \alpha \cdot e^{\beta x} + \gamma$$

These formulas are still frequently used to smooth data, especially at older ages (Horiuchi and
Coale, 1982). Box 9.1 presents an application of equation (9.1) to extrapolate survivors in a
life table beyond the final age whose $l(x)$ value could be calculated directly.[1]

It has been observed, however, that at oldest ages (over age 80 or 90), death rates often
increase at a diminishing rate, and the Gompertz or the Makeham function fit to younger ages
tends to over predict mortality (Vaupel et al., 1979; Horiuchi and Coale, 1990). Perks (1932)

Box 9.1 *Fitting a Gompertz Law of Mortality to Estimate Survivors at Older Ages*

General Equation: $l(x) = C \cdot a^{b^x}$ (derived from equation (9.1))

Parameters C, a, and b can be estimated from the last three values of the life table survival function, $l(y), l(y+n)$, and $l(y+2n)$

$$b = \left(\frac{\ln \dfrac{l(y+2n)}{l(y+n)}}{\ln \dfrac{l(y+n)}{l(y)}} \right)^{\frac{1}{n}} ; \quad a = \exp\left(\frac{\ln \dfrac{l(y+n)}{l(y)}}{b^y(b^n - 1)} \right); \quad C = l(y) \cdot \exp(-b^y \cdot \ln a)$$

Example: Austria, males, 1992

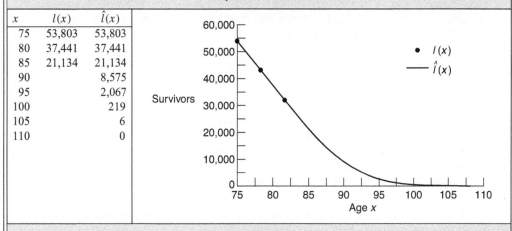

x	$l(x)$	$\hat{l}(x)$
75	53,803	53,803
80	37,441	37,441
85	21,134	21,134
90		8,575
95		2,067
100		219
105		6
110		0

$$b = \left(\frac{\ln \dfrac{l(85)}{l(80)}}{\ln \dfrac{l(80)}{l(75)}} \right)^{\frac{1}{5}} = 1.09543; \quad a = \exp\left(\frac{\ln \dfrac{l(80)}{l(75)}}{b^{75}(b^5 - 1)} \right) = .99933;$$

$$C = l(75) \cdot \exp(-b^{75} \cdot \ln a) = 100{,}819;$$
$$\hat{l}(x) = 100{,}819 \cdot .99933^{1.09543^x}$$

proposed a logistic model that can then be used to represent the sub-exponential growth at oldest ages. The simplest form of a logistic curve is:

$$\mu(x) = \frac{\beta \gamma^x}{1 + \beta \gamma^x}$$

If this formula is used for the death rate, then the complement of the death rate is:

$$1 - \mu(x) = \frac{1}{1 + \beta \gamma^x}$$

and

$$\frac{\mu(x)}{1 - \mu(x)} = \beta \gamma^x$$

In this case, $\ln[\mu(x)/(1 - \mu(x))]$ (i.e., the logit of $\mu(x)$) is a linear function of age.

At the youngest ages, on the contrary, the mortality rate decreases rapidly with age. Bourgeois-Pichat (1946 and 1951) suggested decomposing infant mortality into an underlying, or endogenous, component and an exogenous component depending on the individual's environment (e.g., accidents or infections). He fitted the cumulative proportion dead in a cohort by age n (in days) between the end of the first month and the end of the first year by the formula:

$$q(n) = a + b[\ln(n + 1)]^3$$

with the constant a representing the endogenous process. Deviations from this model have been documented, however, and appear related to breast-feeding practices (Knodel and Kintner, 1977). Lantoine and Pressat (1984) suggested an alternative specification of the formula.

A comprehensive mathematical formula for mortality at all ages is necessarily complex. For example, Heligman and Pollard (1980) found that eight parameters are needed to model the probability of dying between age x and $x + 1$:

$$\frac{{}_1q_x}{{}_1p_x} = A^{(x+B)^C} + De^{-E(\ln(x)-\ln(F))^2} + GH^x$$

The first term (parameters A, B, and C) captures mortality in early life. The coefficient C is negative so that this first term decreases very rapidly with age and becomes very small after childhood. The last term in the sum is similar to the logistic formula for older ages. The second term of the sum accounts for the "accident hump" that is often observed in young adult ages (typically more marked for males than females).

The main difficulty in identifying a law of mortality valid for different populations originates in variations in the age pattern of mortality from different causes of death (Sutter and Tabah, 1952). The age pattern of aggregate mortality reflects the respective importance of specific causes (Preston, 1976a), which varies across populations (e.g., prevalence of car accidents or malaria). A universal law of mortality can only apply to intrinsic or endogenous mortality (Carnes et al., 1996). However, there is probably no cause of death or disease that is not influenced by environmental or behavioral factors.

Fitting mathematical functions to age patterns of mortality requires accurate data on mortality at certain ages. Often, there are no data at all and levels of mortality must be inferred from other information, for example, changes in the size of cohorts from one census to the next. Tabular representations of model age patterns were developed to deal with situations of missing, inadequate, or inaccurate data.

9.1.2 Tabular representations

These tabular representations take the form of "model life tables." They present all of the normal life table functions for populations at a particular "level" of mortality, often indexed by life expectancy at birth. Their utility is predicated on the existence of high correlations among sets of death rates drawn from different populations. Such correlations have been widely observed among populations with good data. That is, when death rates are high at ages 1–4, they also tend to be high at ages 40–4 and 80–4.

The first published set of model life tables was prepared by Valaoras for the United Nations (1955). The empirical basis was a collection of 158 observed life tables for each sex. The set of life tables used in construction of the models was not subjected to a rigorous data quality check.

Furthermore, a method of construction was employed that produced biases in the estimated relations. For these reasons, this set of model life tables is no longer used.

The set of model life tables used most frequently today was constructed by Coale and Demeny in 1966 (second edition, 1983). They improved upon the United Nations system by using a larger, better-screened empirical basis and by constructing different sets of models that recognized regional variations in the relationship between the level and the age pattern of mortality. The method of construction, however, may appear fairly crude by today's statistical standards.

First, 326 male and 326 female empirical mortality schedules were collected, each of which was based on a combination of registered deaths and a population recorded by age in a census. At each age, the values of $_nq_x$ were ranked from lowest to highest, producing for each rank a preliminary model life table. Each actual table was then compared with a composite table having a similar level of mortality, and the difference in rates between the two tables was plotted as a function of age. Visual examination of these deviations was used to screen tables with poor data. For the remaining 192 tables, four patterns were identified. Interestingly, countries in each of these four categories were geographically clustered. Four sets of model life tables were then constructed, one for each region of Europe from which the data principally derived.

The first set of tables, based on the pattern found in nine tables from Sweden (before 1920), Norway, and Iceland, is called North. It exhibits low infant mortality and low mortality above age 50 (figure 9.1). The second set of tables, labeled South because it is based on 22 tables mostly from Spain, Portugal, and Southern Italy, is characterized by high mortality under age 5 and above age 65, but low mortality between age 40 and 60. The third set, East, is based on 31 tables from Austria, Germany, Northern Italy, Hungary, and Poland. Mortality rates are

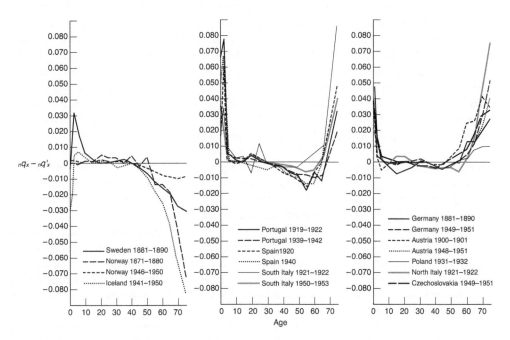

Figure 9.1 Typical deviations with age in the North, South and East regional models
Source: Coale and Demeny, 1983: 11.

Table 9.1: *Infant mortality rates for females by life expectancy at birth and region (per thousand)*

Model	e_0^o				
	30.00	40.00	50.00	60.00	70.00
West	256.11	178.22	118.79	71.16	31.16
North	224.30	156.92	106.02	66.28	32.64
East	306.50	216.83	147.40	89.70	40.96
South	228.81	172.52	130.97	94.91	59.11

Source: Coale and Demeny, 1983.

high in infancy and increasingly high above age 50. The fourth pattern (West) is made of the remaining 130 tables from Western Europe, overseas European populations, and mid-twentieth century Japan and Taiwan. It is considered free of substantial deviations.

Coale and Demeny model life tables make up a "double entry" system: each table is constructed based on a region (North, South, East, and West) and a value of e_{10}^o. Within each regional model, life tables are ranked by mortality "levels," ranging from 1 to 24, with higher mortality "levels" corresponding to higher values of e_{10}^o. The extent of regional variation in age pattern can be inferred from table 9.1, which compares infant mortality rate ($_1q_0$) for female populations at the same level of life expectancy at birth (30, 40, 50, 60, and 70) across regions.

The life table that is selected from a single age-specific mortality rate is thus very sensitive to the choice of a regional model. To choose the appropriate one, we need some independent information on the age pattern of mortality. Lacking such information, inferences are often drawn from the mortality experienced by neighboring countries with better data. This borrowing is made on the assumption that neighboring countries would have similar epidemiological environments, which would be reflected in their cause of death distributions and hence their age patterns of mortality. Preston (1976a) shows that Southern European countries contributing to the South model had high mortality rates from diarrhea. This pattern may best represent the mortality pattern of today's Central America, South Asia, the Middle East, and parts of sub-Saharan Africa where diarrheal death rates are high. None of the empirical tables used by Coale and Demeny incorporated an incidence of mortality from malaria as high as that in contemporary Tropical Africa. But because the age pattern of mortality from malaria resembles to some extent that of mortality from tuberculosis, the preferred Coale and Demeny regional model in tropical Africa is often the North, reflecting a high incidence of mortality from tuberculosis in late nineteenth- and early twentieth-century Northern Europe. The West model is the most general and hence the preferred model when the analyst feels that available information is insufficient to justify selecting a more specific model.

The Coale and Demeny model life tables represent a substantial improvement over the United Nations system. They have been widely used and still represent a standard against which actual tables or subsequent models are compared. Their popularity increased with the second revision, which extended the model to higher ages. Each edition presents stable population age distributions corresponding to a particular model life table and an assumed rate of increase or gross reproduction rate.

A note of caution on their use is in order. Model life tables are extremely convenient because they provide not only predicted values of $_nq_x$ but a full life table. Within a regional model, it is possible to "select" a life table based on any life table value. For example, we may select a life table from an estimated infant mortality rate. By construction, however, these model life tables are supposed to provide the "best" estimates of $_nq_x$ from an estimate of e_{10}^o. There is no guarantee that they will provide the best estimate of, say, $_5q_{40}$ from an estimate of infant mortality; providing such an estimate would have required a different method of construction. In most cases, this constitutes a minor concern.

A bigger problem may arise at highest and lowest mortality levels, outside the range of empirical data on which the model tables were constructed. The highest level of life expectancy at birth in the original tables was 75.2 years for the West region, and only 69.8 years for the South region. Evaluation studies showed that the extrapolation to very high mortality levels performed poorly, as exemplified by the paradoxical difference between life expectancy at age 10 in a model life table – recalculated from the predicted $_nq_x$ – and the initial value of e_{10} that was used to predict those values. The difference could reach several years in some instances (Bhat, 1987), cautioning against using Coale and Demeny tables for extreme values of life expectancy at birth. Coale and Guo (1989) issued a revision of the tables at low levels of mortality, using more recent data. Preston, McDaniel, and Grushka (1993) have produced a set of life tables for high mortality populations.

Lederman and Breas (1959) took the most general approach to the problem of reducing empirical redundancies in the life table. They applied factor analysis to nearly the same data as that used by the United Nations (1955). Factor analysis identifies the minimum number of dimensions (factors) that efficiently represent a more complex data set, here the set of age-specific probabilities $_nq_x$ with originally one dimension per age group. They found that three factors explained more than 90 percent of the variance. The first factor appeared as a fairly homogeneous combination of probabilities at different ages and could be interpreted as the general level of mortality. The second factor represented primarily the relation between child and adult mortality. The third factor was related to mortality at "extreme" ages. Results of the analysis provided convincing evidence that the variation in mortality patterns could not be expressed by simple systems with very few parameters. The interpretation of the factors also contributed to understanding the dimensions of mortality (Bourgeois-Pichat, 1963). The analysis has been influential but the model tables produced from it (Le Bras, 1968; Lederman, 1969) remain little used, in part because the data on which they are based are old and flawed. The tabulated system consist of seven sets of single-entry tables (i.e., tables using a single indicator of mortality) and two sets of double-entry tables.

A limitation, common to all the systems discussed so far, is that their empirical basis consists almost exclusively of the experience of developed countries. Most applications of model life tables, however, are addressed to developing countries with incomplete data. The United Nations (1982) thus published a set of model life tables for developing countries, applying a combination of previous approaches (graphical examination, selection into clusters, and principal components analysis) to data collected by the Organization for Economic Cooperation and Development (OECD, 1979). OECD data consisted of 143 life tables for males and females collected from 54 countries in Africa, 50 in Latin America, and 39 in Asia. Many of these tables, however, were of poor quality. The United Nations applied rigorous consistency checks, retaining only 72 of the original 286 tables (and only Tunisia in Africa). As in Coale and Demeny's system, a regional clustering of mortality patterns emerged from the analysis. For each region, tables were prepared in increments of life expectancy at birth. Associated stable populations by age were also tabulated.

The United Nations system consists of five "regions" (figure 9.2). One is Latin America, which includes data not only from Latin America but also from the Philippines, Sri Lanka,

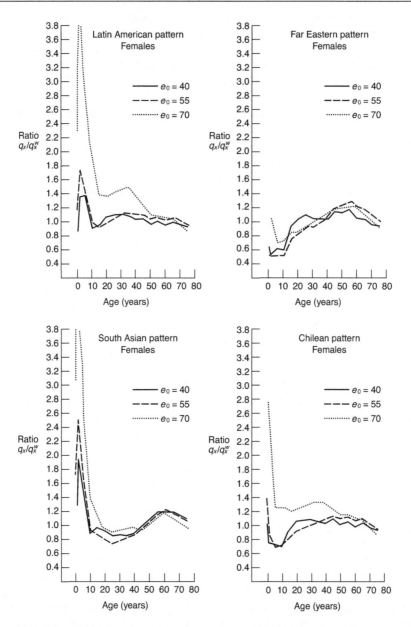

Figure 9.2 Deviations from Coale and Demeny West region for the Latin American, far Eastern, South Asian and Chilean patterns (females)
Source: United Nations, 1982: 12.

and Thailand. It is characterized by high mortality (relative to the West model of Coale and Demeny) during infancy, childhood, and young adult years, but lower mortality at older ages. A second cluster only consisted of data from Chile (1950, 1960, and 1970), characterized by extremely high infant mortality (possibly due to respiratory disease). A third pattern is South Asia (based on data for South and West Asian countries and Tunisia), with high mortality at extremes of age, below 15 and above 60. The fourth pattern is Far East (which included East Asian countries, but also Malaysia, Guyana, and Trinidad and Tobago). This pattern is characterized by high mortality at older ages, possibly due in part to a high incidence of death from tuberculosis or hepatitis B. The last pattern is a General pattern, based on all tables meeting data quality standards.

9.1.3 Relational models

The third category of model age pattern of mortality, relational models, combines features of both the tabular approach of model life tables and the mathematical approach. Relational models consist of a tabulated "standard" mortality function and a mathematical rule for relating that standard to mortality in any population. The complexity of age patterns of mortality is captured through the mortality standard, and the model parameters capture deviations from the standard. These models thus require fewer parameters than mathematical mortality functions.

The first such model was developed by Brass (1971) and is based upon a logit transformation[2] of $q(x)$, the probability of dying before age x:

$$logit[q(x)] = \frac{1}{2} \ln \left[\frac{q(x)}{1 - q(x)} \right]$$

An arithmetic advantage of the transformation is that as $q(x)$ varies from 0 to 1, the logit of $q(x)$ takes all the values between $-\infty$ and $+\infty$. Thus, any predicted value of the logit of $q(x)$ between $-\infty$ and $+\infty$ will map into a value of $q(x)$ itself between 0 and 1. If we can predict the logit of $q(x)$, denoted $Y(x)$, we can then transform $Y(x)$ back and estimate the predicted probability of dying before age x by:

$$\hat{q}(x) = \frac{\exp\left(2\hat{Y}(x)\right)}{1 + \exp\left(2\hat{Y}(x)\right)}$$

Alternatively, the probability of surviving from birth to age x is:

$$\hat{p}(x) = 1 - \hat{q}(x) = \frac{1}{1 + \exp\left(2\hat{Y}(x)\right)} \tag{9.2}$$

Brass proposed a simple relational model to predict $Y(x)$ from the logit of $q(x)$ in the standard population, $Y^S(x)$:

$$\hat{Y}(x) = \alpha + \beta \cdot Y^S(x) \tag{9.3}$$

Brass proposed two standards, labeled a general standard and an African standard. But the system in equation (9.3) can be used with *any* standard (e.g., a Coale and Demeny or a United Nations model life table) that might be thought more appropriate to a particular context. The arithmetic advantages of the logit transformation and the parsimonious specification are attractive, but the model is only useful if it can accurately represent empirical variations in age pattern of mortality. One of the possible tests is to check how well it can reproduce a Coale and Demeny set of model life tables from another model life table in the same family. Several studies have shown that the model performs well in this situation.

Thus, there are two separate features of relational models that determine their success. One is the appropriateness of the standard chosen for the population in question. The other is the appropriateness of the rule that specifies how mortality in the standard is related to mortality in other populations belonging to the same "family."

Although Brass's relational model is easy to use, the selection of the values for the two parameters can be problematic because they do not have an interpretation that is as specific as region and life expectancy at birth in the Coale and Demeny system, for example. We may notice, however, that when α increases, $Y(x)$ increases at all ages and $p(x)$ decreases at all ages (equations 9.2 and 9.3). The parameter α is thus an indicator of the mortality "level," affecting mortality at all ages in the same direction: a higher value of α implies higher mortality (i.e., a lower probability of surviving to any age x as well as a lower probability of surviving between any two ages x and y). To interpret the parameter β, let's first note that both $q(x)$ and $Y(x)$ increase with age and that $Y^S(x)$ is negative at younger ages: the logarithm is negative when the fraction is smaller than one. $Y^S(x)$ equals zero at the age by which half of a birth cohort is dead in the standard population and becomes positive at later ages. When β increases, $Y(x)$ increases at the ages where $Y^S(x)$ is positive, but decreases (becomes more negative) at younger ages where $Y^S(x)$ is negative. Changes in β thus have a different impact at different ages: a higher β increases the slope of the $p(x)$ function (i.e., accelerates the decline with age). Therefore, β is often termed the "slope" of the mortality function, while α represents its "level." Figure 9.3 illustrates the effects of varying α and β in the Brass Logit Model.

If estimates of the probability of surviving to different ages are available, one can compute $Y(x)$ in the population and compare it to the corresponding $Y^S(x)$ at these ages. Since the proposed transformation between $Y(x)$ and $Y^S(x)$ is linear, the two parameters α and β can be estimated using standard linear estimation techniques such as ordinary least squares regression. Once α and β have been estimated, $Y(x)$ and $p(x)$ can be computed at any age from equations (9.2) and (9.3). The model can in this fashion be used to "smooth" empirical data or to complete a partial life table. When no data on actual mortality are available, it is customary to choose a value of β (equivalent to selecting a "region" or "family" in a model life table system) and solve for the level of α using indirect evidence on, for example, the intercensal survival experience of cohorts. A numerical example of the Brass Relational Model is shown in box 9.2.

Ewbank, Gomez de Leon, and Stoto (1983) extended the original logit transformation suggested by Brass. They added two parameters to better represent the shape of mortality in childhood and in adulthood respectively. The transformation of the probability of surviving to age x becomes:

$$T^S(x) = \frac{\left(\dfrac{p^S(x)}{1 - p^S(x)}\right)^{\kappa} - 1}{2\kappa} \qquad \text{when } p^S(x) \geq .5$$

$$= \frac{1 - \left(\dfrac{1 - p^S(x)}{p^S(x)}\right)^{\lambda}}{2\lambda} \qquad \text{when } p^S(x) < .5$$

When κ or λ approach zero, the transformation approaches the classic logit transformation. But using higher values of κ or λ, respectively, allows one to raise the survival probabilities at youngest ages or to lower them at oldest ages.

Relational models have proven extremely useful in a number of comparative studies of mortality. As we saw in section 6.5, Lee and Carter (1992) have constructed a standard designed

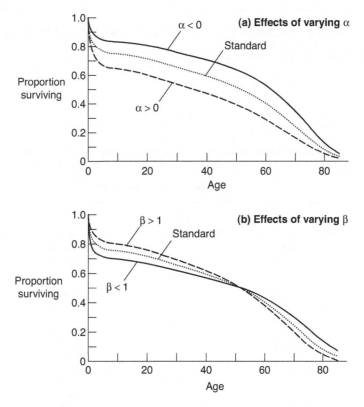

Figure 9.3   Effects of varying the parameters α and β in the Brass Logit Model

to represent the pattern of mortality change in the US during the twentieth century. Himes, Preston, and Condran (1994) present a standard mortality function for use at older ages in low mortality countries and a two-parameter relational model.

In this section, we have presented three ways in which demographers model the age pattern of mortality. The three approaches have been successfully applied to different aspects of the study of mortality and have improved our understanding of human mortality. The traditions of studying age patterns of mortality have also influenced other domains of demographic inquiry, as demographers have also tried to find regularities in age variation in marriage, fertility, or migration.

9.2   Age Patterns of Nuptiality

As a nonrepeatable event, first marriage and its age variations can be approached in ways similar to mortality. Although the force of nuptiality for first marriage cannot be observed directly since two decrements, nuptiality and mortality, are jointly operating on the never-married population, we have seen in sections 3.11 and 4.6 several ways to measure the independent force of nuptiality from empirical data.

In the previous section, we have seen three different approaches taken to model age patterns of mortality. The relational approach, combining empirical and algebraic components, has been the most successful in the analysis of the age patterns of nuptiality.

Box 9.2 *Estimation of Parameters of Brass Relational Model of Mortality*

$q^S(x)$ = probability of dying before age x in the Brass general standard

$$Y^S(x) = \operatorname{logit} q^S(x) = \frac{1}{2} \ln \left[\frac{q^S(x)}{1 - q^S(x)} \right]$$

$q(x)$ = probability of dying before age x in the studied population

$$Y(x) = \operatorname{logit} q(x) = \tfrac{1}{2} \ln \left[\frac{q(x)}{1 - q(x)} \right]$$

$Y(x) = \alpha + \beta \cdot Y^S(x) + \epsilon(x)$; α and β estimated with OLS; $\epsilon(x)$ = error term

Example: US, males, 1991

Age x	$q(x)^S$	$Y^S(x)$	$q(x)$	$Y(x)$
0	0.0000	—	0.0000	—
1	0.1501	−0.8669	0.0100	−2.2986
5	0.2309	−0.6016	0.0120	−2.2050
10	0.2498	−0.5498	0.0132	−2.1560
15	0.2638	−0.5132	0.0148	−2.0981
20	0.2870	−0.4550	0.0211	−1.9179
25	0.3174	−0.3829	0.0292	−1.7518
30	0.3475	−0.3150	0.0380	−1.6153
35	0.3777	−0.2497	0.0488	−1.4853
40	0.4102	−0.1816	0.0621	−1.3572
45	0.4465	−0.1074	0.0783	−1.2330
50	0.4894	−0.0212	0.1009	−1.0935
55	0.5415	0.0832	0.1334	−0.9355
60	0.6035	0.2100	0.1836	−0.7460
65	0.6790	0.3746	0.2566	−0.5319
70	0.7620	0.5818	0.3548	−0.2991
75	0.8500	0.8673	0.4790	−0.0421
80	0.9240	1.2490	0.6228	0.2508
85	0.9710	1.7555	0.7735	0.6142

OLS regression of $Y(x)$ on $Y^S(x)$:

$\alpha = -1.2222$. The level of mortality of US males in 1991 is lower than in the standard

$\beta = 1.2527$. The mortality schedule of US males in 1991 is more concentrated at older ages than in the standard

Data source: National Center for Health Statistics, 1996.

Coale (1971), and Coale and McNeil (1972) examined distributions by age of the proportion of women ever married in many populations and observed considerable variation in the eventual proportion marrying. For example, marriage appeared almost universal in some Asian populations, whereas in some West European populations 20 percent had not married by age 50. The mean age at first marriage also varied from under 15 years in some Asian and African countries to over 25 in some European countries. The more remarkable feature was that the increase of the proportion married for women who ever married were very similar relative to their own mean and standard deviation of age at marriage. More specifically, the proportion of ever-married women by age exhibits a common progression, when divided by the proportion ever-married by age 50 and when age is standardized so that the distributions have the same mean and standard deviation.

As we saw in section 4.6, the proportion ever married at a given age reflects the sum of the cohort's first marriage rates under that age. The similarity of the adjusted proportion ever married suggested that the underlying force of first marriage was following comparable age-specific progression in many populations. Coale and McNeil suggested a relational model to derive the density function of the distribution of women who ever marry by age at marriage, $g(a)$, from a nuptiality standard (constructed from first marriage density in Sweden, 1865–9). The proportion ever-married at age a, $G(a)$, is derived from the proportion in the standard population by:

$$G(a) = C \cdot G^S \left(\frac{a - a_0}{\kappa} \right) \tag{9.4}$$

The parameter a_0 represents the age at which nuptiality "begins" in the population (empirically, it is the age by which approximately 1 percent have married). When the only difference between two age patterns of nuptiality is that age, one pattern can be derived from the other one simply by a horizontal transfer ("sliding") of the proportion ever married by age on the age axis. The second parameter, κ, is an indicator of the spread of the distribution, i.e. how fast women marry after the initial age a_0. The value of κ represents how many years of the population's nuptiality schedule are equivalent to one year of the nuptiality standard. The third factor, C, is a scale factor representing the proportion who eventually marry.

Coale and McNeil's standard density of first marriage has the following form:

$$g_S(x) = 0.19465 \exp\{-0.174(x - 6.06) - \exp[-0.288(x - 6.06)]\} \tag{9.5}$$

They provide tabulated values of $G(a)$ according to different assumed values of C, a_0, and κ. Figure 9.4 shows proportions of women ever married at different ages in the Coale and McNeil nuptiality model, with particular values of C, a_0, and κ.

Rodriguez and Trussell (1980) noted that with the above formulation the mean age at marriage is a function of a_0 and κ, and the variance of the age at marriage is only a function of κ:

$$\mu = \int_0^\infty aG(a)da = a_0 + 11.36\kappa$$

$$\sigma^2 = \int_0^\infty (a - \mu)^2 G(a)da = 43.34\kappa^2$$

The model can thus be reformulated in terms of the mean and the standard deviation of age at marriage in the population. An advantage of this formulation is that it is easier to fit an empirical distribution to a model knowing the mean and variance of the distribution than to solve for a_0 and κ directly.

The double exponential function appearing in equation (9.5) is actually an approximation to the convolution of a normal curve and three exponentials, with exponents in an approximately

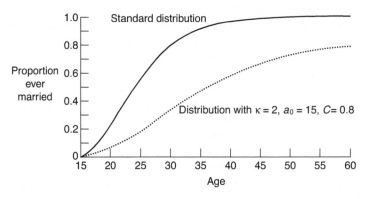

Figure 9.4 Proportion of women ever married in the Coale and McNeil nuptiality model

arithmetic sequence. One can think of the normal curve as representing the age distribution of the population becoming marriageable, while the three exponential terms may represent the distribution of waiting times in different stages of the marriage process, each of which has a constant risk. For example, the first term might represent the time between becoming marriageable and meeting the eventual spouse, the second one the time between meeting and engagement, and the third one the time between engagement and marriage. Empirical attempts to obtain behavioral information based on this model have not been successful because the parameters often take on implausible values in terms of the suggested interpretation. Nevertheless, the model has been useful in "smoothing" data and projecting proportions ever married based on incomplete cohort histories.

9.3 Age Patterns of Fertility

Since marriage is an important part of the fertility process in most populations, it is not surprising that nuptiality schedules have also been instrumental in the development of fertility schedules. An initial approach, based on the behavioral interpretation of the nuptiality schedules, was to derive an age distribution of first birth from an age pattern of nuptiality with the simple addition of a fourth exponential term (representing the waiting time between marriage and conception) and a constant (representing the gestation time). The attempt was not entirely satisfactory because the age patterns with four exponentials terms could not be distinguished from those with three exponentials terms (Trussell, Menken, and Coale, 1982). For practical purposes, Coale and McNeil nuptiality models can also be used as model age patterns of first birth.

A more successful attempt was to derive a relational model of fertility schedule by combining the relational models of nuptiality of Coale and McNeil and a relational model of marital fertility based on two standards. Coale and Trussell (1974) modeled fertility as a convolution of first marriage schedule and an age pattern of marital fertility. If there were no fertility outside of marriage and no marital dissolution, then age-specific fertility rates would simply be:

$$f(a) = G(a) \cdot r(a)$$

where $r(a)$ is the age-specific marital fertility rate and $G(a)$ the proportion married at age a, as in the previous section. Strictly speaking, these two conditions are not met in actual populations but this decomposition provided the framework for the development of Coale and Trussell fertility models. With the existing nuptiality models, the remaining gap was to model the age pattern of marital fertility.

To do this, Coale and Trussell first took advantage of the empirical work on natural fertility by Henry (1961a). Natural fertility is said by Henry to pertain to populations where birth control is not deliberately used. He defined birth control as a couple's behavior that is bound to the number of children already born and that is modified when this number reaches the maximum which the couple does not want to exceed. In Henry's definition, birth control excludes factors that may reduce fertility but are independent of the number of children already born, such as sexual taboos during lactation. Coale and Trussell then observed the departure from an average natural fertility schedule in 43 populations that clearly controlled their fertility. They derived an empirical function of the characteristic deviation by age from natural fertility when couples control their fertility, proposing the following function for $r(a)$, the rate of marital fertility at exact age a:

$$r(a) = M \cdot n(a) \cdot e^{m \cdot v(a)} \qquad (9.6)$$

where $n(a)$ is the rate of childbearing at age a in the average natural fertility schedule from Henry, $v(a)$ represents the age pattern of departure from the natural fertility schedule, and m is an indicator of the extent of departure from natural fertility. The additional term, M, determines the level of marital fertility but doesn't influence the age pattern. It functions in a manner analogous to C in Coale and McNeil's models of nuptiality. The function $v(a)$ has negative values since fertility control has a deflating impact on fertility, a deflation that grows with age. As age increases, couples presumably draw closer to their desired number of children and the proportional reduction of their natural fertility caused by control is also expected to increase. The values of $n(a)$ and $v(a)$ are shown in table 9.2. Additional research has refined estimation of the natural fertility schedule and the schedule of departures from it, but has little affected applications of the model (Xie, 1990; Xie and Pimentel, 1992).

An empirical schedule can be fitted by estimating the values of m and M. Several approaches can be used to estimate the two parameters. The simplest one is to apply standard linear estimation techniques, such as ordinary least squares, to the following relationship:

$$\ln\left(\frac{r(a)}{n(a)}\right) = \ln(M) + m \cdot v(a)$$

which is derived by taking the logarithm of both sides of equation (9.6). A more sophisticated approach using the maximum likelihood estimation of a Poisson distribution has been

Table 9.2: *Schedules of $n(a)$ and $v(a)$ functions*

	Age group a					
	20–4	25–9	30–4	35–9	40–4	45–9
$n(a)$	.460	.431	.395	.322	.167	.024
$v(a)$	0	−.279	−.667	−1.042	−1.414	−1.671

Source: Coale and Trussell, 1978: 205.

Box 9.3 *Estimation of M and m*

$n(a)$ = Natural fertility rates
$v(a)$ = Age pattern of departure from the natural fertility schedule
$r(a)$ = Observed marital fertility rates $r(a) = M \cdot n(a) \cdot e^{m \cdot v(a)}$

$$\ln\left(\frac{r(a)}{n(a)}\right) = \ln M + m \cdot v(a)$$

Estimation of M and m by using OLS regression

Example: Mali, 1995–6

Age a	$n(a)$	$v(a)$	$r(a)$	$\ln(r(a)/n(a))$
20–4	0.460	0.000	0.350	−0.273
25–9	0.431	−0.279	0.313	−0.320
30–4	0.395	−0.667	0.254	−0.442
35–9	0.322	−1.042	0.212	−0.418
40–4	0.167	−1.414	0.095	−0.564

Plot of $\ln(r(a)/n(a))$ **against** $v(a)$

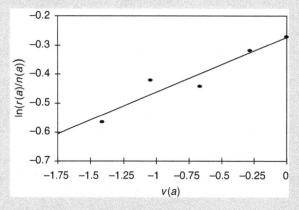

Regression coefficients
Intercept

$\ln M = -0.275$
or $M = .760$

Slope
$m = 0.189$

Interpretation: The level of marital fertility at age 20 to 24 in Mali in 1995–6 is about 76 percent that of natural fertility, and there is little deviation from natural fertility schedule

Data source: Coulibaly, S. et al. 1996. *Enquête Démographique et de Santé, Mali 1995–6*. Calverton, Md., USA: Cellule de Planification et de Statistique du Ministère de la Santé, Direction Nationale de la Statistique et de l'Informatique et Macro International Inc.

developed by Broström (1985). Box 9.3 shows a detailed example of the estimation of M and m from actual data. As recommended by Coale and Trussell (1978), only age groups from 20–4 to 40–4 are taken into account in the regression.

A major application of these models has been to use the estimated value of m to detect whether some control of fertility is being practiced within marriage (e.g., Knodel, 1988). By Henry's definition of natural fertility, m only captures parity-specific birth control and would not detect the use of contraception to increase birth spacing.[3] Simulations have shown additional limitations of interpreting m as an indicator of birth control (Ewbank, 1993; Okun, 1994). First, m can be affected by other factors such as the age at onset of permanent sterility. Second, one cannot give a specific behavioral meaning to different values of m (e.g., derive the proportion of married couples practicing voluntary control). The value of m can only be compared to zero and interpreted according to whether deviations are "large" or "small." Finally, m is not very sensitive to changes in birth control behavior at low levels. Nevertheless, it provides useful information when data are very limited.

Approaches requiring more complex data have been developed using event history analysis (Trussell and Guinnane, 1993) or, more specifically, cohort parity analysis (David et al., 1988). These aim at detecting statistically significant differences in birth interval length that is presumably attributable to voluntary, parity-specific birth control.

Other model representations of fertility age patterns have been developed, although they are not as widely used as Coale and Trussell's models. Another relational model follows Brass's approach to modeling mortality (Booth, 1984). A transformation of fertility at age x, $Y(x)$ is linearly related to the same transformation of a fertility standard at age x:

$$Y(x) = \alpha + \beta \cdot Y^S(x)$$

But instead of $Y(x)$ being expressed in terms of logits, the preferred transformation of fertility is a double logarithm:

$$Y(x) = \ln(-\ln[f(x)])$$

where $f(x)$ is the proportional cumulative fertility at age x (i.e., the proportion of all births in the lifetime of a cohort of women that have occurred by age x). The standard fertility schedule was taken from a Coale and Trussell schedule corresponding to a high fertility population. Again, the main advantage of this approach is parsimony. On the other hand, α and β do not have a behavioral interpretation. The recommended fertility standard is such that Y^S is equal to zero at around age 24. At that age, $Y(x)$ is therefore equal to α, so the higher is α, the higher the proportional cumulative fertility reached by that age. Thus, α is an indicator of the earliness of the fertility schedule. The parameter β is an indicator of the variance of the schedule; a schedule of $\beta = 1$ has the same variance as the fertility standard. As in the case of mortality, this relational model is particularly useful to smooth or complete an empirical schedule, e.g. to predict the fertility of a cohort which has not yet lived through its reproductive span.

In this chapter, we have concentrated on model age patterns of demographic events. In the study of marital fertility, however, the duration of marriage is clearly another relevant dimension in which empirical regularities could be expected. Page (1977) proposed to decompose the fertility rate at age a, duration of marriage d and time t as the product of a time-period effect, an age effect, and a duration effect:

$$r(a, d, t) = L(t)R(a)D(d)$$

Empirical data suggested that $R(a)$ could be approximated by the natural fertility schedule $r(a)$ while $D(d)$ has the form of an exponential function[4] $\exp(-\sigma d)$. The empirical fit of the model to a long series of Swedish data is spectacular, and remains good when limited to populations with a low incidence of divorce and remarriage or to the once-only and currently married population (Rodriguez and Cleland, 1988). The two parameters of the model are an indicator of the period level of fertility, $L(t)$, and an indicator of how rapidly fertility declines within marriage, σ. They are thus similar to Coale and Trussell model parameters, M and m. The two models can actually be reconciled. Dropping the reference to time:

$$r(a) = M\,n(a)\exp[mv(a)]$$

$$r(a,d) = L\,n(a)\exp[-\sigma d]$$

At each age, age-specific marital fertility rates are a weighted average of age- and duration-specific rates at that age:

$$r(a) = \frac{\int_0^a W^L(a,d)r(a,d)dd}{\int_0^a W^L(a,d)dd}$$

where $W^L(a,d)$ is the number of woman of age a, married for d years. Substituting Page's expression for $r(a,d)$ gives:

$$r(a) = L\,n(a)\frac{\int_0^a W^L(a,d)e^{-\sigma d}dd}{\int_0^a W^L(a,d)dd} \tag{9.7}$$

The integral in the numerator is equal to (by the mean value theorem):

$$\exp[-\sigma d^*(a)]\cdot\int_0^a W^L(a,d)dd,$$

where $d^*(a)/a$ duration is between 0 and a. Page's model thus yields the following expression for $r(a)$:

$$r(a) = L\,n(a)\exp[-\sigma d^*(a)] \tag{9.8}$$

The parallel with Coale and Trussell formulation is obvious and allows an additional insight about the function $v(a)$, the deviation from natural fertility (Trussell, Menken, and Coale, 1982). From equation (9.8), $-v(a)$ appears to be proportional to an "average" duration since first marriage for women aged a. If all marriage was taking place at an age a_0, the duration since first marriage for women aged a would be the same for all women and $-v(a)$ would increase linearly with age. Table 9.2 illustrates that $-v(a)$ increases regularly with age but not quite in a linear fashion, possibly because in all populations there is variation in the age at marriage.

9.4 Model Age Patterns of Migration

Migration often occurs in conjunction with some transition in the life course, such as entry into college, a change of job, or retirement. Since these underlying transitions are more frequent at certain ages than at others, pronounced age selectivity can be expected with respect to migration too. Adult migration rates often peak in the young adult ages. A second lesser peak around retirement age has also become apparent in the more developed countries. Migration rates during childhood reflect parents' migration. Using the mathematical approach equivalent to establishing a "law of mortality," Rogers and Castro (1981) have developed a model of migration by age using a mathematical function with 11 parameters (figure 9.5). Seven of them

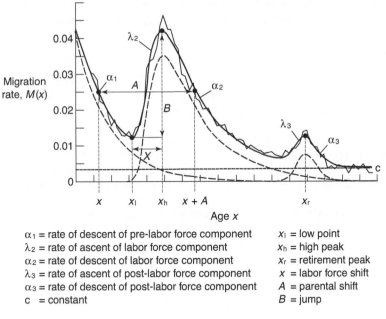

α_1 = rate of descent of pre-labor force component
λ_2 = rate of ascent of labor force component
α_2 = rate of descent of labor force component
λ_3 = rate of ascent of post-labor force component
α_3 = rate of descent of post-labor force component
c = constant

x_l = low point
x_h = high peak
x_r = retirement peak
x = labor force shift
A = parental shift
B = jump

Figure 9.5 The model migration schedule
Source: Rogers and Castro, 1981: 6.

govern the shape of migration by age and the other four represent the intensity of migration. The formula for the migration rate at age x is:

$$m(x) = a_1 \exp(\alpha_1 x) + a_2 \exp\{-\alpha_2(x - \mu_2) - \exp[-\lambda_2(x - \mu_2)]\}$$
$$+ a_3 \exp\{-\alpha_3(x - \mu_3) - \exp[-\lambda_3(x - \mu_3)]\} + c$$

The first term represents the decline in migration rates with age during childhood; a_1 representing the level at birth and of the peak and α_1 the declining slope after birth. Similarly, the second term represents the peak in young adult ages, with a_2 representing the level of the peak, λ_2 and α_2 representing the slope before and after the peak, and μ_2 the peak age. The post-retirement process is represented analogously. In countries where post-retirement migration is unimportant, the schedule can be reduced to four shape parameters and three level parameters.

Although we concentrated in this chapter on age patterns, demographic events can be modeled along other dimensions. As discussed, age is important because the underlying determinants of demographic events vary with age. A more pragmatic reason for the development of age patterns is that age is, in most cultures, a salient individual characteristics, and is thus routinely collected in censuses and surveys. While model age patterns developed rapidly in the 1960s and 1970s, the construction of such models has clearly slowed in recent years. One reason is that these models have satisfied the most immediate needs of demographers reasonably well. These models are still frequently used in population projections (chapter 6) and in indirect estimation techniques (chapter 11). Another reason is that new survey data have become available in many populations that provide more direct evidence about age patterns. This evidence is generally much more informative about fertility and marriage than it is about mortality, and mortality models remain extremely valuable in demography. Dead men tell no tales.

NOTES

1. If the force of mortality follows the two-parameter Gompertz law embodied in equation (9.1) above a certain age y, then the survivorship function, $l(x)$, above that age follows the three-parameter function specified in Box 9.1. The third parameter is a constant adjusting for the number of survivors up to age y.
2. We use the original notation by Brass. In most statistical books now, the factor $1/2$ does not appear in the definition of the logit.
3. Some of the effects of birth spacing will be reflected in the value of M. These effects, however, cannot be separated from some other behaviors, such as breast feeding practices, not related to voluntary birth control.
4. A complication has to be introduced at duration 0 (see Page, 1977 for details).

10 Methods for Evaluating Data Quality

10.1 Statistical Methods for Identifying Coverage Errors
10.2 Statistical Methods for Evaluating Content Errors
10.3 Demographic Methods of Assessing Data Quality

One of the demographer's basic tasks is to produce reliable demographic estimates. Doing so requires having data of high quality or being able to detect and correct errors. Error assessment is useful even if correction is not feasible because it indicates the degree of confidence that can be placed in demographic estimates.

It is useful to know something about the administrative structures that are producing a set of data, e.g., whether registration is mandatory and whether physicians and bureaucrats have incentives to collect data accurately. Similarly, it is useful to know what incentives people have to report themselves accurately in a census or survey or to register vital events. In most industrialized countries, the registration of births and deaths is mandatory and the completeness of birth and death statistics is believed to be very high, though it is rarely tested. The most reliable data are typically derived from countries with population registers, where individuals are followed through time. Data are less accurate in the United States, where there is no register, and where birth and death registration areas were not completed until 1933. Data quality is especially poor for the older black population both because Southern states were among the last to implement mandatory birth registration and because the black population has household structures that are, on average, unusually fluid, thus increasing the difficulties of census enumeration.

It is customary to distinguish two kinds of data errors: coverage errors and content errors. Coverage errors refer to the completeness of inclusion of people or events in the data system. Content errors refer to the accuracy of characteristics recorded in the data system. Misplacement of an event in time would be considered a coverage error if it moved the event across the boundaries defining the units for which estimates are sought. For example, a birth that occurred in 1998 but was registered in 1999 would represent a coverage error in both 1998 and 1999.

There are also two types of approaches to identifying errors: a matching approach, often favored by statisticians, and a demographic approach that relies on accounting identities. The distinction between types of errors and the means of identifying them gives rise to a two-by-two table:

Type of error	Type of approach	
	Matching (statistical)	*Demographic*
Coverage	1	3
Content	2	4

In this chapter, we will deal successively with cells 1–4; cells 3 and 4 are treated simultaneously in section 10.3. Since this is a textbook in demography, we emphasize demographic approaches.

10.1 Statistical Methods for Identifying Coverage Errors

Methods in cell 1 attempt to estimate the completeness of a data source based on case-by- case matching of records in one data source against those in another. The purpose is to ascertain what fraction of records that should have been included in the data system were actually included. There was great enthusiasm for this approach in the 1960s and 1970s as a method for estimating birth rates and death rates in developing countries. The procedure is often referred to as the "dual record system" approach (Krotki, 1978; Marks, 1978). For example, births recorded in a registration system during a certain period can be compared to retrospective reports from a survey of women who are asked about their births during the same period.

The logic of the approach was set down in a classic article by Chandrasekar and Deming (1949). Let us illustrate the approach in the following manner. Suppose that there are data on births in two systems, say, birth registration and a survey of women. After matching the births from the two systems on a case-by-case basis, the following table is produced:

Number of births		In survey	
		Yes	No
Registered	Yes	100 (A)	50 (C)
	No	20 (B)	(D)

So 150 births were registered and 120 births were reported in the survey; 100 events were common to both data systems. One could stop here and say that there were 170 births altogether (150 in the registration system and 20 additional births that were in the survey but that were not included in the registration system). This is in fact what India's Sample Registration System does. But it is almost certain that there are some births in the empty cell (D): births that were missed by both systems. To estimate this number, one can assume that the probability of omission from registration is independent of the probability of omission from the survey:

$$\frac{A}{B} = \frac{C}{D} \quad \text{then} \quad D = \frac{C}{A} \cdot B = \frac{50}{100} \cdot 20 = 10$$

This assumption would lead to the conclusion that there was a total of 180 births during the period considered. This is another way of saying that, based on the match to the survey, registration completeness was $100/120 = 0.8333$. So the total number of births is $150/0.8333 = 180$.

This procedure assumes no correlation between the probability of omission in one source and the probability of omission in the other. This assumption is often unrealistic because in most cases there will be some subgroup that is more likely than average to be omitted from both sources. Suppose that we break the population in this example down into two groups with different probabilities of omission for each group:

Group 1:

Number of births		In survey	
		Yes	No
Registered	Yes	30	30
	No	15	(15)

Group 2:

Number of births		In survey	
		Yes	No
Registered	Yes	70	20
	No	5	(1.4)

Note that the total number of events in cells (A), (B), and (C) is the same as in the earlier example. But suppose we apply the assumption of independence separately to groups 1 and 2. Then the total number of births missed by both data sources would be estimated to be $(15+1.4)=16.4$, which is greater than the 10 estimated before the breakdown. This example illustrates a problem known as "correlation bias," referring to the correlation of omission probabilities across data sources. It is a big enough problem in the US census that matching studies using the assumption of independence typically do not provide satisfactory results, even when applied in subgroups; the correlation bias produces estimated omission rates that are too low according to the results (more reliable in this case) of demographic analysis.

In theory, when faced by this kind of problem, one should obviously disaggregate the population into subgroups wherein the probabilities of omission might not be correlated. However, there will always be the possibility that some unobserved traits will produce a correlation, e.g., not wanting to have one's presence recorded in any data system. Ericksen and Kadane (1985), Bailar (1985), and National Research Council (1999) provide useful discussions of the application of dual record procedures for adjusting the US census.

In addition to correlation bias is the difficulty of identifying what is a correct match. Methods for determining whether any pair of records from the two data sources constitute a true match are presented in Newcombe (1988). In the 1980 US census, the match of individuals from a Current Population Survey to a census individual was "unresolved" for 9 percent of the cases. This is a large proportion in view of the fact that the census undercount itself was only about 2 percent, and it results in much uncertainty. Failing to identify a true match invariably inflates the estimated probability of being missed by both sources and reduces the estimated coverage completeness of both data sources; identifying a false match as true has the opposite effect.

Another major problem encountered by matching studies of birth rates and death rates is termed "out-of-scope" bias. It refers to biases produced when reports in the two systems do not refer exactly to the same time period or geographic entity.

Recognition of these problems has reduced the enthusiasm for using matching studies to evaluate completeness of coverage of births and deaths. They are still a useful tool for evaluating census coverage, especially in subgroups for which demographic analysis cannot be performed.

10.2 Statistical Methods for Evaluating Content Errors

Matching studies for assessing content errors are aimed at assessing either the reliability of the data sources by testing the consistency of information derived from them or the accuracy of one of the two data sources. This second objective can be carried out only if one is fairly certain that one of the two data systems is correct.

Much of demographers' interest is in the quality of data on age, because age is so central to demographic accounts. One simple way to assess the reliability of age data is through reinterview studies, which typically consist of matching a census record with records from a survey conducted shortly after the census. A comparison of such studies in different areas of the world shows that there are some common patterns of errors (Ewbank,1981).

One common error pattern is rounding upward of age. In a study of age accuracy among young children in Ghana in 1963, Caldwell (1966) estimated that age at last birthday was correctly stated for 65 percent of the population, understated for 9 percent of the population, and overstated for 26 percent. Caldwell showed also that age-misreporting varies greatly by age. Overstatement does not begin until age 1, resulting in a large deficit of 1-year-olds.

In an effort to identify correct ages at death, Preston, Elo, Rozenwaike, and Hill (1996) matched a sample of death certificates for elderly African Americans dying in 1985 or 1980 to records for the same individuals in US censuses of 1900, 1910, and 1920, when they were children or young adults. They also matched the death certificates to records from the Death Master File of the Social Security Administration, whose age was believed to be more reliable than the one on death certificates. The characteristics that were used for matching the different records were individual's name, father's name, mother's name, and state of birth.

Table 10.1: *Accuracy of stated age in years, 1963 Ghana registration system. Percent of total persons in age group*

Age	Stated age younger than real age (in years)			Stated age the same as real age	Stated age older than real age (in years)		
	3	2	1		1	2	3
0	—	—	—	99	1	—	—
1	—	—	1	76	23	—	—
2	—	—	1	66	27	5	1
3	—	—	9	63	25	3	—
4	—	1	7	61	25	4	2
5	—	3	11	62	25	—	—
All ages	1	1	7	65	22	3	1

Source: Caldwell, 1966.

Results from this study show that ages at death on death certificates are, on average, understated. Nevertheless, too many deaths were registered at ages 95+. This paradox results from the fact that the number of deaths reported in any age interval is a function not only of the direction of the net age misstatement, but also of the underlying age distribution. As the true age distribution of deaths declines rapidly with age, the base for upward age transfers *into* an age interval becomes much larger than the base for downward transfers *out of* that interval. Thus, the direction of bias in age reporting at an individual level does not inevitably result in the same direction of bias for the population aggregate.

Of course, matching studies focus not only on age but also on all of the characteristics that are normally gathered in the census. Typically, the reliability of different variables is studied through reinterview and postenumeration surveys. One of the most important problems of data quality in the US today relates to race. Many Hispanics do not accept the racial categories offered in the census (Black, White, Asian, etc.), because they don't recognize or accept the distinction between race and ethnicity that is made on the US Census forms. In 1980, 6.3 million people "wrote in" a response to the race question (i.e. they refused to locate themselves in the racial categories designed by the US Census Bureau). In 1990, 9.3 million people, mostly Hispanics, wrote in a response, reflecting the emergence of Hispanics as a distinct ethnic group in the US. These written responses were later statistically allocated to a race. But the original published tables did not include this allocation. The problem of race categorization may bias the computation of race-specific mortality and fertility rates, since the racial/ethnic identification system used in numerators (birth or death statistics) may differ from the system used for the denominators (population at risk). Elo and Preston (1997) show that recorded US Hispanic death rates are too low by about 16 percent because of numerator/denominator incompatibilities in ethnic classification.

10.3 Demographic Methods of Assessing Data Quality

10.3.1 Tests of consistency

All demographic methods for the analysis of data quality are based on demographic accounting identities. These identities are "overdetermined," in the sense that one piece of information is redundant. For example, from the traditional demographic balancing equation (see chapter 1), the change in total population size between two censuses is:

$$\Delta N = B - D + I - O, \qquad (10.1)$$

where all symbols refer to the true count of events. The value of any one element can be inferred from known values of all of the others. If the equation doesn't balance when data are used to estimate the true values, the resulting "error of closure" shows that at least one of the systems is producing erroneous or incompatible data.

A related test of consistency is to apply the same equation for cohorts alive at the first census (and for whom B is thus zero):

$$\Delta N_c = -D_c + I_c - O_c \qquad (10.2)$$

where D_c, I_c and O_c are the true number of deaths, immigrations, and out-migrations in cohort c between two censuses.

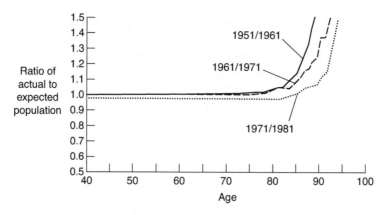

Figure 10.1   Ratio of actual to expected population aged $x+$ at the time of the second census: England and Wales, females
Source: Condran et al., 1991: 52.

A particular version of equation (10.2) has been used extensively to evaluate the consistency of death registration with census counts taken at time t and $t + y$ (Condran et al., 1991):

$$R_c = \frac{N_c(t + y)}{N_c(t) - D_c + I_c - O_c} \tag{10.3}$$

where

$N_c(t)$ is the enumerated size of the cohort at time t,
D_c is the number of intercensal deaths to the cohort,
I_c is the number of intercensal immigrants in the cohort,
O_c is the number of intercensal out-migrants from the cohort.

R_c in equation (10.3) is the ratio of the observed to expected population at the second census. Deviation of R_c from one could be caused by coverage errors and/or age misreporting in any or all of the data sources. Generally, in developed countries, age misstatement is a far more serious problem than undercoverage in censuses or death statistics, especially at older ages, and data on I_c and O_c are usually unreliable. Condran et al. (1991) present simulations showing how different patterns of error affect age patterns of R_c. Figure 10.1 shows the pattern of R_c for England and Wales. The "cohorts" used in this figure are open-ended, e.g., aged 60+ at the first census. Interpreted in light of the simulations, the pattern in figure 10.1 suggests increasing overstatement of age in death statistics as age advances.

These methods are tests of consistency. In order to convert a test of consistency into a test of accuracy, two different options are possible. The first option consists of "privileging" one or more of the data sources, presumably the one(s) that are believed to be more reliable, and using them to evaluate the other(s). The second option, sometimes used in conjunction with the first, involves imposing a model and solving for its parameters. We will discuss these two options in turn.

10.3.2 Data evaluation by "privileging" one or more estimators

The US Census Bureau provides estimates of census completeness by relying principally upon what it terms "demographic analysis." The strategy used is based on the assumption that the correct numbers of births, deaths, and migrations, all derived from noncensus sources, are known. These births, deaths, and migrations are used to estimate the "true" size of each birth cohort at the time of the census, and the comparison of these estimates to the census counts gives an estimate of the coverage error in the census. The true number of people in a cohort is estimated by:

$$\hat{N}_c = B_c - D_c + I_c - O_c, \tag{10.4}$$

where variables in the right-hand side designate estimates of the true numbers and refer to cumulative counts since the cohort was born. This method appears to provide useful estimates for the African American population, but illegal and undocumented immigration produces greater uncertainty for the rest of the population. For an excellent review of demographic analysis as conducted by the US Census Bureau, see Himes and Clogg (1992).

First developed by Vincent (1951), the "extinct generation" method is based on a similar idea, except that cohort deaths are cumulated from the highest rather than from the lowest ages. It reconstructs the size of a cohort at age x by counting all deaths that occurred in that cohort subsequent to age x until the cohort has expired. In formal terms, the number of persons aged x at time t is found by

$$\hat{N}(x, t) = \int_0^\infty D^*(x + a, t + a) \, da, \tag{10.5}$$

where $D^*(x + a, t + a)$ is the recorded number of deaths at age $x + a$ at time $t + a$. (If the cohort is open to migration, then a term, $I^*(x + a, t + a)$, must be subtracted from the $D^*(x + a, t + a)$ term, where $I^*(x + a, t + a)$ is the recorded amount of net migration at age $x + a$ and at time $t + a$.)

The extinct generation method "privileges" only one data source, that of death registration. It has been applied to the African American population for the years 1930–90 (Elo and Preston, 1994). Figure 10.2, pertaining to the female population of 1930, reveals very clearly the degree of preference for reporting different digits in this census. One of the most important applications of the extinct generation method is to estimate mortality at older ages (Kannisto, 1994; Kannisto, 1996; Manton and Stallard, 1997).

A limitation of the extinct generation method is that it cannot be applied to recent generations that are not extinct. By using variable-r equations, however, it is possible to use the logic of extinct generation estimates to relate the size of population to deaths in the period rather than the cohort, using the following equation:

$$\hat{N}(y, t) = \int_y^\infty D^*(x, t) e^{\int_y^x r^*(a,t)da} dx \tag{10.6}$$

Formula (10.6) is very similar to (10.5); the $r^*(a, t)$ term "corrects" the period death series to estimate what it will be in the cohort aged y at time t. Note that, if all growth rates are zero and hence the population is stationary, equation (10.6) collapses to equation (10.5) once we

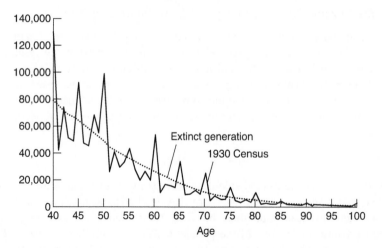

Figure 10.2 1930 census counts and extinct generation estimates, African American females
Source: Elo and Preston, 1994: 441.

recognize that deaths at a particular age will be constant over time in a stationary population. As we saw in chapter 8, equation (10.6) is more often used to evaluate the completeness of death registration than to estimate population counts (Bennett and Horiuchi, 1981). In this case, the population count is being treated as the privileged element, rather than the death count. Of course, it is the relative completeness of the two systems that matters for mortality estimation.

10.3.3   Data evaluation and correction by imposing a model

10.3.3.1 Brass's method for estimating completeness of death registration   The first effort to use population models to make an explicit estimate of data completeness was Brass (1975). The method is addressed to estimating the completeness of death registration. It is based on the simple equality which holds in any closed population (from chapter 1):

$$r = b - d$$

where r, b, and d are the true rates of growth, birth, and death over some defined period. This identity is also valid for the portion of the population above age x:

$$r(x+) = b(x+) - d(x+),$$

or

$$b(x+) = r(x+) + d(x+) \qquad\qquad (10.7)$$

where $r(x+)$ and $d(x+)$ are the growth rate and death rate of the population segment aged x and above, and where $b(x+)$ is the "birth rate" above age x, i.e., the ratio of people achieving age x during a year to the total population above x. This "birth rate" is often estimated from actual data by using the following equation:

$$b^*(x, t) = \frac{N(x, t)}{N(x+, t)} = \frac{\frac{1}{10}(_5N_{x-5}(t) + _5N_x(t))}{\sum_{a=x,5}^{max} {_5N_a(t)}} \qquad\qquad (10.8)$$

Brass imposes the assumption that the population is stable, in which case $r(x+) = r$, i.e., the age-specific growth rate is constant across ages. A second and final assumption is that completeness of death registration, R (the ratio of reported to true deaths), is constant with age. The "true" death rate above age x is therefore equal to:

$$d(x+) = \frac{d^*(x+)}{R}$$

where $d^*(x+)$ is the reported death rate above age x. When substitutions reflecting these assumptions are made in equation (10.7), it becomes:

$$b^*(x+) = r + \frac{1}{R} \cdot [d^*(x+)] \tag{10.9}$$

If the assumptions are exactly correct, then this equation must hold for all ages, and a plot of $b^*(x+)$ against the reported death rate $d^*(x+)$ must follow a straight line. Brass suggests estimating the completeness of death registration by doing a simple linear regression of $b^*(x+)$ on $d^*(x+)$. The intercept of the line is the growth rate, r , and the slope is $1/R$, the reciprocal of the registration completeness R.

In reality, of course, the points described by equation (10.9) rarely follow a straight line. Misreporting of the ages of deaths or of the population, in particular, can greatly affect the points at older ages. These points have a heavy weight in the estimation of the parameters because most of the points below late middle-age are tightly clustered, reflecting the large proportion of deaths that occur at older ages. Brass recommends ignoring the points at older ages that depart too much from linearity.

Results of the method are also sensitive to departures from stability, especially when destabilizing changes have been abrupt (Martin, 1980). In case of rapid mortality decline, the function $r(x+)$ typically rises with age instead of remaining constant. As a result, the estimated slope from equation (10.9) is biased upwards. This leads to underestimation of the registration completeness, R. The estimated value of R might therefore be interpreted as a lower bound for the true rate of completeness when mortality is declining and other assumptions are met. Box 10.1 shows the application of the Brass technique to data from El Salvador.

10.3.3.2 Methods for estimating the completeness of death registration from intercensal survival Preston and Hill (1980) proposed an alternative method for estimating the completeness of death registration that does not require the assumption of stability. It relies on the basic demographic relationship in equation (10.2). This expression, adapted here for a closed population, relates the size of a cohort at a second census to the size of same cohort at a first census and to the intercensal deaths occurring to members of the cohort:

$$N_c(2) = N_c(1) - D_c \tag{10.10}$$

where $N_c(1)$ and $N_c(2)$ are the true numbers in the cohort at census 1 and 2, and D_c is the true number of intercensal deaths occurring to members of the cohort.

The authors assume that the relative completeness of death registration and of the two censuses may vary across data sources but is constant across age within each source. Then the reported numbers in the cohort at census 1 and 2, respectively $N_c(1)^*$ and $N_c(2)^*$, can be

Box 10.1 *Brass Method for Estimating Completeness of Death Registration*

$_5N_x$ = reported mid-year female population aged x to $x + 5$

$_5D_x$ = registered deaths between ages x and $x + 5$ during the considered year

$$N(x+) = \sum_{a=x,5}^{max} {_5N_a}; \qquad N(x) = \frac{_5N_{x-5} + {_5N_x}}{10}; \qquad D(x+) = \sum_{a=x,5}^{max} {_5D_a}$$

$$d^*(x) = \frac{D(x+)}{N(x+)}; \qquad b^*(x) = \frac{N(x)}{N(x+)}$$

Example: El Salvador, females, 1961

x	$_5N_x$	$_5D_x$	$N(x+)$	$N(x)$	$D(x+)$	$d^*(x+)$	$b^*(x+)$
0	214,089	6,909					
5	190,234	610	1,060,164	40,432	6,743	0.0064	0.0381
10	149,538	214	869,930	33,977	6,133	0.0070	0.0391
15	125,040	266	720,392	27,458	5,919	0.0082	0.0381
20	113,490	291	595,352	23,853	5,653	0.0095	0.0401
25	91,663	271	481,862	20,515	5,362	0.0111	0.0426
30	77,711	315	390,199	16,937	5,091	0.0130	0.0434
35	72,936	349	312,488	15,065	4,776	0.0153	0.0482
40	56,942	338	239,552	12,988	4,427	0.0185	0.0542
45	46,205	357	182,610	10,315	4,089	0.0224	0.0565
50	38,616	385	136,405	8,482	3,732	0.0274	0.0622
55	26,154	387	97,789	6,477	3,347	0.0342	0.0662
60	29,273	647	71,635	5,543	2,960	0.0413	0.0774
65	14,964	449	42,362	4,424	2,313	0.0546	0.1044
70	11,205	504	27,398	2,617	1,864	0.0680	0.0955
75+	16,193	1,360					

Plot of $b^*(x+)$ against $d^*(x+)$:

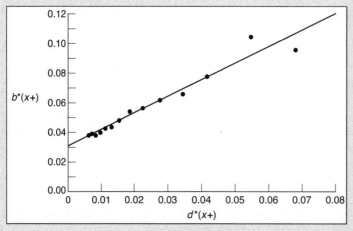

Regression coefficients:

Intercept
$r = 0.0311$

Slope
$1/R = 1.1002$ or $R = .909$

Source: United Nations, 1983: 135.

related to the true values through the following relationships:

$$N_C(1)^* = N_C(1) \cdot E(1),$$

and

$$N_C(2)^* = N_C(2) \cdot E(2)$$

where $E(1)$ and $E(2)$ are the completeness of enumeration at censuses 1 and 2, respectively. The reported intercensal deaths, D_c^* , can be expressed through a similar equation:

$$D_c^* = D_c \cdot R,$$

where R is the completeness of intercensal death registration.

Substituting the reported values into equation (10.10) and rearranging gives the following expression:

$$\frac{N_c^*(1)}{E(1)} = \frac{N_c^*(2)}{E(2)} + \frac{D_c^*}{R},$$

or,

$$\frac{N_c^*(1)}{N_c^*(2)} = \frac{E(1)}{E(2)} + \frac{E(1)}{R} \cdot \frac{D_c^*}{N_c^*(2)} \tag{10.11}$$

As in the Brass method, the values of $E(1)/E(2)$ and $E(1)/R$ can be estimated by using a simple linear regression applied to data on different cohorts. The two observed variables are $N_c^*(1)/N_c^*(2)$ and $D_c^*/N_c^*(2)$. The intercept, $E(1)/E(2)$, is the relative completeness of the two censuses and the slope, $E(1)/R$, is the completeness of death registration relative to that of the first census. The cohorts used in this procedure can be defined in conventional terms or can be open-ended, i.e., born in some specific year or earlier.

It should be noted that this method provides estimates of registration completeness that are not absolute but are relative to that of the first census. This relativity is not a problem for the estimation of mortality because it is sufficient to know only the relative errors in order to adjust mortality rates. A serious problem of the method is its sensitivity to overstatement of age, which tends to distort the estimated relative completeness of death registration. The method has worked better in East Asian populations than in Latin America, where problems of age ascertainment are generally more severe.

Hill (1987) developed a modification of this method that is designed to be less sensitive to age misreporting. Rather than focusing on changes in the size of cohorts from census to census, it focuses on changes in the size of age groups. It is based on equation (10.7) with allowance for differences in census coverage and for incompleteness of death registration.

10.3.3.3 Estimation of mortality at older ages by imposing a model life table system

As we saw earlier, misstatement of age is one of the main problems in the estimation of mortality rates at older ages. These ages have become increasingly important in the study of mortality because such a high fraction of the population around the world achieves them. Fortunately, age misreporting does not affect the crude death rate of a population. If age misreporting is present only at older ages, say above age 65, then the crude death rate for the population aged 65 and above will not be affected. By imposing a particular model life table system on mortality at older ages and solving for the "level" of mortality within the model life table system, the age-specific death rates in the model can be substituted for the flawed rates that have been recorded (Elo and Preston, 1994).

The basic assumption of this method is that the reported crude death rate above a certain age is a valid estimate of the true rate. The second assumption is that when age misreporting occurs in the censuses, it introduces the same proportionate pattern of error at both censuses, so that the intercensal age-specific growth rates remain accurate.

The first step in applying the method consists of identifying the highest age, Y, below which data are consistent, for example by using one of the consistency checks described earlier in this chapter. Reported age-specific death rates below that age can be retained in the construction of a complete eventual life table. The second step requires the use of a model life table system at older ages. Given a particular system, one must identify a table within that system that is consistent with the reported crude death rate above Y. The expression for the death rate above age Y is the following:

$$DR_{Y+} = \frac{\int_Y^\infty N(a)\mu(a)da}{\int_Y^\infty N(a)da} \qquad (10.12)$$

Because $N(a)$ is believed to be distorted at ages above Y, it is desirable to substitute into (10.12) the basic age distributional equation using variable-r relations (equation 8.1):

$$N(a) = N(Y)e^{-\int_Y^a r(x)dx} \frac{p(a)}{p(Y)}$$

Thus:

$$DR_{Y+} = \frac{\int_Y^\infty e^{-\int_Y^a r(x)dx} p(a)\mu(a)da}{\int_Y^\infty e^{-\int_Y^a r(x)dx} p(a)da} = \frac{\int_Y^\infty e^{-\int_Y^a r(x)dx} d(a)da}{\int_Y^\infty e^{-\int_Y^a r(x)dx} p(a)da} \qquad (10.13)$$

where $r(x)$ is the reported growth-rate at age x, $d(a)$ are model life table deaths at age a, and $p(a)$ is the number of survivors to age a in the model life table. Equation (10.13) (actually, the discrete approximation to (10.13), which appears even more complex) is then used to select the model life table that is consistent with the reported age-specific growth rates and the reported crude death rate above age Y. As life expectancy increases within the model life table system, the value of the right-hand side will decrease until a value equaling the observed crude death rate on the left-hand side is achieved.

10.3.3.4 Use of three or more censuses

10.3.3.4 Use of three or more censuses   An alternative to the Census Bureau's "demographic estimates" consists in using an age/period/cohort model of census counts to estimate the true size of a cohort (Preston et al., 1998). Unlike the Census Bureau's "demographic estimates," which ignore census counts altogether in estimating the true size of the population, this procedure uses census counts themselves, in combination with registered deaths, in order to identify systematic census errors and to produce estimates of cohort size at each census date.

The objective is to estimate the true size of a cohort at its initial appearance in a census, and to reconstruct the cohort size at subsequent censuses by subtracting intercensal deaths from that initial count and adding intercensal net migrations.

By making the assumption that there is an age-specific error constant over time, and a period-specific error which is constant over age, the reported census counts can be related to the true counts with the following equation:

$$C_{it} = \alpha_a \tau_t X_{it} + \varepsilon_{it} \tag{10.14}$$

where

C_{it} is the observed number of people enumerated in cohort i in the census taken
    at time t,
X_{it} is the true size of the population in cohort i at time t,
α_a is the completeness of census coverage at age a,
τ_t is the completeness of census coverage at time t, and
ε_t is a residual that is mean zero conditional on age, time period and cohort.

If we relate X_{it} to γ_i, the true size of the cohort when it first appeared, and to D_{it}, the cumulative deaths and net emigrations in cohort i between its first appearance and time t, it appears that we can obtain consistent estimates of α, τ, and γ by minimizing the error term in equation (10.14) with respect to parameters α_a, τ_t, and γ_i:

$$Min \sum_i \sum_t (C_{it} - \alpha_a \tau_t (\gamma_i - D_{it}))^2 \tag{10.15}$$

Thus, equation (10.15) can be used to derive the value of initial cohort sizes. As in the Census Bureau "demographic estimates," this procedure is based on the assumption that death registration is accurate. However, the assumption of accurate birth registration is replaced by the statistical model specified in equation (10.14), which makes the estimated true size of the cohort at first appearance a function of how large it was at each census where it appeared. When applied to the African American population, this procedure has provided a strong confirmation of the basic validity of Census Bureau estimates of census undercounts for African Americans.

Another approach to using multiple observations on the same cohort and intercensal deaths was developed by Luther and Retherford (1988). It aims at developing a set of correction factors for age-specific population counts at two or more censuses, for intercensal births and for age-specific intercensal deaths, so that the resulting corrected counts of births, deaths, and survivors satisfy the traditional demographic balancing equation for cohorts. To implement the method, one first needs to supply a preliminary set of correction factors by using available demographic information regarding coverage of the different data sources or by privileging one data source over the other. This preliminary set of factors will not necessarily be consistent, i.e., it may not necessarily satisfy the demographic balancing equations. From this plausible yet inconsistent set of correction factors, the procedure estimates a consistent set of correction factors that is statistically "closest" to the set of preliminary factors.

This method offers flexibility in the sense that, unlike the age/period/cohort model described above, no particular assumption needs to be made in order to implement the procedure. The final estimates, however, will be highly dependent on the original set of correction factors, whose estimation is left to the choice of the analyst.

11 Indirect Estimation Methods

> 11.1 Estimation of Child Mortality from Information on Child
>   Survivorship: The Brass Method
> 11.2 Estimation of Adult Mortality Using Information on Orphanhood
> 11.3 The Sisterhood Method for Estimating Maternal Mortality
> 11.4 Estimating Mortality and Fertility from Maternity Histories
> 11.5 Indirect Estimation Methods Using Age Distributions at Two Censuses

The previous chapter described methods that aim at detecting data errors, principally by examining the consistency among demographic data sources. For close to half of people in the world today, however, these consistency checks cannot be applied because registration systems are poor or nonexistent. Demographers fill this gap with indirect estimation methods that are based upon censuses or surveys alone. These are principally used to provide estimates of mortality, which help to assess the social and health progress of a population, to identify the effectiveness of government programs, to locate high-risk groups, and even to understand the impact of health-related behaviors. Because mortality estimates are central to demographic accounting, they also help to inform estimates of fertility and population growth.

Some methods that are traditionally considered "indirect" have been dealt with in earlier chapters. This chapter focuses on additional methods of two sorts: those based upon reports of kin survival; and those based on two censuses. For a full comprehension of these methods, it is important to understand the logic behind them. Therefore, we will focus not only on the mechanics of the methods, but also on the demographic identities on which they are based.

11.1 Estimation of Child Mortality from Information on Child Survivorship: The Brass Method

11.1.1 Description of the method

One method that revolutionized mortality estimates in less-developed countries and that is still a very commonly-used procedure is the Brass method for estimating child mortality from reports of mothers about the survivorship of their children (Brass, 1975). It is based on interviews with women, who are asked a minimum of two retrospective questions: the number of live-born children they have given birth to, and the number of those children that have survived. These questions were asked in US Censuses of 1900 and 1910, in the Brazilian census of 1940, and in several postwar African surveys. The data were put to little use, however, before Brass's development of a technique for analyzing the results. The questions are now on the UN's list of recommended items on national censuses.

Brass's idea was to translate the proportion dead into a conventional life-table-type measure. A simple example will illustrate how the translation occurs. Suppose that in a population, the life table is:

Age x	l_x	$q(x) = {}_xq_0 = 1 - l_x/l_0$
0	1000	.000
1	880	.120
2	850	.150
3	840	.160
4	835	.165
5	830	.170
10	800	.200

Suppose further that all childbearing occurs at exact age 19.5. Then if we asked women in this population about the survivorship of their children, the proportion of children dead to women at a particular age, y, would be close to the life table value of the proportion dead among children aged $(y - 19.5)$. For example, the proportion of children dead among 20-year-old women (i.e., women who were aged 20.5 years, on average) would be close to $q(1)$. In a very orderly world, we might observe the following proportions dead by age of woman:

Age of women at last birthday	Average exact age	Duration since childbearing = age of children	Proportion dead among children ever born	Life table value
20	20.5	1	.120	$q(1)$
21	21.5	2	.150	$q(2)$
22	22.5	3	.160	$q(3)$
23	23.5	4	.165	$q(4)$
24	24.5	5	.170	$q(5)$
29	29.5	10	.200	$q(10)$

Let's now be more realistic, and suppose that childbearing is more spread out in age. Imagine that we interview women whose exact age is 25.0, and ask them how many children ever born and children surviving they have. Suppose that their 200 births had been distributed by age in the manner shown in the table below, i.e., 20 births occurred at age 20.0 (five years earlier), 30 at age 21.0 (four years earlier), and so on. If their children were exposed to the life table cited earlier, then we should observe the number reported dead in the right-hand column:

Age of women at birth x	Years since birth $a = 25 - x$	Number of births $B(a)$	$q(a)$	Number of dead children $B(a)^*q(a) = D(a)$
20.0	5	20	.170	3.40
21.0	4	30	.165	4.95
22.0	3	40	.160	6.40
23.0	2	50	.150	7.50
24.0	1	60	.120	7.20
Sum		200		29.45

So these women aged 25.0 would report 29.45 dead children among their 200 children ever born, and the proportion dead would be $d_{25} = 29.45/200 = 0.147$. Referring to the different values of $q(a)$, we see that this value of 0.147 would equate to the probability of dying before about age 1.9. So the proportion of children dead among children ever born to these women is very close to $q(2)$, i.e., it is weighted towards younger ages because births have been relatively recent and because cumulative mortality rises at a slower pace as age advances. If the births had been evenly distributed, we would have obtained the following results:

Age of women at birth x	Years since birth $a = 25 - x$	Number of births $B(a)$	$q(a)$	Number of dead children $B(a)*q(a) = D(a)$
20.0	5	40	.170	6.8
21.0	4	40	.165	6.6
22.0	3	40	.160	6.4
23.0	2	40	.150	6.0
24.0	1	40	.120	4.8
Sum		200		30.6

In this case, the ratio of children dead to children ever born would be $d_{25} = 30.6/200 = 0.153$, or about $q(2.3)$. It corresponds to the probability of dying before an age somewhat higher than in the previous example because children had been exposed to the risk of dying for a longer period. So the ratio, d_x, is a function of both the mortality level ($q(a)$ function) *and* of the distribution of births in the life histories of women, $B(a)$. This latter distribution is clearly a product of the age-pattern of fertility.

More formally, the proportion dead among children ever born to women aged i is:

$$d_i = \frac{D_i}{B_i} = \frac{\int_0^{i-\alpha} D_i(a)da}{\int_0^{i-\alpha} B_i(a)da} \tag{11.1}$$

where

B_i = total number of children born to women aged i at the time of survey,
D_i = total number dead among children born to women aged i at time of survey,
$D_i(a)$ = number of deaths among children born a years before the survey
          to women aged i at time of survey,
$B_i(a)$ = number of births a years before the survey to women aged i at time of survey, and
α = earliest age of childbearing.

Equation (11.1) can be rewritten as follows:

$$d_i = \frac{\int_0^{i-\alpha} B_i(a) \cdot \frac{D_i(a)da}{B_i(a)}}{\int_0^{i-\alpha} B_i(a)da} = \frac{\int_0^{i-\alpha} B_i(a) \cdot q(a)da}{B_i} = \int_0^{i-\alpha} c_i(a) \cdot q(a)da \tag{11.2}$$

where $c_i(a)$ is the proportion of births to women aged i that occurred a years earlier $(B_i(a)/B_i)$. One can see in equation (11.2) that d_i is a weighted average of $q(a)$, the weights being the time distribution of births born in the past to women aged i at the time of the survey. Since $q(a)$ is a rising function (the cumulative probability of dying increases with age), and since older women's births will have occurred longer ago, d_i will be higher at older ages of women. For example, d_{20} is based on very recent births and on children at very young ages, whereas d_{45} is based on more distant experience. Surely, d_{20} will be lower than d_{45} in the absence of rising mortality or some other unusual circumstance.

Using the mean value theorem in equation (11.2), we obtain the following expression:

$$d_i = \int_0^{i-\alpha} c_i(a) \cdot q(a)da$$

$$= q(a^*) \cdot \int_0^{i-\alpha} c_i(a)da$$

$$= q(a^*) \tag{11.3}$$

According to equation (11.3), there must be some age a^* between 0 and $i - \alpha$ at which $d_i = q(a^*)$. This relationship forms the basic logic of Brass approach, which consists of establishing a set of correspondences between i, the age of reporting mothers, and a^*, the age of children whose mortality is most precisely identified by reports of women aged i.

If we assume that $q(a)$ is linear, then $q(a) = K + j \cdot a$, and the correspondences between i and a^* are obvious:

$$d_i = \int_0^{i-\alpha} c_i(a) \cdot q(a)da$$

$$= \int_0^{i-\alpha} c_i(a) \cdot [K + j \cdot a]da$$

$$= K \cdot \int_0^{i-\alpha} c_i(a)da + j \cdot \int_0^{i-\alpha} c_i(a) \cdot a\, da$$

$$= K + j \cdot A_b = q(A_b) \tag{11.4}$$

where A_B is the mean length of time since birth of children. That is, the proportion dead among children ever born to women aged i will precisely identify $q(a)$ at a value of a equal to the mean length of time since their children's birth, A_b. This length A_b obviously rises with age of women, because older women will have had more distant births.

Brass established a set of correspondences between ages of mothers and ages of their children, and these correspondences have been widely used by all subsequent analysts:

Age of women i	Age of children for whom cumulative mortality is best identified
15–19	1
20–4	2
25–9	3
30–4	5
35–9	10
40–4	15
45–9	20

These correspondences, however, are not exact. They depend, as shown earlier, on the nature of reproductive histories in a particular group of women who are reporting their births. So Brass developed adjustment factors, k_i , that attempt to adjust for the particular reproductive histories of a group of women. These adjustment factors are based on comparisons of cumulative parities across women in different age groups. The ideal data for establishing the adjustment factors would be $c_i(a)$, which could be obtained from the reproductive history of each group of reporting women. However, this information is often not available. In its absence, we must infer it from a comparison across cohorts.

The parity measures used in the adjustment procedure are the following:

$P_1 = P_{15-19}$ = mean number of children ever born to all women in age group 15–19
$P_2 = P_{20-4}$ = mean number of children ever born to all women in age group 20–4
$P_3 = P_{25-9}$ = mean number of children ever born to all women in age group 25–9

The basic adjustment factor in Brass's approach depends on P_1/P_2, which is an index of the earliness of fertility, hence of the amount of children's exposure to the risk of mortality. The higher is P_1/P_2, the longer ago were children born, and the higher fraction will be dead, given a certain life table $q(a)$ function. For example, suppose that there are two populations with same value of $d_{20-4} = .170$. But suppose that their childbearing histories differed:

Population	P_1/P_2
A	.3
B	.1

Which population has higher mortality? The answer is population B, because it has the same proportion dead in spite of children's shorter exposure to the risk of mortality.

Brass adjustment factors were developed by simulation. He took a simulated fertility and child mortality regime, slid the fertility schedule along the age axis, and identified the number of children ever born and children surviving by age of woman produced by each combination of fertility and mortality schedules. He then identified how much error there was in the estimation of $q(x)$ based on the age correspondences shown earlier, and then derived adjustment factors based on P_1/P_2. Sullivan (1972) developed a set of adjustment factors based on a wider range of fertility and mortality conditions. Trussell (1975) has also developed a set of adjustment factors that are now more commonly used. We reproduce in table 11.1 his set of coefficients that pertains to the "West" Coale and Demeny model. The full set of coefficients pertaining to different mortality models can be found in table 47 of the UN *Manual X* (United Nations, 1983: 77).

It is clear that proportions of children surviving to the date of the survey are not a product of mortality conditions at the date of the survey, but the result of mortality conditions in the past. If mortality is constant, of course, the past is not different from the present. If mortality has been changing, however, it is important to identify the time period to which Brass-type estimates most closely pertain. Following on the work of Griffith Feeney, Coale and Trussell (1977) simulated linear mortality declines and used the simulations to develop formulas for the estimation of the reference period, $t(x)$ (number of years prior to the survey), to which the values of $q(x)$ most predictably refer. These equations have the same format as those for the estimation of the adjustment factors k_i. We show in table 11.2 the coefficients for the Coale

Table 11.1: *Coefficients for estimation of child mortality adjustment factors, Trussell variant, mortality model West*

Age group of mothers	Index	Age of child	Coefficients		
	i	x	a_i	b_i	c_i
15–19	1	1	1.1415	−2.7070	.7663
20–4	2	2	1.2563	.5381	−.2637
25–9	3	3	1.1851	.0633	−.4177
30–4	4	5	1.1720	.2341	−.4272
35–9	5	10	1.1865	.3080	−.4452
40–4	6	15	1.1746	.3314	−.4537
45–9	7	20	1.1639	.3190	−.4435

Estimation equations:
$$k_i = a_i + b_i \cdot P_1/P_2 + c_i \cdot P_2/P_3$$
$$q(x) = k_i \cdot d_i$$

Source: United Nations, 1983: 77.

Table 11.2: *Coefficients for estimation of the reference period, $t(x)$, to which the values of $q(x)$ most reliably refer*

Age group of mothers	Index	Age of child	Coefficients		
	i	x	a_i	b_i	c_i
15–19	1	1	1.0970	5.5628	−1.9956
20–4	2	2	1.3062	5.5677	.2962
25–9	3	3	1.5305	2.5528	4.8962
30–4	4	5	1.9991	−2.4261	10.4282
35–9	5	10	2.7632	−8.4065	16.1787
40–4	6	15	4.3468	−13.2436	20.1990
45–9	7	20	7.5242	−14.2013	20.0162

Estimation equation for $t(x)$, number of years prior to the survey:
$$t(x) = a_i + b_i \cdot P_1/P_2 + c_i \cdot P_2/P_3$$

Source: United Nations, 1983: 78.

and Demeny "West" model. Coefficients for other regional models can be found in table 48 of *Manual X* (United Nations, 1983: 78).

11.1.2 Sources of errors and misinterpretation in Brass-type estimates

Because Brass's approach has become so influential, it is useful to consider some of the errors to which it is subject. One source of error arises simply from misreport of the number of children ever born and children dead. These numbers are often understated, and it is generally presumed that dead children are more likely to be understated than children surviving, because a dead child is not present to remind the mother of the birth. Women may also have an aversion to mentioning a dead child or referring in any way to his or her absence. Women may also be confused about whether they should count a stillbirth (they should not) or a child that died shortly after birth (they should). These two categories are often not readily distinguished and women's reports about them show unusually high unreliability.

Possible sources of bias that give rise to overstatement of mortality include the report of still births as live births and the omission of living children who moved away from their mother's household. The latter problem is probably more severe for older women, and therefore, it is sometimes recommended to omit older women from the analysis. To improve data quality, it is recommended to ask more specific questions about how many males and females are living at home or away and, directly, about how many have died. Information on the sex of child also allows estimates of sex-specific mortality.

A second alleged problem with the Brass approach pertains to changes in mortality levels. These changes are a source of error if the estimate of $q(x)$ is taken to pertain to mortality conditions at the time of the survey. But we have seen that this assignment is not necessary and that means exist to properly "date" the estimates. Thus, such an error is not intrinsic to the method but is the fault of the analyst.

Changes in fertility levels, however, may and usually do bias results. In order to properly interpret the proportion of children dead, we would ideally be able to observe the reproductive histories of each cohort of reporting women. However, these data are often unavailable, and we usually infer that information by comparing the cumulative average number of births across cohorts. When fertility declines at younger ages, the period P_1/P_2 ratio will underestimate P_1/P_2 in the cohort aged 20–4 simply because fertility was higher in the cohort at age 15–19 than it was for those who are currently 15–19. The downwardly biased P_1/P_2 ratio will produce too high a level of estimated mortality; children's exposure will appear more recent than it actually was.

Results from the Brass method are usually too high for the estimate of $q(1)$ based on women aged 15–19. This bias results from the fact that younger women have a high proportion of first births, which generally have above-average risks of mortality, and from selection by socioeconomic status, since early childbearers tend to come from lower socioeconomic strata with higher mortality risks. For example, Ewbank (1982) found that $q(1)$ was too high by 20 percent in Bangladesh because of birth order differences. The small number of births to women aged 15–19 can also lead to erratic estimates of the proportion of children dead, resulting in poor $q(1)$ estimates. The first-birth bias also extends into the age interval 20–4, although it is attenuated. Ewbank (1982) offers some strategies for estimating and correcting the bias.

A final source of bias can come from selective mortality among mothers. Only women who survive are able to report their children's experience in a census or a survey. If child survival experience among dead mothers is different from that among surviving mothers (i.e. if there is no independence between mortality of children whose mother died and mortality of children whose mother is surviving), then the survivors will provide a biased estimate of child mortality in the population.

The direction of the bias depends on the relative risk of child mortality among children of dead mothers relative to that of children of surviving mothers. If dead mothers had higher mortality among their children, then d_i would be biased downward. This is the likely direction of bias because the death of a mother is likely to raise risks for children. Also, in the context of the AIDS epidemic, with the virus being transmitted from mothers to children, there is certainly no independence between mortality risks of mothers and those of children, and mortality risks at different ages are positively correlated across social groups in nearly all populations; both impoverished women and impoverished children have excessive risks of death.

Fortunately, the bias from selective mortality is typically small (except in populations with high HIV prevalence) because female mortality is low in the childbearing interval. Even when e_0^o is as low as 50 years, the probability of surviving from 20 to 45 is approximately 0.83 (from model life tables). Furthermore, women who have died will have contributed an unusually small number of births to their cohort at any age because of their shortened lives. But the bias introduced in populations where HIV is prevalent can be severe because of the high intergenerational correlation in death risks that HIV introduces. Ward and Zaba (1998) simulate the likely biases and suggest some procedures for correcting them.

Box 11.1 shows a detailed application of the Brass method to data from Zimbabwe.

11.1.3   Variants of the Brass approach

Brass's approach has been very influential in demography (Feeney, 1991). Several other methods for estimation of childhood mortality are based on the same general idea, with different degrees of complexity (Hill, 1991). The first alternative consists of doing the calculations using proportions of children dead classified by mother's duration of marriage (i.e., time since first marriage) instead of age. The advantage of this approach, introduced by Jerry Sullivan, is that in some populations, marital duration may be better reported than age because it refers to a more recent event. Another advantage is that fertility changes or social differentials at younger ages are often caused by variation in marital behavior, marriage duration-specific fertility rates being somewhat more stable. As a result, the cross-sectional P_1/P_2 ratio might be less distorted when computed from data classified by marriage duration. The procedure is similar to the Brass procedure using data classified by age described above, except for the use of different sets of estimation coefficients. The sets of appropriate coefficients are reported in tables 56 and 57 of *Manual X* (United Nations, 1983: 82–3). For populations where marriage is less salient because of a high volume of nonmarital childbearing, Hill and Figueroa (1999) has developed a method based on time since first birth.

A very simple variant consists of collecting information about births in the last twelve months only. The proportion surviving gives an estimate of $_1L_0/l_0$ in the life table. However, it is argued that this method generally gives mortality estimates that are too low, perhaps because of the reluctance to report recent deaths, or because of difficulties with identification of the reference period.

A similar approach consists of asking women in the reproductive ages about the survival of their most recent birth. A selection bias makes this approach risky. Consider all the births that occurred two years earlier. Those children who died were likely to have been replaced by another birth, if for no other reason than the foreshortened period of lactation and non-ovulation

Box 11.1 *Estimation of Child Mortality from Information on Children Ever Born and Children Surviving (Brass Method)*

Data required:
W_i = total number of women in age group i (irrespective of marital status)
B_i = number of children ever born reported by women in age group i
S_i = number of children surviving reported by women in age group i

Computational procedure: $D_i = B_i - S_i$ = number of children dead to women in age group i
$d_i = D_i / B_i$ = proportion of children dead for mothers in age group i
$P_i = B_i / W_i$ = average parity per woman in age group i

Example: Zimbabwe, 1994, both sexes

Mother's age group	Index i	W_i	B_i	S_i	D_i	d_i	P_i
15–19	1	1,472	250	236	14	0.0560	0.17
20–4	2	1,269	1,396	1,282	114	0.0817	1.10
25–9	3	915	2,159	1,995	164	0.0760	2.36
30–4	4	871	3,388	3,101	287	0.0847	3.89
35–9	5	661	3,391	3,074	317	0.0935	5.13

Calculation of probability of dying and surviving:
a_i, b_i, c_i = coefficients for estimation of child mortality multipliers (West model coefficients shown here)
$k_i = a_i + b_i \cdot P_1/P_2 + c_i \cdot P_2/P_3$
$q(x) = k_i \cdot d_i$ = probability of dying from age 0 to x, for children of women in age group i
$l(x) = 1 - q(x)$ = probability of surviving from age 0 to x

Mother's age group i	a_i	b_i	c_i	k_i	d_i	Corresponding child age x	$q(x) = k_i \cdot d_i$	$l(x)$	Mortality level (West model)
1	1.1415	−2.7070	0.7663	1.0808	0.0560	1	0.0605	**0.9395**	18.6
2	1.2563	−0.5381	−0.2637	1.0503	0.0817	2	0.0858	**0.9142**	17.6
3	1.1851	0.0633	−0.4177	1.0001	0.0760	3	0.0760	**0.9240**	18.6
4	1.1720	0.2341	−0.4272	1.0090	0.0847	5	0.0855	**0.9145**	18.4
5	1.1865	0.3080	−0.4452	1.0265	0.0935	10	0.0960	**0.9040**	18.3
			$P_1/P_2 =$	0.1544					
			$P_2/P_3 =$	0.4662					

Estimation of reference period:
a_i, b_i, c_i = coefficients for estimation of reference period (West model coefficients shown here)
$t(x) = a_i + b_i \cdot P_1/P_2 + c_i \cdot P_2/P_3$ = number of years before the survey date to which $q(x)$ refers
Reference date = date of survey − $t(x)$. In this example, the date of survey is 1994.7

Age group	Index i	Age x	a_i	b_i	c_i	$t(x)$	Reference date
15–19	1	1	1.0970	5.5628	−1.9956	1.0	**1993.7**
20–4	2	2	1.3062	5.5677	0.2962	2.3	**1992.4**
25–9	3	3	1.5305	2.5528	4.8962	4.2	**1990.5**
30–4	4	5	1.9991	−2.4261	10.4282	6.5	**1988.2**
35–9	5	10	2.7632	−8.4065	16.1787	9.0	**1985.7**

Data source: Central Statistical Office [Zimbabwe] and Macro International Inc., 1995. *Zimbabwe Demographic and Health Survey, 1994*, Calverton, Md.: Central Statistical Office and Macro International Inc.

among their mothers. Therefore, their death would not be reported, and mortality estimates produced by the approach would be biased downwards.

A more promising and widely-used variant of the Brass approach consists in collecting information about the survival of the "preceding birth," i.e., the birth that preceded a birth just occurring (Brass and Macrae, 1984). The idea here is to interview women at the time of birth about the outcome of their previous birth, usually in a hospital or clinic. The proportion dead is usually converted into an estimate of $q(2)$, since the proportion dead approximates this value when birth intervals average about 30 months, a common value. The fact that only women giving birth in institutions are interviewed raises, of course, an immediate problem of selection bias. These women have children who will usually have had better health conditions, and the resulting $q(2)$ might underestimate the true mortality conditions in the population. The bias may not be large, however, if a large proportion of the population is giving birth in institutions. By nature of the data collection strategy, no information is gathered on births that come last in a woman's childbearing history. The main advantage of the method is its timeliness and simplicity, which has allowed some institutions to collect the data on a continuous basis. Instead of having to mount periodic surveys, this method permits an easy and fairly up-to-date monitoring of child mortality.

With additional data on ages of surviving children such as one would find in a household census file, it is possible to use another variant of the Brass method, developed by Preston and Palloni (1977). These additional data permit a more accurate assessment of reproductive histories of women, and make unnecessary the use of synthetic cohort comparisons with the P_1/P_2 ratio. In effect, women's reproductive histories are inferred from the age distribution of surviving children. This inference is especially useful when estimates of child mortality by social class (e.g., husband's occupation) are sought, since P_1/P_2 ratios in a period can give highly misleading indicators of the actual P_1/P_2 ratio in a cohort. Results of the method are not biased by fertility trends, unlike Brass's original approach.

A problem with the method, however, is that it is sensitive to age-selective omission and misreporting of ages of children. It should therefore be applied only if the quality of data on age is judged acceptable.

11.2 Estimation of Adult Mortality Using Information on Orphanhood

11.2.1 Description of the method

Brass methods dominate child mortality indirect estimation, with extensions to all retrospective inquiries, because in many instances, mothers give reasonably accurate reports about their children. There is no equivalently powerful method for adults, or more generally for individuals aged above 5 or 10 years. A battery of methods exists, which are adapted to data availability and data quality problems. These methods all work very well if data are good and assumptions are met, but most of them are very sensitive to errors in data and violation of assumptions. The main reason is that adult mortality is a rather infrequent event, even in high mortality population. For example, in Guatemala in 1985, the death rate above age 5 is .0060, compared to a death rate below age 5 of .0212 (Keyfitz and Flieger, 1990: 310). Small violations of assumptions and small departures from accuracy in data can produce relatively large impacts on the implied mortality levels of adults.

In spite of these limitations, the logic of the Brass approach to childhood mortality has been extended to the estimation of adult mortality based on survey questions on the survival of parents. The developments are primarily attributable to Brass himself and his students, Kenneth Hill and Ian Timaeus. However, the pioneering effort to use orphanhood information to make inferences about adult mortality was made by Louis Henry (1960). The logic of the approach is the same as for children, and the operationalization is very similar: a simple question about the survivorship of the respondent's mother and father is asked in a survey or in a census. The survivorship status of one's parents up to the time of the survey, together with the age of the respondent, provides well-defined indicators of mortality outcomes and the duration of exposure required to interpret them.

Suppose that childbearing always occurred at age 30. Then the proportion of persons aged 20 with a surviving mother is an estimate of $_{20}p_{30}^{F}$, the female probability of surviving from age 30 to 50. The likelihood that a particular mother's mortality will be reported upon in the survey is directly proportional to her number of surviving children who are eligible for inclusion in the survey. Thus to use the proportion of mothers who survived as an estimator of the population's survivorship requires the assumption that adult mortality is not associated with the number of surviving children, including whether or not a woman had any children at all.

Of course, childbearing does not occur to women at a single age, but is spaced over a period of some 35 years. The general expression for the number of non-orphans aged y at time t in a closed population is:

$$NO(y, t) = B(t - y) \cdot p(y) \cdot p_M(y) \tag{11.5}$$

where

$B(t - y) =$ the number of births y years ago/(i.e., at time $t - y$),
$p(y)$ $\quad =$ the probability that a child born y years ago survived to age y,
$p_M(y)$ $\quad =$ the probability that a mother of a child born y years ago survives y years since giving birth.

By its multiplicative format, this expression assumes independence of the survival probabilities of mother and child.

Similarly, the expression for the number of persons aged y at time t in a closed population is:

$$N(y, t) = B(t - y)p(y) \tag{11.6}$$

Then:

$$\Pi(y, t) = \frac{NO(y, t)}{N(y, t)} = \frac{B(t - y) \cdot p(y) \cdot p_M(y)}{B(t - y) \cdot p(y)} = p_M(y) \tag{11.7}$$

where $\Pi(y, t)$ is the proportion of non-orphans aged y at time t. The proportion non-orphaned gives a direct estimate of mothers' survival probability. Let us see how that probability is connected to the underlying population life table, assuming that survival probabilities are the same for mothers as for all women and ignoring multiple births, which do not affect the account.

Define $W_{t-y}(t)$, the number of living women at time t who gave birth at time $t - y$:

$$W_{t-y}(t) = \int_{15}^{50} B(x, t - y) \cdot {}_y p_x dx \tag{11.8}$$

where

$B(x, t - y) =$ the number of births to women aged x at time $t - y$,

$_yp_x$ $\quad\quad = $ the probability of surviving from x to $x + y$ in the female cohort life table for the cohort aged x at time $t - y$.

The total number of women who gave birth at time $t - y$, $W_{t-y}(t - y)$, is simply equal to the total number of births at time $t - y$. Thus:

$$p_M(y) = \frac{W_{t-y}(t)}{W_{t-y}(t - y)} = \int_{15}^{50} \frac{B(x, t - y)}{B(t - y)} \cdot {_yp_x}\, dx = \int_{15}^{50} v(x, t - y) \cdot {_yp_x}\, dx \quad \text{(11.9)}$$

where $v(x, t - y)$ is the proportionate age distribution of mothers at birth at time $t - y$.

Combining equations (11.7) and (11.9) gives:

$$\Pi(y, t) = \int_{15}^{50} v(x, t - y) \cdot {_yp_x}\, dx \quad\quad\quad \text{(11.10)}$$

Thus, the proportion of people aged y at time t with a living mother is a weighted average of adult female survival probabilities, with weights being the age distribution of mothers at childbirth y years earlier. As in the Brass method, the proportion of the population with surviving kin confounds actual mortality conditions with the shape of the fertility function. The left-hand side of equation (11.10) is provided by a survey of the population, and it is used to estimate a feature of the adult female mortality function.

Once again, to interpret the proportion with surviving mothers as a pure measure of mortality, we must adjust for effects of fertility. Suppose again that the $_yp_x$ function is linear in x which is typically not a bad assumption over a wide range of adult ages: $_yp_x = K - j \cdot x$. Then

$$\Pi(y, t) = \int_{15}^{50} v(x, t - y) \cdot [K - j \cdot x]\, dx$$

$$= K - j \cdot \int_{15}^{50} v(x, t - y) \cdot x\, dx$$

$$= K - j \cdot M^*$$

or

$$\Pi(y, t) = {_yp_{M^*}} \quad\quad\quad\quad \text{(11.11)}$$

where M^* is the mean age of mothers at childbearing at time $t - y$.

Equation (11.11) is not a bad approximation, but it is possible to improve upon it while making the implementation of the method more user-friendly. Analogously to Brass child mortality procedures, a set of correspondences is established between the ages of reporting children and ages of mothers:

Age of offspring	Mortality function estimated from orphanhood reports for this age
15–19	l_{45}/l_{25}
20–4	l_{50}/l_{25}
25–9	l_{55}/l_{25}
30–4	l_{60}/l_{25}
	(note that the same beginning age is kept)

Once again, the estimates need to be tailored to fertility circumstances of a particular population by means of adjustment factors. Instead of being based on P_1/P_2, these are based on M^*, the mean age of mothers at childbirth. As before, M^* is usually estimated on the basis of current fertility, $M^*(t)$, rather than on fertility at the time of birth of each surviving cohort of children interviewed, $M^*(t-y)$, as equation (11.11) requires. (Where this latter information is available, of course, it should be used.) Usually, this mean age at birth is calculated from a question on "births last year," by age of mother. It is not equal to the mean age of the fertility schedule, because M^*, unlike the mean age of the fertility schedule, is affected by the age distribution of women. Note that if M^* is estimated from "births last year" tabulated by current age, women were on average half a year younger when they gave birth, so that one must subtract 0.5 years from the mean age obtained in order to obtain the correct value of M^*.

Hill and Trussell (1977) have designed the following adjustment equation which converts proportions non-orphaned into conventional probabilities of surviving:

$$_y P_{25} = a_y + b_y \cdot M^* + c_y \cdot {}_5\Pi_{y-5} \tag{11.12}$$

where

$_y P_{25}$ = the female probability of surviving from age 25 to $25 + y$,
M^* = the mean age of mothers at childbirth,
$_5\Pi_{y-5}$ = the proportion of people aged $(y-5)$ to y whose mother is alive, and
a_y, b_y, and c_y = adjustment factors.

Once again, the set of adjustment factors are produced by simulations using model schedules of mortality and fertility. The coefficients are included in box 11.2, which shows a detailed example of the estimation procedure using the orphanhood method with data from Swaziland in 1986. Note that the coefficients on M^* are positive: the older are mothers at childbirth, given a certain proportion orphaned, the higher is the implied life table survivorship.

This method can also be used to estimate male mortality from information on paternal orphanhood, but results are often more disappointing. The relationship between fathers and children is, on average, less durable than that between mothers and children. Consequently, people may have poorer information about the survival of their physiological fathers.

11.2.2 Problems and biases associated with the orphanhood method

One problem associated with the method is that the estimated mortality does not refer to specific time periods; it provides direct information about cohort mortality, not period mortality. This is not a problem if mortality has been constant, but in most cases, the estimates represent average measures over a somewhat lengthy (and varying) period of exposure. A method to "date" the estimates has been developed by Brass and Bamgboye (1981), but it is not as straightforward as for the Brass child mortality technique.

A potential bias already noted arises from the fact that only surviving children can report about the survivorship of their mothers. This selection effect probably biases survival estimates upwards because mortality risks across generations in the same family are likely to be positively correlated. The bias may be offset in part by the tendency for poor women, whose mortality risks are usually above average, to have higher fertility.

Perhaps the most serious drawback of the method is a problem that has been termed the "adoption effect." This term refers to the tendency to give reports not about the biological mother but about the social mother who may have adopted the respondent after the death of the actual mother. This bias is very problematic below age 15, when children are not reporting for themselves. The interviewer will often assume that the mother is living, which leads to implausibly low mortality below age 15. For this reason, the method is designed primarily to be used with reports from offspring aged 15 and older. This "adoption" problem affects other ages also, but it becomes relatively less important as mortality itself makes bigger inroads among aging cohorts.

Another source of potential bias is misreporting of respondent's age, the indicator of parental exposure to the risk of death. In applying the method separately by sex of respondents, it has often been found (e.g., in Latin America and South Asia) that mother's mortality appears higher from daughters' reports than from sons'. While this difference could result from a real survival advantage of having sons, it could also be simply due to different patterns of age reporting between the sexes. It appears that women's ages are often understated relative to men's, perhaps because of women's efforts to appear youthful or the prestige associated with achieving older ages for men.

11.2.3   Variants of the orphanhood method

When there is information on orphanhood at two surveys of the same population, it is possible to avert the time indeterminacy of estimates and produce survival probabilities that pertain specifically to the intersurvey period (Preston and Chen, 1984). This method is based on a simple extension of the variable-r equations developed in chapter 8. The following equation expresses the number of non-orphans aged x at time t in terms of risk functions and growth rates at time t:

$$NO(x, t) = NO(0, t) \cdot e^{- \int_0^x [r_{NO}(a,t) + \mu_{NO}(a,t) + \mu_M(a,t)] \, da} \qquad \textbf{(11.13)}$$

where

$NO(x, t)$ = the number of non-orphans aged x at time t (i.e., the number of persons whose natural mother is still living),

$r_{NO}(a, t)$ = the growth rate of the number of non-orphans at age x at time t,

$\mu_{NO}(a, t)$ = the force of mortality of non-orphans aged a at time t,

$\mu_M(a, t)$ = the force of mortality of mothers of non-orphans aged a at time t.

Box 11.2 *Estimation of Adult Mortality from Information on Orphanhood, Hill and Trussell Variant*

Data required:
$_5N_y$ = Number of respondents aged y to $y + 5$
$_5NO_y$ = Number of respondents aged y to $y + 5$ with mother alive (non-orphans)
$_5B_y$ = Number of children born in past year to women aged y to $y + 5$ at time of interview

Intermediate indexes:
$$M^* = \frac{\sum_{y=15,5}^{45}(y+2)\cdot _5B_y}{\sum_{y=15,5}^{45} {_5B_y}} = \text{mean age of mothers at childbirth.}$$

$$_5\Pi_y = \frac{_5NO_y}{_5N_y} = \text{proportion of respondents aged } y \text{ to } y + 5 \text{ with mother alive.}$$

Estimation equation:
$_yP_{25} = a_y + b_y \cdot M^* + c_y \cdot {_5\Pi_{y-5}}$ = female probability of surviving from age 25 to $25 + y$
a_y, b_y, c_y : Coefficients for estimation of female survivorship probabilities

Example: Swaziland, 1986

Age y	$_5N_y$	$_5NO_y$	$_5B_y$	$(y+2)\cdot {_5B_y}$	$_5\Pi_y$	Coefficients			$_yP_{25}$	West mortality level
						a_y	b_y	c_y		
15	75,358	71,510	3,234	54,978	0.9489					
20	58,097	52,579	6,576	144,672	0.9050	−0.1798	0.00476	1.0505	0.9444	20.0
25	46,852	39,887	5,240	141,480	0.8513	−0.2267	0.00737	1.0291	0.9018	18.8
30	35,515	27,721	3,403	108,896	0.7805	−0.3108	0.01072	1.0287	0.8518	18.3
35	30,927	21,412	2,146	79,402	0.6923	−0.4259	0.01473	1.0473	0.7856	17.8
40	24,437	14,102	874	36,708	0.5771	−0.5566	0.01903	1.0818	0.7015	17.7
45	22,663	10,837	411	19,317	0.4782	−0.6676	0.02256	1.1228	0.5839	17.4
50	16,096	5,799			0.3603	−0.6981	0.02344	1.1454	0.4767	18.7
Sum			21,884	585,453						

$M^* = 585,453/21,884 = 26.75$ years
Example of calculation of $_yP_{25}$:
$$_{20}P_{25} = a_{20} + b_{20} \cdot M^* + c_{20} \cdot {_5\Pi_{15}}$$
$$= -0.1798 + 0.00476 \cdot 26.75 + 1.0505 \cdot 0.9489$$
$$= 0.9444$$
Data source: Swaziland. Central Statistical Office. *Report on the 1986 Swaziland Population Census, Vol. 1: Statistical Tables*. Mbabane, Swaziland, Central Statistical Office, 1988.

The corresponding equation for the entire population is:

$$N(x, t) = N(0, t) \cdot e^{-\int_0^x [r(a,t)+\mu(a,t)]\,da} \tag{11.14}$$

Assuming that $\mu_{NO}(a, t) = \mu(a, t)$, and dividing equation (11.13) by equation (11.14) gives:

$$\frac{NO(x, t)}{N(x, t)} = \Pi(x, t) = e^{\int_0^x [r_{NO}(a,t)-r(a,t)+\mu_M(a,t)]\,da} \tag{11.15}$$

Rearranging equation (11.15) gives:

$$\Pi(x) \cdot e^{\int_0^x [r_{NO}(a) - r(a)] \, da} = e^{-\int_0^x [\mu_M(a)] \, da}$$

$$\Pi(x) \cdot e^{\int_0^x r_\pi(a) \, da} = \Pi^*(x)$$

(11.16)

where

$\Pi(x)$ = the observed proportion non-orphaned at age x (geometric mean of the proportions observed at age x at two surveys),

$r_\pi(a)$ = the growth rate of the proportion non-orphaned at age a,

$\Pi^*(x)$ = the proportion of non-orphaned at age x in a stationary population based on the force of mortality of mothers during the intersurvey period.

Note that if mortality and ages of childbearing have been constant, $r_\pi(a)$ will be zero at all ages and $\Pi(x)$ will be an unbiased estimate of $\Pi^*(x)$. In other cases, once the growth correction is performed, the converted proportion can be used as an input into the Brass orphanhood procedure. The resulting mortality estimates pertain to the intercensal or intersurvey period, and therefore, there is no need for "dating" the estimates.

Table 11.3 presents an application of the method to data from Panama, and compares it to the traditional orphanhood method. The proportion non-orphaned rose at almost every age between 1977 and 1980, indicating that mortality was declining. Applying the Brass orphanhood method to the growth-corrected proportions non-orphaned results in lower mortality estimates (i.e., higher "levels" of mortality in the West model life table system). This result is consistent with the fact that the traditional orphanhood method provides mortality estimates that pertain to the past. An improvement in mortality is also suggested by the improved "levels" of mortality in the West model life table system at younger ages in columns (6) and (7), when the cross-sectional, uncorrected estimates are used, and where younger ages represent more recent experience. In contrast, the "levels" associated with the growth-corrected orphanhood proportions (col. 8) show no such trend and are gratifyingly consistent. Other applications of this procedure are presented in Robles (1996).

Other ways of averting the time indeterminacy of Brass's original procedure involve collecting supplementary information relative to the timing of death of parents who have died. Chackiel and Orellana (1985) suggest asking specific questions about the date of death of the parents, which allows one to directly estimate the time location of the mortality estimates. However, respondents are often unable to accurately provide answers to this question, a problem that has limited the use of the method in regions like sub-Saharan Africa. A more promising method is based on a question about whether orphanhood occurred before or after marriage, asked to people aged 25 or more (Timaeus, 1991a). Such a question is less precise than Chackiel and Orellana's question about parents' date of death, but it seems to be more accurately reported by respondents. This method has shown promising results when applied to data from some African and Latin-American countries (Timaeus, 1991b, 1996).

There is an alternative way of using orphanhood logic to estimate adult mortality without asking a direct question about orphanhood. This procedure uses instead standard information provided by the Brass child mortality question on numbers of children surviving. The basis of the method is the recognition that, in a closed population, the number of surviving children reported by mothers is equal to the number of non-orphans in the population (Preston, 1980).

Table 11.3: *Estimates of adult mortality via orphanhood methods applied to Panama, 1977–80*

Age	Proportion non-orphaned		Growth rate of proportion non-orphaned, 1977–80	Cumulation of growth rates to midpoint of interval	Adjusted proportion 1977–80	"Level" of mortality based upon proportions orphaned in:		
	7-1-77	5-11-80				1977	1980	1977–80
	(1)	(2)	(3)	(4)	(5)*			
0–4	.9960	.9949	−.00039	−.00097	.9945	—	—	—
5–9	.9844	.9903	.00210	.00331	.9906	20.6	21.5	22.4
10–14	.9753	.9794	.00147	.01224	.9894	20.7	22.0	23.0
15–19	.9556	.9608	.00191	.02069	.9782	20.3	20.9	22.7
20–4	.9195	.9316	.00459	.03694	.9604	19.7	20.5	22.6
25–9	.8908	.8967	.00232	.05422	.9435	19.9	20.3	22.9
30–4	.8157	.8450	.01240	.09101	.9093	18.9	20.1	23.0
35–9	.7618	.7746	.00585	.13664	.8806	19.2	19.9	23.5
40–4	.6166	.6781	.03340	.23477	.8177	18.0	19.8	23.9

* This column is derived by multiplying the geometric mean of columns (1) and (2) by exp{col(4)}

Source: Preston and Chen, 1984.

Starting from this identity, an expression relating the proportion of the total population with living mother to the female life table is derived:

$$\frac{NO}{N} = \int_0^\infty c(x) \int_\alpha^\beta v(a) \cdot {}_x p_a \, da \, dx$$

or, in discrete terms:

$$\frac{NO}{N} = \sum_{x=0}^\infty {}_5 c_x \sum_{a=15}^{45} {}_5 v_a \cdot \frac{5 \cdot l_{a+5+x}}{{}_5 L_a} \tag{11.17}$$

where

NO/N = the proportion of the total population that is not orphaned, i.e., the number of surviving children reported by mothers divided by the total size of the population,

${}_5 c_x$ = the proportionate age distribution of the total population,

${}_5 v_a$ = the proportionate age distribution of women at birth, and

${}_5 L_a$ and l_a = functions in a model life table system.

Because movement to better mortality conditions monotonically raises the right-hand side of equation (11.17), there is only one level of mortality in a life table system that will make the right-hand side equal the left-hand side. The method consists in finding, from a model life table system, the mortality level that satisfies the equality in equation (11.17).

Unlike the direct orphanhood method, this method yields only one estimate of adult female mortality, and it best identifies e_{25}^o or e_{30}^o. The reference period in most developing countries will be about 10 years earlier. Although the method is subject to the adoption bias and to errors of omission, its main advantage is the wide availability of the data required. It is principally designed to be used as a last resort when no other data are available.

11.3 The Sisterhood Method for Estimating Maternal Mortality

Techniques similar to the orphanhood method rely on reports of the survivorship of spouses or siblings. These are typically subject to greater inaccuracies in reporting. The link between brothers and sisters may not be as strong as the mother–child link, so some people might not know with certainty whether their siblings are surviving or not. They might also be unaware of siblings who died in childhood. Similarly, divorced adults might loose touch with their ex-spouses and not know about their survivorship.

One kin survival method has gained greater currency, in part because of growing interest in maternal mortality. The sisterhood method (Graham, Brass and Snow, 1989) is a cause-specific development of the technique for estimating general mortality, based on the survivorship of sisters. From proportions of sisters who died in childbirth, the method provides estimates of the lifetime risk of maternal mortality in the presence of other causes of death.

Let us define $N(i)$, the number of sisters ever at risk of maternal death reported by respondents in age group i, and $D^m(i)$, the number of maternal deaths among those sisters. Assume for purposes of model development that fertility and mortality have been constant. For practical reasons, $N(i)$ will be collected by inquiring how many sisters have ever married (or are aged over 15), and $D^m(i)$ will be the number of sisters, among these, who have died during pregnancy, childbirth, or the postpartum period of six weeks after childbirth.

The method relates $\Pi^m(i) = D^m(i)/N(i)$, the proportion of adult sisters dead from maternal causes, reported by respondents aged i, to $q^m(w)$, the lifetime risk of maternal death. If there are no births after age 50, the lifetime risk of maternal death can be expressed as $q^m(50)$. In order to establish the relationship between $\Pi^m(i)$ and $q^m(50)$, two demographic models are used:

- *standard fertility and mortality schedules* that allow one to model a distribution of z, the difference between ages of siblings and respondents (Hill and Trussell, 1977). It can be demonstrated that z has a symmetrical distribution, $\theta(z)$, about a mean of zero if the reproductive life of the mothers of respondents is completed.
- *a maternal mortality model* that allows one to relate $q^m(i)$, the probability of dying from maternal causes before age i, to $q^m(50)$, the probability of maternal death by the end of the reproductive period. The relationship between $q^m(i)$ and $q^m(50)$ can be expressed as:

$$q^m(i) = c(i) \cdot q^m(50) \tag{11.18}$$

where $c(i)$ represents the proportion of maternal deaths occurring before age i, according to the standard schedule of maternal mortality.

The proportion of sisters dead from maternal causes $\Pi^m(i)$, reported by respondents aged i is equal to:

$$\Pi^m(i) = \int_{-\infty}^{+\infty} \theta(z) q^m(i+z) dz \tag{11.19}$$

By combining equations (11.18) and (11.19), $\Pi^m(i)$ can be related to the lifetime risk of maternal mortality $q^m(50)$.

$$\Pi^m(i) = q^m(50) \cdot \int_{-\infty}^{+\infty} \theta(z) \cdot c(i+z) \, dz \tag{11.20}$$

We see from equation (11.20) that $\Pi^m(i)$ differs from $q^m(50)$ by a factor which only depends on the two demographic models. If the age i of respondents is high enough, say 60 and over, all sisters have graduated from the risk of maternal mortality. The function $c(i+z)$ is in this case equal or near 1 for any possible value of z, and $\Pi^m(i)$ at those ages is a good estimator of $q^m(50)$. However, if the age of the respondents is under 60, some sisters would still be at risk of maternal death. The function $c(i+z)$ will be less than one for some values of z, and $\Pi^m(i)$ will in this case underestimate $q^m(50)$. Thus, the proportions need to be adjusted in order to give ultimate estimates of the lifetime risk of mortality. Fertility and mortality models are used to calculate the adjustment factors $A(i)$:

$$A(i) = \int_{-\infty}^{+\infty} \theta(z) \cdot c(i+z) \, dz \tag{11.21}$$

The set of adjustment factors $A(i)$, applicable to any population, is shown in box 11.3. As expected, $A(i)$ equals 1.00 above age 60, and goes down for younger age groups.

Dividing each proportion of dead sisters by those adjustment factors, we are able to derive separate estimates of the lifetime risk of maternal mortality, $q^m(50)$, for each age-group i:

$$q^m(50) = \frac{D^m(i)}{N(i) \cdot A(i)} \tag{11.22}$$

Variations in $q^m(50)$ by age of respondents can in theory be interpreted in terms of time trends in maternal mortality. The reference period, T_i, to which each estimate refers, was computed from fixed fertility and mortality models. This set of T_i is an average approximation designed to be used for various populations without specific adjustment. By summing deaths across age groups, one can obtain an overall single estimate of the lifetime risk of maternal mortality for all age groups:

$$Q^m(50) = \frac{\sum_i D^m(i)}{\sum_i N(i) \cdot A(i)} \tag{11.23}$$

For the estimation of the reference period to which this overall single estimate refers, Graham, Brass and Snow (1989) propose to use the following estimation equation, using reports from women under age 50 only:

$$T = \frac{\sum_i N(i) \cdot A(i) \cdot T(i)}{\sum_i N(i) \cdot A(i)} \tag{11.24}$$

In practice, T tends to be approximately 12 years; that is, the overall estimate of lifetime risk approximates mortality conditions 12 years or so before the survey.

The sisterhood method is easy to implement. However, it is not free of problems (Garenne and Friedberg, 1997). The estimates are sensitive to the assumption of independence between the number of siblings and their survival probabilities, and the models of mortality and fertility used to calculate the adjustment factors may not suit the studied population. Reporting errors may be large, especially if a maternal death occurred many years before the survey. The definition of a maternal death is based on the timing of death relative to pregnancy, rather than on specific pregnancy-related conditions, so that some nonmaternal deaths will be classified as maternal. Often, the sample size of the survey will be too small to allow any interpretation of differences in $q^m(50)$ among age groups. Thus, it is preferable to rely on $Q^m(50)$, the overall estimate of the lifetime risk of maternal mortality. A detailed example of the application of the sisterhood method is shown in box 11.3.

An alternative survey procedure for estimating maternal mortality, based upon more intensive inquiries about the conditions surrounding sisters' deaths, is presented by Rutenberg and Sullivan (1991). Using a logic similar to the sisterhood method, Hill (1981) suggested taking advantage of information on the residence of siblings to estimate the volume of out-migration.

11.4 Estimating Mortality and Fertility from Maternity Histories

11.4.1 Estimation of child mortality from complete maternity histories

One of the most common ways of estimating mortality in countries with no or deficient vital registration is the use of complete maternity histories. This method consists of taking a survey of women of reproductive ages and asking them about the birth and death of all children born to them. Mortality rates can then be directly computed from the analysis of the survival of different birth cohorts.

Box 11.3 *The Sisterhood Method for Estimating Maternal Mortality*

$N(i)$ = number of ever-married sisters reported by women in age group i

$D^m(i)$ = number of ever-married sisters who died from maternal mortality

$A(i)$ = adjustment factor, estimated from fertility and mortality models

$q^m(50) = \frac{D^m(i)}{N(i) \cdot A(i)}$ = lifetime probability of dying from maternal causes, for sisters of respondents in age group i

$Q^m(50) = \frac{\sum_i D^m(i)}{\sum_i N(i) \cdot A(i)}$ = lifetime probability of dying from maternal causes, single estimate for all women included in the survey

$T_i =$ reference period, in years, to which each $q^m(50)$ refers, computed from fixed models of $\theta(z)$ and $q(x)$

$T = \frac{\sum_i N(i) \cdot A(i) \cdot T(i)}{\sum_i N(i) \cdot A(i)}$ (for $i < 50$) = reference period to which the single estimate $Q^m(50)$ refers

Example: Gambia, 1987

Age group i	Number of respondents	$N(i)$	$D^m(i)$	$A(i)$	$N(i) \cdot A(i)$	$q^m(50)$	T_i
15–19	320	493*	4	0.107	53	0.076	5.7
20–4	263	405*	6	0.206	83	0.072	6.8
25–9	275	427	11	0.343	146	0.075	8.1
30–4	265	414	11	0.503	208	0.053	9.7
35–9	214	334	12	0.664	222	0.054	11.7
40–4	157	238	11	0.802	191	0.058	14.3
45–9	158	233	10	0.900	210	0.048	17.5
50–4	140	202	2	0.958	194	0.010	21.2
55–9	133	215	9	0.986	212	0.042	25.6
60+	238	373	15	1.000	373	0.040	35.2
All			91		1,892	0.048	11.7

$Q^m(50) = 91/1,892 = .048$

$T = 11.7$ years

The lifetime risk of dying from pregnancy-related causes in Gambia is about 1 in 21, and it refers to a period about 12 years prior to the survey

* For those age groups, the total number of sisters who will ultimately enter the reproductive period is underestimated. It can be adjusted by multiplying the number of respondents in these age groups by the average number of sisters reaching the reproductive period reported in the age groups 25+, i.e., 1.54

Source: Graham, W. et al., 1988. *Indirect Estimation of Maternal Mortality: The Sisterhood Method*. CPS Research Paper 88–1, London School of Hygiene and Tropical Medicine.

This strategy has been extensively used by the World Fertility Survey (WFS) and Demographic and Health Survey (DHS) programs, even though the data collection involved is much more time consuming than that required for the traditional Brass question: 20–30 minutes on a questionnaire, versus 2–5 minutes for the Brass question (Sullivan, 1990). The advantage of this strategy is that it provides detailed information on child mortality (Wunsch, 1983). It permits the computation of age-specific mortality rates of children and the explicit estimation of trends in child mortality.

In addition, the data collected through maternity histories permit the analysis of various factors associated with child mortality, including age of mother, birth order of the child, and birth interval. For example, the analysis of maternity histories collected by WFS has shown the key role of birth intervals in child mortality (Hobcraft et al., 1985). Maternity histories often include socioeconomic characteristics of the father, mother, and household, permitting multivariate analyses through hazard models, logit regression methods, or other approaches.

The estimation of child mortality from maternity histories, although evaluated *directly* from the counts of births and deaths, is included in this chapter on *indirect* methods because it is subject to various biases that are not present in conventional direct mortality estimation based upon the traditional combination of census and vital registration data.

First, the analysis of maternity histories is subject to selection biases. Obviously, only surviving women are interviewed, and therefore, no information is collected on the mortality conditions of those who have been orphaned. Child mortality estimates in periods more distant from the survey are based on the experience of younger and younger women because older women (e.g., ages 50+) are usually excluded from such surveys. This selectivity by age of women is illustrated in figure 11.1. If a survey of women aged 15–50 is carried out, say, on January 1, 1990, the maternity histories of these women will provide information on birth cohorts born between 1955 and 1989. The Lexis diagram shows that earlier birth cohorts are born to younger women, in contrast to the more representative reporting for more recent births. Since first-order births typically have a higher risk of death, the resulting child mortality estimates for earlier periods might be overestimated, and the estimated mortality decline might appear larger than it actually is. To limit this problem, it is recommended to analyze child mortality rates for time periods up to only 15 years before the survey (Hill, 1991).

The most important problem related to the analysis of maternity histories refers to what is termed "recall" errors. When maternity histories are collected, women are asked to recall events that occurred up to several decades earlier. Consequently, they may simply not remember some births at all, or be unable to locate them precisely in time. The reported ages or dates may therefore be rounded to exact numbers, introducing biases into the data set. Age rounding is particularly problematic for the computation of the infant mortality rate, for which deaths must be precisely allocated to periods before or after the child's first birthday. Of course, no allocation whatsoever is possible if only the Brass questions are asked.

A similar approach has been used for the estimation of adult mortality, using retrospective questions about the deaths of household members asked during a single-round survey. Such procedures have yielded less success than the analysis of maternity histories because, even in high-mortality countries, adult mortality rates are low enough to produce large sampling variability in small-scale survey data. In addition, under-reporting of adult deaths in such surveys is very common and often makes it impossible to estimate adult mortality with a reasonable degree of precision (Hill, 1991).

11.4.2 *Estimation of fertility from complete maternity histories*

Complete maternity histories can also be used to estimate fertility levels and trends. The computation of age-specific fertility rates for different time periods is straightforward when such data are available. The numerator and denominator of fertility rates must pertain to the

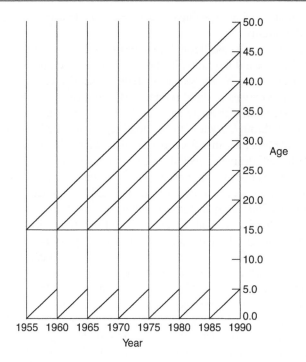

Figure 11.1 Lexis diagram for cohorts of women aged 15–50 in 1990 and for cohorts of their offspring between the ages of 0 and 5

same exposure segment defined in terms of ages of women and calendar periods. The numerator consists of a count of births and the denominator a count of person-years.

This use of maternity histories can produce good estimates of age-specific fertility rates, but it gives little information on the trend in the total fertility rate. As illustrated in figure 11.1, if the sample includes women from age 15 to 50, the TFR can be computed only for the most recent period. To obtain a longer set of TFRs, the survey must include age groups beyond age 50. As a substitute, models of age patterns of fertility are sometimes employed.

As in the context of child mortality estimation, the main biases associated with the use of maternity histories for fertility estimation are related to errors in the retrospective declaration of births. The two main possible sources of distortion are omission of births and misplacement of births in time. Although the extent of under-reporting is acceptable in some cases (Garenne, 1994), errors of misplacement of births in time is a very common problem in maternity histories in less developed countries. Several methods have been proposed to correct for these errors (Brass, 1975; Potter, 1977), none of them highly satisfactory when the errors are substantial. In section 11.5.3, we will present a method for estimating period fertility rates from the comparison of the women's age-specific parities at two surveys, which offers the advantage of being insensitive to misplacement of births in time.

11.5 Indirect Estimation Methods Using Age Distributions at Two Censuses

Many indirect methods are based on the observation of the population at two censuses. In chapter 10, we encountered the use of two-census methods to assess the quality of death registration. All of the variable-r methods developed in chapter 8 are also based on intercensal comparisons. In this section, we will study some other methods based on the same logic.

The basic idea behind all two-census methods is in fact very simple and relies upon the balancing equation of population growth adapted for cohorts. In a closed population, the difference between the size of a cohort at the first census and its size at the second census corresponds to the number of deaths in the cohort. Thus, intercensal methods principally consist of tracking birth cohorts at two census dates, using age as a marker of cohort membership. If the two censuses are separated by ten years, a birth cohort present at the first census should be 10 years older at the second census. Of course, age misreporting can create spurious flows into and out of cohorts.

The most simple intercensal method consists in calculating for each cohort the proportion surviving the intercensal period ("survivorship ratios") and recognizing that the ratio maps directly onto a cohort life table function for the intercensal period. For example, in case of a 5-year intercensal period:

$$\frac{{}_5N_{x+5}(t+5)}{{}_5N_x(t)} = \frac{{}_5L_{x+5}}{{}_5L_x} \tag{11.25}$$

where

$_5N_x(t) =$ the number of people aged x to $x+5$ at time t; and
$_5L_x \quad =$ the number of person-years lived between age x and $x+5$ in the life table pertaining to the intercensal period.

By chaining together the ratios at different ages, it is possible to reconstruct the life table beyond age 5. For a complete life table, we would also need the intercensal births, $B[t, t+5]$, and compute the following ratio:

$$\frac{{}_5N_0(t+5)}{B[t, t+5]} = \frac{{}_5L_0}{5 \cdot l_0} \tag{11.26}$$

In many cases, though, data on intercensal births are not available or are seriously flawed, and the method will produce only a life table starting at age 5.

Despite its apparent simplicity, the estimation of adult mortality through this approach is not straightforward. In many cases, censuses are separated by a number of years that makes it difficult to compute survival ratios or to chain them together. Unless migration adjustments are made, the apparent number of deaths is spuriously inflated by out-migration and deflated by immigration. Since adult mortality is low (much less than 1 percent per year in most of the world), small differences in the completeness of coverage in the two censuses can make it appear that mortality was exceptionally high or low. Age misreporting can produce some very erratic sequences of survivorship ratios, including some ratios greater than one, which is not humanly possible. Age misreporting is a major obstacle to the successful implementation of the basic intercensal method, and the techniques described in this section are basically addressed to minimizing its effects on mortality estimates.

11.5.1 Estimation of intercensal mortality by using cumulation and projection

One way to deal with the problems introduced by age misreporting is to introduce a system of model life tables, which imposes a structure on the set of age-specific survival rates. The idea behind this method is to find the structure that is most consistent across cohorts with the observed data, and to assume that this mortality structure is what actually prevailed in the population. The procedure was developed by Coale and Demeny (United Nations, 1983: 208). They proposed dealing with the cumulated age distribution, rather than with individual age groups, because it is less vulnerable to age misreporting.

For example, assume that we observe the population in 5-year age groups at censuses in 1980 and 1990. We would have the following array of data:

$$
\begin{array}{ll}
{}_5N_0(1980) & {}_5N_0(1990) \\
{}_5N_5(1980) & {}_5N_5(1990) \\
{}_5N_{10}(1980) & {}_5N_{10}(1990) \\
\cdots\cdots & {}_5N_{15}(1990) \\
\cdots\cdots & \cdots\cdots
\end{array}
$$

The idea is simply to find the level of mortality that successfully survives the population aged 0+ in 1980 to 10+ in 1990. After choosing an initial model life table (usually indexed by life expectancy at birth), the population aged 10+ in 1990 is estimated by "projecting" forward the population aged 0+ in 1980. For example, if we use $e_0^o = 50.0$ years for the initial model life table, the appropriate estimation equation is:

$$
N_{10+}^{50}(1990) = {}_5N_{10}^{50}(1990) + {}_5N_{15}^{50}(1990) + {}_5N_{20}^{50}(1990) + \cdots
$$

$$
= {}_5N_0(1980)\frac{{}_5L_{10}^{50}}{{}_5L_0^{50}} + {}_5N_5(1980)\frac{{}_5L_{15}^{50}}{{}_5L_5^{50}} + {}_5N_{10}(1980)\frac{{}_5L_{20}^{50}}{{}_5L_{10}^{50}} + \cdots \quad \textbf{(11.27)}
$$

where

$N_{10+}^{50}(1990)$ = the estimated population above age 10 in 1990, obtained from projection with a life expectancy at birth of 50 years, and

${}_5L_x^{50}$ = the person-years lived between ages x and $x + 5$, taken from a model life table with a life expectancy at birth of 50 years.

As we choose higher values, v, for the life expectancy at birth in the model life table system, the value for $N_{10+}^{v}(1990)$ will increase. By varying the level of mortality in the model life table system, one can find the level, v^*, at which $N_{10+}^{v^*}(1990)$ will equal the observed N_{10+} (1990). This procedure is affected by age misreporting that transfers people across the age-10 boundary at the second census. Thus, it is desirable to repeat the process beginning with other initial ages at first census (5, 10 . . .). Coale and Demeny recommend taking the median of the first nine estimates to obtain a single e_0^o estimate.

This method is appealing because it requires only a limited number of assumptions: that the population is closed to migration (or adjusted for net international migration), that the two censuses are equally complete, and that mortality belongs to a certain family of model life tables. As a practical matter, violations of the third assumption are far less consequential for estimating overall mortality indexes, such as life expectancy at age 10, than are violations of the first two assumptions.

The method is also affected by age misstatement, which is common in many countries. In general, age overstatement will produce too favorable a level of mortality, with the biases increasing with age at initial estimate; more people will appear to survive the intercensal period than actually do because some "migrate" into a cohort from younger ages. Cumulation limits to some extent problems associated with age overstatement at older ages.

The method just described is sometimes called "forward projection", although the same logic could have been followed with "backward" projection. Palloni and Kominski (1984) have shown that, contrary to a common intuition, the two methods don't necessarily lead to the same estimates because age distributional information is weighted differently when starting with the second census than when starting with the first. Box 11.4 shows a detailed example of the forward survival method applied to data from Indonesia. Heuveline (1998) uses a variant of this approach to estimate the deathtoll of the Khmer Rouge regime in Cambodia, where 25 percent of the population is believed to have died in less than 4 years. The same logic can be used to estimate intercensal net migration assuming that we have a perfect estimate of intercensal mortality (Shryock and Siegel, 1973: 595–6).

11.5.2 Integrated system for demographic estimation from two age distributions

The "forward projection" method just described was based on the choice of an existing tabulated model life table to estimate the mortality level of a population. We present now a two-census method which uses instead a mathematical representation of relationships among mortality rates within a model life table system. Important additional products of the method are an estimate of the crude birth rate and of the true age distribution. This method uses the Brass logit transformation discussed in chapter 9. As we saw in that chapter, the assumption is that within a model life table system, one can represent any life table as a simple transformation of another:

$$\ln\left[\frac{q(a)}{p(a)}\right] = \alpha + \beta \cdot \ln\left[\frac{q_s(a)}{p_s(a)}\right] \tag{11.28}$$

where $q_s(a)$ and $p_s(a)$ are the $q(a)$ and $p(a)$ functions in a "standard" life table. α and β are the parameters that relate the standard life table to any other life table in the mortality family. The higher is α, the higher is mortality relative to the standard; the higher is β, the higher is adult mortality relative to that in childhood. Equation (11.28) can be simplified by substituting $1 - p(a)$ for $q(a)$ and by exponentiating:

$$\frac{1 - p(a)}{p(a)} = e^\alpha \left[\frac{q_s(a)}{p_s(a)}\right]^\beta$$

or

$$\frac{1}{p(a)} = e^\alpha \left[\frac{q_s(a)}{p_s(a)}\right]^\beta + 1 \tag{11.29}$$

We also know from chapter 8 that, in a closed population:

$$c(a) = b e^{-\int_0^a r(x)dx} p(a)$$

Box 11.4 *Estimation of Intercensal Mortality by Using Projection and Cumulation: Example with a 10-year Intercensal Period and 5-year Age Intervals*

$_5N_x(t)$ = population aged x to $x + 5$ at time t

$_5N_x(t+10)$ = population aged x to $x + 5$ at time $t + 10$

$N_{x+}(t+10) = \sum_{a=x}^{\infty} {_5N_a(t+10)}$ = population aged x and above at time $t + 10$

$_5L_x^v$ = person-years lived between ages x and $x + 5$ in the model life table with mortality level v

$_5N_x^v(t+10) = {_5N_{x-10}(t)} \cdot \dfrac{_5L_x^v}{_5L_{x-10}^v}$ = projected population aged x to $x + 5$ at time $t + 10$, with mortality level v

$N_{x+}^v(t+10) = \sum_{a=x}^{\infty} {_5N_a^v(t+10)}$ = projected population aged x and above at time $t + 10$, with mortality level v

Strategy:

For each age group, find v_1 and v_2 so that $N_{x+}^{v_1}(t+10) \leq N_{x+}(t+10) \leq N_{x+}^{v_2}(t+10)$ and use linear interpolation to estimate the level of mortality v^*, implied by the observed number of people aged x and above at time $t + 10$:

$$v^* = v_1 + (v_2 - v_1) \cdot \frac{N_{x+}(t+10) - N_{x+}^{v_1}(t+10)}{N_{x+}^{v_2}(t+10) - N_{x+}^{v_1}(t+10)}$$

Example: Indonesia, males, intercensal period 1980–90; United Nations model life tables, South Asian pattern

Age x	$_5N_x$ (1980.83)	$_5N_x$ (1990.83)	N_{x+} (1990.83)	Projection with $e_0^o = 51$			with $e_0^o = 53$	with $e_0^o = 55$	with $e_0^o = 57$	e_0^o interpolated
				$\dfrac{_5L_x^{51}}{_5L_{x-10}^{51}}$	$_5N_x^{51}$ (1990.83)	N_{x+}^{51} (1990.83)	N_{x+}^{53} (1990.83)	N_{x+}^{55} (1990.83)	N_{x+}^{57} (1990.83)	
0	10,815,974	10,760,859								
5	10,832,383	11,928,095								

10	9,131,871	11,044,127	**66,684,518**	0.92380	9,991,847	**66,639,725**	**67,020,691**	67,388,390	67,743,731	51.2
15	7,512,541	9,520,440	**55,640,391**	0.97682	10,581,279	**56,647,878**	56,932,078	57,209,872	57,481,942	<51.0
20	5,978,576	7,583,305	**46,119,951**	0.98011	8,950,243	**46,066,599**	**46,322,124**	46,573,223	46,820,487	51.4
25	5,612,684	7,457,150	**38,536,646**	0.97621	7,333,848	37,116,356	37,352,495	37,585,409	**37,815,628**	>57.0
30	4,022,625	6,584,325	**31,079,496**	0.97116	5,806,184	29,782,509	30,000,090	30,215,514	**30,429,300**	>57.0
35	4,190,944	5,788,441	**24,495,171**	0.96359	5,408,333	23,976,325	24,176,263	24,375,046	**24,573,150**	56.2
40	3,644,053	4,010,254	**18,706,730**	0.95089	3,825,067	**18,567,992**	**18,747,575**	18,927,090	19,106,967	52.5
45	3,012,756	3,723,922	**14,696,476**	0.93048	3,899,605	**14,742,925**	14,904,216	15,066,246	15,229,439	<51.0
50	2,717,883	3,289,190	**10,972,554**	0.89864	3,274,709	**10,843,320**	**10,980,541**	11,119,302	11,260,002	52.9
55	1,720,501	2,321,621	**7,683,364**	0.85235	2,567,910	7,568,611	**7,679,611**	**7,792,683**	7,908,167	53.1
60	1,559,230	2,219,069	**5,361,743**	0.78756	2,140,493	5,000,701	5,085,490	5,172,482	**5,261,973**	>57.0
65	811,113	1,329,162	**3,142,674**	0.69878	1,202,250	2,860,208	2,917,461	2,976,641	**3,038,008**	>57.0
70	689,074	945,876	**1,813,512**	0.58786	916,605	1,657,958	1,695,242	1,733,987	**1,774,398**	>57.0
75+	688,422	867,636	**867,636**	0.33873*	741,353	741,353	758,663	776,719	**795,636**	>57.0

* = T^{51}_{75}/T^{51}_{65}

Overall estimate of e^o_0 for the entire male population for the period 1980–90:

Median of the first nine interpolated e^o_0 values

$\bar{e}^o_0 = 52.5$ years

Data source: United Nations, Demographic Yearbook (various years); United Nations, 1982. Model Life Tables for Developing Countries. New York: United Nations.

or

$$\frac{1}{p(a)} = \frac{be^{-\int_0^a r(x)dx}}{c(a)} \qquad (11.30)$$

Combining equation (11.29) and (11.30), and setting $e^{\alpha} = K$ and $\beta = 1$, we have:

$$\frac{e^{-\int_0^a r(x)dx}}{c(a)} = \frac{1}{b} + \frac{K}{b}\left[\frac{q_s(a)}{p_s(a)}\right] \qquad (11.31)$$

The assumption that $\beta = 1$ implies that the slope of the $p(a)$ function in the studied population is the same as that in the standard life table. This may be a reasonable assumption for estimation purposes, because data are often too flawed to allow estimates of both α and β, and because the major issue is to estimate the "level" of mortality relative to a standard.

Equation (11.31) is in fact a simple linear function, where the reciprocal of the intercept corresponds to the birth rate of the population, and where the ratio of the slope to the intercept is an estimate of the level of mortality relative to the chosen standard. The information needed for the left-hand side of the equation can be taken from two censuses, and the variable on the right hand side, $q_s(a)/p_s(a)$ is obtained from the assumed standard life table. Fitting a simple linear regression to these observations will produce the two desired estimates. Note that the function $c(a)$ can be estimated through a linear interpolation, using $(_5c_{a-5} + _5c_a)/10$. Also, if an independent and reliable estimate of child mortality is available (for example, by using the Brass child survival method), then it is possible to limit the analysis to above age 5 and to use the following equation:

$$\frac{p^*(5)e^{-\int_0^a r(x)dx}}{c(a)} = \frac{1}{b} + \frac{K}{b}\left[\frac{q_s^5(a)}{p_s^5(a)}\right], \qquad \text{with } a \geq 5 \qquad (11.32)$$

where $p^*(5)$ is the independent estimate of the survival to age 5, and where q_s^5 and p_s^5 are the probability of dying before or of surviving to age a in the standard life table, conditional on survival to age 5.

This method has been applied to data from India and South Korea (Preston, 1983). Like other intercensal methods, the estimate of the mortality level is sensitive to intercensal migration, to differential census coverage and to age misstatement. There is also a certain level of arbitrariness in selecting points used to fit the line.

Heligman (1985) uses the method to estimate the "true" age distribution of the population. The estimated level of mortality allows one to reconstruct the entire intercensal life table though equation (11.28). This estimated life table, along with the estimated birth rate and the recorded age-specific growth rates, can then be used as input in the basic variable-r equation to reconstruct the age distribution:

$$_5C_a^* = be^{-\int_0^{a+2.5} r(x)dx}\frac{_5L_a}{l_0} \qquad (11.33)$$

The comparison of the estimated age structure to the observed one (more precisely, to the mean of the two observed distributions) can be used to detect errors in age distributions, especially those produced by age misreporting.

11.5.3 The iterative intracohort interpolation procedure for estimating intercensal age schedules

The iterative intracohort interpolation procedure is based on the same idea: the comparison of the population age or duration structure at two censuses gives information about attrition or accession during the intercensal period. It is, however, a more general method that can be applied to various data configurations and to various demographic processes, including mortality, fertility, marriage and mobility. The objective of the method is to estimate the (unobserved) set of intercensal rates that produced the observed intercensal changes in the status of the population classified by age or duration between the two dates. It does so using maximum likelihood reasoning.

Iterative intracohort interpolation was first developed by Coale (1984) as a refinement of the basic variable-r procedure. By estimating with greater precision the number of person-years lived at a certain age during the intercensal period, the original interpolation method permitted the relaxation of the assumption that the age-specific growth rates are constant over time during the intercensal period. It often produced more reliable results than the basic variable-r procedures, especially when applied to population structures that are highly irregular. It was then generalized to other demographic processes (Coale et al., 1985) and applied to relationships that do not use variable-r equations (Coale, 1985). Finally, Stupp (1988) clarified and simplified the procedure. The iterative nature of the procedure is in fact its greatest strength relative to other methods.

Before generalizing the procedure to various types of demographic accounts, we will first briefly describe the application of the procedure to the estimation of age-specific fertility rates from parity at different ages, adapted from Stupp's simplification of the method (Stupp, 1988). The data needed here are simply the mean parity of women at different ages in the population at two different censuses or surveys.

We first need to recognize that when following a cohort through time, the cohort's parity at the second census is equal to the cohort's parity at the first census incremented by the sum of the intercensal age-specific fertility rates for that cohort. An initial estimation of intercensal age- and cohort-specific rates is performed by using linear interpolation, i.e., by assuming that for each cohort, parity increases linearly during the intercensal period. This is done by simply assigning the total intercensal increment in each cohort to the various ages proportionately to the time spent in each age. The age- and cohort-specific fertility rates thus estimated will however differ for each cohort. Since the method aims at producing one set of intercensal rates that apply to all cohorts, these differences are resolved by producing a weighted average at each age of the fertility rates of the different cohorts, with the weights proportional to a cohort's exposure time in an age interval. Through this procedure, we obtain a first set of "average" age-specific fertility rates.

The next step is to apply this first set of "average" age-specific fertility rates to each cohort during the intercensal period. The estimated parity at the second census date for a particular cohort will most likely differ from the observed one. Therefore, a second set of age- and cohort-specific rates needs to be estimated. This is done by observing the proportionate discrepancy between the observed and predicted (i.e., based on the estimated fertility rates) intercensal change in parity for each cohort. This discrepancy is then assumed to prevail in each age interval occupied by the cohort during the period. By adjusting the cohort's fertility rates in this fashion, a second set of "average" age-period fertility rates is obtained. The procedure is then reiterated until the set of rates is stable from one iteration to the other. When this happens,

Table 11.4: *Classification of events to which the intracohort interpolation procedure applies*

Type of event	Example	Status variable required (at two dates [a])	Outcome
(1) Recurrent	• lifetime births • lifetime moves • lifetime marriages	average cumulative number of occurrences of the event, by age or duration	age- or duration-specific rate of occurrence
(2) Nonrecurrent	• first marriage • first birth • death	proportion of persons having experienced the event, by age or duration	age- or duration-specific rate of occurrence

[a] The length of the intercensal period must be a multiple of the length of the age interval.

the resulting fertility rates will indeed agree with the set of mean parities at the two census dates.

This indirect procedure can be applied to many events, including particular events for which no direct method exists because the occurrence of an event is not registered. For example, it has been used successfully to estimate the rates of leaving parental homes in some East Asian and European countries (Zeng et al., 1994), overcoming the fact that departures from parental home are not registered in any of these countries. Table 11.4 shows the different types of event for which the iterative intracohort interpolation method can estimate age schedules when data exist on the cumulative number of events of a particular kind from two censuses or surveys.

For recurrent events, the method produces synthetic estimates of age-specific rates. From these, the cumulative number of lifetime events at various ages can be derived because the initial conditions are specified; the cumulative number of lifetime events at birth is, by definition, zero. Likewise, the proportion experiencing nonrecurrent events such as first marriage or first birth can also be derived. In these cases, estimation of age-specific rates requires the assumption that there is no correlation between the probability of experiencing the event and the probability of being present at the censuses (i.e., that there is no differential mortality or migration).

In the case of mortality estimates, a different approach is required since the living population is never surveyed about whether it is dead. In this case, the intracohort interpolation method must be applied to absolute numbers of survivors by age. Assuming that the rate of occurrence of the event is constant within each age interval, the number of survivors at two dates in a closed population can be related to age-specific occurrence rates as in the following example (adapted from equation 3.10):

$$_1N_{x+2}(t+2) = {_1N_x(t)} \cdot e^{-\left\{ \frac{{_1M_x}}{2} + {_1M_{x+1}} + \frac{{_1M_{x+2}}}{2} \right\}}$$

(11.34)

where

$_1N_x(t)$ = number of survivors aged x to $x+1$ at time t,

$_1M_x$ = intercensal rate of occurrence of the event between age x and $x+1$.

Rearranging equation (11.34) gives:

$$-\ln\{_1N_{x+2}(t+2)\} = -\ln\{_1N_x(t)\} + \frac{_1M_x}{2} + {}_1M_{x+1} + \frac{_1M_{x+2}}{2} \qquad \textbf{(11.35)}$$

Equation (11.35) relates the numbers of survivors to intercensal occurrence rates in an additive way, which allows one to apply the intracohort interpolation method. As shown in equation (11.35), the "status variable" is in this case $-\ln(_nN_x)$, analogous to mean parity in the example developed earlier.

12 Increment–Decrement Life Tables

Alberto Palloni, University of Wisconsin

12.1 Introduction

In chapter 3 we studied the life table as a tool to describe mortality. A life table can be used to describe *any* event whereby individuals under observation transit from one state to another. In the case of mortality the event is death and the two states under consideration are "alive" (state 1) and "dead" (state 2).

The mortality process studied in chapter 3 can be thought as representing a model resting on the following assumptions:

a. *Simple state space*: There are only two possible states that individuals can occupy;
b. *Event is proper*: All individuals eventually transit from state 1 to state 2;
c. *Destination state is "absorbing"*: Nobody who moves from state 1 to state 2 ever goes back to state 1.

Most demographic phenomena consist of events that cannot be represented and comprehended by such a basic model. To represent the marriage process, for example, we need to modify assumption (a) by increasing the number of possible states to include single, married, widowed, and divorced. These states are clearly not absorbing because people who enter them may subsequently leave them.

Chapter 4 discussed modifications to the simple life table procedure to handle one important generalization, namely, the introduction of multiple and competing destination states. This is an extension that removes assumption (a). However, the multiple decrement model continues to be restrictive since it relies on the other two assumptions, namely, that all destination states are absorbing (no reverse flows are possible), and that the events are proper, that is, everyone will experience the event under study or, equivalently, everybody will exit from state 1. Of these assumptions, that preventing reverse flows is most problematic for demographic computation. Section 12.2 describes increment–decrement life table models that enable us to understand events with non-absorbing states and reverse flows. Section 12.3 introduces an example, discusses computational choices for the calculations to estimate an increment–decrement table, and suggests interpretations for the results. In the remaining sections of the chapter we formalize and generalize relations between quantities in any increment–decrement table.

12.2 Increment–Decrement Life Tables

In this section we review examples of three phenomena that can be fruitfully analyzed with generalized increment–decrement tables.

12.2.1 Marriage and divorce

The process of union formation and dissolution is the prime example of interrelated events that can be understood with a simple increment–decrement model. To keep the illustration simple we will neglect the existence of consensual unions and assume that all unions are formally sanctioned. We will also overlook equally important complexities raised by the fact that union formation and dissolution involve not just one but two individuals. In what follows we focus on women exposed to marriage.

In most populations a majority of, but not necessarily all, women will eventually marry. Some but not all among those who marry will experience a divorce (permanent separation) or widowhood due to the death of their partner. Finally, some marriages will be terminated as a consequence of the death of the woman herself. The multistate representation of these events is graphically displayed in figure 12.1 (Schoen, 1988). Women who marry for the first time cannot return to the single state, and thus there is only a one directional arrow linking the state "single" with the state "married". By contrast, those who divorce or separate and those who experience widowhood may remarry, and this possibility is reflected by two-directional arrows. As always, death is an absorbing state and there are no reverse flows from the state, "dead."

In this representation, the passage of time is measured by the age of the woman and one does not necessarily need to account for the time spent in each state as an important dimension of the problem. That is, the model assumes that remarriage and divorce depend on time only through the age of the woman and not through the duration that they have spent in any state. If this assumption is violated, special procedures to handle both age and duration dependence are needed.

Of interest to those studying marriage change and family formation are questions such as the following: what is the expected time before the first marriage? What is the probability

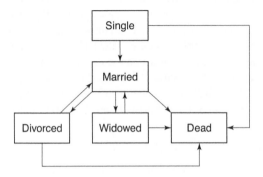

Figure 12.1 Multistate representation of marriage and marriage disruption

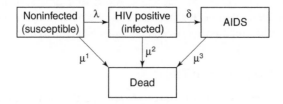

Figure 12.2 Multistate representation of HIV/AIDS

that a first marriage will eventually end up in a divorce? What is the average number of marriages that a woman will experience during her lifetime? What is the expected number of years before a first marriage breaks up by divorce? Answers to these questions may enable investigators to understand better the effects of social and economic forces on family formation and organization.

12.2.2 HIV/AIDS

Because of its very nature, the HIV epidemic admits a simple multistate representation (Palloni, 1996). Individuals in a population exposed to HIV can occupy one of three states: susceptible (noninfected), HIV-positive and asymptomatic (contracted virus but with no symptoms of AIDS), and AIDS (full-blown symptoms of AIDS). As always, death is an absorbing state. A graphic representation appears in figure 12.2. The force of infection, λ, is the instantaneous rate of infection or HIV incidence; the force of incubation, δ, is the instantaneous rate of incubation or AIDS incidence; and the quantities μ^i ($i = 1, 2, 3$) are, respectively, the forces of mortality for individuals who are susceptible, infected, and with AIDS. As in any application of life table procedures, our interest is to use observed events, namely, becoming infected, developing AIDS, and dying, to estimate the underlying rates, λ, δ, and μ^i.

This example shares an important feature with simple life table representations: there are no reverse flows, as individuals who become infected will remain infected for life. As before, death is an absorbing state. However, not everybody in the population is likely to become infected. Indeed, an important quantity to be estimated is the ultimate proportion of individuals who are likely to become infected.

In the case of HIV/AIDS the issue of time dependence is more complicated than in the case of marriage. Indeed, while the force of infection is mainly dependent on the age of individuals, the force of incubation is driven by the duration in the state (duration of infection) as much as it is by age. By the same token, the risk of mortality once AIDS is contracted, μ^3, is almost entirely associated with duration of infection and only weakly dependent on age.

As in the case of marriage, an understanding of the HIV/AIDS epidemic requires us to answer questions that increment–decrement tables can address very precisely: what proportion of a cohort will eventually contract the virus? What is the average age at which individuals in a cohort will contract the virus? What fraction of the cohort will contract the virus before reaching age x? What fraction of the cohort will develop AIDS before age y?

12.2.3 Health, chronic illnesses, and disability

An important and lively current debate in the study of health and mortality revolves around the idea that as improvements in survivorship and life expectancy continue, the health of those

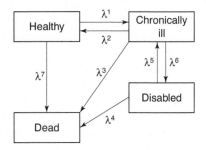

Figure 12.3 Multistate representation of chronic illness and disability

individuals benefited by these improvements may deteriorate (Fries, 1980; Singer and Manton, 1994). Is it generally true, for example, that the time spent ill or disabled is longer now than it was when life expectancy was around 60 years? Could it be that when they reach their retirement age baby boomers will experience higher life expectancy but also higher prevalence of ill-health and disability than their parents did at similar ages? If this is so, what kind of pressure will there be on resources to keep a minimum standard of well-being?

A simple way to understand the events and relations involved and indeed to begin to answer these questions is, once again, through an increment–decrement representation (Rogers et al., 1990). This is shown in figure 12.3. We assume that all individuals start out in the state "healthy" and that they can transit first to the state "chronically ill" and from there to the state "disabled." As most disability is caused by chronic illnesses, we will neglect the possibility of a flow from "healthy" to "disabled." As in the case of marital status, reverse flows are possible as individuals can recover from either disability or chronic illnesses.

Strategic factors that will shape the answers to the questions formulated before are the set of transition rates, λ^1 and λ^2. These are, respectively, the rate of incidence of chronic illness and the rate of recovery. To the extent that λ^1 remains invariant over time but λ^2 decreases, we should expect that a growing fraction of the population will be occupying the state "chronically ill" or "disabled." Note also that if λ^3 or λ^4 are reduced (death rates fall among the ill and disabled) and all the other rates remain unchanged, we should expect a similar result, namely, an increase in the prevalence of chronic illness and disability. Understanding the factors that determine these rates is then a key to providing evidence for or against the idea that morbidity is increasing or expanding.

There are a number of other examples and illustrations that we could have used. Paramount among these are applications to multiregional life tables, where the analyst is interested in modeling migration flows between and within geographic regions as well as mortality (Rogers, 1995b).

12.3 Estimation of Increment–Decrement Life Tables

12.3.1 Children's experiences of marriage, consensual unions, and disruptions

A controversial topic in the current demographic and sociological literature is related to the changing dynamic of union formation and dissolution. Over the past twenty years or so the rate of entrance into consensual unions has increased sharply. This is thought by some to be responsible for increasing rates of childbearing out of wedlock. In addition, some researchers believe that consensual unions are more likely to end up in eventual separation and that, even if they lead to a marriage, the latter is subject to an increased chance of divorce. These transformations certainly influence the family structure and material well-being of couples, but are thought to produce particularly salient consequences for the early experiences of children. Because children's early life experiences have potentially large effects on their later life behaviors and activities, it becomes important to describe children's patterns of exposure to different types of family contexts dictated by their parents' union history.

We can shed some light on this issue by summarizing the experiences of children at various ages as a function of one (or both) of their parents' union status (see Bumpass and Lu, 2000). For simplicity, we choose to work with their mother's union status. Thus, the study population consists of children whose mother's union history will determine the family context which children encounter at a given point in their life. Since the most strategic issues associated with a child's living arrangements have to do with early life impact, we are justified to focus our attention on children's experiences between exact ages zero and 15. Similarly, since the main hypotheses suggest that the most important contrasts are associated with children who experience life with a single mother, with a mother in a consensual union, or with a mother in a marriage, we will neglect altogether all states created by mortality. As a consequence we start with a simplified representation of the marriage process displayed in figure 12.4. In this figure the states are numbered sequentially and the transition rates to and from any of them are indexed so that the first superscript always corresponds to the state of origin and the second to the state of destination. The corresponding rates for these transitions, $\lambda^{ij}(x)$, are associated with children, not with adult women and/or men, and refer to the rate at which children whose mothers are in state i at age x move to state j in the small age interval $(x, x + \delta x)$. Thus, $\lambda^{12}(x)$ is the rate at which children who live with mothers who are not in a union experience a change between ages x and $x + \delta x$ and begin to live with mothers who are cohabiting but not married. Similarly, $\lambda^{23}(x)$ is the rate at which children who live with a mother in a consensual union move between ages x and $x + \delta x$ to a family context characterized by a mother who is married.

Relative to the marital status example given before, the state-space representation in figure 12.4 is both simpler and more complicated. The illustration is more complicated because we now explicitly consider the existence of consensual unions as different from marriages. This complication is justified by the increasing importance of consensual unions and the increased prevalence of children who live with cohabiting parents who are not legally married.

The state-space representation, however, is also simpler since we neglect altogether the effects of mortality. In fact, not only have we omitted an absorbing state for death (of the child), but we also overlook the distinction, for example, between a child whose mother is not in a union due to death of a spouse or partner (widowhood) and a child whose mother is not

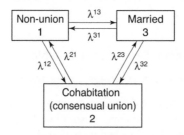

Figure 12.4   Multistate representation of children's experience with family contexts

in a union due to a divorce or separation. This decision is probably inconsequential since we are only interested in the evolution of the phenomena in a range of maternal ages (15 to 55) where adult mortality is very low. Thus, the rates λ^{21} and λ^{31} will reflect primarily the risk of separation (from consensual unions) and divorce (from marriage). By the same token, we do not distinguish among women in the non-union state according to the nature of their previous union. Instead, we lump together divorced mothers with those who were in a cohabiting union. This is tantamount to assuming that any heterogeneity in the transition rates out of this state (non-union) can be legitimately ignored or, equivalently, that the processes of union or marriage formation for those whose previous union was a cohabitation is essentially the same as it is for those whose previous union was a marriage. If this were not a realistic assumption – and, in all likelihood, it is not so – we should distinguish the existence of two disruption states.

12.3.2 Estimation of rates

The National Survey of Family Growth (NSFG) is a nationally representative survey of households in the United States implemented periodically by the National Center for Health Statistics. The goal of the survey is to retrieve information on fertility and related health issues. The NSFG-5 fielded in 1995 includes 10,847 female respondents who are 15–44 years of age in 1995 (Potter et al., 1997). Since the NSFG-5 elicits union and fertility histories for the women in the sample, we are able to reconstruct their children's experience of cohabitation, marriage, or union disruption (Bumpass and Lu, 2000). With the retrospective information on events that occurred during the period 1990–4, we calculate observed single-year age-specific rates for every relevant age and flow displayed in figure 12.4. These rates, which we will denote $_1M_x^{ij}$, correspond to the ratios $_1D_x^{ij}/_1N_x^i$ of observed transitions from i to j in the age interval x to $x + 1$ ($_1D_x^{ij}$) to the estimated midperiod population in state i in the age group ($_1N_x^i$). These rates are displayed in table 12.1.[1] Just as the mortality rates $_1M_x$'s defined in chapter 3 were the basis for the life tables in the two-state case, so the $_1M_x^{ij}$'s rates will be the basis for life tables associated with each state in figure 12.4. Thus, in this application we will have one life table for children whose mothers are not in a union (state 1 or "non-union"), one for children whose mothers are in a consensual or cohabiting union (state 2, "cohabitation"), and one for children whose mothers are married (state 3, "married"). As in chapter 3, the central quantities in these tables are the corresponding probabilities of experiencing the events.

Recall now the procedure used when there are only two states to consider, origin and destination, and only one flow from origin to destination. In this case we only focused on quantities describing the exits or the flow away from the origin state. To do so we calculated values of $_1M_x$'s and added an assumption about the behavior of the underlying risk to estimate the values of $_1q_x$, $_1d_x$, and $_1L_x$. For example, with the assumption that $l(x)$ is linear over one-year intervals, we could uniquely estimate $_1q_x$ from $_1M_x$ for every age group, and then derive the quantities $_1d_x$ and $_1L_x$.[2] Although we did not describe the procedure quite in these terms, we could say that for each age (other than age 0) in the life table we have three equations in three unknowns. The three equations in the linear case are:

$$l(x + 1) = l(x) - {}_1d_x$$
$$_1d_x = {}_1M_x \cdot {}_1L_x \tag{12.1}$$
$$_1L_x = .5 \cdot [l(x) + l(x + 1)]$$

Table 12.1: *Observed values of* $_1 M_x^{ij}$ *for the states and flows represented in figure* 12.4

Age	1 (non-union) Destination		2 (cohabitation) Destination		3 (marriage) Destination	
	2	3	1	3	1	2
0	.0777	.0421	.0968	.1460	.0121	.0086
1	.0858	.0405	.0984	.1411	.0211	.0082
2	.1068	.0350	.0759	.1468	.0196	.0069
3	.1054	.0354	.0829	.1639	.0210	.0045
4	.0832	.0475	.0656	.1282	.0216	.0084
5	.0939	.0497	.0555	.1433	.0214	.0076
6	.0617	.0469	.0506	.1229	.0251	.0022
7	.0808	.0580	.0471	.1326	.0201	.0078
8	.0507	.0305	.0655	.1387	.0196	.0027
9	.0621	.0375	.0815	.1430	.0215	.0031
10	.0854	.0411	.0508	.1370	.0201	.0049
11	.0435	.0343	.0855	.1149	.0186	.0032
12	.0656	.0521	.0880	.0896	.0260	.0043
13	.0427	.0313	.0812	.1307	.0204	.0071
14	.0837	.0314	.0851	.0712	.0260	.0066

Source: NSFG-5. See also Bumpass and Lu, 2000.

Since for each age x, $l(x)$ is known – a result of the recursion that starts from an arbitrary radix or value for $l(0)$ – the three unknowns are $l(x + 1)$, $_1 d_x$ and $_1 L_x$. One can easily verify that the solution for $_1 d_x$ is

$$_1 d_x = l(x) \cdot \frac{_1 M_x}{1 + .5 \cdot _1 M_x}$$

or, equivalently,

$$l(x + 1) = l(x) \cdot \frac{1 - .5 \cdot _1 M_x}{1 + .5 \cdot _1 M_x} \tag{12.2}$$

This implies that

$$_1 q_x = \frac{_1 M_x}{1 + .5 \cdot _1 M_x},$$

the kernel of the empirical solution to the two-state life table in chapter 3.

We can proceed in an analogous way in the multistate case provided that we account for the fact that at each age there could be more than one flow. To do this most efficiently, it is convenient to introduce more notation. We define the following quantities:

$l^i(x)$ is the number of individuals in state i at exact age x;
$_1 d_x^{ij}$ is the number of individuals moving from state i to state j between ages x and $x + 1$;
$_1 L_x^i$ is the number of person-years lived in state i between ages x and $x + 1$.

The reader should verify that the following equalities hold for all ages:

$$l^i(x+1) = l_i(x) + \sum_j {}_1d_x^{ji} - \sum_j {}_1d_x^{ij} \qquad \text{Equation of type I}$$

$${}_1d_x^{ij} = {}_1M_x^{ij} \cdot {}_1L_x^i \qquad\qquad\qquad \text{Equation of type II} \qquad \textbf{(12.3)}$$

$${}_1L_x^i = .5 \cdot [l^i(x) + l^i(x+1)] \qquad\qquad \text{Equation of type III}$$

Since in the representation of figure 12.4 we have three different states, for each age group we will need three equations of type I, and also three equations of type III. Similarly, since there is a total of six flows or transitions, we will need six equations of type II. This amounts to a total of twelve equations. The unknowns will be three values of $l^i(x+1)$, three values of ${}_1L_x^i$ and six values of ${}_1d_x^{ij}$ or, equivalently, six values of the conditional probabilities ${}_1q_x^{ij}$.[3]

To generate estimates of the quantities we seek, ${}_1q_x^{ij}$, we need to solve a system of twelve equations in twelve unknowns for each age. This is certainly not a trivial task but it is not intrinsically difficult. Indeed, and as we show below, calculation of the solution involves consecutive operations of inversion of a matrix, one for each age group (except for age zero). Although the matrix inversion operation is not always smooth, there are a number of software packages that can handle the assignment very efficiently (see section 12.7).

Using the rates displayed in table 12.1 we solve the system of equations, one for each age group, and then proceed to calculate the quantities $l^i(x)$, ${}_1d_x^{ij}$, and ${}_1L_x^i$ for all three relevant states. All calculations are based on a radix of $l^i(0) = 1,000$ for all i, that is, we arbitrarily assume that we start with a synthetic cohort of 3,000 children aged 0, one thousand in each state. For accurate estimates, of course, it would be necessary to know the actual distribution of children at birth among the states.

Table 12.2 displays the values of ${}_1q_x^{ij}$, and table 12.3 displays the values of $l^i(x)$ and ${}_1d_x^{ij}$. In table 12.2 the values in the first of the three columns associated with each state correspond to the conditional probabilities of remaining in that state at the end of each one-year interval. Thus, in the first age group and for state 1, the value in the first column is .8902 ($= 1 - .0657 - .0441$). Although the values of ${}_1L_x^i$ are implicit in table 12.3, we omit them to avoid excessive cluttering. Finally, the estimated expected durations at age zero spent in each of the three states are displayed in table 12.4.[4]

12.3.3   Interpretation of estimates

For each origin state i and for each age x, the conditional probabilities of moving from state to state, ${}_1q_x^{ij}$, displayed in table 12.2 add up to 1.0, as they should. Thus, for example, the three possible transitions for a child aged zero who lived with a mother not in a union are: (a) to continue to experience the same living arrangement with probability .8902, or (b) to live with a cohabiting mother with probability .0657 or, finally, (c) to live with a married mother with probability .0441. Combining the conditional probabilities in table 12.2 with radices $l^i(0) = 1,000$ for each i leads to the figures displayed in table 12.3. According to this table, at exactly age 5 there are 837 children in state 1, 604 in state 2, and 1,559 in state 3. Note that these numbers add up to 3,000 since there is no child mortality in our representation, and all 3,000 children in the original cohort must be in one of the three states at every age.

The columns ${}_1d_x^{ij}$ also have straightforward interpretations. Thus, reading down the column ${}_1d_x^{12}$ we find that among the 837 children who lived with a mother not in a union at exact

Table 12.2: *Estimated values of $_1q_x^{ij}$ for the states and flows represented in figure* 12.4

Age	1 (non-union) Destination			2 (cohabitation) Destination			3 (married) Destination		
	1	2	3	1	2	3	1	2	3
0	.8902	.0657	.0441	.0823	.7868	.1308	.0117	.0080	.9802
1	.8850	.0724	.0427	.0841	.7898	.1261	.0199	.0080	.9721
2	.8711	.0900	.0381	.0651	.8032	.1317	.0183	.0070	.9747
3	.8723	.0879	.0398	.0705	.7839	.1456	.0196	.0049	.9756
4	.8800	.0715	.0485	.0574	.8259	.1167	.0202	.0083	.9714
5	.8686	.0800	.0514	.0485	.8217	.1298	.0199	.0077	.9724
6	.8988	.0540	.0472	.0455	.8418	.1127	.0236	.0027	.9738
7	.8723	.0696	.0581	.0416	.8371	.1213	.0187	.0078	.9735
8	.9237	.0443	.0320	.0583	.8162	.1254	.0187	.0029	.9784
9	.9076	.0533	.0391	.0712	.8003	.1285	.0204	.0033	.9763
10	.8832	.0736	.0432	.0449	.8304	.1247	.0188	.0052	.9760
11	.9270	.0381	.0349	.0758	.8195	.1047	.0178	.0032	.9789
12	.8918	.0571	.0511	.0775	.8394	.0832	.0244	.0046	.9710
13	.9304	.0374	.0322	.0720	.8102	.1178	.0197	.0067	.9736
14	.8945	.0736	.0318	.0756	.8582	.0663	.0245	.0070	.9685

Source: NSFG-5. See also Bumpass and Lu, 2000.

Table 12.3: *Estimated values of $l^i(x)$ and $_1d_x^{ij}$ for the states and flows represented in figure* 12.4

Age	State i								
	i = 1 (non-union)			i = 2 (cohabitation)			i = 3 (married)		
	$l^1(x)$	$_1d_x^{12}$	$_1d_x^{13}$	$l^2(x)$	$_1d_x^{21}$	$_1d_x^{23}$	$l^3(x)$	d_x^{31}	d_x^{32}
0	1,000	66	44	1,000	82	131	1,000	12	8
1	984	71	42	861	72	109	1,155	23	9
2	966	87	37	760	49	100	1,274	23	9
3	915	80	36	706	50	103	1,378	27	7
4	875	63	42	641	37	75	1,484	30	12
5	837	67	43	604	29	78	1,559	31	12
6	787	43	37	576	26	65	1,637	39	4
7	772	54	45	531	22	64	1,696	32	13
8	728	32	23	512	30	64	1,761	33	5
9	736	39	29	454	32	58	1,810	37	6
10	737	54	32	409	18	51	1,854	35	10
11	704	27	25	403	31	42	1,893	34	6
12	717	41	37	363	28	30	1,920	47	9
13	714	27	23	355	26	42	1,931	38	13
14	728	54	23	327	25	22	1,945	48	14
15	724	—	—	348	—	—	1,928	—	—

Source: NSFG-5. See also Bumpass and Lu, 2000. Calculated from table 12.2. Note that the sum of $l^i(x)$ for each row should be equal to 3,000. Discrepancies are due to rounding.

Table 12.4: *Expected duration (or waiting time) by state and state of origin*

State of origin (at age 0)	Expected number of years to be lived in state $j =$		
	1 (non-union)	2 (cohabitation)	3 (married)
All	4.0	2.7	8.3
1	8.0	2.5	4.6
2	2.8	5.3	6.9
3	1.3	.6	13.1

Source: First row calculated from table 12.3. Row entries do not always add to 15.0 due to rounding.

age five, 67 experience a change and begin living with a mother who is in a cohabiting union. Similarly, 43 of the original 837 children who were in state 1 at exact age 5 begin living with a married mother between their fifth and sixth birthdays. A similar interpretation applies to the other columns.

The functions $l^i(x)$ are not always monotonically decreasing, reflecting the fact that at every age and for each state there are both decrements and increments. Thus, it should be clear that it is not possible to use $l^i(x)/l^i(0)$ as a measure of the probability, for a newborn in state i, of remaining in state i at age x. Similarly, the ratios $l^i(x+k)/l^i(x)$ no longer measure the conditional probabilities of remaining in state i. One can, however, use the ratios

$$l^i(x) \Big/ \sum_i l^i(0)$$

to represent the probability that a newborn will *be* in state i at age x. For example, the probability that a newborn will live with a married mother at age 10 is .618 ($=1854/3000$).

There are two types of life expectancy, or expected waiting times, that can be derived from increment – decrement life tables. The first is an *unconditional* expected duration representing the average duration of time lived in a particular state, regardless of origin. According to table 12.4, the expected number of years spent in states 1, 2, and 3 by the members of our fictitious cohort are respectively 4.0 years, 2.7 years, and 8.3 years. This means that a member of the original cohort (regardless of his/her starting state) is expected to live 4.0 years of his life between ages zero and 15 (exactly) with a mother who is not in a union, 2.7 years with a mother in a cohabiting union, and the remaining years with a mother in a marriage. These figures add up to 15.0; we have accounted fully for all of the first 15 years of life.

The second kind of waiting time or duration in a state is called "conditional," and it is important to understand the difference between unconditional and conditional waiting times or duration (Schoen, 1988). The unconditional duration or life expectancy in state j at age x, $e^j(x)$ – the number of years of life to be lived in state j after age x – can be directly calculated from the values of $_1L_y^j$ ($y \geq x$) implicit in table 12.3. By construction these values are additive. In particular,

$$\sum_j e^j(0) = e(0)$$

In our case this is fifteen years since there is no child mortality.

By contrast, the conditional expectations or conditional duration, $\Psi^{ij}(x)$ – the expected number of years to be lived in state j by those who are in state i at exact age x – must be estimated using the trajectory followed by members of the cohort who occupy state i at exact age x and then calculating the time spent in state j. These calculations are tedious but not intrinsically difficult.

Suppose that there are $l^i(x)$ children who are in state i at exact age x. We then estimate a new set of life tables for a cohort with $l^i(x)$ members who start in state i and for whom the starting age is not zero but age x. From these newly estimated life tables we will obtain unconditional expectations or values $e^j(y)$ for all j and for $y \geq x$. These values are associated with the $l_i(x)$ children in the new initial cohort, not with the original cohort of children. To avoid confusion we will label these unconditional expectations $\epsilon^j(y)$ for $y \geq x$. It follows that the quantities we seek, $\Psi^{ij}(x)$, are indeed the values $\epsilon^j(x)$. It also follows that the total number of years lived after exact age x by those who are in state i at age x must equal

$$\sum_j \psi^{ij}(x)$$

The values displayed in the first row of table 12.4 correspond to $e^j(0)$ whereas those in the remaining rows are the quantities $\Psi^{ij}(0)$.[5] An interesting feature revealed by these quantities is that children born to a married mother will spend most of their first fifteen years of life in such a state, whereas those born to mothers not in a union or in a cohabiting union will spend much of their first fifteen years of life in those same states.

12.4 Formalization and Generalization of Relations

We now examine more closely the nature of the functions $l^j(x+1)$ and $_1d_x^{ij}$ and explore key interrelations between them.

12.4.1 The nature of $_1d_x^{ij}$

What is $_1d_x^{23}$ in our illustration? It is the number of children who reached exact age x with a mother in a cohabiting union and whose mother was married when they (the children) reached age $x+1$. This quantity is a result of a multiplicity of flows, some involving only one transition, others involving more than one transition, some involving moves away from state 3 and others moves into state 3. For example, it includes children whose mothers were in a union at age x and then married at age $x+\delta$ ($0 < \delta < 1$) and stayed married until age $x+1$. But it also includes children whose mothers experience a potentially more complicated sequence of moves such as: cohabiting when the child is age x, marrying when the child is $x+\delta$ ($0 < \delta < 1$), divorcing when the child is $x+\delta'$ ($\delta < \delta'$), entering another cohabiting union at age $x+\delta''$ ($\delta < \delta''$) and, finally, marrying again and staying married until the child reaches age $x+1$. Thus, $_1d_x^{23}$ is affected not just by flows *into* state 3 but also by those *out* of it. The quantity, therefore, *excludes* individuals who start in state 2, move to 3, and then exit this state without reentering it before attaining age $x+1$. It also excludes individuals with multiple transitions, such as the one described before but with an extra transition out of state 3 without reentry before age $x+1$. It is clear then that if rates of exits *out* of state 3 were lower, the quantity $_1d_x^{23}$ could be higher.

In most applications either the time intervals are very short or the rates are so low that the likelihood that an individual will experience multiple events in a single time interval is remote. But even in the most conservative case, that is, when only one move per individual per time interval is permitted, $_1d_x^{ij}$ is no longer to be considered a measure of pure decrements, except when j is an absorbing state.

12.4.2 The nature of $l^i(x+1)$

We already noted that the function $l^i(x+1)$ in table 12.3 is not strictly decreasing with age. For example, the value attained by $l^3(x)$ at age 7 (=1696) represents an increase relative to the value of $l^3(6)$ (=1637). This occurs because $l^3(x)$ reflects the ebb and flow of marriage as well as of the other phenomena. In the case of state 3, between ages six and seven there is a decrement of about 39 caused by divorces, and another decrement of 4 caused by transitions toward cohabitation. But there are also increments of 37 and 65 accounted for by transitions from state 1 and state 2 respectively. Clearly, the function $l^i(x+1)$ is influenced by the magnitude of the transition rates (into and out of the state) and also by the magnitude attained by the functions $l^j(x)$ for all j different from i.

12.4.3 General linkages

These linkages between the various states are rendered more fully if we construct a matrix containing the sources of *increments* and *decrements* for each state i. This matrix, which we call $l(x+1)$, contains as elements the values ${}^i l^j(x+1)$, the number of individuals who were in state i at exact age x and end up in state j by age $x+1$. For $i \neq j$ the function ${}^i l^j(x+1)$ is equivalent to ${}_1 d_x^{ij}$; indeed, these values represent the number of individuals who move from state i to state j in the age interval. By contrast, the values of the function ${}^i l^i(x+1)$ represent the survivors of the original "cohort" of individuals who started out in state i at age x. Therefore it must be a strictly decreasing function of age that depends on the initial value ${}^i l^i(x)$ on the one hand, and on the decrements consisting of all those individuals who moved out of state i, namely

$$\sum_{j \neq i} {}_1 d_x^{ij},$$

on the other.

We can now establish the link between the elements of $l(x+1)$ and those of $l(x)$ via the quantities ${}_1 d_x^{ij}$. In a very general situation when we have non-absorbing states $i = 1, \ldots, k$:

$$l(x+1) = l(x) - D(x) \tag{12.4}$$

or, in longhand:

$$
\begin{pmatrix}
{}^1 l^1(x+1) & {}^1 l^2(x+1) & \cdots & {}^1 l^k(x+1) \\
{}^2 l^1(x+1) & {}^2 l^2(x+1) & \cdots & {}^2 l^k(x+1) \\
\cdots & \cdots & \cdots & \cdots \\
{}^k l^1(x+1) & {}^k l^2(x+1) & \cdots & {}^k l^k(x+1)
\end{pmatrix}
=
\begin{pmatrix}
{}^1 l^1(x) & 0 & \cdots & 0 \\
0 & {}^2 l^2(x) & \cdots & 0 \\
\cdots & \cdots & \cdots & \cdots \\
0 & 0 & \cdots & {}^k l^k(x+1)
\end{pmatrix}
$$

$$
-
\begin{pmatrix}
\sum_{j} {}_1 d_x^{1j} & -{}_1 d_x^{12} & \cdots & -{}_1 d_x^{1k} \\
-{}_1 d_x^{21} & \sum_{j} {}_1 d_x^{2j} & \cdots & -{}_1 d_x^{2k} \\
\cdots & \cdots & \cdots & \cdots \\
-{}_1 d_x^{k1} & -{}_1 d_x^{k2} & \cdots & \sum_{j} {}_1 d_x^{kj}
\end{pmatrix}
$$

The matrix $D(x)$ is a matrix of increment and decrements. Quantities in the diagonal entries, the cells (i, i), are decrements associated with state i (the sum of all the $_1d_x^{ij}$ or exits out of i). By contrast, quantities in off-diagonal columns, the cells (i, j), are increments for state i.

The matrix equation (12.4) preserves all the information contained in equation of type I in expression (12.3). The diagonal elements of matrix $l(x + 1)$ will always be smaller than the corresponding elements at age x since the values in the diagonal of matrix D are all decrements. They are like the $l(x)$'s in a simple death process.[6] The number of individuals who are in state i at exactly age $x + 1$, which we symbolize as $l^i(x + 1)$, must be the sum of the elements in the corresponding column of the matrix $l(x+1)$. Thus, for example, $l^1(x+1)$ is simply the sum of the elements of the first column of $l(x + 1)$, namely $^1l^1(x + 1) + ^2l^1(x + 1) + \cdots + ^kl^1(x + 1)$. However, the similarities with the simple life table stop there. In particular, it is not the case that the sum of decrements for state i over all ages x will add up to $l^i(0)$, as is in fact the case in the single decrement table. Since each of the quantities $_1d_x^{ij}$ expresses a frequency of events, the ratio to the number of years lived or total exposure in the interval $(x, x + 1)$ will represent a rate. In the notation of the life table we ought to have that

$$_1m_x^{ij} = \frac{_1d_x^{ij}}{_1L_x^i}$$

where $_1d_x^{ij}$ is the number of transitions from state i to state j in the age interval, $_1L_x^i$ is the total number of person-years lived by those who were in state i during the age interval in a stationary population, and $_1m_x^{ij}$ are transition rates for the stationary population.

The observational counterpart to $_1m_x^{ij}$ are the quantities $_1M_x^{ij}$, or the ratios $_1D_x^{ij}/_1N_x^i$ of observed transitions from i to j in the age interval to the estimated midperiod population in the age group.

Just as we can arrange the values of $_1d_x^{ij}$ in a matrix, so we can create a matrix for the values of the observed transition rates, $_1M_x^{ij}$:

$$M(x) = \begin{pmatrix} \sum_j {}_1M_x^{1j} & -_1M_x^{12} & -_1M_x^{13} & \cdots & -_1M_x^{1k} \\ -_1M_x^{21} & \sum_j {}_1M_x^{2j} & -_1M_x^{23} & \cdots & -_1M_x^{2k} \\ \cdots & \cdots & \cdots & \cdots & \cdots \\ -_1M_x^{k1} & -_1M_x^{k2} & -_1M_x^{k3} & \cdots & \sum_j {}_1M_x^{kj} \end{pmatrix} \qquad (12.5)$$

which is obtained when we divide the quantities in the matrix $D(x)$ by the corresponding values of exposure. This matrix equation is equivalent to equation of type II in expression (12.3).

Let us assume that the functions representing the number of survivors in each state are linear between any two ages, that is, that the values of $_1L_x^i$ can be generated as the average of $l^i(x)$ and $l^i(x + 1)$. Similarly, we assume that the values $_1L_x^{ij} = .5 \cdot (^il^j(x + 1))$ are a good representation of the number of person-years lived in the age interval $(x, x + 1)$ by those who moved from state i to state j. If so, we can arrange the values of $_1L_x^{ij}$ in a matrix and use matrix notation again to write the following:

$$L(x) = .5 \cdot [l(x) + l(x + 1)] \qquad (12.6)$$

a matrix equivalent of equation of type III in expression (12.3).

Substituting (12.6) into (12.5) we shall obtain the solution for $l(x + 1)$ as:

$$l(x + 1) = l(x) \cdot [I - .5 \cdot M(x)][I + .5 \cdot M(x)]^{-1} \qquad \textbf{(12.7)}$$

where I is the identity matrix and the superscript "-1" stands for the inverse of the matrix. This is a formal solution to the simultaneous equations we introduced in expression (12.4). Note that expression (12.7) is the matrix equivalent of the two-state solution where

$$l(x + 1) = l(x) \cdot \frac{1 - .5 \cdot {}_1M_x}{1 + .5 \cdot {}_1M_x}$$

To calculate $l^i(x + 1)$ associated with each state we need to solve for the corresponding values using expression (12.7) for each age group. As in the two-state case, these values are sufficient to calculate all other quantities of interest. The process cannot get started, however, unless we specify a radix, $l^i(0)$, which in our example was set to be $l^j(0) = 1{,}000$ for all j.

We showed that calculations needed to construct increment–decrement life tables are, in principle at least, fairly simple: one needs to invert a matrix for each and every one of the age groups or time intervals considered relevant, and then calculate the quantities of interest from the resulting estimates. These quantities are then assembled in the form of life tables, one for each state. With a few states (less than four) and a handful of age groups, matrix inversion presents few difficulties, and can be done expeditiously with a hand calculator. When the number of states and age groups is larger, however, matrix inversion becomes tedious and can be better handled by a computer. In the last section of this chapter we provide some suggestions regarding software to accomplish these tasks.

12.4.4 Introduction of mortality or other absorbing states

Although in examples such as the one considered above, it is in principle justified to neglect the existence of an absorbing state, this may not always be the case. For example, to model the dynamics of HIV/AIDS or of health conditions at older ages, we will need to explicitly introduce mortality.

The introduction of an absorbing state presents no added difficulties but does require a suitable redesign of matrices and vectors, one that facilitates interpretations and simplifies numerical manipulations. If we were to introduce mortality in the example of children's family life experiences we would need to include an additional state and all associated transitions. The matrices would normally be arranged in such a way as to have death as the last state to be considered (the last row in matrices $l(x)$, $l(x + 1)$, $M(x)$). By convention we set the last row of matrices $l(x + 1)$, $D(x)$, and $M(x)$ to zero to reflect inactivity in the absorbing state. Aside from these changes in the design of our matrices, no other modifications are required.

12.4.5 Closing the multistate table

As in the case of a simple life table, the calculation of quantities corresponding to the last age group or duration presents some difficulties. In chapter 3 we saw that to close the table we needed to assume that the population was stationary above some high age, ω. This enabled us to set the following equation:

$$_\infty L_\omega = \frac{l(\omega)}{_\infty M_\omega} \qquad \textbf{(12.8)}$$

to solve for the unknown value of the number of person-years lived.

In the multistate case we proceed in an analogous fashion. The only difference is that we must now account for several states of interest, $i = 1, 2, \ldots, k$. Thus in the example of marriage and union formation and dissolution we need to apply equation (12.8) three times because there are three values $_\infty L_\omega^i$ for which we need to solve. As the reader must have guessed, the operation involved is simply a matrix multiplication:

$$L(\omega) = l(\omega) \cdot [M(\omega)]^{-1} \qquad (12.9)$$

where $L(\omega)$ and $l(\omega)$ are diagonal matrices. $M(\omega)$ is a $(k \times k)$ matrix constructed by taking into account only k non-absorbing states.

12.5   The Simplest Case: A Two-state System

In this section we briefly review the explicit solution for the two-state case. We do this because the expressions for the relevant quantities are revealing of the dynamics of the process and of the consequences of some of the underlying assumptions.

Suppose we have a two-state system with no absorbing state. The solution for the conditional probabilities of staying in states 1 and 2 in the age interval x to $x + 1$ ($_1 p_x^{11}$ and $_1 p_x^{22}$) and of moving from state 1 to state 2 and from state 2 to state 1 in the age interval x to $x + 1$, ($_1 q_x^{12} = 1 - {}_1 p_x^{11}$ and $_1 q_x^{21} = 1 - {}_1 p_x^{21}$), are:

$$_1 p_x^{11} = \frac{1 + .5 \cdot {}_1 M_x^{21} - .5 \cdot {}_1 M_x^{12}}{1 + .5 \cdot {}_1 M_x^{21} + .5 \cdot {}_1 M_x^{12}} \qquad\qquad _1 q_x^{12} = \frac{_1 M_x^{12}}{1 + .5 \cdot {}_1 M_x^{21} + .5 \cdot {}_1 M_x^{12}}$$

$$_1 p_x^{22} = \frac{1 + .5 \cdot {}_1 M_x^{12} - .5 \cdot {}_1 M_x^{21}}{1 + .5 \cdot {}_1 M_x^{21} + .5 \cdot {}_1 M_x^{12}} \qquad\qquad _1 q_x^{21} = \frac{_1 M_x^{21}}{1 + .5 \cdot {}_1 M_x^{21} + .5 \cdot {}_1 M_x^{12}}$$

The reader should verify that this solution results from expression (12.7) with the following 2×2 matrix $M(x)$:

$$M(x) = \begin{pmatrix} _1 M_x^{12} & -{}_1 M_x^{12} \\ -{}_1 M_x^{21} & _1 M_x^{21} \end{pmatrix}$$

A comparison of the conditional "survival" probabilities for this case with those obtained in the simple life table is revealing. The expression for the conditional probability of moving from state 1 to state 2 in the simple life table is given by the ratio $_1 M_x / (1 + .5 \cdot {}_1 M_x)$, which is approximately equal to the product of $_1 M_x \cdot (1 - .5 \cdot {}_1 M_x)$. This product expresses directly the implications of the assumption of linearity: it is tantamount to requiring that all events occur at the midpoint of the interval, at which point there should be a fraction of approximately $(1 - .5 \cdot {}_1 M_x)$ of the original survivors who will be exposed to an attrition given by $_1 M_x$.

In the case of a two-state system with two flows the conditional probability of moving from state 1 to state 2 can be interpreted analogously. We first survive individuals in state 1 at age x up to the middle of the interval $(x, x + 1)$. We do this by using the quantity $(1 - .5 \cdot {}_1 M_x^{12})$. We then apply the rate $_1 M_x^{12}$ and the factor $(1 - .5 \cdot {}_1 M_x^{21})$, the latter accounting for the fact that some individuals who move from 1 to 2 will experience a move back to the original state. Thus the probability that an individual in state 1 at exact age x is in state 2 at exact age $x + 1$, $_1 q_x^{12}$, is:

$$_1 M_x^{12} \cdot (1 - .5 \cdot {}_1 M_x^{21}) \cdot (1 - .5 \cdot {}_1 M_x^{12})$$

which, when the rates are small, is approximately equal to:

$$\frac{{}_1M_x^{12}}{1 + .5 \cdot {}_1M_x^{21} + .5 \cdot {}_1M_x^{12}}$$

An analogous derivation results in the second equation for ${}_1q_x^{21}$.

12.6 Alternative Solutions: The Case of Constant Rates

The solution expressed by equation equation (12.7) rests on the assumption that the functions ${}^il^j(x)$ are linear in unit intervals. This implies that the underlying risk $\mu^{ij}(a)$ in the unit interval, $(x \leq a \leq x+1)$, is increasing. In some cases it may be more accurate and convenient to assume that the rates are approximately constant in an interval. This implies that $l(x)$'s are nonlinear (exponential) functions of age. An analogous consequence follows in the multistate case: all the quantities ${}^il^j(x+1)$ become an exponential function of the rates ${}_1M_x^{ij}$. The only caveat here is that we are dealing with an array of functions and that the expressions involve matrices, not scalars. Indeed, the solution for the matrix $l(x+1)$ is now

$$l(x + 1) = l(x) \cdot \exp\{-M(x)\} \qquad\qquad (12.10)$$

where $l(x+1)$, $l(x)$ and $M(x)$ are the same matrices defined before. Expression (12.10) is somewhat meaningless without a definition for the matrix-valued exponential function. Just as in the one-dimensional case, the function $\exp(q)$, where q is any real number, can be expressed as an infinite series of the form $(1 + q + q^2/2! + q^3/3! + \cdots)$, so it is possible to define $\exp(Q)$, where Q is an n × n matrix, as

$$\exp(Q) = I + Q + [Q]^2(1/2!) + [Q]^3(1/3!) + \cdots$$

In most cases the rates will be sufficiently small that only the first or first two elements in the series will be necessary to approximate well the quantity on the left of the expression. If so, the solution for the multistate life table system is even simpler than in the case when $l(x+1)$ was assumed to be linear. This is because no matrix inversion and at most one matrix multiplication is required.

How is one to choose between alternative procedures to estimate the required conditional probabilities of an increment–decrement table? A good answer would be that under very general conditions, the linear method is to be preferred on the grounds of simplicity and ease of calculations. However, it is known that the assumption of linearity leads to a fair amount of inaccuracy when the underlying risks are decreasing rapidly (Schoen, 1988), and that it may even lead to outright impossibly negative values when some or all of the transition rates are very large (Hoem and Funck-Jensen, 1982; Nour and Suchindran, 1984). Thus, the exponential method, or alternatively the so-called "mean duration of transfer method" (Schoen, 1988), are to be preferred on the grounds of consistency.

12.7 Programs for the Calculation of Increment–Decrement Life Tables

There a number of computer programs available for calculation of increment–decrement life tables. In the late seventies, Willekens wrote a quite general program implementing the linear solution, but unfortunately it was not made widely available. The first program to be quite broadly accessible was designed and written by Robert Schoen. The corresponding Fortran code is fully included in his book (Schoen, 1988). The main limitation of this program is that it restricts estimation and calculations to a four-state multistate system.

More recently, Andrei Rogers, a pioneer in the application of increment–decrement tables procedures, made available a DOS-compatible program that performs fairly general calculations using the assumption of linearity (Rogers, 1995b). Since the program runs on any PC with minimum memory requirements, it is an attractive option. Its only limitation is that the number of output functions associated with the estimated life tables is fairly restricted.

Pete Tiemeyer and Glen Ulmer, two former Ph.D. students at the Center for Demography and Ecology, University of Wisconsin, wrote a C++ program that can run on any PC with minimal memory and hard disk space requirements. The program implements the linear solution and can handle any number of states and time intervals (Tiemeyer and Ulmer, 1991). Finally, it outputs a very large number of functions and outcomes. The program with accompanying instructions for installation and implementation is freely available from the authors.

Inevitably each empirical application will demand attention to special conditions, data inputs and outputs. Most of the available software is not general or flexible enough to handle a very broad class of applications or to implement alternative solutions (exponential instead of linear). Thus, in most cases it will be up to the researchers to create their own tool for estimation and calculation of increment–decrement tables. Our suggestion is to use general software packages such as STATA, S-PLUS, or MATLAB that are conducive to mixing preprogrammed routines (such as matrix inversion) with user-defined subroutines (for example those required to estimate conditional life expectancies).

NOTES

1. In this notation $_1M_x^{ij}$ corresponds to the transition rate between state i and state j in the age group $x, x+1$. The rates $\lambda^{ij}(x)$ are the continuous version of the $_1M_x^{ij}$'s.
2. The reader should remember that the assumption that $l(x)$ is linear in one-year intervals is equivalent to assuming that $_1a_x = .5$, and that $\mu(x)$ is a monotonically increasing function of x.
3. It is important to remember that the system of equations in (12.3) rests on the assumption that we know the values of M_x^{ij}. Normally this requires that the observed rates be identical to the ones in the stationary population.
4. The quantities displayed in tables 12.2, 12.3, and 12.4 were obtained using the matrix solution discussed later in this chapter. These estimates are slightly different from those that one would obtain solving the system of 12 equations for each age group. Because of these differences, the empirical relations between estimated quantities (such as $_1d_x^{ij}$ and $_1M_x^{ij}$) do not exactly correspond to what is implied by the expressions in equation (12.3).
5. Notice that for each j in the table, $e^j(0)$ is NOT equal to the weighted average of the values $\Psi^{ij}(0)$ for $i = 1, 2, 3$.
6. Because $D(x)$ is a matrix of decrements AND increments, there is no compelling justification to write expression (12.4) with a negative sign. We could have just as well have written $l(x) + D(x)$ and changed the sign of the cells of the matrix $D(x)$.

References

Alho, J. M. 1998. *A Stochastic Forecast of the Population of Finland*. Helsinki: Statistics Finland.

Arriaga, Eduardo. 1968. *New Life Tables for Latin American Populations in the Nineteenth and Twentieth Centuries*. Population Monograph Series No. 3. Berkeley: Institute of International Studies, University of California.

——— . 1984. "Measuring and Explaining the Change in Life Expectancies," *Demography*, 21(1): 83–96.

——— . 1989. "Changing Trends in Mortality Decline During the Last Decades," pp. 105–29 in Lado Ruzicka, Guillaume Wunsch, and Penny Kane, eds., *Differential Mortality: Methodological Issues and Biosocial Factors*. Oxford, England: Clarendon Press. International Studies in Demography.

Arthur, W. B. and J. W. Vaupel. 1984. "Some General Relationships in Population Dynamics," *Population Index*, 50(2): 214–26.

Bailar, A. B. 1985. "Comment to Ericksen and Kadane," *Journal of the American Statistical Association*, 80(389): 109–14.

Bennett, N. G. and S. Horiuchi. 1981. "Estimating the Completeness of Death Registration in a Closed Population," *Population Index*, 47(2): 207–21.

Bernardelli, H. 1941. "Population Waves," *Journal of the Burma Research Society*, 31(1): 1–18.

Bhat, M. P. 1987. *Mortality in India: Levels, Trends, and Patterns*. Unpublished Ph.D. Dissertation, University of Pennsylvania.

Bhrolchain, M. N. 1992. "Period Paramount? A Critique of the Cohort Approach to Fertility," *Population and Developpement Review*, 18(4): 599–619.

Bogue, D. J., E. E. Arriaga, D. L. Anderton, and G. W. Rumsey. 1993. *Readings in Population Research Methodology*. New York: United National Population Fund.

Bongaarts, J. 1978. "A Framework for Analyzing the Proximate Determinants of Fertility," *Population and Development Review*, 4(1): 105–32.

——— . 1982. "The Fertility-inhibiting Effects of the Intermediate Fertility Variables," *Studies in Family Planning*, 13(6–7): 179–89.

——— . 1994. "Population Policy Options in the Developing World," *Science*, 263: 771–6.

Bongaarts, J. and G. Feeney. 1998. "On the Quantum and Tempo of Fertility," *Population and Development Review*, 24: 271–91.

Bongaarts, J. and S. Greenhalgh. 1985. *An Alternative to the One-child Policy in China*. New York: Population Council. Center for Policy Studies Working Paper No. 115.

Bonynge, Francis. 1852. *The Future Wealth of America*. New York.

Booth, H. 1984. "Transforming the Gompertz for Fertility Analysis: The Development of A Standard for the Relational Gompertz," *Population Studies*, 38(3): 495–506.

Bourgeois-Pichat, J. 1946. "De la Mesure de la Mortalité Infantile," *Population*, 1(1): 53–68.

——— . 1951. "La Mesure de la Mortalité Infantile. II, Les Causes de Décès," *Population*, 6(3): 459–80.

——— . 1963. "Application of Factor Analysis to the Study of Mortality," in *Emerging Techniques in Population Research*, proceedings of a round table of the thirty-ninth annual conference of the Milbank Memorial Fund, Sept. 18–19, 1962. New York: Milbank Memorial Fund.

Bourgeois-Pichat, J. and S. A. Taleb. 1970. " Un Taux D'accroissement Nul pour les Pays en Voie de Développement en L'an 2000. Rêve ou Réalité ?," *Population*, 25(5): 951–74.

Brass, William. 1971. "On the Scale of Mortality," pp. 69–110 in W. Brass, ed., *Biological Aspects of Demography*. London: Taylor and Francis Ltd; New York: Barnes & Noble Inc.

—————. 1975. *Methods for Estimating Fertility and Mortality from Limited and Defective Data, Based on Seminars Held 16–24 September 1971 at the Centro Latinoamerico De Demografia (Celade) San Jose, Costa Rica*. Chapel Hill, NC: International Program of Laboratories for Population Statistics.

—————. and E. A. Bamgboye. 1981. *The Time Location of Reports of Survivorship: Estimates for Maternal and Paternal Orphanhood and the Ever-widowed*. London, England, University of London, London School of Hygiene and Tropical Medicine, Centre for Population Studies. CPS Working Paper no. 81–1.

—————. and S. Macrae. 1984. "Childhood Mortality Estimated from Reports on Previous Births Given by Mothers at the Time of a Maternity: Preceding-births Technique," *Asian And Pacific Census Forum*, 11(2): 5–8.

Broström, G. 1985. "Practical Aspects on the Estimation of the Parameters of Coale's Model for Marital Fertility," *Demography*, 22(4): 625–31.

Bumpass, Larry L. and Hsien-Hen Lu. 2000. "Trends in Cohabitation and Implications for Children's Family Contexts in the United States," *Population Studies*, 54(1): 29–41.

Caldwell, J. C. 1966. "A Study of Age Misstatement among Young Children in Ghana," *Demography*, 3(2): 477–90.

Cannan, E. 1895. "The Probability of a Cessation of the Growth of Population in England and Wales during the Next Century," *The Economic Journal*, 5: 505–15. Also in *Population and Development Review*, 4(4): 695–704.

Carnes, B. A., S. J. Olshansky, and D. Grahn. 1996. "The Search for a Law of Mortality," *Population and Development Review*, 22(2): 231–64.

Chackiel, J. and H. Orellana. 1985. "Adult Female Mortality Trends from Retrospective Questions about Maternal Orphanhood Included in Censuses and Surveys," pp. 39–51 in *International Population Conference, Florence, 1985, 5–12 June*. Congres International de la Population, Volume 4. Liege, Belgium, International Union for the Scientific Study of Population.

Chandrasekar, C. and W. E. Deming. 1949. "On a Method of Estimating Birth and Death Rates and the Extent of Registration," *Journal of the American Statistical Association*, 44: 101–15. Laboratories of Population Statistics Reprint Series No. 1.

Chiang, C. L. 1968. *An Introduction to Stochastic Processes in Biostatistics*. New York: Wiley.

—————. 1978. *Life Table and Mortality Analysis*. Geneva: World Health Organization.

Coale, Ansley J. 1957. "A New Method for Calculating Lotka's r–The Intrinsic Rate of Growth in a Stable Population," *Population Studies*, 11(1): 92–4.

—————. 1969. "The Decline of Fertility in Europe from the French Revolution to World War II," in S. B. Behrman, L. Corsa, and R. Freedman, eds., *Fertility and Family Planning: A World View*, Ann Arbor: University of Michigan Press.

—————. 1971. "Age Patterns of Marriage," *Population Studies*, 25(2): 193–214.

—————. 1972. *The Growth and Structure of Human Populations*. Princeton: Princeton University Press.

—————. 1974. "The History of Human Population," *Scientific American*, 123(3): 41–51.

—————. 1981. "A Reassessment of World Population Trends," pp. 35–8 in *International Population Conference, Manila 1981, 1983 Proceedings*. Liège: International Union for the Scientific Study of Population.

—————. 1984. "Life Table Construction on the Basis of Two Enumerations of a Closed Population," *Population Index*, 50(2): 193–213.

—————. 1985. "An Extension and Simplification of a New Synthesis of Age Structure and Growth," *Asian And Pacific Census Forum*, 12(1): 5–8.

—————. and P. Demeny, with B. Vaughan. 1983. *Regional Model Life Tables and Stable Populations*. New York: Academic Press.

—————. and G. Guo. 1989. "Revised Regional Model Life Tables at Very Low Levels of Mortality," *Population Index*, 55(4): 613–43.

_____ , A. M. John, and T. Richards. 1985. "Calculation of Age-specific Fertility Schedules from Tabulations of Parity in Two Censuses," *Demography*, 22(4): 611–23.

_____ and D. R. McNeil. 1972. "The Distribution by Age of the Frequency of First Marriage in a Female Cohort," *Journal of the American Statistical Association*, 67(340): 743–9.

_____ . and J. Trussell. 1974. "Model Fertility Schedules: Variations in the Age Structure of Childbearing in Human Populations," *Population Index*, 40(2): 185–258.

_____ and _____ . 1977. "Annex I: Estimating the Time to Which Brass Estimates Apply," *Population Bulletin of the United Nations*, No. 10: 87–9.

_____ and _____ . 1978. "Technical Note: Finding Two Parameters that Specify a Model Schedule of Marital Fertility," *Population Index*, 44(2): 202–13.

_____ and C. Y. Tye. 1961. "The Significance of Age-patterns of Fertility in High Fertility Populations," *Milbank Memorial Fund Quarterly*, 39(4): 631–46.

Collett, D. 1994. *Modeling Survival Data in Medical Research*. London: Chapman & Hall.

Condran, G. A., C. Himes, and S. H. Preston. 1991. "Old Age Mortality Patterns in Low-mortality Countries: An Evaluation of Population and Death Data at Advanced Ages, 1950 to the Present," *Population Bulletin of the United Nations*, No. 30: 23–60.

Cox, D. R. 1972. "Regression Models and Life Tables," *Journal of the Royal Statistical Society, Series B*, No. 34: 187–220.

Das Gupta, P. 1993. *Standardization and Decomposition of Rates: A User's Manual*. Washington, DC: US Government Printing Office.

David, P. A., T. A. Mroz, W. C. Sanderson, K. W. Wachter, and D. R. Weir. 1988. "Cohort Parity Analysis: Statistical Estimates of the Extent of Fertility Control," *Demography*, 25(2): 163–88.

Day, J. C. 1996. *Projections of the Population of the United States, by Age, Sex, Race, and Hispanic Origin: 1995 to 2050*. Bureau of the Census Current Population Reports Series P-25/1130. Washington, DC: US Government Printing Office.

Deparcieux, A. 1746. *Essai sur les Probabilités de la Durée de la Vie Humaine*. Paris: Guérin Frères.

Dorn, H. F. 1950. "Pitfalls in Population Forecasts and Projections," *Journal of the American Statistical Association*, 45(251): 311–34.

Easterlin, R. 1980. *Birth and Fortune*. New York: Basic Books.

Elandt-Johnson, R. C. and N. L. Johnson. 1980. *Survival Models and Data Analysis*. New York: Wiley.

Elo, I. T. and S. H. Preston. 1994. "Estimating African-american Mortality from Inaccurate Data," *Demography*, 31(3): 427–58.

_____ and _____ . 1997. "Racial and Ethnic Differences in Mortality at Older Ages," pp. 10–42 in L. Martin, and B. Soldo, eds., *Racial and Ethnic Differences in the Health of Older Americans*. Washington, DC: National Academy Press.

Ericksen, E. P. and J. B. Kadane. 1985. "Estimating the Population in a Census Year: 1980 and Beyond," *Journal of The American Statistical Association*, 80(389): 98–109.

Ewbank, D. C. 1981. *Age Misreporting and Age-selective Underenumeration: Sources, Patterns, and Consequences for Demographic Analysis*. Washington, DC, National Academy Press, Committee on Population and Demography Report No. 4.

_____ . 1982. "The Sources of Error in Brass's Method for Estimating Child Survival: The Case of Bangladesh," *Population Studies*, 36(3): 459–74.

Ewbank, D. C. 1993. "Coarse and Refined Methods for Studying the Fertility Transition in Historical Populations," pp. 345–60 in D. Reher and R. Schofield, eds., *Old and New Methods in Historical Demography*. Oxford: Clarendon Press.

_____ , J. C. Gomez de Leon, and M. A. Stoto. 1983. "A Reducible Four-parameter System of Model Life Tables," *Population Studies*, 37(1): 105–27.

Feeney, G. 1991. "Child Survivorship Estimation: Methods and Data Analysis," *Asian and Pacific Population Forum*, 5(2–3): 51–5, 76–87.

Feeney, G. and W. Feng. 1993. "Parity Progression and Birth Intervals in China: The Influence of Policy in Hastening Fertility Decline," *Population and Development Review* 19(1): 61–101.

Fries, J. F. 1980. "Aging, Natural Death and the Compression of Morbidity," *New England Journal of Medicine*, 303: 130–5.

Garenne, Michel. 1994. "Do Women Forget Their Births? A Study of Maternity Histories in a Rural Area of Senegal (Niakhar)," *Population Bulletin of the United Nations*, No. 36: 43–54.

_____ and F. Friedberg. 1997. "Accuracy of Indirect Estimates of Maternal Mortality: A Simulation Model," *Studies in Family Planning*, 28(2): 132–42.

Gini, C. 1924. "Premières Recherches sur la Fécondité de la Femme," pp. 889–92 in *Proceedings of the International Mathematics Congress*, vol. 2.

Gompertz, B. 1825. "On the Nature of the Function Expressive of the Law of Mortality," *Philosophical Transactions*, 27: 513–85.

Grabill, W. H., C. V. Kiser, and P. K. Whelpton. 1958. *The Fertility of American Women*. New York: Wiley.

Graham, W., W. Brass, and R. W. Snow. 1989. "Estimating Maternal Mortality: The Sisterhood Method," *Studies in Family Planning*, 20(3): 125–35.

Graunt, J. 1662. *Natural and Political Observations Mentioned in a Following Index, and Made Upon the Bills of Mortality*. London. Republished with an Introduction by B. Benjamin in the *Journal of the Institute of Actuaries*, 90: 1–61 (1964).

Greville, T. N. E. 1943. "Short Methods of Constructing Life Tables," *Record from the American Institute of Actuaries*, No. 32: 29–42.

Hajnal, J. 1953. "Age at Marriage and Proportion Marrying," *Population Studies*, 7(2): 111–36.

Halley, E. 1693. "An Estimate of the Degrees of the Mortality of Mankind," *Philosophical Transactions*, 17: 596–610, 653–6.

Heligman, Lawrence. 1985. *The Modelling of Age Patterns of Mortality and the Use of Such Models to Evaluate the Quality of Recorded Census Age Distributions*. Dissertation in Demography. Philadelphia: University of Pennsylvania.

Heligman, L. and J. H. Pollard. 1980. "The Age Pattern of Mortality," *Journal of the Institute of Actuaries*, vol. 107, Part 1, No. 434: 49–80.

Henry, Louis. 1953. *Fécondité des Mariages: Nouvelle Méthode de Mesure*. Travaux et Documents de l'INED, Cahier No.16. Paris: Presses Universitaires de France.

_____ . 1957. "Fécondité et Famille. Modèles Mathématiques (I)," *Population*, 12(3): 413–44.

_____ . 1960. "Mesure Indirecte de la Mortalité des Adultes," *Population*, 15(3): 457–66.

_____ . 1961a. "Some Data on Natural Fertility," *Eugenics Quarterly*, 8(2): 81–91.

_____ . 1961b. "Fécondité et famille. Modèles mathématiques (II)," *Population*, 16(1): 27–48 and 16(2): 261–82.

_____ . 1964. "Mortalité Intra-utérine et Fécondabilité," *Population*, 19(5): 899–940.

_____ . 1969. "Schéma de Nuptialité: Déséquilibre des Sexes et Âge au Mariage," *Population*, 24(6): 1067–122.

Heuveline, Patrick. 1998. " 'Between One and Three Million': Towards the Demographic Reconstruction of a Decade of Cambodian History (1970–1979)," *Population Studies*, 52(1): 49–65.

Hill, Kenneth. 1981. "A Proposal for the Use of Information on Residence of Siblings to Estimate Emigration by Age," *IUSSP Papers*, 18: 19–34.

_____ 1987. "Estimating Census and Death Registration Completeness," *Asian and Pacific Population Forum*, 1(3): 8–13.

_____ . 1991. "Approaches to the Measurement of Childhood Mortality: a Comparative Review," *Population Index*, 57(3): 368–82.

_____ and M. E. Figueroa. 1999. *Child Mortality Estimation by Time Since First Birth*. Baltimore, Md.: Hopkins Population Centers on Population WP 99–05.

_____ and J. Trussell. 1977. "Further Developments in Indirect Mortality Estimation," *Population Studies*, 31(2): 313–34.

Himes, Christine L. and Clifford C. Clogg. 1992. "An Overview of Demographic Analysis as a Method for Evaluating Census Coverage in the United States," *Population Index*, 58(4): 587–607.

――――, S. H. Preston, and G. A. Condran. 1994. "A Relational Model of Mortality at Older Ages in Low Mortality Countries," *Population Studies*, 48(2): 269–91.

Hobcraft, J., J. W. McDonald, and S. O. Rutstein. 1985. "Demographic Determinants of Infant and Early Child Mortality: A Comparative Analysis," *Population Studies*, 39(3): 363–85.

Hoem, J. M. 1972. "Inhomogeneous Semi-Markov Processes, Select Actuarial Tables, and Duration-Dependence in Demography," pp. 251–96 in T. N. Greville, ed., *Population Dynamics*. New York: Academic Press.

――――― and U. Funck-Jensen. 1982. "Multistate Life Table Methodology: A Probabilistic Critique," in K. C. Land and A. Rogers, eds., *Multidimensional Mathematical Demography*. New York: Academic Press.

Hoogendyk, C. G. and G. F. Estabrook. 1984. "The Consequences of Earlier Reproduction in Declining Populations," *Mathematical Biosciences*, 71: 217–35.

Horiuchi, Shiro and A. J. Coale. 1982. "A Simple Equation for Estimating the Expectation of Life at Old Ages," *Population Studies*, 36(2): 317–26.

――――― and ―――――. 1990. "Age Patterns of Mortality for Older Women: An Analysis Using the Age-specific Rate of Mortality Change with Age," *Mathematical Population Studies*, 2(4): 245–67.

――――― and S. H. Preston. 1988. "Age-Specific Growth Rates: The Legacy of Past Population Dynamics," *Demography*, 25(3): 429–41.

Kalbfleisch, J. D. and R. L. Prentice. 1980. *The Statistical Analysis of Failure Time Data*. New York: Wiley.

Kannisto, Vaino. 1994. *Development of Oldest-old Mortality, 1950–1990: Evidence from 28 Developed Countries*. Odense Monographs on Population Aging; no. 1. Odense: Odense University Press.

―――――. 1996. *The Advancing Frontier of Survival: Life Tables for Old Age*. Odense Monographs on Population Aging, No. 3. Odense: Odense University Press.

Karmel, P. H. 1947. "The Relation Between Male and Female Reproduction Rates," *Population Studies*, 1(3): 249–74.

Keyfitz, Nathan. 1966. "A Life Table that Agrees with the Data," *Journal of the American Statistical Association*, 61(314):305–12.

―――――. 1968a. "A Life Table that Agrees with the Data II," *Journal of the American Statistical Association*, 63(324): 1252–68.

―――――. 1968b. *Introduction to the Mathematics of Population*. Reading, Mass.: Addison-Wesley.

―――――. 1971. "On the Momentum of Population Growth," *Demography*, 8(1): 71–80.

―――――. 1972. "On Future Population," *Journal of the American Statistical Association*, 67(338): 347–63.

―――――. 1981. "The Limits of Population Forecasting," *Population and Development Review*, 7(4): 579–93, 728–9.

―――――. 1985 (2nd edn.). *Applied Mathematical Demography*. New York: Wiley.

――――― and W. Flieger. 1968. *World Population: An Analysis of Vital Data*. Chicago: University of Chicago Press.

Keyfitz, Nathan and W. Flieger. 1990. *World Population Growth and Aging: Demographic Trends in the Late Twentieth Century*. Chicago and London: University of Chicago Press.

――――― and J. Frauenthal. 1975. "An Improved Life Table Method," *Biometrics*, No. 31: 889–99.

Kim, Young J. and Robert Schoen. 1993. "Crossovers that Link Populations with the Same Vital Rates," *Mathematical Population Studies*, 4(1): 1–19.

―――――. 1997. "Population Momentum Expresses Population Aging," *Demography*, 34(3): 421–8.

―――――. 2000. "On the Quantum and Tempo of Fertility: Limits to the Bongaarts–Feeney Adjustment," *Population and Development Review*, 26(2), forthcoming.

――――, Robert Schoen, and P. Sandara Sarma. 1991. "Momentum and the Growth-Free Segment of a Population," *Demography*, 28(1): 159–76.

Kiser, C. V., W. H. Grabill, and A. A. Campbell. 1968. *Trends and Variations in Fertility in the United States*. Cambridge: Harvard University Press.

Kitagawa, E. M. 1955. "Components of a Difference between Two Rates," *Journal of the American Statistical Association*, 50(272): 1168–94.

Knodel, J. 1988. *Demographic Behavior in the Past: A Study of Fourteen German Village Populations in the Eighteenth and Nineteenth Centuries*. New York: Cambridge University Press.

_____ and H. Kinner. 1977. "The Impact of Breast Feeding Patterns on Biometric Analysis of Infant Mortality," *Demography*, 14(4): 391–409.

Krotki, K. J. 1978. "The Role of PGE/ERAD/ECP Surveys among Endeavors to Secure Improved Demographic Data," pp. 1–52 in K. J. Krotki, ed., *Developments in Dual System Estimation of Population Size and Growth*. Edmonton, Canada: University of Alberta Press.

Lantoine, C. and R. Pressat. 1984. "Nouveaux Aspects de la Mortalité Infantile," *Population*, 39(2): 253–64.

Le Bras, Hervé. 1968. "Nouvelles Tables de Mortalité: Présentation d'un Cahier de l'I.N.E.D.," *Population*, 23(4): 739–44.

_____ . 1976. "Lois de Mortalité et Âge Limite," *Population*, 31(3): 655–92.

Ledermann, Sully. 1969. *Nouvelles Tables-types de Mortalité*. INED Travaux et documents, cahiers no. 53. Paris: Presses Universitaires de France.

_____ and J. Breas. 1959. "Les Dimensions de la Mortalité," *Population*, 14(4): 637–82.

Lee, R. D. 1993. "Modeling and Forecasting the Time Series of US Fertility: Age Distribution, Range, and Ultimate level," *International Journal of Forecasting*, 9(2): 187–202.

_____ . 1998. "Probabilistic Approaches to Population Forecasting," pp. 156–90 in W. Lutz, J. W. Vanpel, and D. A. Ahlburg, eds., *Frontiers of Population Forecasting*, supplement to *Population and Development Review*, vol. 24.

_____ and L. R. Carter. 1992. "Modeling and Forecasting US Mortality," *Journal of the American Statistical Association*, 87(419): 659–71.

_____ and S. Tuljapurkar. 1994. "Stochastic Population Forecasts for the United States: Beyond High, Medium, and Low," *Journal of the American Statistical Association*, 89(428): 1175–89.

_____ and S. Tuljapurkar. 1998. "Uncertain Demographic Futures and Social Security Finances," *American Economic Review*, 88(2): 237–41.

Leridon, H. 1977. *Human Fertility: The Basic Components*. Chicago: University of Chicago Press.

Leslie, P. H. 1945. " On the Use of Matrices in Certain Population Dynamics," *Biometrika*, 33: 183–212.

Lewis, E. G. 1942. "On the Generation and Growth of a Population," *Sankhya*, 6: 93–6.

Lexis, W. 1875. *Einleitung ein die Theorie der Bevölkerungs-Statistik*. Strasbourg: Trubner.

Lopez, Alvaro. 1961. *Problems in Stable Population Theory*. Office of Population Research, Princeton University, Princeton, New Jersey.

Lotka, A. J. 1939. *Théorie Analytique des Associations Biologiques. Part. II. Analyse Démographique avec Application Particulière à l'Espèce Humaine*. Actualités Scientifiques et Industrielles, No. 780. Paris: Hermann et Cie.

Luther, Norman Y. and Robert D. Retherford. 1988. "Consistent Correction of Census and Vital Registration Data," *Mathematical Population Studies*, 1(1): 1–20.

Lutz, W. and S. Scherbov. 1992. "Sensitivity of Aggregate Period Life Expectancy to Different Averaging Procedures," *Population Bulletin of The United Nations*, No. 33: 32–46.

Makeham, W. M. 1860. "On the Law of Mortality and the Construction of Annuity Tables," *Assurance Magazine*, 8: 301–10.

Manton, K. G. and E. Stallard. 1997. "Non-white and White Age Trajectories of Mortality: Evidence from Extinct Cohort Analyses, 1950 to 1992," pp. 15–40 in K. S. Markides and M. R. Miranda, eds., *Minorities, Aging, and Health*. Thousand Oaks, Calif.: Sage Publications.

Marks, E. S. 1978. "The Role of Dual System Estimation in Census Evaluation," pp. 156–88 in K. J. Krotki, ed., *Developments in Dual System Estimation of Population Size and Growth*. Edmonton, Canada: University of Alberta Press.

Martin, L. G. 1980. "A Modification for Use in Destabilized Population of Brass's Technique for Estimating Completeness of Death Registration," *Population Studies*, 34(2): 381–95.

McFarland, David. 1969. "On the Theory of Stable Population: A New and Elementary Proof of the Theorems under Weaker Assumptions," *Demography*, 6(3): 301–22.

Menken, J. A. 1977. "Current Status of Demographic Models," *Population Bulletin of the United Nations*, No. 9: 22–34.

Merli, Giovanna. 1998. "Mortality in Vietnam, 1979–1989," *Demography*, 35(3): 345–60.

Mode, C. J. 1985. *Stochastic Processes in Demography and their Computer Implementation*. Berlin and New York: Springer Verlag.

National Center for Health Statistics [NCHS]. 1968. "United States Life Tables by Causes of Death: 1959–61," *Life Tables: 1959–1961*, vol. 1, no. 6. Washington, DC.

_____ . 1996. *Vital statistics of the United States, 1992. Volume II, Mortality, Part A*. Hyattsville, Md.

National Research Council. 1999. *Measuring a Changing Nation*. National Academy Press, Washington DC.

National Research Council. 2000. *Beyond Six Billion: Forecasting the World's Population*. National Academy Press, Washington DC, forthcoming.

Newcombe, Howard B. 1988. *Handbook of Record Linkage: Methods for Health and Statistical Studies, Administration, and Business*. Oxford, New York: Oxford University Press.

Nour, E. S. and C. M. Suchindran. 1984. "The Construction of Multi-State Life Tables: Comments on the Article by Willekens et al.," *Population Studies*, 38: 325–8.

Okun, B. S. 1994. "Evaluating Methods for Detecting Fertility Control: Coale and Trussell's Model and Cohort Parity Analysis," *Population Studies*, 48(2): 193–222.

Organization for Economic Cooperation and Development [OECD]. 1979. *Mortality Project Annotated Bibliography on the Sources of Demographic Data, vols. 1–3*. Paris, Organization for Economic Cooperation and Development.

Page, H. J. 1977. "Patterns Underlying Fertility Schedules: A Decomposition by Both Age and Marriage Duration," *Population Studies*, 31(1): 85–106.

Palloni, Alberto. 1996. "Demography of HIV/AIDS," *Population Index*, 62(4): 601–52.

_____ and R. Kominski. 1984. "Estimation of Adult Mortality Using Forward and Backward Projections," *Population Studies*, 38(3): 479–93.

Parlett, B. 1970. "Ergodic Properties of Populations, I: the One Sex Model," *Theoretical Population Biology*, 1: 191–207.

Pearl, R. 1933. "Factors in Human Fertility and their Statistical Evaluation," *The Lancet*, 225: 607–11.

_____ and L. J. Reed. 1920. "On the Rate of Growth of the Population of the United States since 1790 and its Mathematical Representation," *Proceedings of the National Academy of Science*, 6: 275–88.

Perks, W. 1932. "On Some Experiments in the Graduation of Mortality Statistics," *Journal of the Institute of Actuaries*, 63: 12–57.

Pollard, J. H. 1982. "The Expectation of Life and its Relationship to Mortality," *Journal of the Institute of Actuaries*, 109: 225–40.

_____ . 1988. "On the Decomposition of Changes in Expectation of Life and Differentials in Life Expectancy," *Demography*, 25(2): 265–76.

Potter, F. J., F. G. Iannachione, W. D. Mosher, R. E. Mason, J. D. Kavee, and S. L. Botman. 1997. "National Survey of Family Growth Cycle 5: Design, Estimation and Inference," *Vital and Health Statistics, Series 2*. Hyattsville, Md. US National Center for Health Statistics [NCHS].

Potter, J. E. 1977. "Problems in Using Birth-history Analysis to Estimate Trends in Fertility," *Population Studies*, 31(2): 335–64.

Pressat, Roland. 1972. *Demographic Analysis; Methods, Results, Applications*. Chicago: Aldine-Atherton.

_____ . 1995. *Eléments de Démographie Mathématique*. Paris, France: Association Internationale des Démographes de Langue Française [AIDELF].

Preston, Samuel H. 1972. "Interrelations Between Death Rates and Birth Rates," *Theoretical Population Biology*, 3: 162–85.

—— . 1974. "Effect of Mortality Change on Stable Population Parameters," *Demography*, 11(1): 119–30.

—— . 1976a. *Mortality Patterns in National Populations*. New York: Academic Press.

—— . 1976b. "Family Sizes of Children and Family Sizes of Women," *Demography*, 13(1): 105–14.

—— . 1980. "Estimating Adult Female Mortality from Reports on Number of Children Surviving," *Asian and Pacific Census Forum*, 6(4):5–8.

—— . 1983. "An Integrated System for Demographic Estimation from Two Age Distributions," *Demography*, 20(2): 213–26.

—— . 1986. "The Relation between Actual and Intrinsic Growth Rates," *Population Studies*, 40(3): 343–51.

—— . 1987a. "Estimation of Certain Measures in Family Demography Based upon Generalized Stable Population Relations," pp. 40–62 in J. Bongaarts, ed., *Family Demography: Methods and Their Application*. Cambridge: Cambridge University Press.

—— . 1987b. "Relations Among Standard Epidemiologic Measures in a Population," *American Journal of Epidemiology*, 126(2): 336–45.

—— . 1988. "Reply to Wachter," *Population Studies*, 42(3): 495–501.

—— and N. Bennett. 1983. "A Census-Based Method for Estimating Adult Mortality," *Population Studies*, 37(1): 91–104.

—— and N. Chen. 1984. *Two-census Orphanhood Methods for Estimating Adult Mortality, with Application to Latin America*. Unpublished manuscript.

—— and A. J. Coale. 1982. "Age Structure, Growth, Attrition and Accession: A New Synthesis," *Population Index*, 48(2): 217–59.

—— , I. T. Elo, A. Foster, and H. Fu. 1998. "Reconstructing the size of the African-American Population by Age and Sex, 1930–1990," *Demography*, 35(1): 1–21.

—— , I. T. Elo, I. Rosenwaike, and M. Hill. 1996. "African-American Mortality at Older Ages: Results of a Matching Study," *Demography*, 33(2): 193–209.

—— and M. Guillot. 1997. "Population Dynamics in an Age of Declining Fertility," *Genus*, 53(3–4): 15–31.

—— and K. Hill. 1980. "Estimating the Completeness of Death Registration," *Population Studies*, 34(2): 349–66.

—— , C. Himes and M. Eggers. 1989. "Demographic Conditions Responsible for Population Aging," *Demography*, 26(4): 691–704.

—— , N. Keyfitz, and R. Schoen. 1972. *Causes of Death: Life Tables for National Populations*. New York: Seminar Press.

—— , A. McDaniel, and C. Grushka. 1993. "New Model Life Tables for High-Mortality Populations," *Historical Methods*, 26(4): 149–59.

—— and A. Palloni. 1977. "Fine-tuning Brass-type Mortality Estimates with Data on Ages of Surviving Children," *Population Bulletin of the United Nations*, No. 10: 72–91.

—— and Michael Strong. 1986. "Effects of Mortality Declines on Marriage Patterns in Developing Countries," pp. 88–100 in United Nations, *Consequences of Mortality Trends and Differentials*. United Nations Population Study, No. 95, United Nations. New York.

Pritchett, H. S. 1891. "A Formula for Predicting the Population of the United States," *Quarterly Publication of the American Statistical Association*, No. 2: 278–86.

Reed, L. and M. Merrell. 1939. "A Short Method for Constructing an Abridged Life Table," pp. 43–51 in D. Smith and N. Keyfitz, eds., *Mathematical Demography*. New York: Springer Verlag, 1977.

Robles, A. 1996. "Mortalidad adulta entre poblaciones indígenas y no indígenas de Guatemala y Bolivia," *Notas De Población*, 24(64): 33–61.

Rodriguez, G. and J. Cleland. 1988. "Modelling Marital Fertility by Age and Duration: An Empirical Appraisal of the Page Model," *Population Studies*, 42(2): 241–57.

_____ and J. Trussell. 1980. "Maximum Likelihood Estimation of the Parameters of Coale's Model Nuptiality Schedule," *World Fertility Survey Technical Bulletin*, No. 7. Woorburg: International Statistical Institute.

Rogers, A. 1995a. "Population Projections: Simple vs. Complex Models," *Mathematical Population Studies*, 5(3): 197–292.

_____ . 1995b. *Multiregional Demography*. Chichester, West Sussex: John Wiley & Sons.

_____ and L. J. Castro. 1981. *Model Migration Schedules*. International Institute for Applied Systems Analysis, Laxenburg, Austria.

_____ , R. Rogers, and A. Belanger. 1990. "Longer Life but Worse Health? Measurement and Dynamics," *The Gerontologist*, 30: 640–9.

Rutenberg, N. and J. M. Sullivan. 1991. "Direct and indirect estimates of maternal mortality from the sisterhood method," pp. 1, 669–96 in *Demographic and Health Surveys World Conference, August 5–7, 1991, Washington, DC*, proceedings, vol. 3. Columbia, Maryland.

Ryder, N. 1965. "The Cohort as a Concept in the Study of Social Change," *American Sociological Research*, 30: 854–61.

_____ . 1986. "The History of Cohort Fertility in the United States," *Population and Development Review*, 12(4): 617–44.

Schoen, Robert. 1988. *Modeling Multigroup Populations*. New York: Plenum Press.

Sheps, M. C. and J. A. Menken. 1973. *Mathematical Models of Conception and Birth*. Chicago: University of Chicago Press.

Shryock, H. and J. Siegel. 1973. *The Methods and Materials of Demography*. Washington, DC: US Government Printing Office.

Singer, B. S. and K. Manton. 1994. "What's the Fuss About the Compression of Morbidity?," *Chance*, 7(4): 21–30.

Smith, D. P. and N. Keyfitz (eds.). 1977. *Mathematical Demography: Selected Papers*. Berlin: Springer Verlag.

Smith, H. L., S. P. Morgan, and T. Koropecky-Cox. 1996. "A Decomposition of Trends in the Nonmarital Fertility Ratios of Blacks and Whites in the United States," *Demography*, 33(2): 141–51.

Stoto, M. 1983. "The Accuracy of Population Projections," *Journal of the American Statistical Association*, 78(381): 13–20.

Stover, J. 1998. "Revising the Proximate Determinants of Fertility Framework: What Have We Learned in the Past Twenty Years?," *Studies in Family Planning*, 29(3): 255–67.

Stupp, P. W. 1988. "Estimating Intercensal Age Schedules by Intracohort Interpolation," *Population Index*, 54(2): 209–24.

Sullivan, J. M. 1972. "Models for the Estimation of the Estimation of the Probability of Dying between Birth and Exact Age of Early Childhood," *Population Studies*, 26(1): 79–97.

Sullivan, J. M. 1990. "The Collection of Mortality Data in WFS and DHS Surveys," pp. 48–63 in Jacques Vallin, Stan D'Souza, and Alberto Palloni, eds., *Measurement and Analysis of Mortality: New Approaches*, New York/Oxford, England: Oxford University Press.

Sutter, Jean and Léon Tabah. 1952. "La Mortalité, Phénomène Biométrique", *Population*, 7(1): 69–94.

Tiemeyer, Peter and Glen Ulmer. 1991. *MSLT: A Program for the Computation of Multistate Life Tables*. Center for Demography & Ecology working paper 91-34. University of Wisconsin-Madison, Nov.

Timaeus, Ian M. 1991a. "Estimation of Adult Mortality from Orphanhood Before and since Marriage," *Population Studies*, 45(3): 455–72.

_____ . 1991b. "Measurement of Adult Mortality in less Developed Countries: A Comparative Review," *Population Index*, 57(4): 552–68.

_____ . 1996. "New Estimates of the Decline in Adult Mortality since 1950," in Ian Timæus, J. Chackiel, and L. Ruzicka, eds., *Adult Mortality in Latin America*. International Studies in Demography. Oxford: Clarendon Press.

Trussell, J. 1975. "A Re-estimation of the Multiplying Factors for the Brass Technique for Determining Childhood Survivorship Rates," *Population Studies*, 29(1): 97–107.

Trussell, J. and T. Guinnane. 1993. "Techniques of Event History Analysis," pp. 181–205 in D. Reher and R. Schofield, eds., *Old and New Methods in Historical Demography*. Oxford: Clarendon Press.

⸺ , J. Menken, and A. J. Coale. 1982. "A General Model for Analyzing the Effect of Nuptiality on Fertility," pp. 7–27 in L. T. Ruzicka, ed., *Nuptiality and Fertility*. Liège: Ordina Editions.

⸺ , J. Strickler, and B. Vaughan. 1993. "Contraceptive Efficacy of the Diaphragm, the Sponge and the Cervical Cap," *Family Planning Perspectives*, 25(3): 100–5.

Tuljapurkar, S. 1992. "Stochastic Population Forecasts and Their Uses," *International Journal of Forecasting*, Special Issue, 8(3): 385–91.

United Nations. 1955. *Age and Sex Patterns of Mortality: Model Life Tables for Underdeveloped Countries*. New York: United Nations.

⸺ . 1958. *Multilingual Demographic Dictionary*. United Nations Population Studies, No. 29.

⸺ . 1967. *Manual IV: Methods of Estimating Basic Demographic Measures from Incomplete Data*. New York: United Nations.

⸺ . 1982. *Model Life Tables for Developing Countries*. New York: United Nations. Population Studies no. 77.

⸺ . 1983. *Manual X: Indirect Techniques for Demographic Estimation*. New York: United Nations.

⸺ . 1989. *World Population Prospects, 1988*. New York: United Nations.

⸺ . 1991. *World Population Prospects, 1990*. New York: United Nations.

⸺ . 1994. *The Age and Sex Distribution of the World Population: The 1994 Revision*. New York: United Nations.

⸺ . 1995. *World Population Prospects: The 1994 Revision*. New York: United Nations.

⸺ . 1996. *Demographic Yearbook 1994*. New York: United Nations.

⸺ . 1997. *World Population Prospects: The 1996 Revision*. New York: United Nations.

⸺ . 1999. *World Population Prospects: The 1998 Revision*. New York: United Nations.

Van Imhoff, E. and N. Keilman. 1991. *LIPRO 2.0: An Application of a Dynamic Demographic Projection Model to Household Structure in the Netherlands*. Publications of the Netherlands Interdisciplinary Demographic Institute (NIDI) and the Population and Family Study Centre (CBGS) No. 23. Berwyn, Penn./Lisse, Netherlands: Swets and Zeitlinger.

Vaupel, J. W. 1997. "The Remarkable Improvements in Survival at Older Ages," *Philosophical Transactions of the Royal Society of London*, series B, 352(1363): 1799–804.

⸺ , K. G. Manton, and E. Stallard. 1979. "The Impact of Heterogeneity in Individual Frailty on the Dynamics of Mortality," *Demography*, 16(3): 439–54.

Verhulst, P. F. 1838. "Notice sur la Loi que la Population Suit dans son Accroissement," *Correspondance mathématique et physique*, 10: 113–21.

Vincent, Paul. 1951. "La Mortalité des Vieillards," *Population*, 6(2): 181–99.

Wachter, K. W. and C. E. Finch. 1997. *Between Zeus and the Salmon: The Biodemography of Longevity*. Washington, DC: National Academy Press.

Ward, Patrick and Basia Zaba. 1998. *The Effect of HIV-1 on the Estimation of Child Mortality Using the Children Ever Born /Children Surviving Technique*. Paper presented at the International Union for the Scientific Study of the Population [IUSSP] seminar on Measurement of Risk and Modeling the Spread of AIDS. Copenhagen, 2–4 June, 1998.

Whelpton, P. K. 1928. "Population of the United States, 1925–1975," *The American Journal of Sociology*, 31: 253–70.

⸺ . 1936. "An Empirical Method for Calculating Future Population," *Journal of the American Statistical Association*, 31: 457–73.

White, K. M. and S. H. Preston. 1996. "How many Americans are alive because of twentieth-century improvements in mortality?," *Population And Development Review*, 22(3): 415–29, 603, 605.

World Health Organization. 1977. *Manual of Mortality Analysis: A Manual on Methods of Analysis of National Mortality Statistics for Public Health Purposes*. Geneva, World Health Organization, Division of Health Statistics, Dissemination of Statistical Information.

Wunsch, G. 1983. "Maternal and Child Health in the Developing Countries: Problems of Data Collection," *World Health Statistics Quarterly. Rapport Trimestriel De Statistiques Sanitaires Mondiales*, 36(1): 62–71.

Xie, Y. 1990. "What is Natural Fertility? The Remodeling of a Concept,"*Population Index*, 56(4): 656–63.

_____ and E. E. Pimentel. 1992. "Age Patterns of Marital Fertility: Revising the Coale–Trussell Method," *Journal of the American Statistical Association*, 87(420): 977–84.

Zeng, Y., A. J. Coale, M. K. Choe, L. Zhiwu, and L. Li. 1994. "Leaving the Parental Home: Census-based Estimates for China, Japan, South Korea, United States, France, and Sweden," *Population Studies*, 48(1): 65–80.

Index